PHOTOGRAPHING PLACES

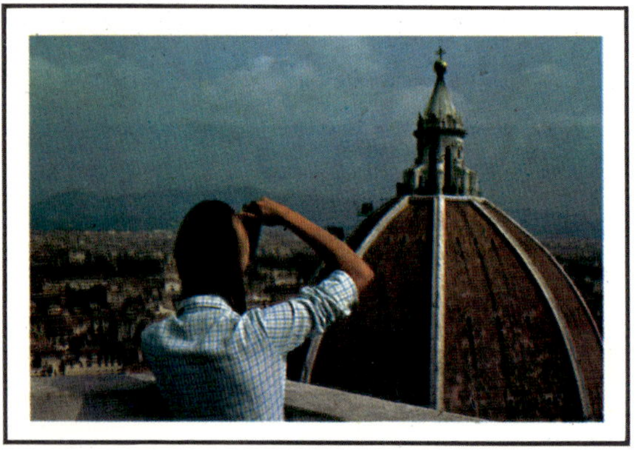

CENTURY PUBLISHING

LONDON

PHOTOGRAPHING PLACES

CAMILLO SEMENZATO

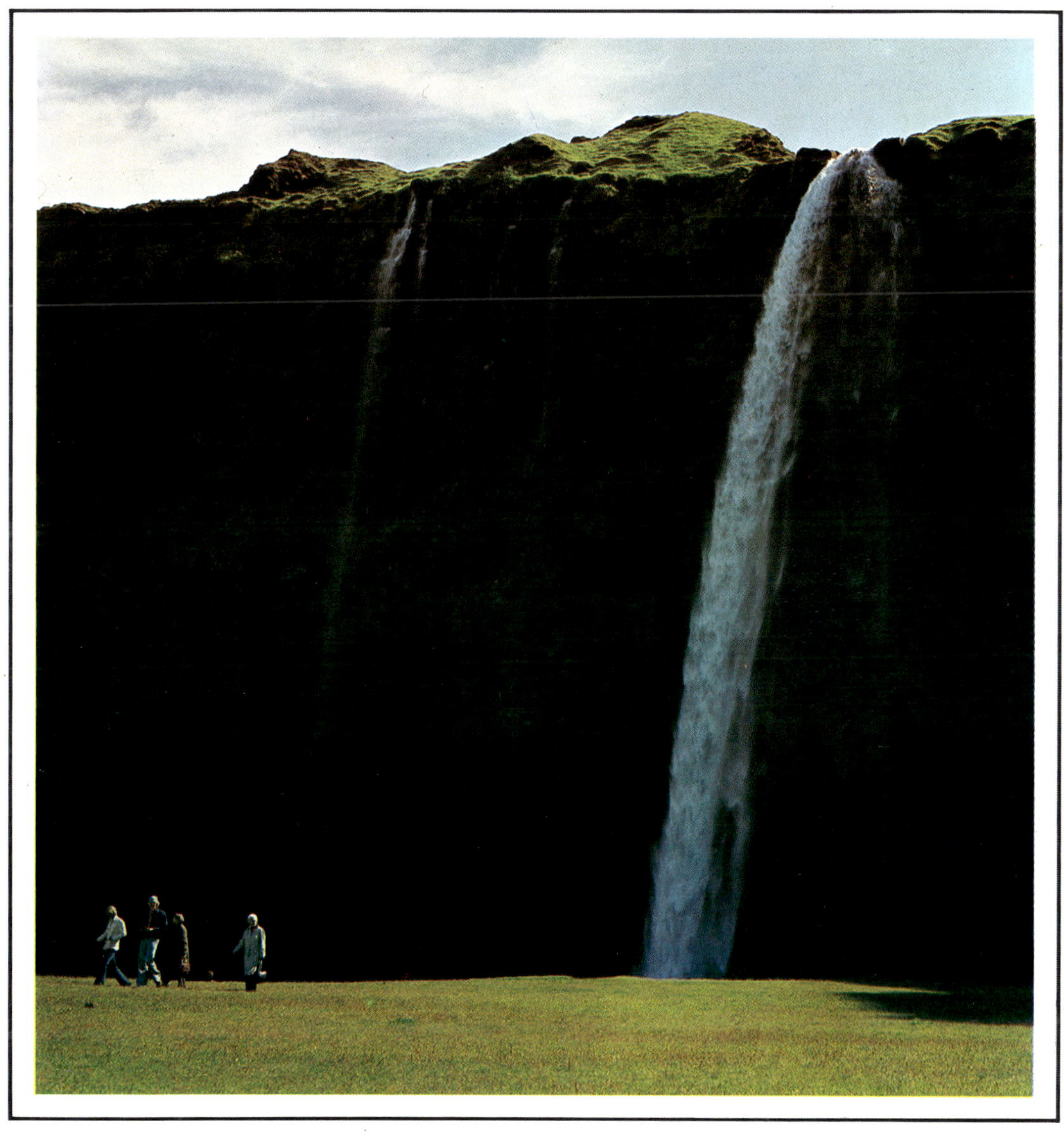

Translated by Valerie Palmer

First published in Great Britain in 1983 by
Century Publishing Co. Ltd,
76 Old Compton Street, London W1V 5PA

ISBN 0 7126 0201 1

Printed and bound in Italy by
Arnoldo Mondadori Editore, Verona

CONTENTS

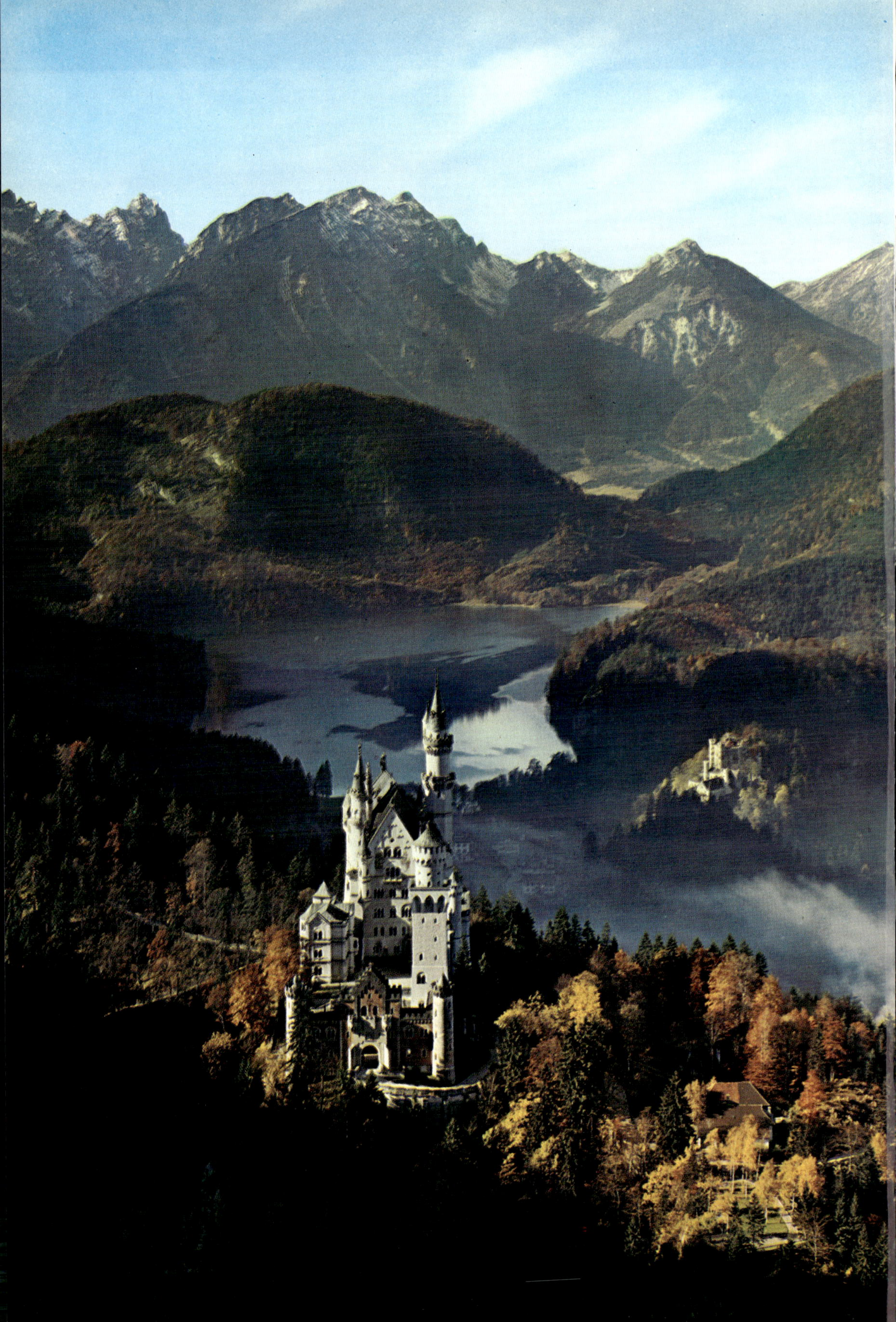

Foreword

A volume on landscape photography is not just an opportunity to specify technical details, it provides a chance for us to reexamine some general ideas on the possibilities for self-expression open to the photographer in this field. It also helps to clarify some ideas on the aesthetics of photography and how man feels about his relationship with nature. Obviously, it is not intended to be a treatise on aesthetics or a philosophical discourse, but we believe that it is a good idea for anyone involved in a creative activity to probe deeply into the issues involved. For that matter, photographers and photographic critics frequently do so, and not always in a way that is helpful to the layman. Immersed as they are in their own poetry, tastes and individual ideas – as artists often tend to be – they risk being one-sided and extremist. This in our opinion is a serious mistake in a field which should be open and give pleasure, not just to the initiated, but to the amateur as well.

Nowadays, in speaking of photography, one is addressing an enormous public, extending well beyond the limits of specialization and professionalism to include a growing number of people who use this very modern and universal means to tackle the eternal problems of art and creation.

Of course, we know that not all amateurs will become great photographers, just as not all those who paint become great artists. But we also know that dignity and creative pleasure know no barriers and that everyone has within him an aesthetic dimension and artistic potential which are only waiting to be developed. The fact that this can not only be useful but necessary to the life of the individual needs no emphasis here. Every true amateur must already have experienced from within some of the satisfaction which these activities can offer.

This book therefore aims to assist him, not just, as we have said, in offering technical advice but in clarifying his thoughts, if necessary, and encouraging him to persevere in a dimension which involves not only his technical skill but those spiritual resources and personal qualities which no one can disregard when they turn to the world of art.

PERCEIVING THE LANDSCAPE

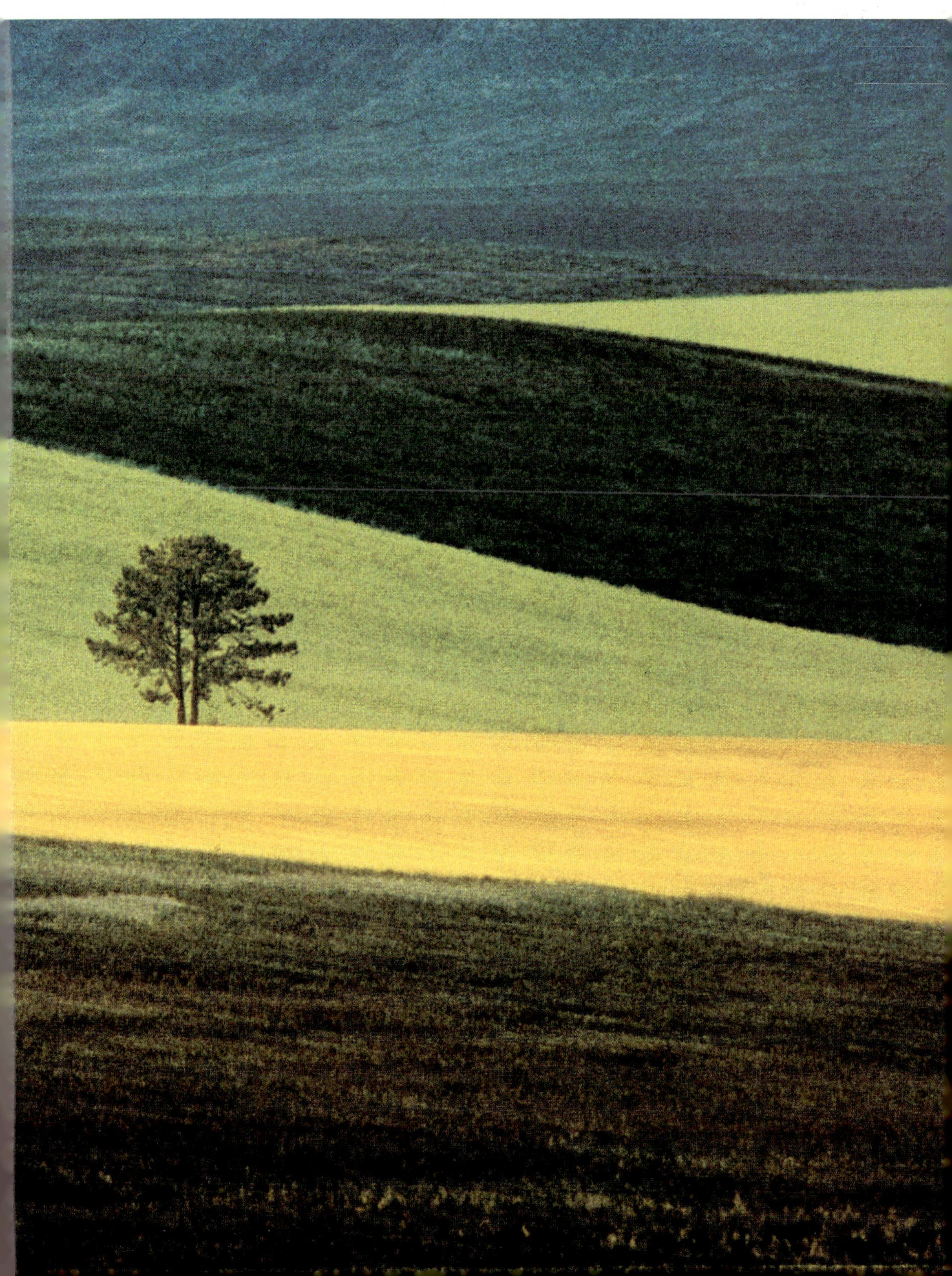

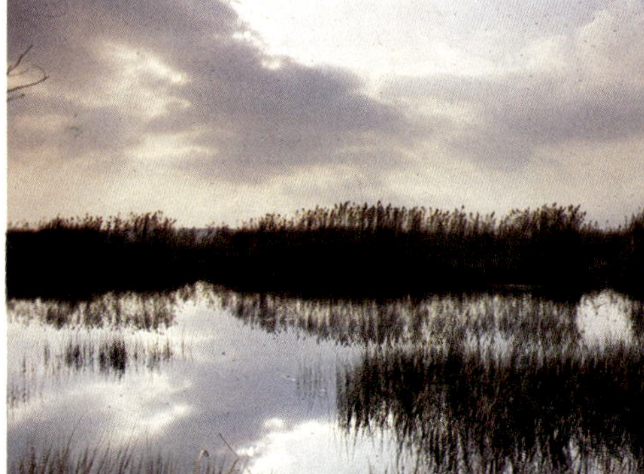

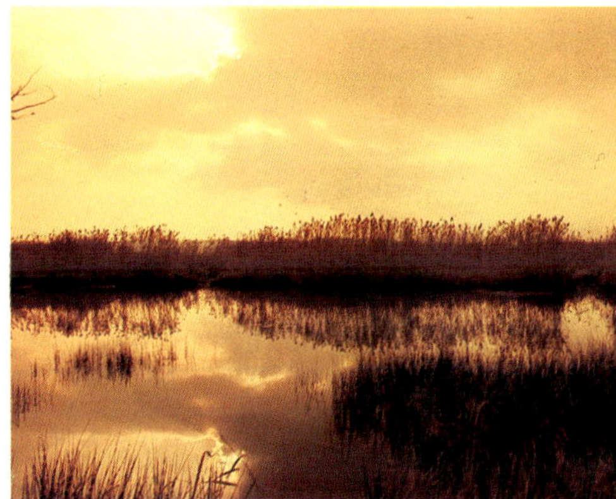

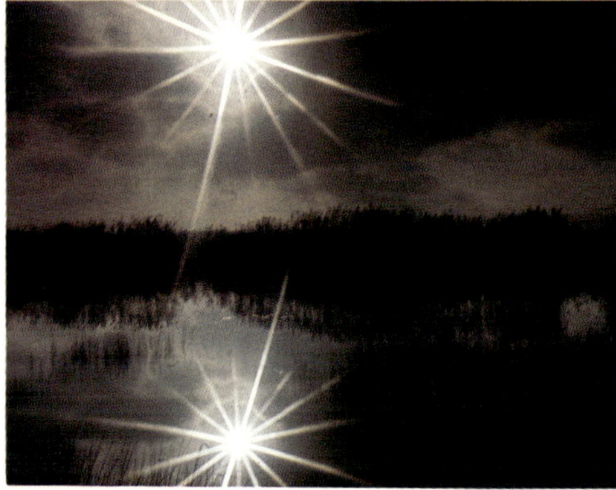

Photography as an art

This book does not claim to produce artists, or photographic artists. That is not to say that some of our readers may not become great photographers – and we should be very flattered if our reflections were able to assist them, even to a very limited extent, in doing so. But that is not our aim. We are well aware that art, at the highest levels, cannot be taught. It is the product of various factors: strength of character, originality, sensitivity and perseverance – which are frequently beyond the capabilities of the amateur, whatever his field of interest. The great artist and the great photographer can be produced by a combination of factors which are often unpredictable in their essence, in their amalgamation and in their development. But we should be less than honest if we were to state modestly that our only aim was to suggest a few basic rules which would be sufficient to bring the capabilities of each individual up to a level of bare adequacy.
There is no limit to improvement and there is a vast, intermediate range of possibilities between the highest achievements and barely mediocre results.
There is never a clear-cut distinction or qualitative barrier between the great, committed artist and the modest craftsman or still more modest amateur, but a very gradual series of results, already above a certain level which need not be very high, but which can be worthy of consideration and more than satisfying for those achieving them. Not only that, but while the great artist or photographer can produce some mundane works along with a series of masterpieces, by the same token the amateur, the humble photographer, can come up with some exceptional results along with a series of insignificant ones.
Photography as a means of communication is so intensively used today that it is all too easy to come across mediocre results, for example in newspapers, periodicals and in illustrated books. We are sure that many amateur photographers, equipped with a minimum of experience and sensitivity, would do better than some professional photographers who are accustomed to vulgarizing their products without any regard for culture or good taste.
We are sure, in fact, that many would be capable of improving on the general run of products in which photography is reduced to a mere, effortless means of mechanical reproduction.
On the contrary, we know that despite the mechanical components and technical

On the two preceding pages, a landscape by Franco Fontana.

On the opposite page, the same landscape, at the same time of day, photographed in natural light, with a graduated grey filter, with a sepia filter and with a graduated grey filter plus a cross screen. Whilst discussion of these filters will be dealt with later in the book, notice here the strikingly different results which can be obtained simply by changing a mechanical accessory – in confirmation of the interpretational freedom which the photographer, too, like any other artist, can generally achieve.

The photograph on the right, showing the Eiffel Tower at dusk, taken with a film for artificial light plus a cross screen, and the photograph below showing lighting effects obtained by moving the camera in different directions at night with the lens wide open, further confirm this freedom which can be carried to the limits of artificiality, even if we shall mainly be concentrating on the simplest and least sophisticated uses of photographic technique.

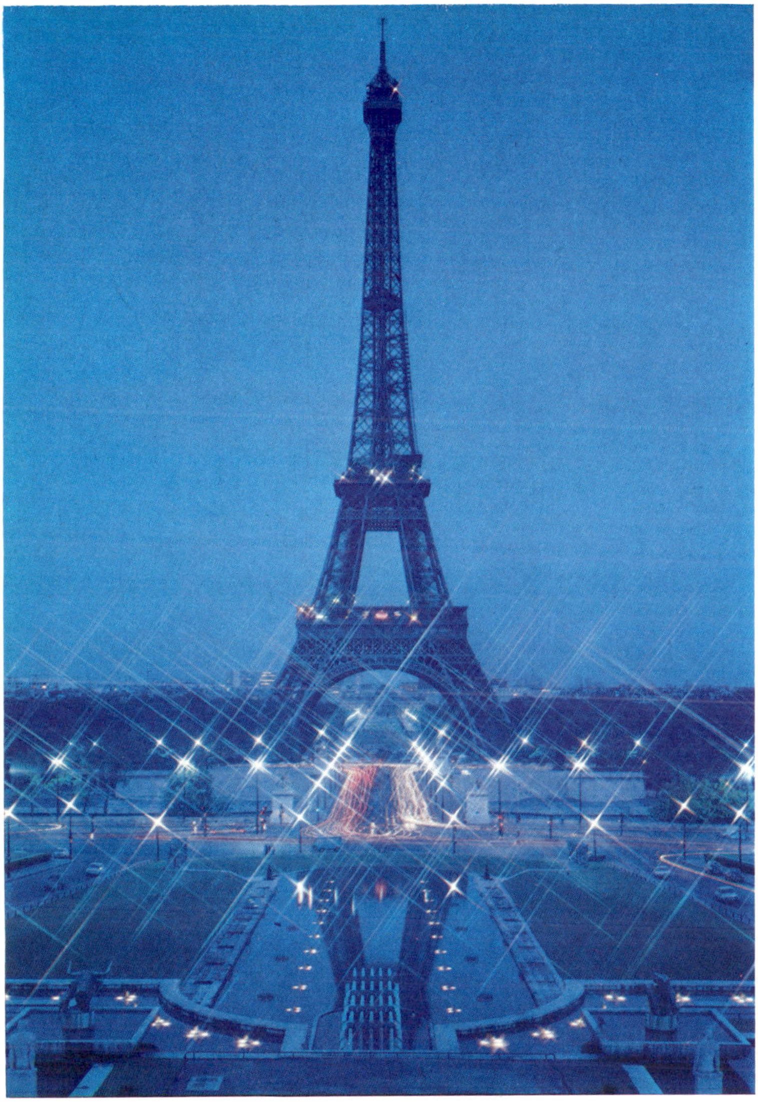

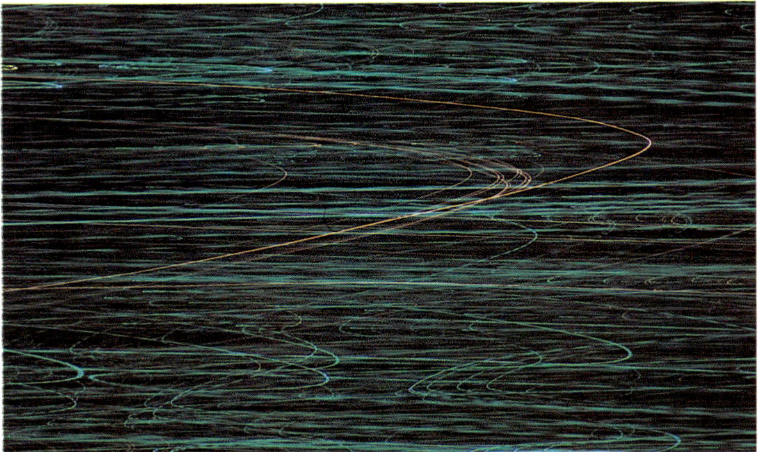

constraints by which photography is tied, from the choice of lens to the format and type of film, use of filters etc., the photographer has an instrumental freedom and a range of expressive possibilities which, even if not comparable to that which many craftsmen of the past enjoyed in other fields, is nonetheless more than sufficient to allow him scope for personal interpretation and hence creative originality. There is, in fact, no doubt that if on the one hand you need a theme, a precise datum to produce a good photograph — and we shall be seeing how important this is, above all for landscapes — on the other hand, it is the executor, the photographer, who must instil the characteristics of his choice, his own interpretation and possibly his own personality, into the material. On these will depend the quality or otherwise of his compositions. Faced with reality, with nature or with a landscape, a painter — in a field which has particular affinities with photography — has enormous technical freedom, even though he too is bound by certain objective components: the format of the canvas, for example; the types of colours available to him; the size of the brush, etc. The greater freedom which a painter enjoys is due to the fact that these very technical materials impose on him a deformation, an alteration of the subject matter, to make it more expressive and effective. A realist painter can respect absolutely the reality of the theme he is dealing with, whilst altering certain relationships, proportions and colours, if this enables him to portray it more effectively. There are also those artists who are not required to imitate more or less faithfully

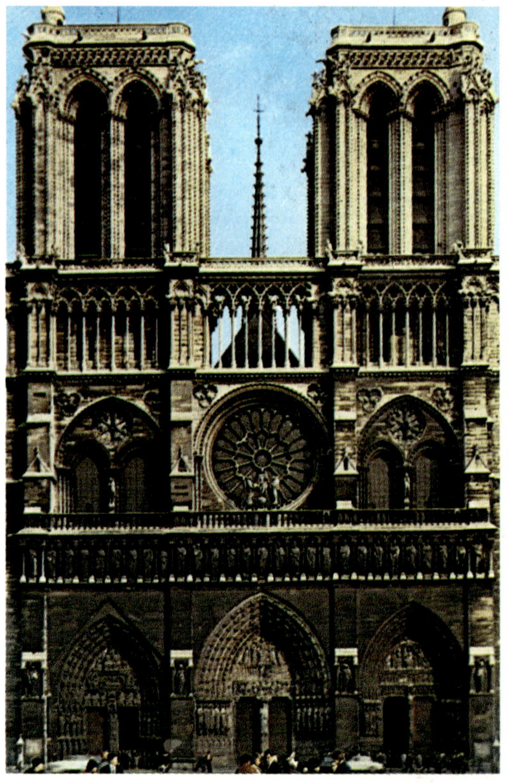

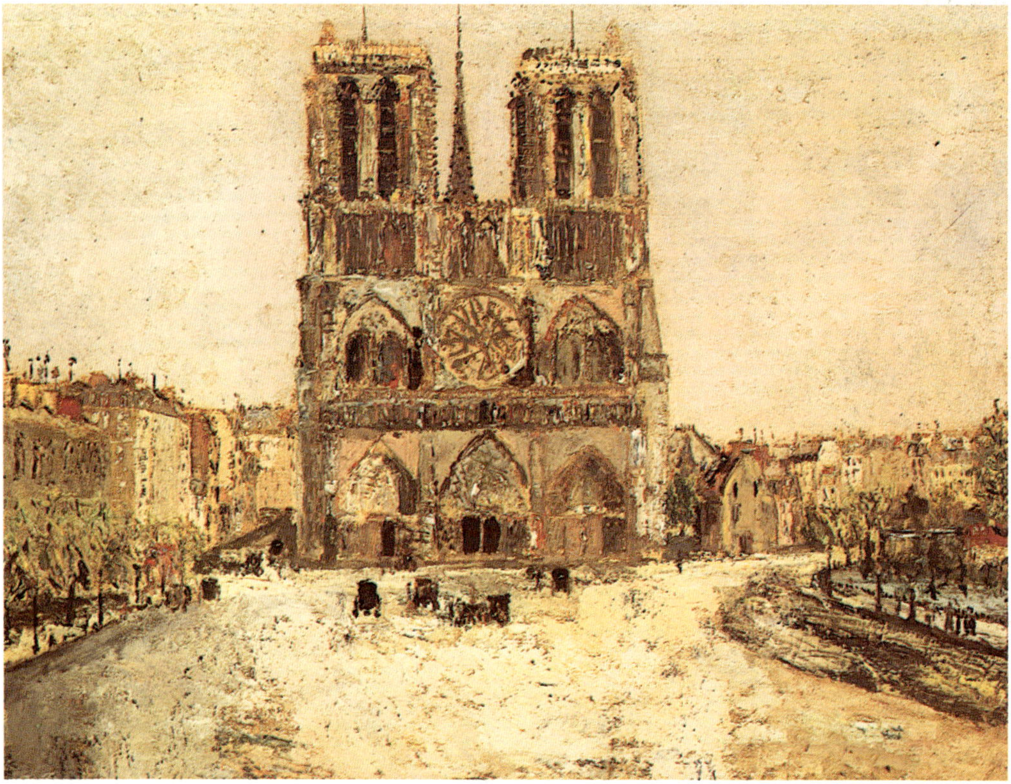

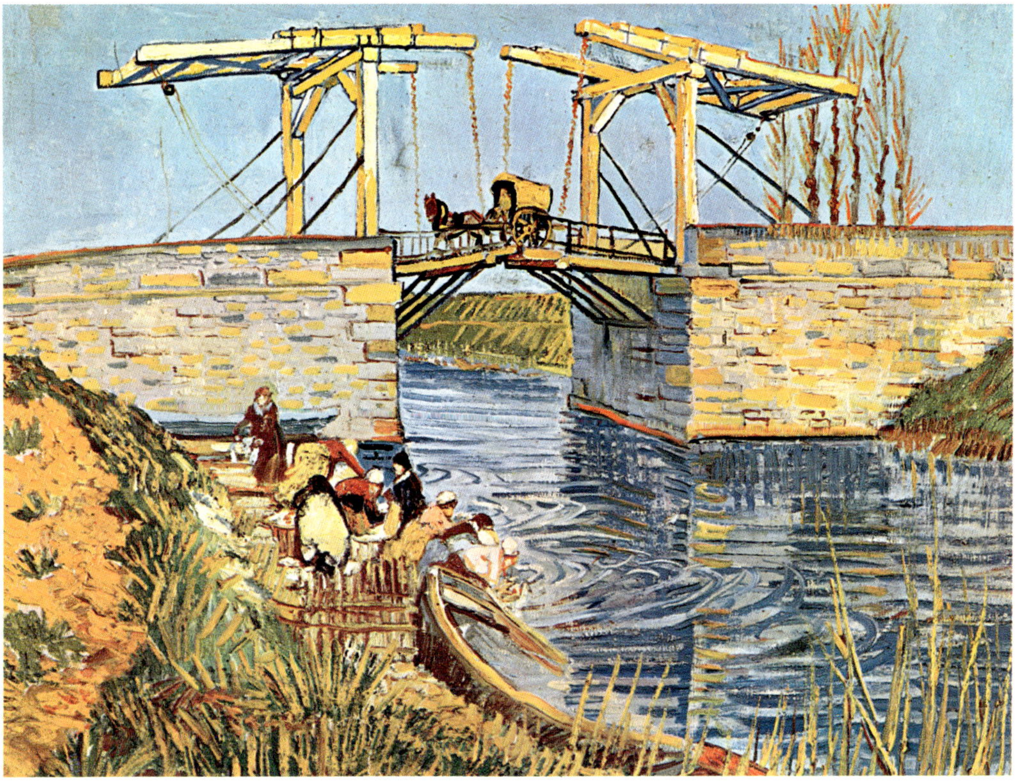

On the opposite page, the façade of Notre Dame in Paris and below, the same subject seen through the eyes of a famous Post-Impressionist painter: Maurice Utrillo. In this case the interpretational freedom of the artist is evident: the façade of the cathedral seems a mere support for the airy brush strokes of the artist, who is not interested in reproducing the details of reality which would have deprived the picture of the powerful sense of atmosphere which characterizes it.

the theme they have chosen but interpret it in a way that is at times deeply subjective, to the extent that the original data, the reality, are highly approximate.

As we shall see, the photographer also has a chance to alter or even disarrange the natural data, for example at the developing and printing stages, but he normally tends to respect them far more, given that photography has an essentially reproductive and documentary role and this is the area in which his skills are generally best employed. So many other means are available of creating an abstract composition, which are freer and more suitable than the camera. But if one wishes to document reality, then photography will seem to be the most efficient technical means available and in some cases, such as aerial, underwater and other types of scientific photography, quite irreplaceable.

But even when the photographer sets himself an exclusively, or primarily, reproductive goal, he can bring into play a whole range of elements, from the choice of theme to its composition, the use of a given type of lens, a given aperture, or film, as well as the processes of developing and printing, which enable him to add a personal touch to the photograph

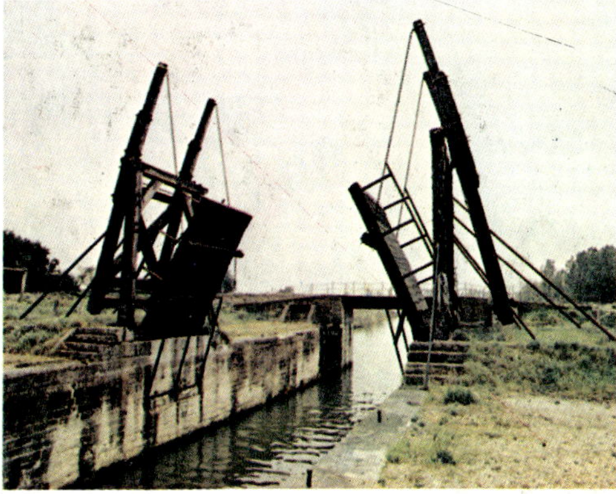

On this page, the drawbridge at Langlois as it really is, and in a famous interpretation by Van Gogh. To the artist, the picture of the bridge seems merely a pretext for producing the expressive tension of his colours. The painting is a graphic demonstration of the transfiguring power of art.

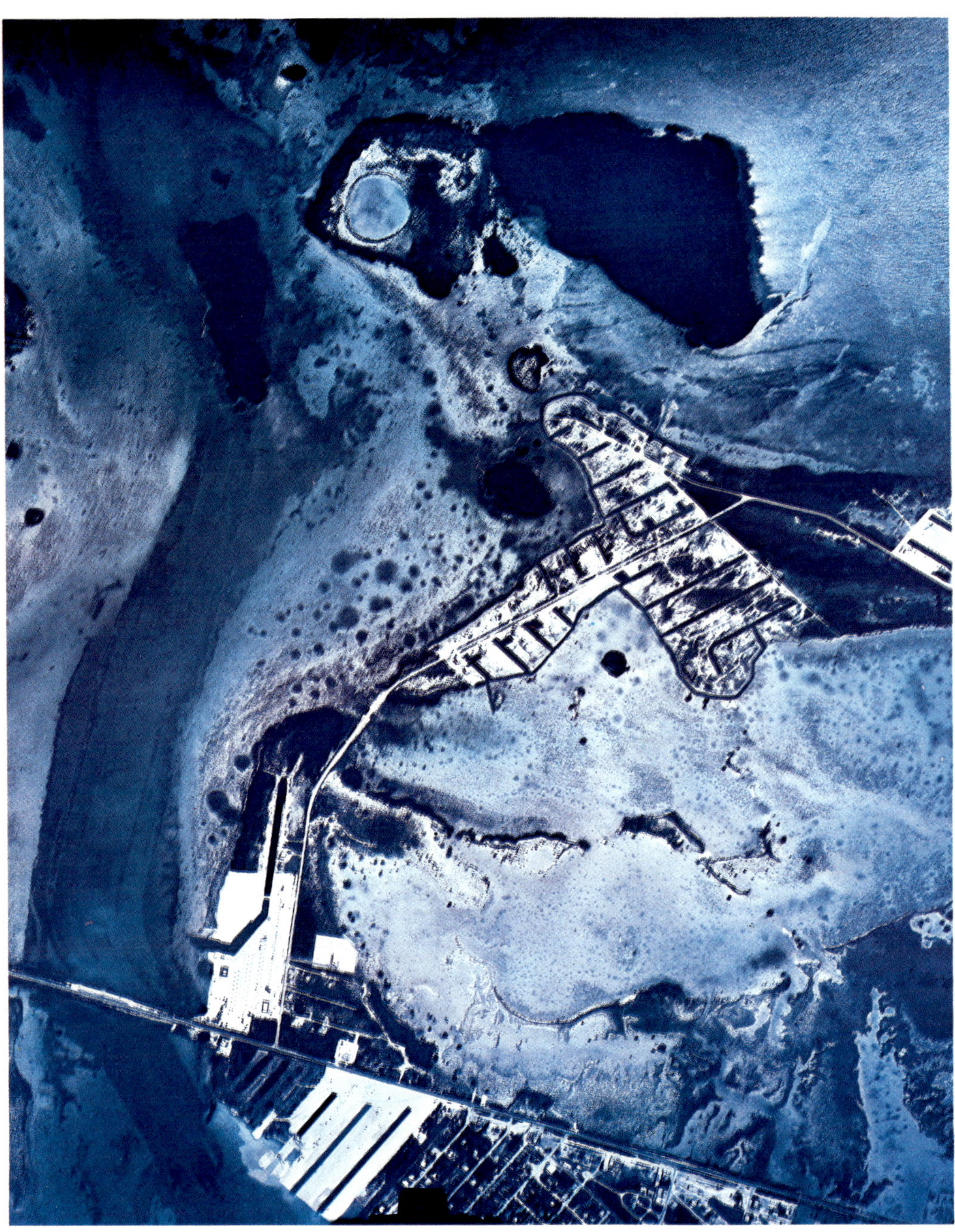

which will always be visible, even if he himself is not specifically aware of it. But this is the hallmark, as we have said, of that interpretational and creative freedom which is one of the necessary preconditions to any achievement being placed on an aesthetic plane. The mechanical nature of the reproductive means which the photographer uses can arouse the suspicion, and in some even the conviction, that photography is a product with very limited artistic potential. But you need only consider the means available to the photographer to personalize his image, to be fully convinced of the contrary.

Aerial photograph of Key West in Florida using techniques to emphasize blue light. It is a typical example of a photograph taken for documentary purposes, to show up the configuration of the coral reefs and the topography of the shallow waters.

The search for aesthetic quality

It is worth devoting a few words, once and for all, to the subject of aesthetic values. There is a tendency in society now to run down the aesthetic value of a product in favour of its social or economic implications. This is the almost inevitable consequence of a recent period of idolatry of the aesthetic and a sublimation of works of art and artists, which placed them above all other values.
It is not our wish to argue here with these typical attitudes of contemporary culture, nor to adopt a position either for or against them, but merely to point out that a reassessment of aesthetic values, even if it can seem desirable from a certain point of view, absolutely cannot lead to their negation. However important the useful and the good may be, in an economic and social context, one absolutely cannot exclude the presence of the beautiful. Any achievement, whatever its purpose, cannot avoid being classified according to a criterion of beauty, which it will be up to the moralist, the economist or the sociologist to establish how constructive it is, but which certainly exists in its own right and accordingly must respect certain rules and fixed values.
We therefore believe that a search for aesthetic quality, apart from being legitimate, is essential. For that matter, we instinctively make aesthetic judgements all the time, even about facts and achievements which do not really seem to elicit serious criticism.
A further investigation of what is meant by aesthetics and art would lead us far beyond the limits of our discussion and we are confident that the reader will accept the empirical nature of what has been said and would not press us to make distinctions which are interesting but superfluous on this occasion.
What we most wish to emphasize is that no photographs can avoid being judged in terms of aesthetics, not even the most scientific or documentary ones, because even these, apart from their technical quality, (which is not to be confused with their aesthetic value but is always a prerequisite for it) can have a greater or lesser aesthetic quality. With the same means and for the same purpose, one can take more or less beautiful photographs and the difference is all the more important, the more closely such photographs are concerned with the very broad field of advertising.

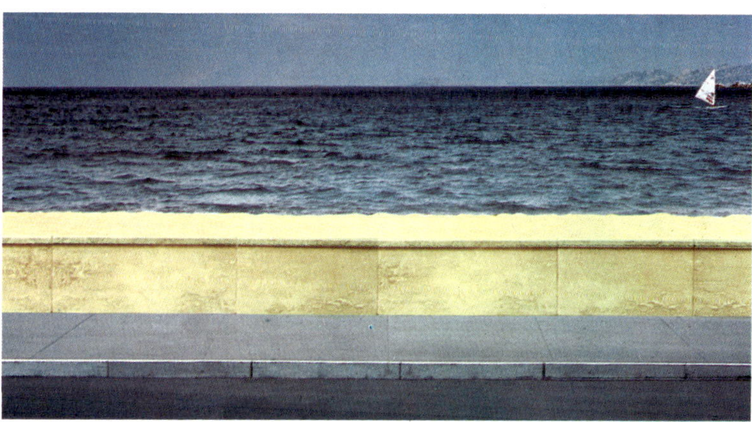

E' BELLO AVERE UNA RITMO.

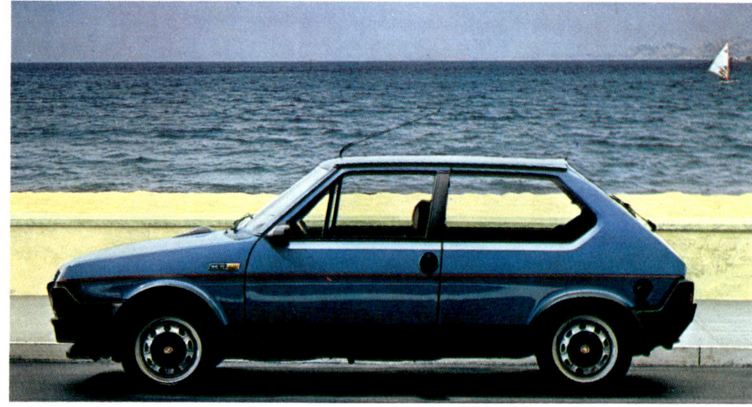

A typical example of a photograph used for advertising purposes. In a photograph of this kind, as in the one on the opposite page, the aesthetic component is clearly wholly subordinated to other aims. Note, however, that together with technical correctness of execution, which must be wholly suited to the purpose required, these pictures are not without an intrinsic formal quality, which goes to show that any type of functionality must also be backed up by good interpretational skills.

The space of the landscape

If you assign to photography a primarily reproductive role, that is of adhering to reality, even if this is not its only purpose but merely the one which seems best suited to its technical requirements, it must be understood that it will never be a reproduction but an interpretation of reality. This becomes clear when one is dealing with landscape photography. A landscape, in fact, can never be contained in a photograph. Nor can a portrait, a figure or a still life. No object can realistically be contained in a photograph; but the disproportions, the conditioning, the adaptations of the thing portrayed in the photograph, are more obvious in the landscape than elsewhere. You need only think of a typical characteristic of landscapes, which is their sense of space and atmosphere. Even a still life or a portrait has a spatial and atmospheric dimension, but it is not comparable to that of a landscape.

We do not merely *look* at a landscape; we travel though it, breathe it, live it. The same relationship is found between landscapes and other dimensions of reality, as between architecture and other figurative expressions. Painting and sculpture also have a material space, but this has objectively minimal dimensions which only the power of suggestion can make us expand in the imagination, while architectural space is concrete, is there before us. It invites us to walk through it and arouses thoughts in us which directly involve not just our eyes, but, as it were, the totality of our senses. This does not mean that architecture is a higher or richer form of art than others, but simply that given the unity of artistic values, whatever the dimension in which they are expressed and the often misleading opinions which have dominated the world of art criticism, architecture expresses itself in a language which is typical of it and which other forms of art possess to a different degree. The sense of space, therefore, which is certainly one of the most characteristic elements in landscapes, is physically irreproducible in the small and sometimes minute format of a photograph. It can only be suggested, evoked, but clearly then it is no longer a reproduction, but an interpretation.

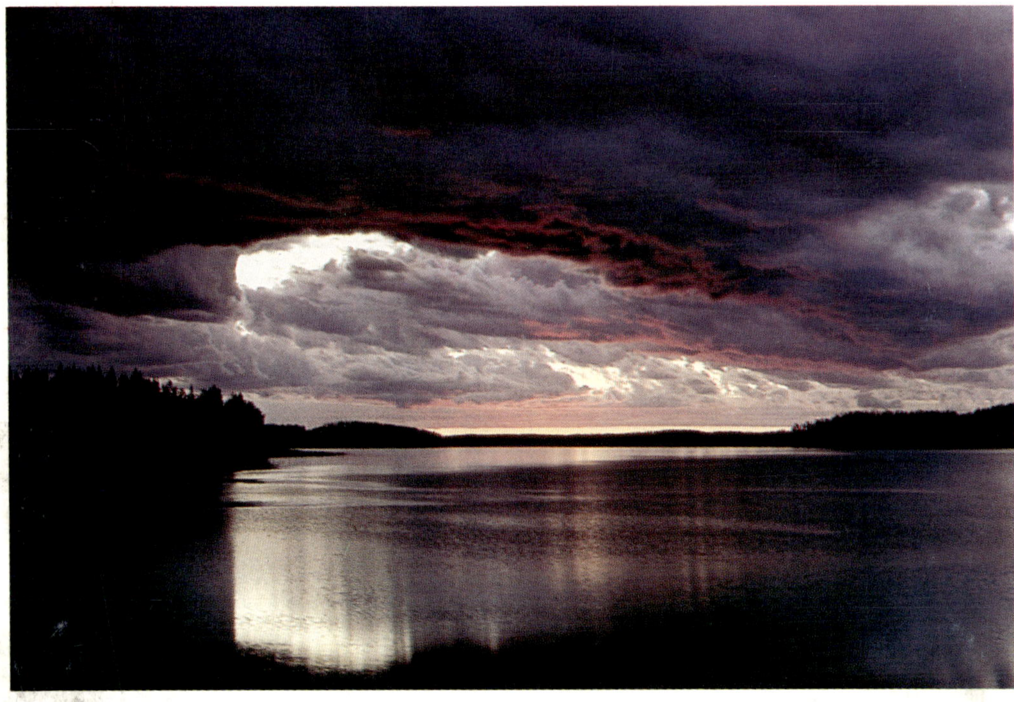

Above, effect of clouds over a stretch of water. Space is indicated by the scenographic "wing" effect of the clouds.

Opposite page, fallow deer at S. Rossore, Pisa (photo taken with a Hasselblad 250 mm lens from a hide). Both these photographs owe much of their effect to the interpretation of space, shown in very different ways. In the first case the space is made up of strong contrasts of light and colour which show the mobility of the planes composing it; in the second, the gradation of atmospheric tones gives what is known in painting as "aerial perspective."

Obviously, interpretation is very much open to the subjectiveness and creative freedom of the artist. This in fact is why so-called "realist" painters, or those who have devoted themselves most conscientiously to imitating reality, have never been able to reduce their creativity to mere technical application; their overriding personality always manifests itself in the most original fashion – and so it is with photographers. However, landscape painting was not present throughout the history of painting. Some cultures – particularly religion-based ones such as medieval Christianity or Moslem culture – ignored landscapes altogether and therefore gave a wholly different meaning to space. On those rare occasions when paintings from these periods contain landscapes in some form they are portrayed in such a way as to exclude a direct relationship with reality as we see it.

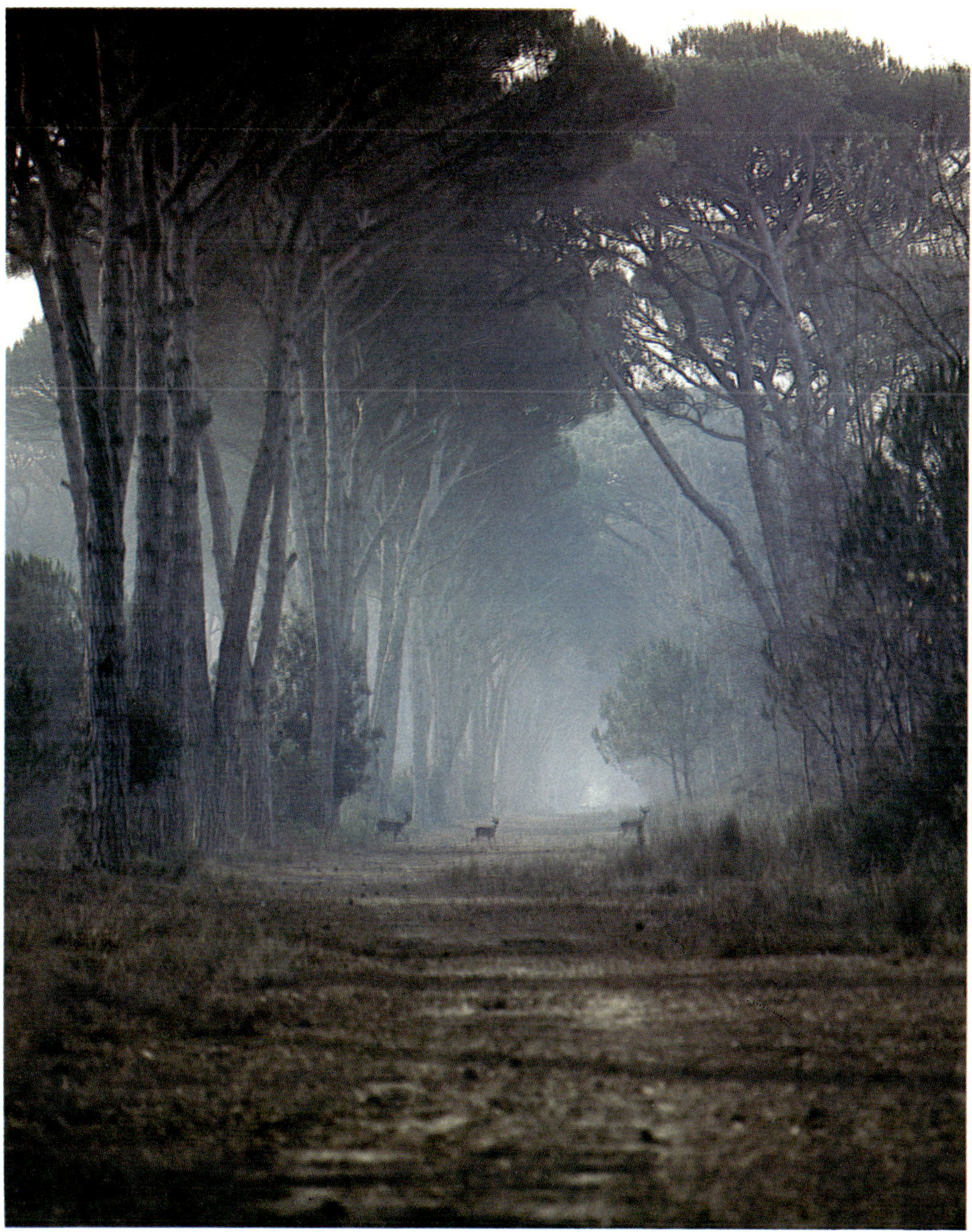

Analogies between painting and landscape photography

Some quite extraordinary analogies may be established between painting and landscape photography. Painters can be described as the first landscape photographers in history. From them, an intelligent photographer can obtain very valuable ideas, even today, not so much from a technical point of view, of course, but certainly in terms of the type of reflection and mental processes involved, after which the technical application might seem a mere mechanical corollary.

Landscape painters, in short, have had to complete a process of identification, of choice and adaptation which is often identical to the one a photographer must complete. Remembering that some of these landscape painters have touched the highest peaks of artistic expression, one can readily understand how useful an exercise it is, in every respect, whether formal, historical, psychological, etc., to understand their language.

No cultured person, no artist, even if he is operating at amateur level, can fail to appreciate what a wealth of experience, teachings and stimuli is contained in the masterpieces of the past. Certainly, the most significant works of our time, or those very near to our time, may be regarded as the most useful for us to know in that they can give us more "up-to-date" and functional information on our problems, but we cannot ignore or underestimate what could be called the eternal universality of man, namely everything which unites us in an extraordinary variety of art forms to the men of all times and all nations, with the result that no human experience is lost to us, or superfluous. Thus if the paintings in the paleolithic "cathedrals," that is, the prehistoric paintings in the caves of the Pyrenees and the Massif Central in France or certain paintings in Pompeii, Egypt, or China can be meaningful to us and can be described as "modern," how much more accessible to us will be a work by Canaletto, who was painting in the first half of the eighteenth century, or Constable, who was active in the last century. Finally there is another aspect which can show us how valuable an experience of the masterpieces of the past can be, namely the refinement of our taste and critical capacity. It would be a serious mistake to think that the critical sense is quite separate from the creative sense, as if criticism involved only passivity, and creation only initiative. Anyone familiar with the history of art will know that painting did not always have the descriptive character typical of it in more recent times. In some periods, painting, like every other artistic

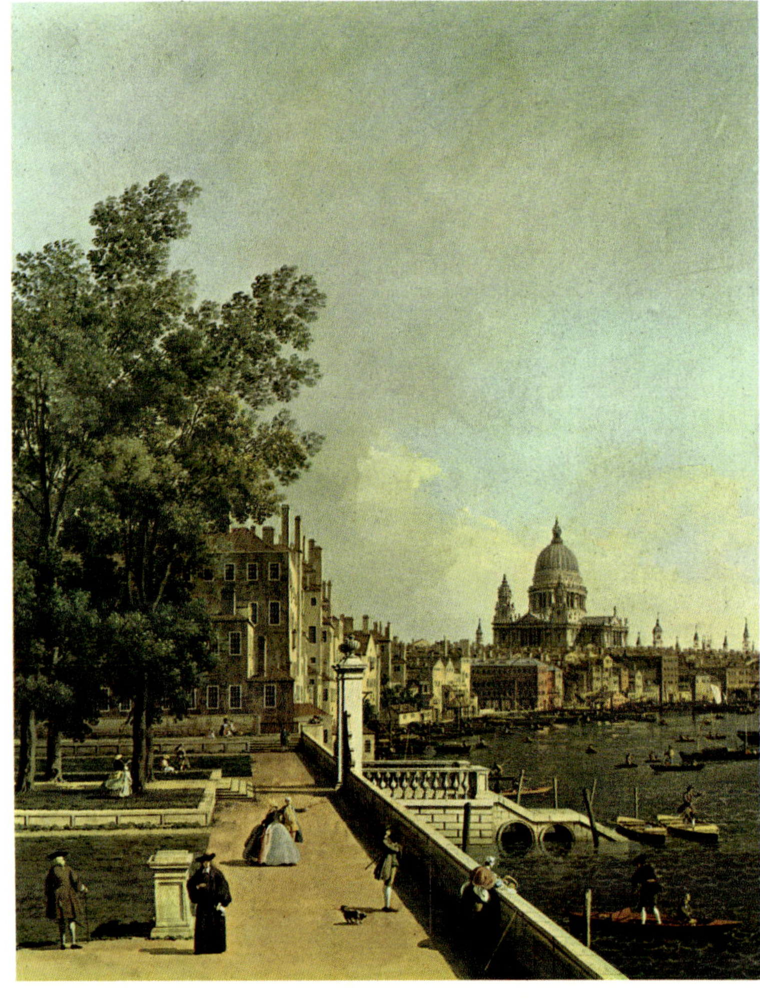

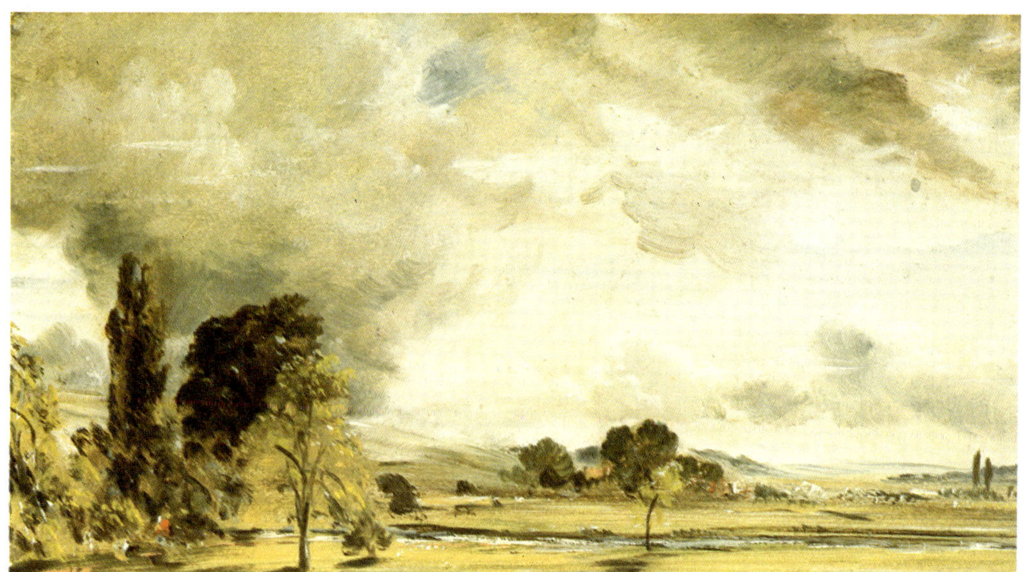

On the opposite page, detail from a famous painting by Canaletto showing The Thames from the terrace of Somerset House. *It is obvious that Canaletto in the eighteenth century still relied on a geometric type of perspective formation, in which all the details were thoroughly sharp, and despite this the light achieved a profound visual unity, joyful and vibrant.*

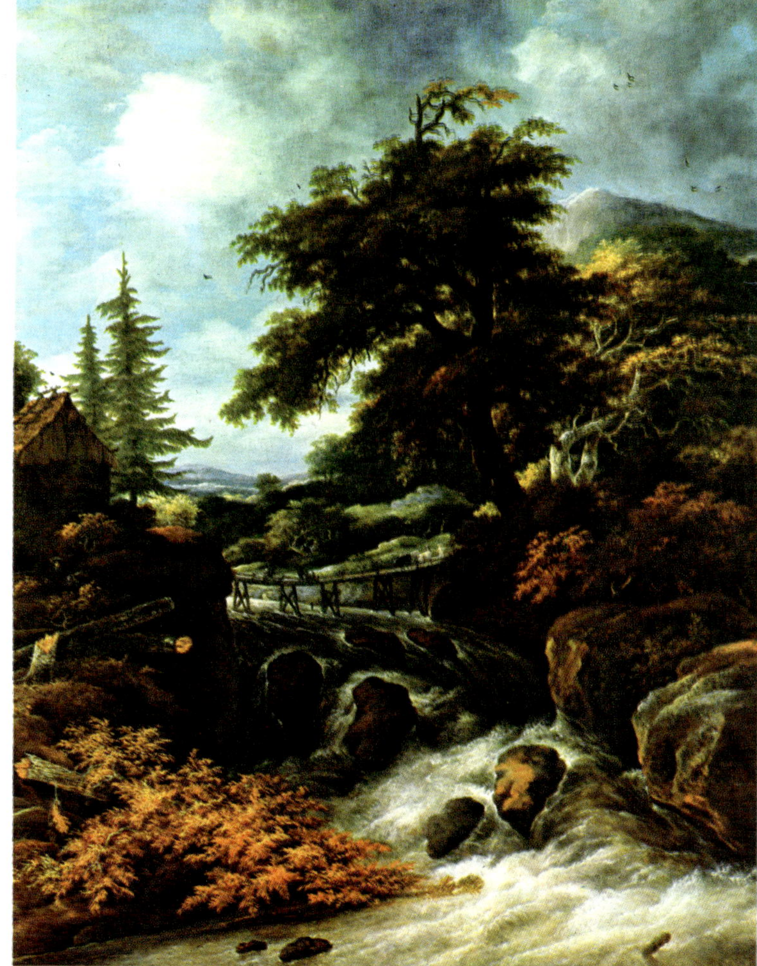

Above, John Constable, A View at Salisbury, *1829. Constable relied for the representation of space on a profound sense of atmosphere, by which he showed the solemn movement of the English sky.*

Right, Jacob van Ruysdael, Waterfall near a hut in Hilly Country. *This artist is regarded as the leading exponent of seventeenth-century Dutch painting and he interpreted space by dramatic and romantic contrasts of different masses of colour.*

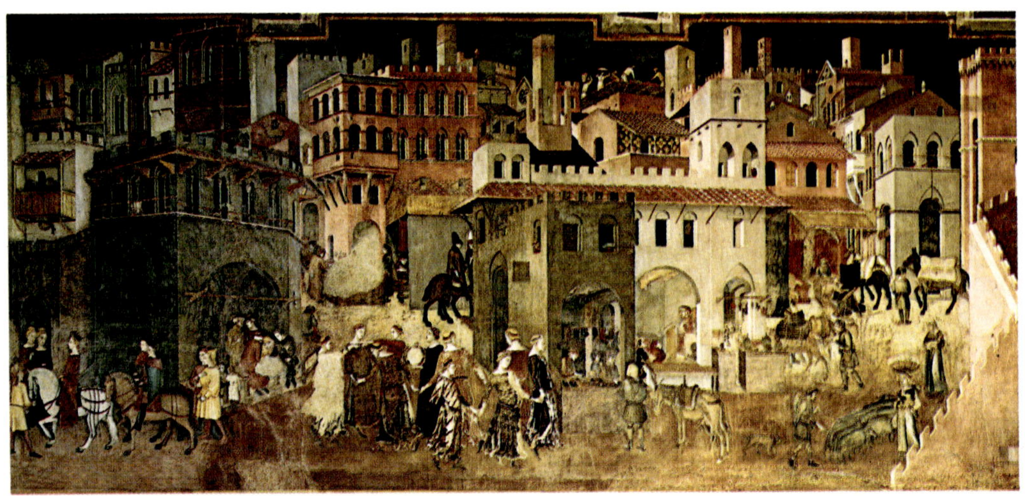

expression, played an exclusively or primarily religious, politico-religious or magical role and artists worked not to embellish an environment, which in the final analysis is what a painter tends to do even today when he paints a picture, but to teach truths, express concepts of power or arouse feelings of adoration and prayer. Landscape painting developed naturally in those times where the description of nature, its beauties and the relationship which man shared with it, assumed a prevailing importance; it is no accident that, as happened to the Dutch painters of the seventeenth century, landscape painting developed alongside still life and portrait painting and in fact these genres (portrait, still life, landscape) more or less appeared together and grew out of a celebration of reality – the *joie de vivre* of an opulent Holland which after long years of sacrifice and wars had won her freedom. Even before the Dutch made landscape painting one of the key genres of their pictorial civilization and spread it throughout Europe as a sign of their merchant, middle class and democratic spirit, landscapes had known moments of glory, although not in their own right. They are already found in the realist studies of the Gothic period, when, without abandoning certain religious preconceptions and traditional

Above, Ambrogio Lorenzetti, Allegory of Good Government, *Palazzo Pubblico, Siena. This great fresco, painted in the first half of the fourteenth century, is one of the first examples of the interpretation of an urban landscape which is fantastic overall, but realistic in many details. Medieval painting, which for very many centuries was tied to symbolism and mystic abstraction, only developed an interest in the concrete aspects of life later on. This drew the artists' attention to the world of nature and thus to landscapes.*

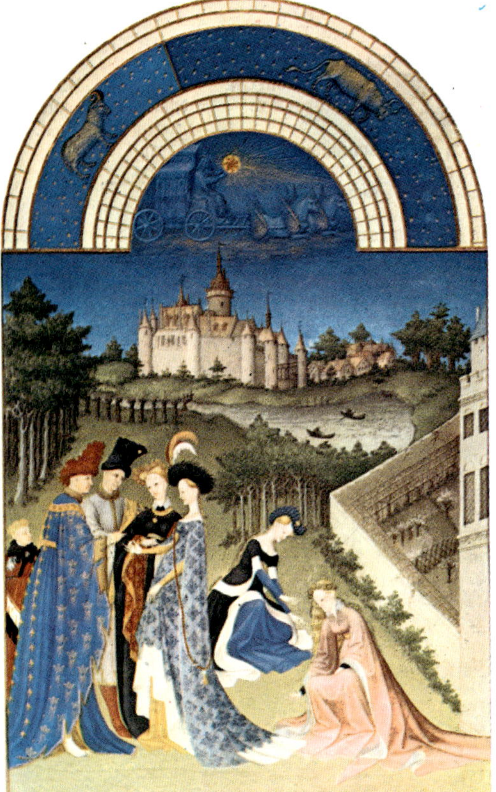

Left, Paul de Limbourg, April, *from* Les Très Riches Heures *of the Duc de Berry. Note how despite the attention of the painter at the beginning of the fifteenth century to the figures and the marvellously natural environment, fantastic elements still prevail.*

On the opposite page, Giorgione da Castelfranco, The Tempest. *This is the first representation of a scene in which nature, the atmosphere, the landscape, prevail over the very meaning of the representation, which has been lost. It is also a classic example of "aerial perspective."*

precepts, which excluded a genuine reality for fear of vulgarity, men had begun to discover nature.
No one can forget the view of the streets of Siena painted by Ambrogio Lorenzetti in the *Allegoria del Buon Governo* (Allegory of Good Government) in the Palazzo Pubblico with the cavalcade passing out of the city gates towards a landscape of hills and countryside in which one never ceases to recognize not specific places, but even more importantly, the very spirit of the countryside of Siena.
Nor can one forget the castles and estates where the peasants are at work, the meadows and forests where cavalcades of knights and ladies meet, in the illustrations of the *Très Riches Heures* of the Duc de Berry. Midway between chivalry and astrology, these pictures contain very vivid references to nature and landscapes, which the subsequent painting by the primitive Flemish artists from Van Eyck to Bosch were to assimilate. But in these works, although they were so far ahead of their time in their interest in reality – as in the more conscious Tuscan painting of the Renaissance which created the laws of perspective governing the vision of space – the landscape was subordinated to other interests, other values, above all religious ones, or the humanist values being extolled by the Renaissance. This also happens with the painters of the Venetian school, who are the most mature in terms of their interest in landscapes. In their paintings, from Bellini to Titian, the dominant motif, whether religious or allegorical and humanistic, leaves ever greater room for the definition of the landscape, which invades their themes to an increasing extent, even literally, until we come to *The Tempest* painted by Giorgione, in which even the enigmatic meaning of the canvas seems to dissolve in a nocturnal vision illuminated by the lightning flashes of a summer storm. Here, discovery of the landscape does not just denote an interest in reality but an appreciation of its inner being, its transformation into states of mind, its melting into the moments of our existence.
However, with the continuation, even in *The Tempest* by Giorgione, of purposes extraneous to the landscape as such, which in these and other cases assumes a purely allegorical role, with the use of the landscape as an element subordinated to other meanings of the painting, we have to admit that we are still a long way from a landscape which is specifically reproduced, even if it is very realistically interpreted.
The paintings of the fifteenth and sixteenth centuries already contain faithful reproductions of landscape details, which have a counterpart in reality, but the realism of these paintings hardly ever concerns them as a whole, but only the details, such as flowers, plants, rocks, water, clouds etc. All the elements which make up the picture seem true-to-life, each in its own right, but it is the imagination which links them together in landscapes which are nearly always imaginary, despite having all the characteristics of real landscapes.

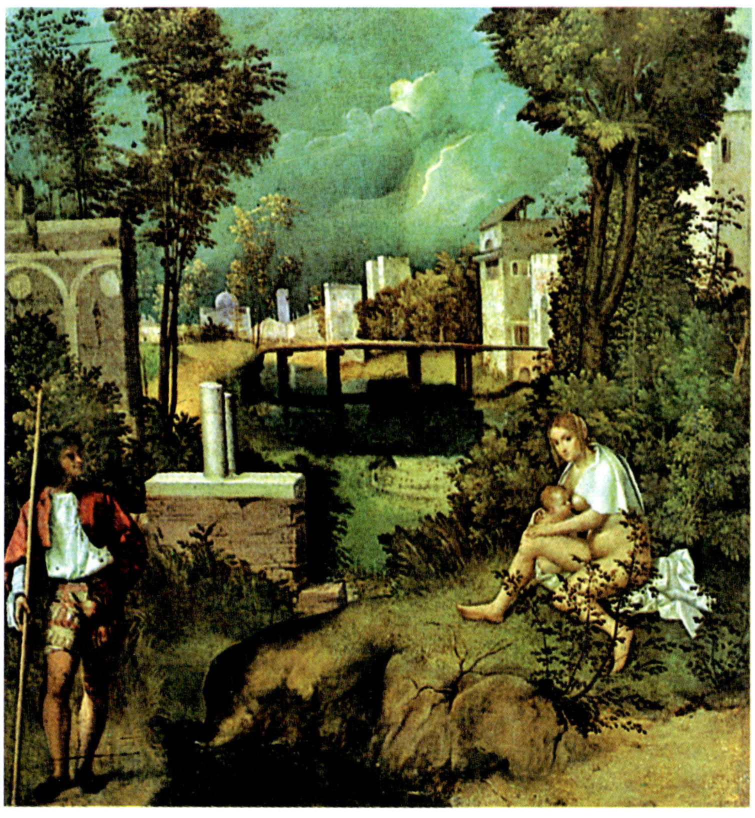

Two- and three-dimensional space

It is worth clarifying the definition of "landscape." Generally, when this word is used it is easy to understand what is meant, but a moment's reflection can lead us to some important considerations. Landscape originally meant a "tract of land" and the definition therefore refers to a territory, a natural environment of variable size, but always relatively large. An unavoidable characteristic of a landscape would therefore seem to be "space." Space has been shown in paintings in very many different ways. In some periods and civilizations, space was seen in two-dimensional terms, that is, height and width alone, which qualify a surface, without the dimension of depth. This happened, for example, in Byzantine painting which for long periods was purely "two-dimensional," above all because it represented symbols, which were devoid of true substance, and hence thickness or real depth. Clearly, in this type of interpretation, even the elements of the landscape such as houses, trees or rocks, could only be symbolic, described purely on the surface and without body or depth. Even oriental painting was at times two-dimensional, and this was because it was more interested in certain profiles, movements and attitudes than in a global representation of reality. Interest in the material world developed above all in the Renaissance. In the fifteenth century the Tuscan artists got to grips with the problem of reproducing space and solved it by organizing their view according to the geometrical rules of perspective, which became a fundamental part of their art. From the Renaissance to the nineteenth century, painting always portrayed a three-dimensional space, in which depth was emphasized in

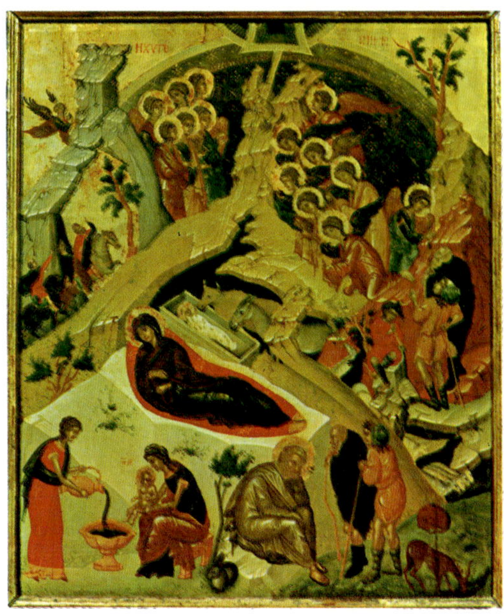

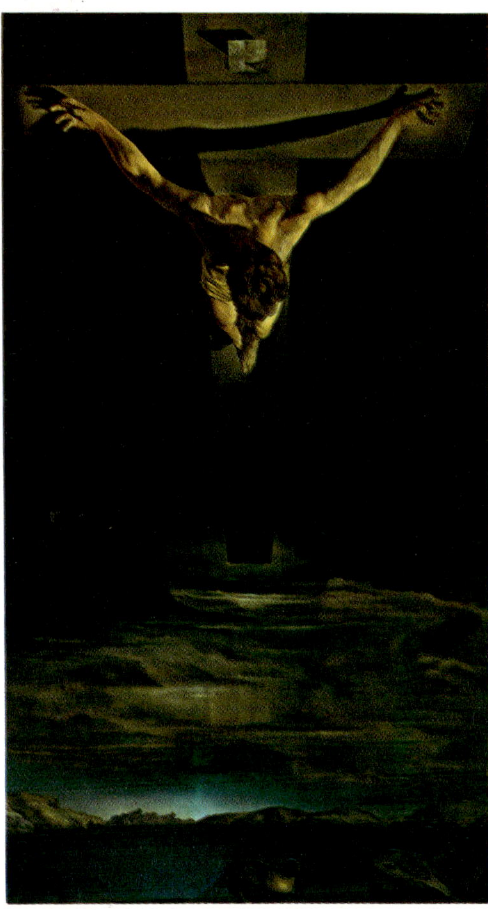

Above, a typical Byzantine painting representing the Nativity. Byzantine art was faithful for centuries to a tradition which interpreted space in a totally symbolic way, barely suggesting the depth of the planes and flattening everything on to the same surface.
Left, this painting by Salvador Dali, representing the Christ of St. John of the Cross, is a clear example of three-dimensional representation, carried to levels of virtuosity.

On the opposite page, above: this photograph, which shows a picture of the sun through a delicate framework of grasses, is an example of the extreme flattening produced by telephoto lenses and shows how, even in photography, one can achieve an almost totally two-dimensional representation of space.
At the opposite extreme, the photograph below, showing a sunset in the lagoon, gives us an interpretation of the depth of space, that is, of its three-dimensionality, purely in terms of chromatic values, that is, the different tones of light, given that there is no geometrical support for perspective in the picture.

various ways. But at the end of the nineteenth and above all in our own century, anti-academic currents tended to deny three-dimensional space in favour of forms of symbolism and abstraction which led once again to the negation of depth. Paintings by Matisse, Klee, Miró and many others, are often only developed on the surface, showing no thickness or relief. However much photography, having a primarily documentary and reproductive role, may have tended to remain faithful to a three-dimensional interpretation of space, there have been attempts to relate it to the most *avant-garde* stages of painting, by trying to obtain effects of the annihilation of depth.

In any case, even ignoring the experiments which have been carried out in specific environments in the name of aestheticism, the language of photography has undoubtedly been affected by what was happening in other artistic sectors, suggesting forms of expression which took account of similar experiments even when they continued to have a primarily reproductive, not abstract role.

We shall be taking a look later on at some photographers who have approached abstractionism, whilst respecting certain elements of reality.

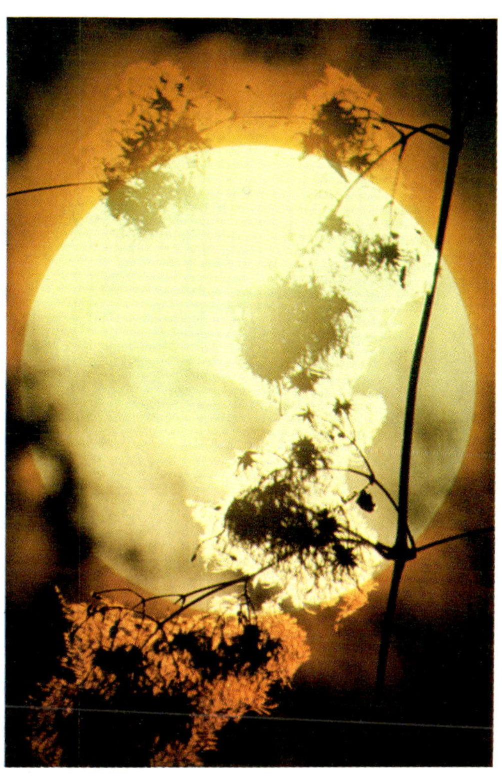

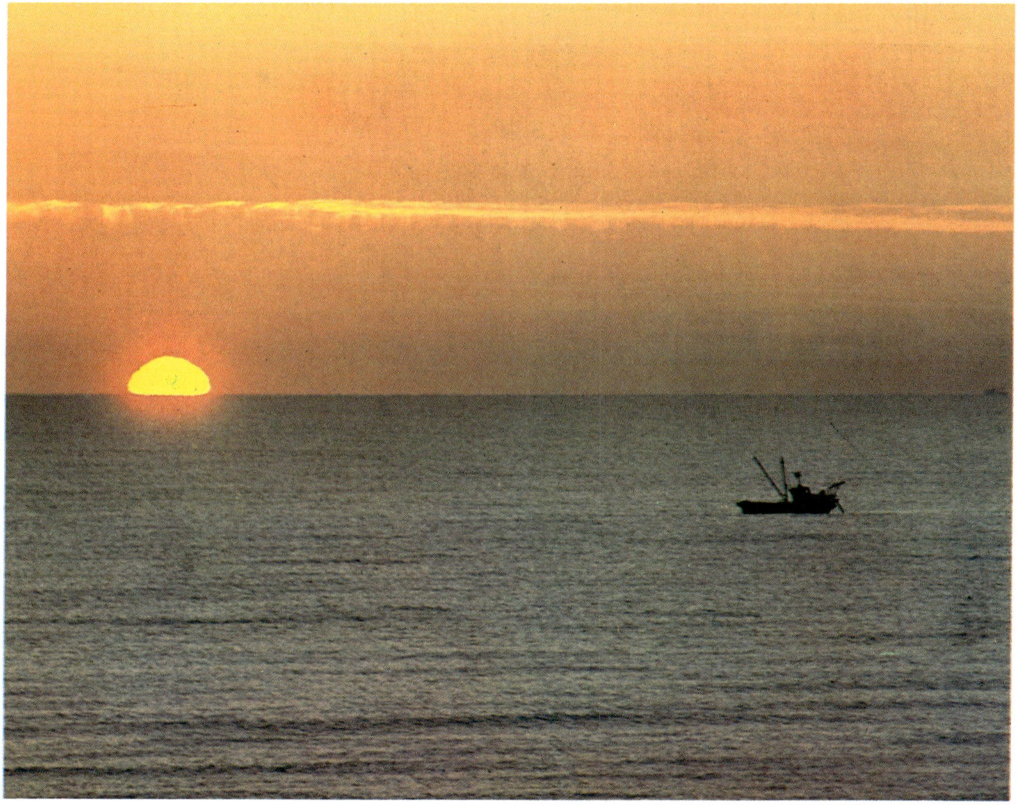

The application of the rules of perspective to the representation of space was not a mere technical device for the artists of the Renaissance. It coincided with a new conception of man and the universe; it was a way of comprehending reality in rational terms and therefore had moral, scientific and philosophical implications. Some of the leading artists of the period, such as Piero della Francesca, were also treatise writers and it was partly on account of their prestige that the rules of perspective were considered a vital part of any artist's training until comparatively recently. These rules were studied increasingly in all their possible applications until, in the seventeenth and eighteenth centuries, they found an ideal field of application in stage design. In those centuries, classified as the Baroque and Rococo periods in the history of art, the theater was one of the major art forms, in which one of the prevailing aspects of the culture of that time – a tendency to ostentation, emphasis and imagination – could be developed to the full.

Right from the outset, perspective was akin to theatrical sets, in that it had to create an artificial impression of three-dimensional space within the two-dimensional limits of a flat surface, and the first stage designers were already applying

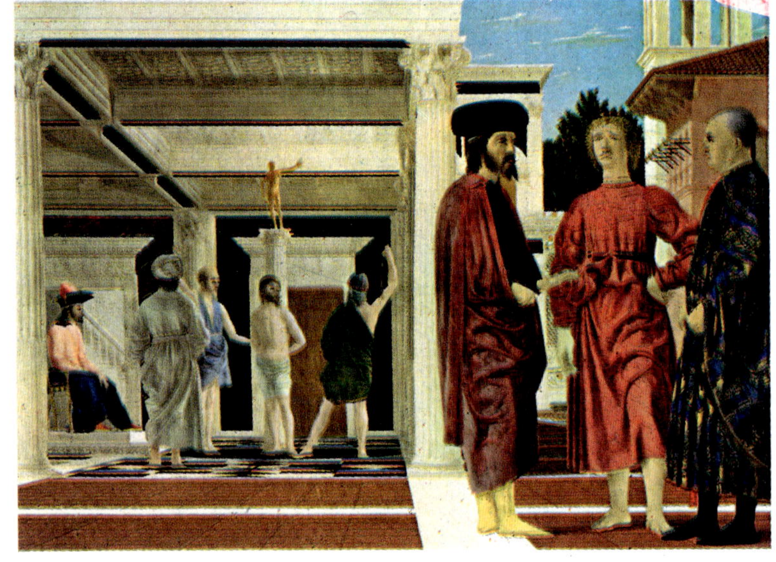

Above, Piero della Francesca, Flagellation of Christ. *This work is symbolic of the use of geometrical perspective by Tuscan artists in the Renaissance. The application of linear perspective seems here to be demonstrating a theorem, it is so neat and regular. Far from being a mere technical invention, perspective becomes a lyrical theme, in which space, thus represented, achieves an order which is ideal in its purity and heroic in its grandeur. The representation of reality by means of perspective was a pretext for extolling human reason and the absolute powers which man seemed to possess in relation to nature. The technique of perspective was studied not only for aesthetic and formal purposes, but with the fervour dedicated to a new science.*

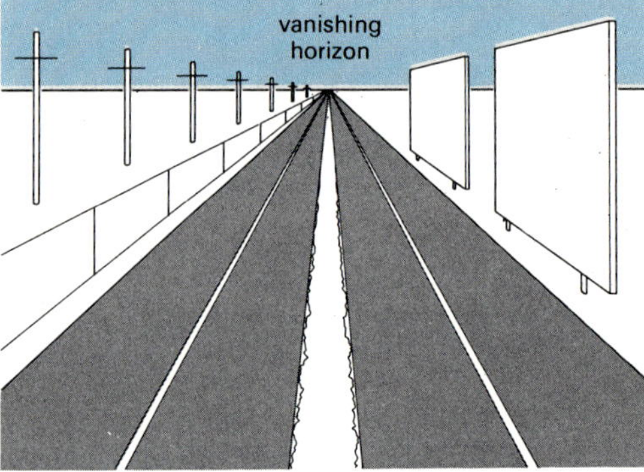

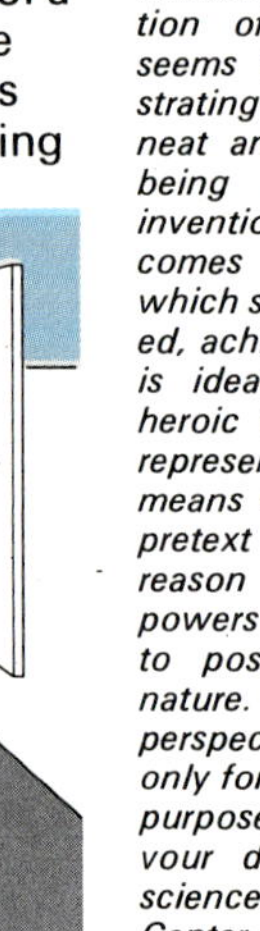

Center, example of central perspective with a single vanishing point.

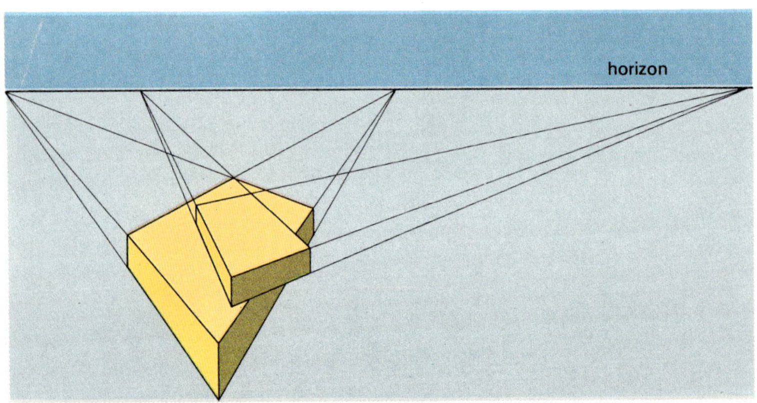

Below, example of perspective with several vanishing points.

On the opposite page, map of a hypothetical complex of four parallelepipeds, showing the cardinal points for orientation. Underneath, a diagram of how the appearance of the same parallelepipeds changes when seen from various viewpoints: from the south, east, south-east, south-west and north-east.

these rules in fairly simple form in the sixteenth century. But as experience of the subject was built up, together with an interest in increasingly complex and surprising scenes, the art of feigning space by a careful articulation of wings and other perspective devices became increasingly elaborate, and stage design came to influence all other art forms, including architecture and, of course, painting. Stage designers, architects and painters now seemed like expert producers who knew how to organize vanishing points, movements and lights. Although perspective is based on a single and indisputable principle from a scientific point of view, it can be variously interpreted and applied. To the uninitiated, this may seem absurd, and even art historians have not always been fully aware of it. But the perspective used by Masaccio, for example, is different from that of Piero della Francesca or Mantegna, or Tiepolo. Perspective is a means of reproducing the depth of space on a flat surface, using an imaginary network of lines going out from a frame which is chosen as the setting for the view and meeting at a single point, placed at a distance representing infinity. The various figures need therefore only be placed within this network for them to acquire the size which derives mathematically from their distance.

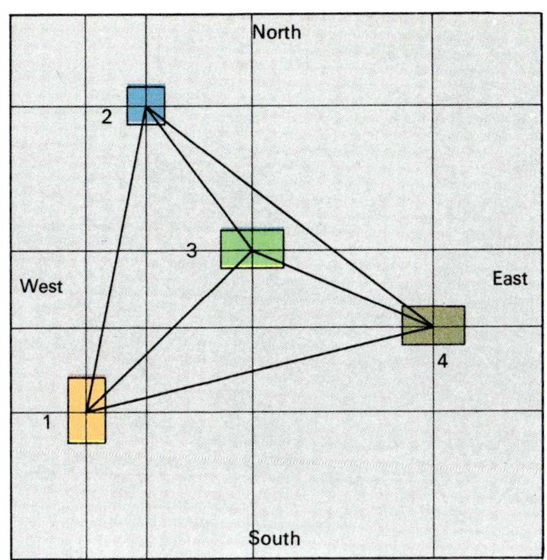

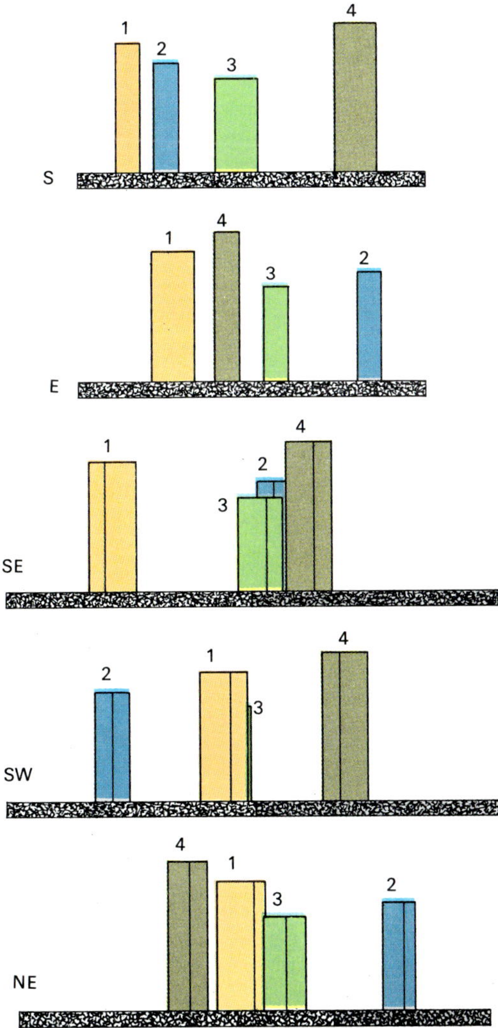

Up to this point, the rules of perspective are one and immutable. But the proportions of the frame may well be varied, that is, we can broaden our visual base, or narrow it down at will. Photographers can readily understand this problem by a simple reference to the lenses they use. As these are mechanical devices, it is obvious that they subject one's view to a precise mathematical organization of proportions. But the result a wide-angle gives is radically different from that, for example, of a normal lens. The visual pyramid created by the wide-angle (every system of perspective can be reduced to a visual pyramid) has a very broad base and therefore a relatively modest height. Conversely, the visual pyramid of a normal lens has a relatively small base but a far greater height, or rather, a longer focal length. Thus while a wide-angle can cover a very broad space which is even more than that of normal, human vision, the other lens can only select a slice of our view, but to compensate for this, the imaginary oblique lines marking the pyramid or perspective will distort the spaces and objects reproduced much less than the wide-angle, which invariably alters them a great deal, particularly the near ones.

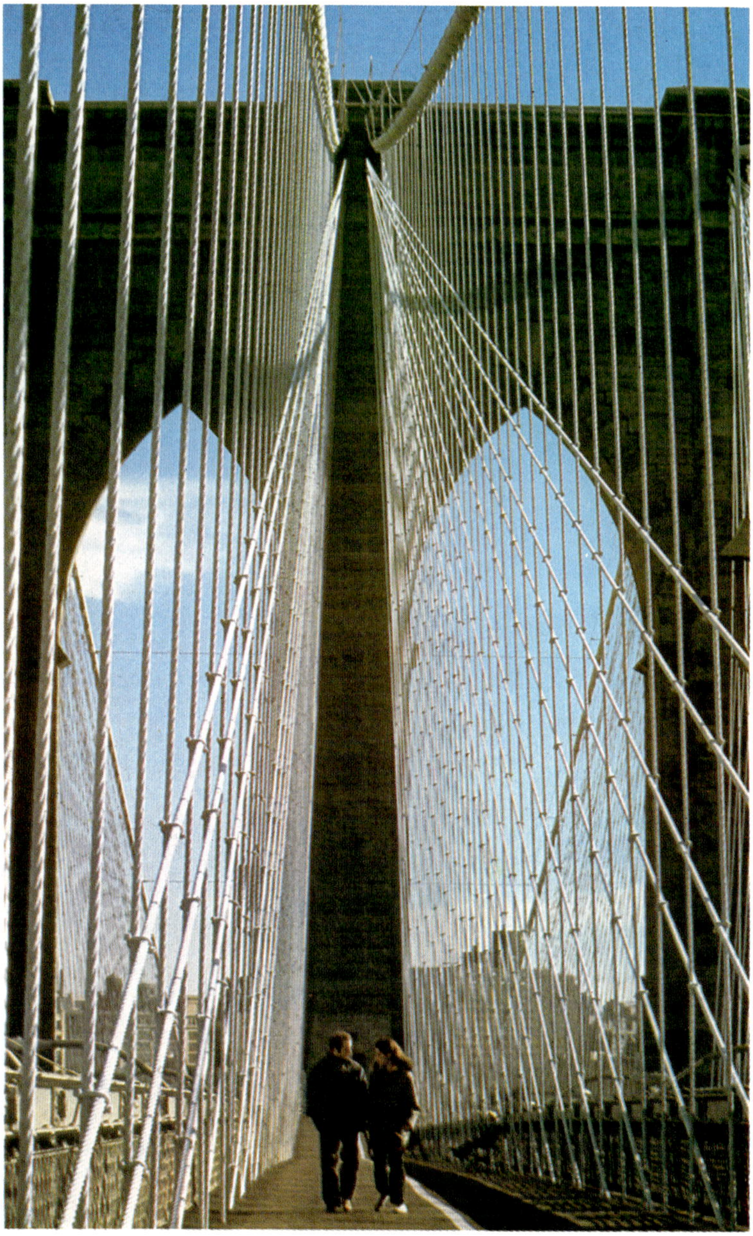

vanishing point, or the vertex of the geometrical pyramid, which can be placed at the center of the picture, or in any other position, higher up, or farther down. Clearly, in this case, the perspective relationship of the things reproduced will change, as it does when a normal camera is tilted backwards or forwards. Furthermore, up to now, we have been speaking of a single vanishing point and a single visual pyramid, but more than one vanishing point can be used if desired, as painters have always known, even if they have only made limited use of this expedient. The stage designers of the eighteenth century who created their sets with two or more vanishing points were very well aware of this.
In short, when speaking of geometrical perspective, one must consider its great variety of applications which does not depend on the whim of the artists, nor their desire to invent new formulae at all costs, but on the visual habits, aesthetic canons and figurative

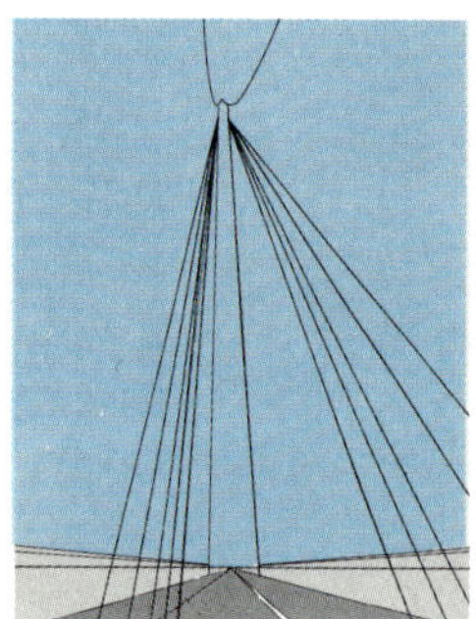

Variations in perspective

The wide-angle and other lenses available to the photographer will therefore have radically different uses as well as results, to which we shall be returning later in the book. We have mentioned them now merely to clarify, with data which are easily controllable by photographic practice, this apparent absurdity of the existence of different geometrical perspectives. It is worth noting that up to now we have been referring purely to geometrical perspectives, which are not the only type, and we shall be seeing that there are others, which are very widely used in both painting and photography. Another difference in the use of perspective can depend on the

On the opposite page, an unusual shot of Brooklyn Bridge in New York, with a diagram of its vanishing point (on the right). It is a typical example of the use of linear elements which in themselves produce a geometric type of spatial perspective.

On this page, examples of variations in perspective, according to the lens used, applied to the same view of the Christianhavn quarter in Copenhagen. In the top photograph, taken with a wide-angle lens, the presence of two different perspective vanishing points is evident, illustrated in the drawing below it. The other photographs, taken with lenses of increasing focal lengths, show the progressive reduction in evidence of the two big axes of perspective.

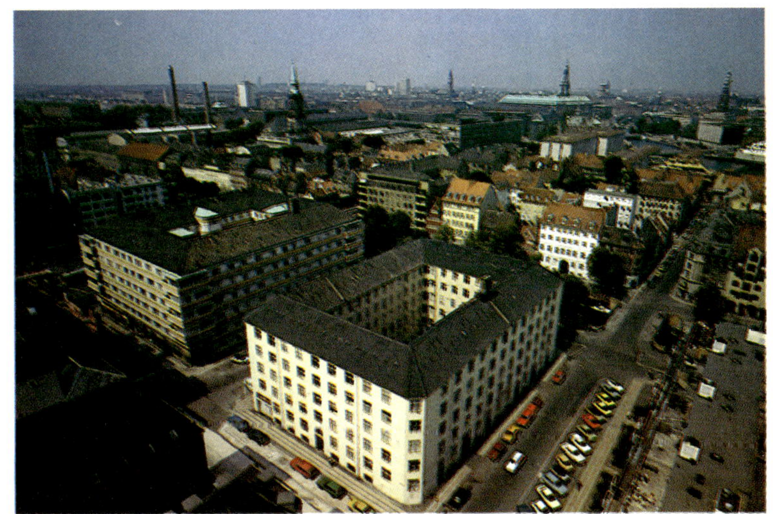

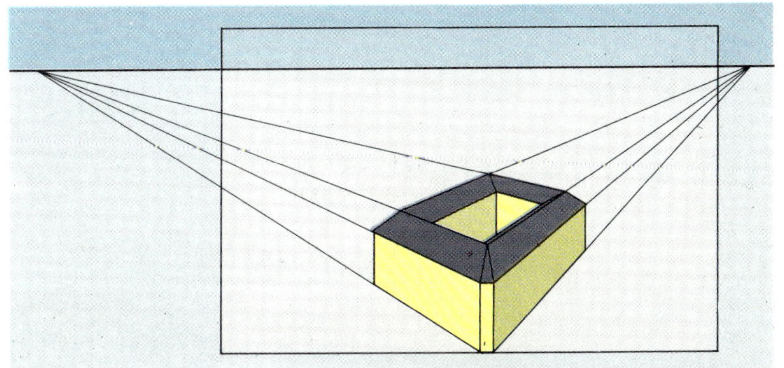

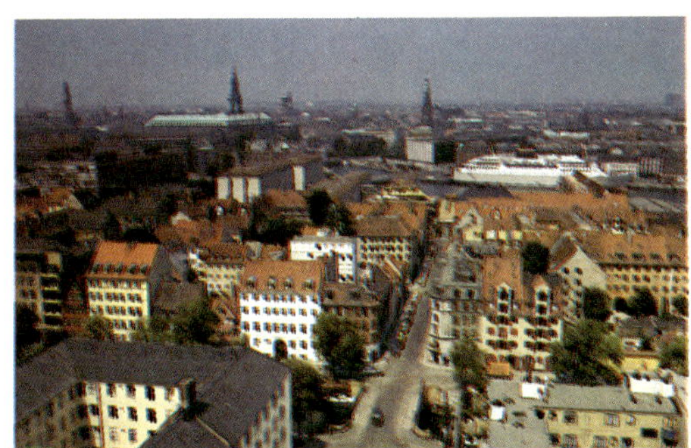

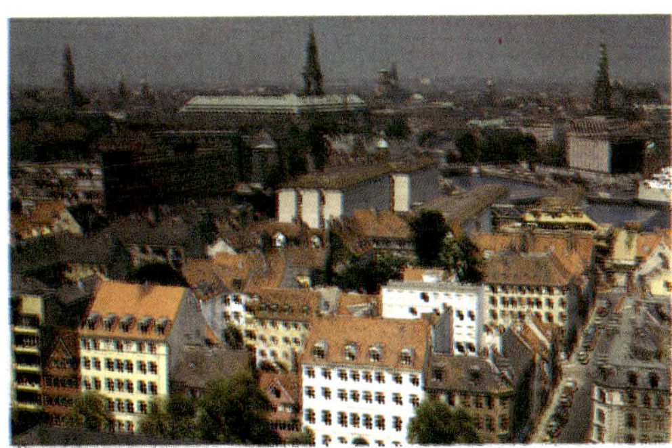

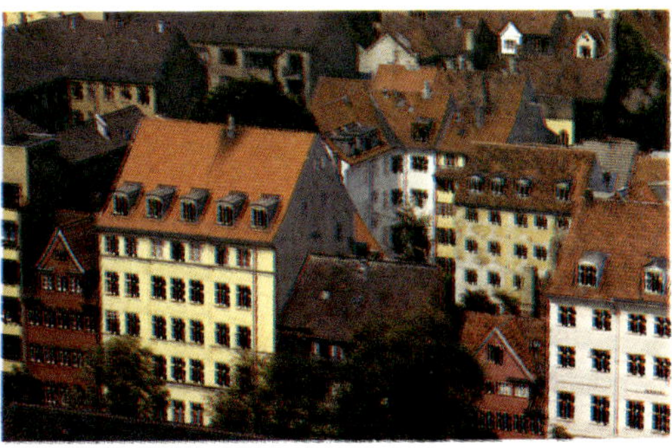

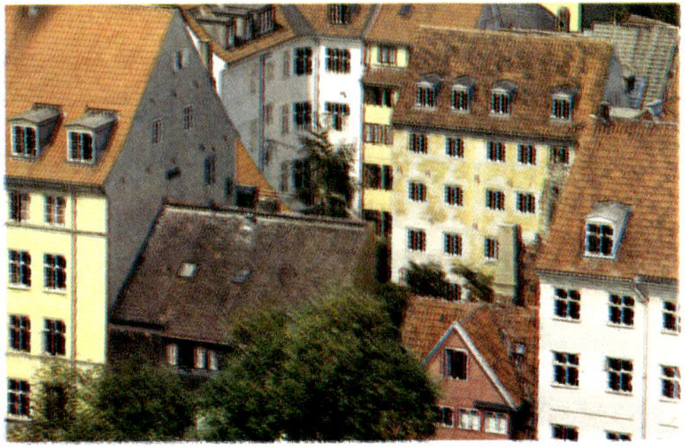

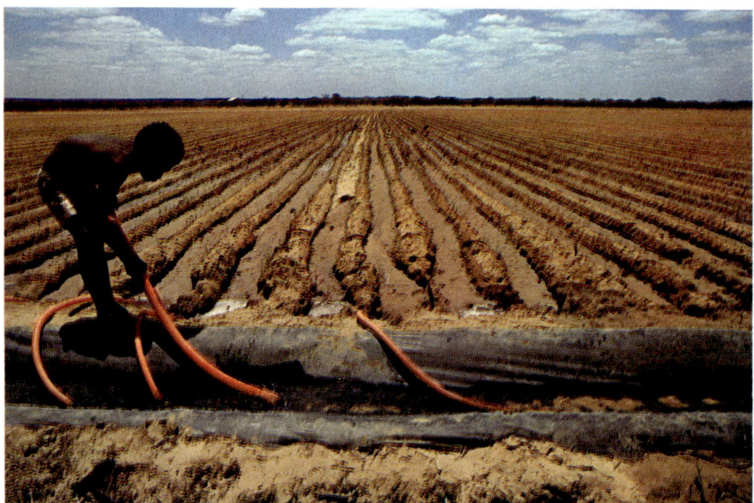

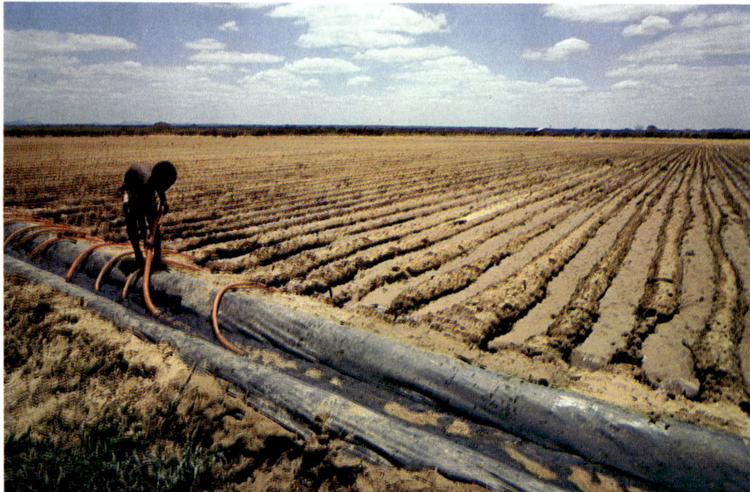

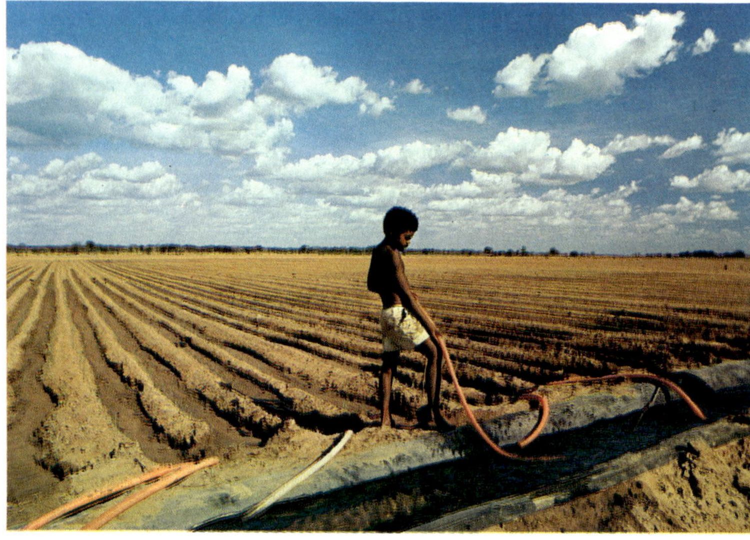

traditions prevailing at the time, which led artists to follow one system rather than another according to their aims, in the same way that photographers choose their lenses for different purposes.

This analogy between the use of lenses and the geometrical perspective used by artists may appear forced. But it will seem clearer if you consider black-and-white photography in particular, where the representation of space is often assisted by a geometrical arrangement of shapes, that is, where the typically geometrical language of lines, profiles and shapes is often heavily emphasized.

Not always, in fact, only in some cases, is the subject treated suited to a geometrical interpretation and it is in these cases that the lines of perspective become a vital part of the photograph. What tends to happen more often, is that the landscape does not lend itself to any particular geometrization.

But the photographer cannot ignore absolutely the optical laws governing his lens, which will inevitably condition the rendering of his image by flattening the space or extending its depth, and lengthening or foreshortening every detail. His problem will be in knowing how to make the most of this conditioning in artistic terms, by transforming what could be a technical

limitation into a means of reinforcing the result.
The choice of lens, therefore, and of the perspective one wishes to use in the frame is enormously important. It can never be accidental and must be subordinated to a precise purpose which should take into account both what one in fact wishes to show in the photograph, and the type of interpretation one wishes to give it.
In the field of painting, the infinite variety of perspective solutions, the different use made of them each time according to the period and the artist, testify to the possibilities inherent in the interpretation of space.
Space can be a vital part of the landscape, and in many cases the photographer may be interested in suggesting its size in order to describe it as fully as possible. Panoramic landscapes are those required to be exhaustive, even from a geographical point of view, and therefore reproduced in their entirety.
But in very many other cases this documentary aspect may not be necessary, and it may seem much more useful to evoke a certain atmosphere, a certain characteristic of the landscape through some details of it.
The physical value of a space, its actual measurements, may not even be the most important thing. There is no denying that the vastness of a seascape or an alpine panorama viewed from a mountain top have a particular evocative force on account of their sheer size. But in very many other cases, the depth and vastness of a space can be suggested by a detail from it which, by virtue of being limited, is easier to achieve.
It must not be forgotten that one of the obstacles to the representation of large spatial dimensions is

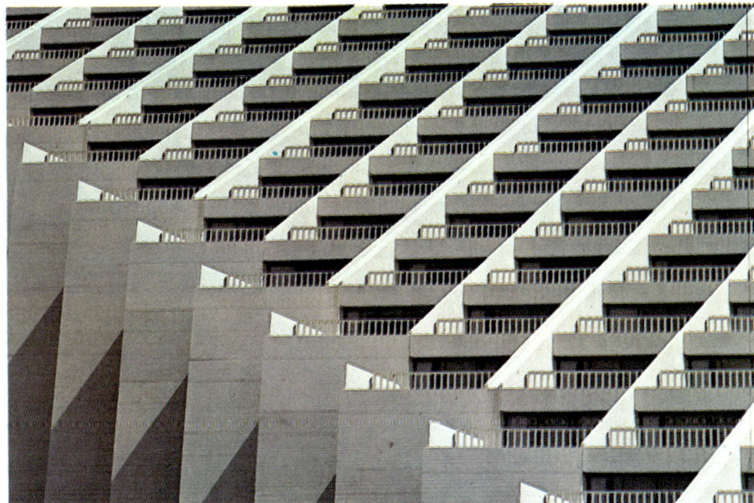

The photographs on the opposite page, depicting an irrigation system in the state of Pernambuco in Brazil, show three different ways of positioning the vanishing point: central, shifted to the right, and shifted to the left.

Above, detail of the Hyatt Regency Hotel in San Francisco. It is a clear example of typically geometric indications being used to show spatial perspective.
Below, a mollusc farm. Another example of a geometrical interpretation of spatial perspective, which is so clearly defined that it can be particularly well set off by a black-and-white photograph.

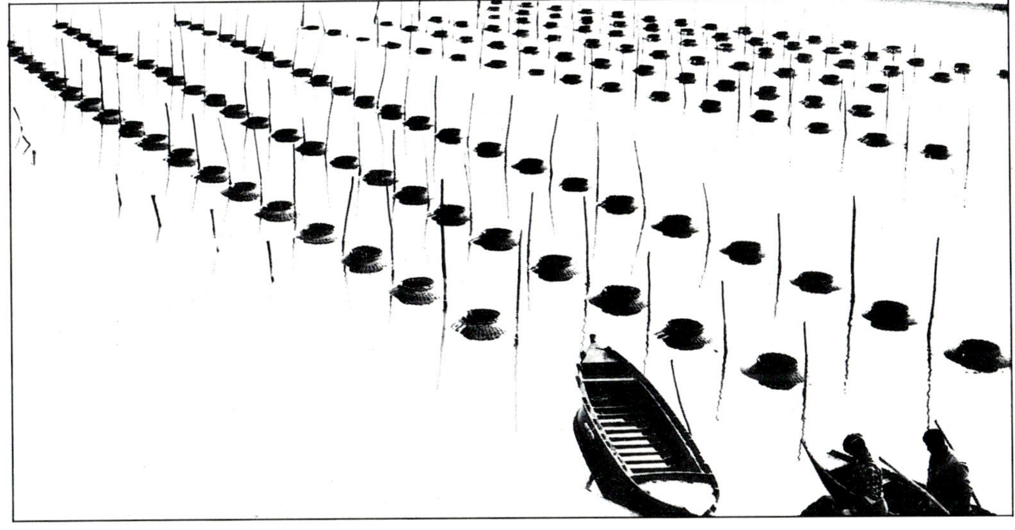

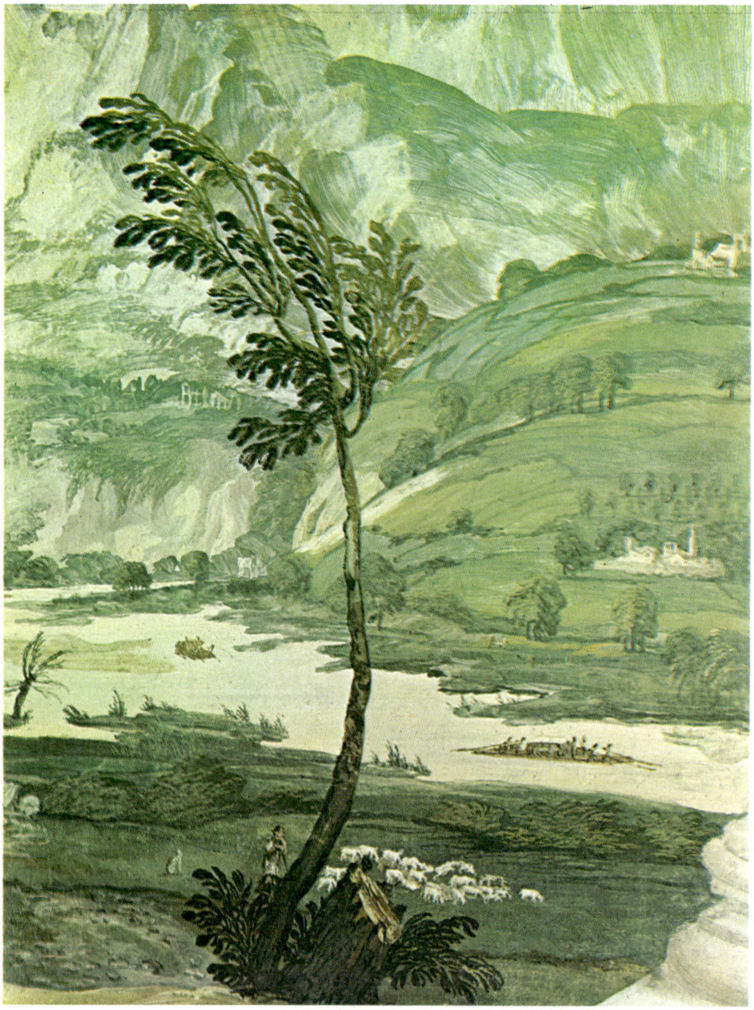

not the entire landscape, but a detail from it.

Apart from the geometrical perspective, there are other types of perspective, or more precisely other ways of representing spatial depth. At the end of the fifteenth century, the Venetian painters who had by then assimilated the geometrical perspective used by the Tuscan artists, had already begun to show spatial depth in a more empirical fashion, through the use of colour and tonal variations. This process reached maturity with the painter Giorgione da Castelfranco. If we were to examine some of his famous works, such as *The Tempest,* already mentioned, according to the rules of geometrical perspective used by the Tuscans, we would find his paintings full of anomalies, if not plain errors. The fact is that Giorgione and the other Venetian

the actual format in which they must be contained and the limited focal length of most, commonly-used portable cameras. To photograph a landscape, we repeat, the ideal formats are those of the big cameras which also have a longer focal length. If excellent results can be achieved even with ordinary portable cameras, this is because one can use adaptations, one of the most obvious of which is to limit the width of the field of view by reproducing

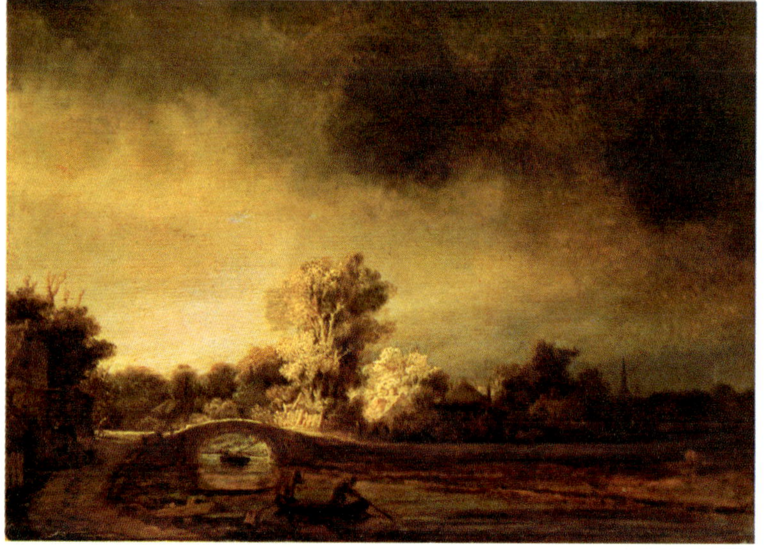

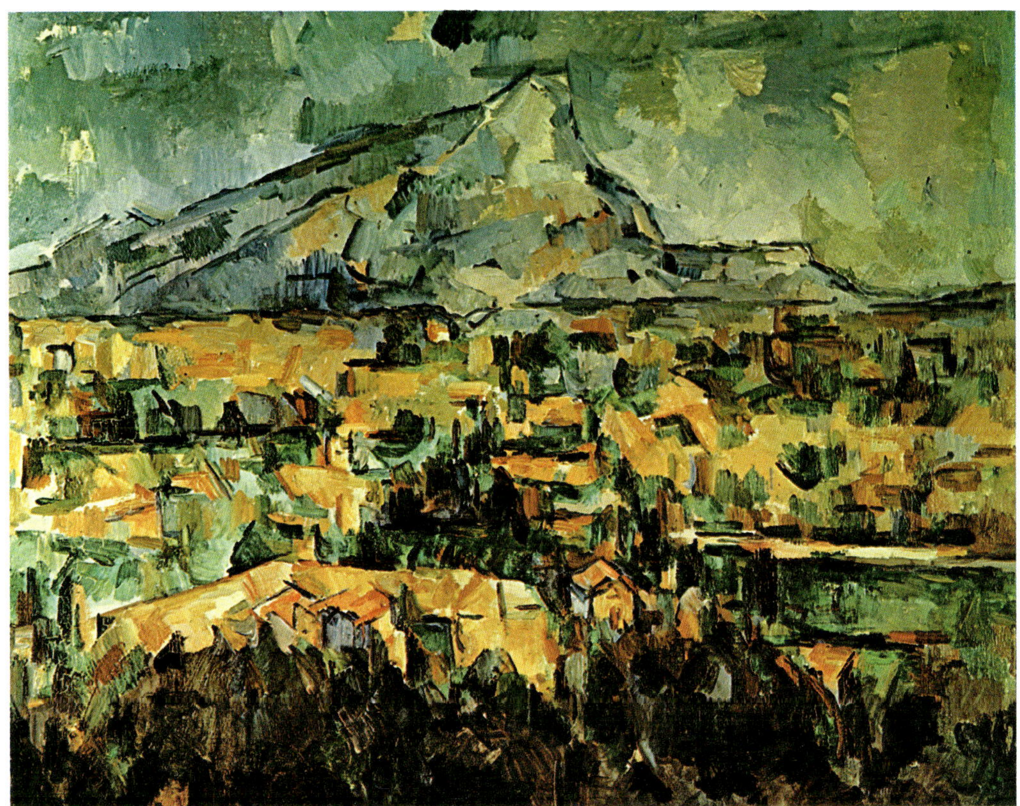

On the opposite page, above, detail of an imaginary landscape painted by Veronese, in the Villa at Masèr. As nearly always happens in sixteenth-century painting, the landscapes are basically fantastic. But all the details composing them, from the trees to the water and mountains, are suggested by reality. Note the uniform tone of this painting, which helps create that sense of balance and serenity which is typical of the art of Veronese.
Below, The Stone Bridge *by Rembrandt, a painting in which the artist entrusts the effects of spatial depth to the dramatic opposition of light and shade.*

Above, the Saint-Victoire Mountain *by Paul Cézanne shows us the prevailing interest of the painter in capturing the colour components of the landscape, to the extent that, while the shape is suggested, he breaks it down into a multitude of brilliant facets.*

painters were not just interested in perspective as a framework, as a dimension about which one could make abstract theories, but as an experience of nature and atmosphere.
Colour, which in the Tuscans tends to be nearly always very clear and applied on a well-defined ground with a limited play of different tones, in the Venetians is blended, is rich and full of subtleties, passages and tonal variations, and it undoubtedly lends itself better to a representation of reality which is complex and eludes simplification in its composition.
The Venetians created spatial depth by varying the tones of colours which, in the distance, assumed softer, subtler values, producing what has been defined as "aerial perspective," or a perspective based on aerial values, which we can equally well call "tonal" perspective, because it is the play of different tones which produces these aerial values.
It was, above all, in the seventeenth century that landscape painting developed into its various branches. The painters dealing with this genre specialized in one area or another. There were painters like Claude Lorrain and Nicolas Poussin, who worked on largely imaginary landscapes which conjured up a distant, mythical age, as did the painters of Arcadia. There were painters specializing in marine subjects or the Dutch countryside, or the regions of the south, with generous concessions on the one hand to the realism of the life of the peasants and on the other to classical folklore, an invariable attribute for many years of the southern landscape. There was also – and this time in Italy thanks to a painter from Calabria, Salvator Rosa – a type of landscape which showed ravines and wild country, rocky precipices and gnarled and sombre forests, evocative of ambushes by brigands.
Speaking of tonal perspective, it will be as well to clarify the terms we are using

because they could generate some confusion in the minds of those accustomed to a rigorously scientific terminology. In speaking scientifically of colour, the use of the word "tone" is equivalent to that of tint, that is, it means the basic quality of the colour, relative to its wavelength: the reason why a yellow is distinguished from a green, or a red. Colours of the same tint, or tone, are also

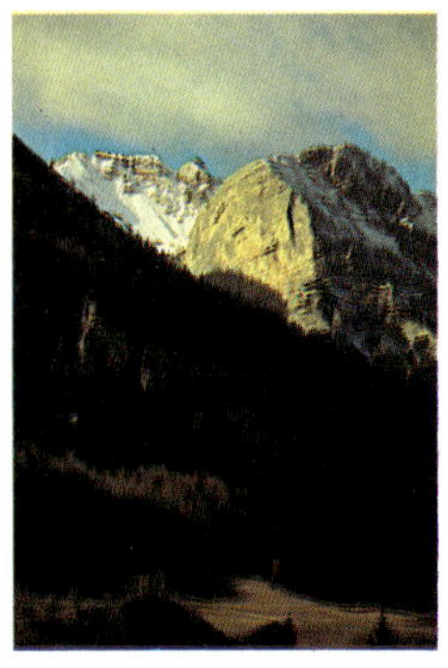

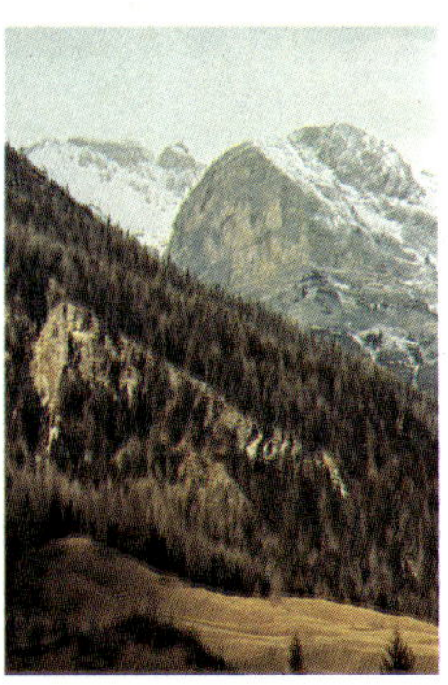

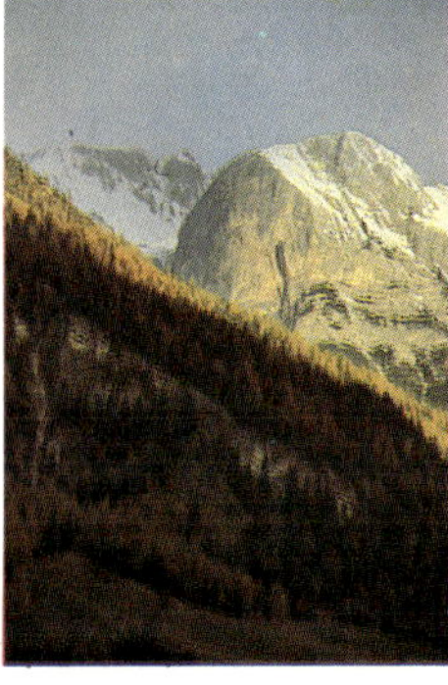

distinguished by the amount of light they possess. A red can be the same red with more or less light, and by the percentage of white or black with which it can be mixed. The larger this percentage, the more the colour is described as desaturated, while if the colour is at maximum purity, it is called saturated. In common usage, however, the word tone, which is associated with the language of music, indicates the strength of a colour, without distinguishing whether this is due to its light, its saturation or the position the colour occupies in relation to others. In speaking of tonal painting, however, it is fairly obvious that one is referring to a type of painting where the variations in colour, whether subtle or intense, prevail over every other formal component (lines, planes, relief).

In colour photography, tonal values are often very important. In these photographs, the values of the lines, the geometrical components for example, may not be obvious or may hardly be there at all, and the masses of colour and their tonal values may be emphasized instead, so that the sense of spatial depth and perspective may be achieved by gradations of colour, as in tonal painting, even without the photographer needing to pay particular attention to it (at the most, he may respect or intensify them), because these values are already present in the reality which he is subjecting to his camera lens.

It would therefore seem that from a technical viewpoint, leaving out of consideration the size of the frame, a photographer has little to learn from the tonalism of painters and that this whole discussion has more academic than practical value. But one need not dwell on the subject for long to understand that the study of tonal values, or the eminently colouristic aspects of the great masters of the past (apart from the Venetians, tonalism is also found in the Flemish artists and influenced broad areas of painting up to the Impressionists) is bound to sensitize the eye of the photographer profoundly and make him aware of the presence of colours and harmonies which might have eluded him before.

Studying the great painters, as well as great photographers, also has this advantage. It makes us notice values which our eyes and minds did not perceive before. They may be compositional, volumetric or spatial values, but also chromatic and tonal ones. We think that the latter are particularly

On the opposite page, above, a seascape by Fulvio Roiter. The photographer has captured a very special moment of light refraction on the sea, set off by the presence of a sailing vessel. Left, variations in the lighting conditions and colours of the same landscape, at three different times of day; dawn, midday, and sunset.

On this page, variations in the lighting conditions and colour in the same landscape as that of the previous page, over the twelve months of the year.

important, not because we wish to create a hierarchy of art forms: a harmony in the composition of lines, for example, is no less important than a harmony in colour tones, and there are some artists who will express themselves better in lines while others will express themselves better in colours. But the observation of colours is very important because, generally speaking, although we like colours a great deal we tend to observe them less than other visual values. Nature, the landscape and reality, provide an inexhaustible fund of ideas, models, harmonies and compositions. In the lights of a single day, in the colours of the different seasons, our most complex and varied feelings can be expressed and the most diverse themes can be capturod: from the most tragic to the most idyllic; from lyricism to romance. Everything is already written. Everything is already there. The important, the difficult part, is knowing how to decipher this mass of lines, shades and shapes which meets our eye at every moment. And this is another reason why learning how to see, like every other type of learning, must be practised on the great masterpieces in which the past is so rich.

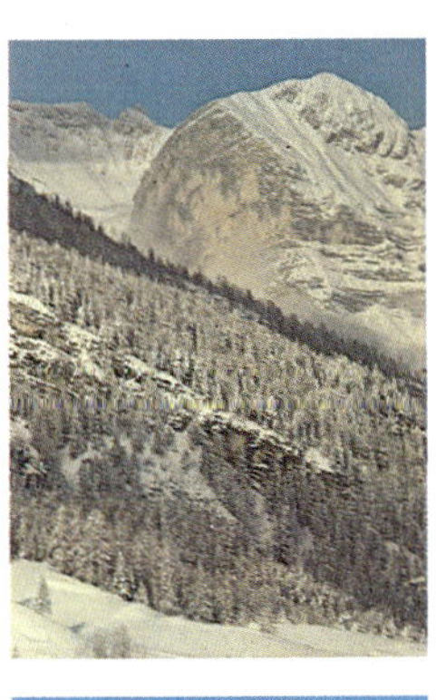
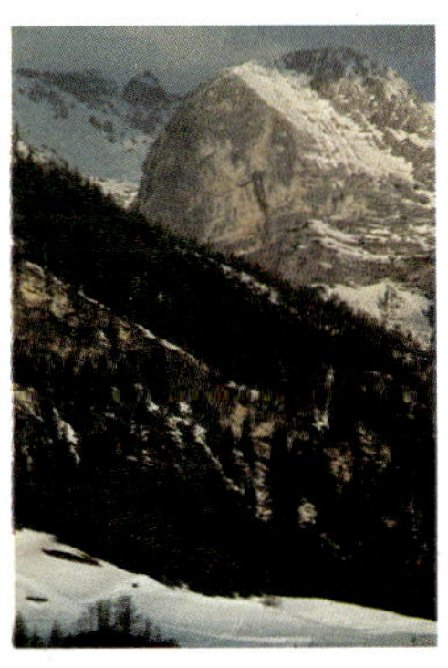
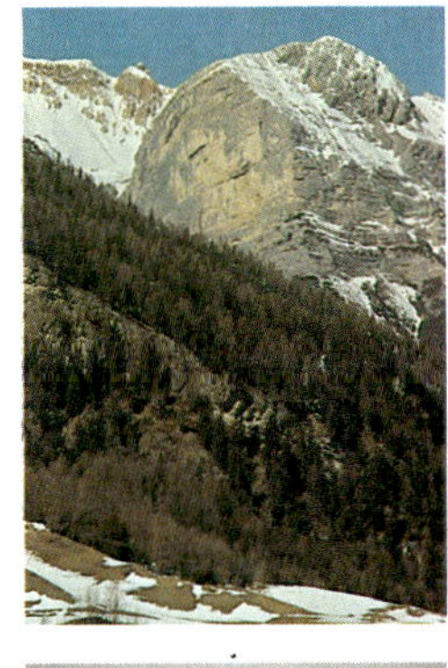
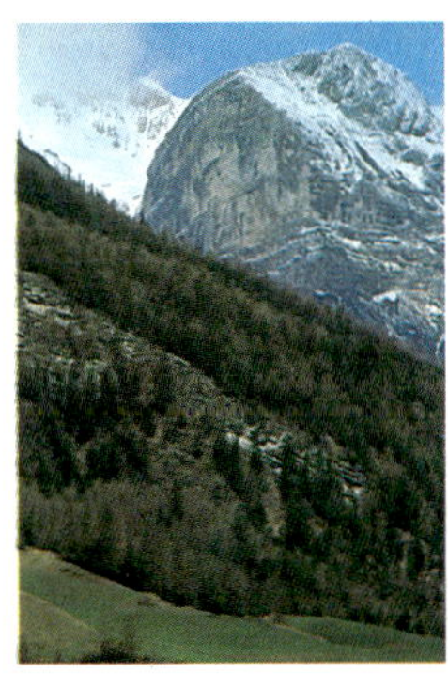
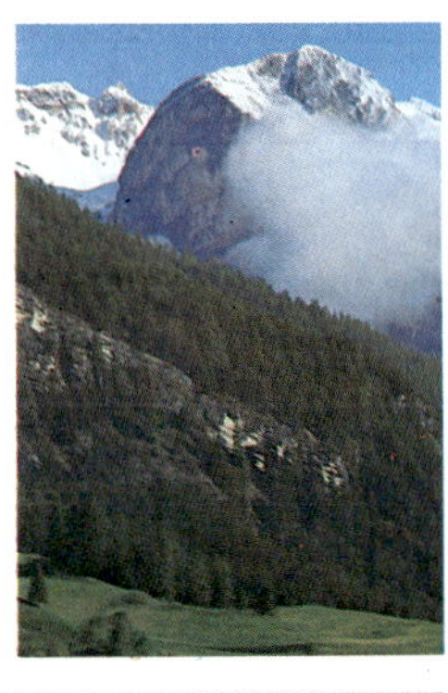
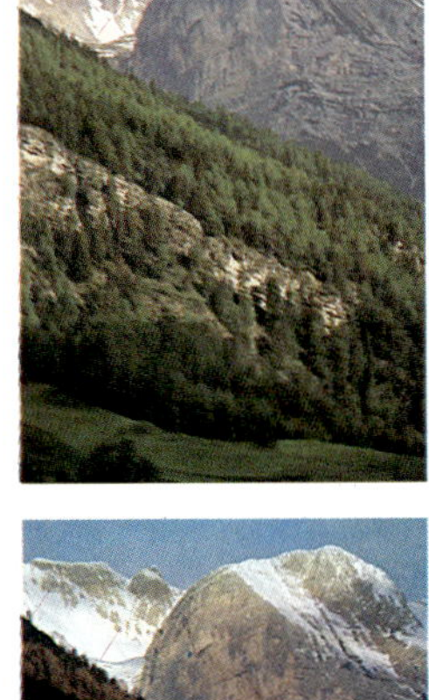
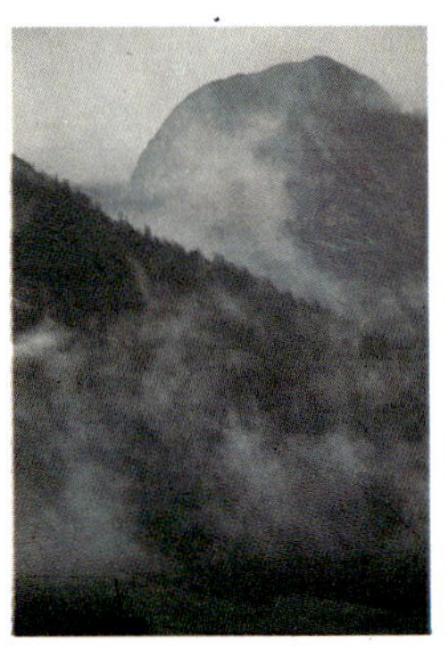
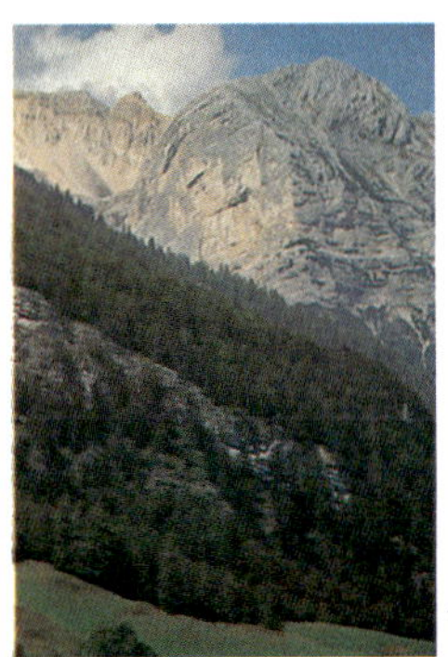
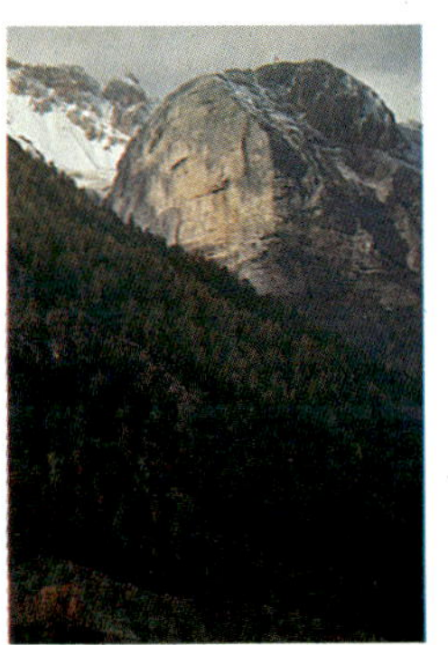
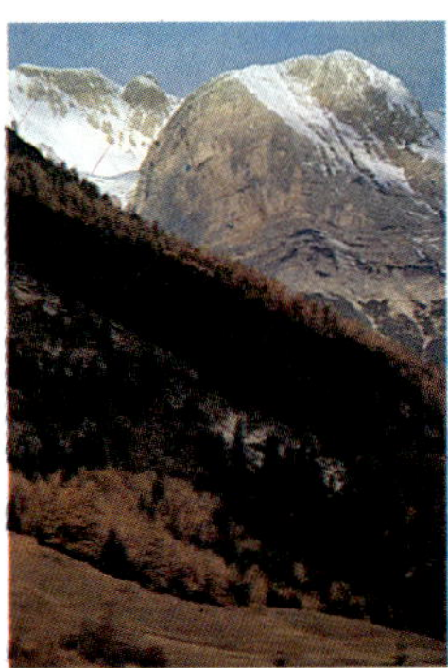
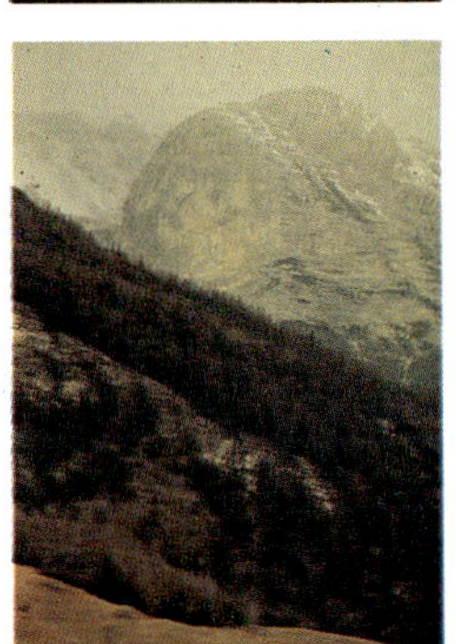
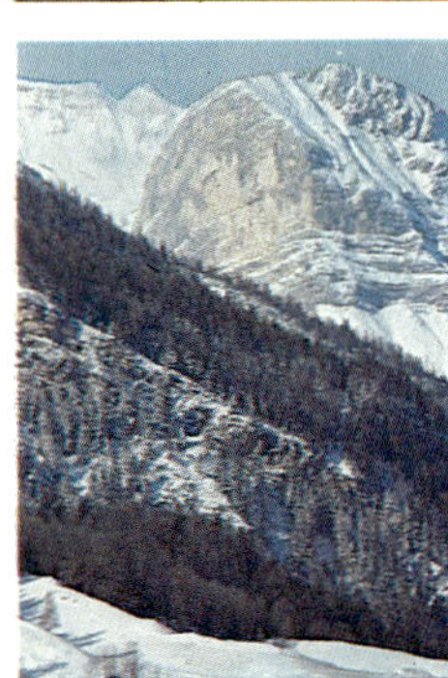

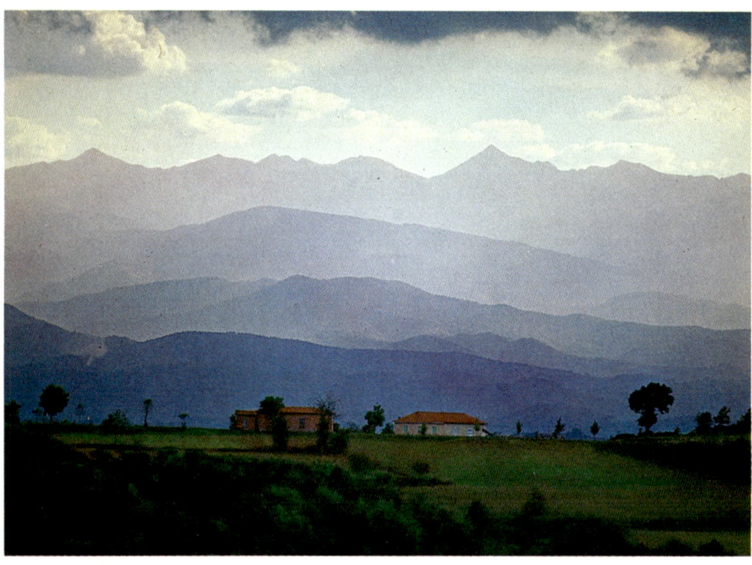

The limits of originality

Choosing one's own particular mode of expression requires a patient exercise of application and humility, which all great artists have had to develop and which is diametrically opposed to an attitude which is all too common today, in which, to do something good, it is sufficient to be original. The assumption that originality is sufficient in itself and that it should therefore be sought after at all costs, can be very damaging both because it pushes the research and efforts of the beginner in the direction of superficiality and because eccentricity, with which originality is nearly always confused, is satisfied with superficial effects and does not submit itself to the patient preparation which is in fact the price to be paid for any apprenticeship. Nowadays, it is almost harder to find someone capable of exercising his profession conscientiously, than someone claiming to excel by his own imagination. And it is also very easy for flights of fantasy to be in bad taste, while a work which is modestly performed has at least the advantage of not offending, apart from being much more respectable through being carried out with greater technical commitment.

One can only be deliberately original when one has achieved sufficient skill, and improvisation and imagination must not be exercised at the expense of correctness. Note, too, that the most original artists very often were not so because they decided to be so, but because they developed certain solutions spontaneously; the originality was already in them before it was looked for as such.

Modesty can never be recommended too highly. It is a sign of sensitivity and intelligence. It is modesty which makes us more receptive to the enrichment which others can give us and urges us to improve our knowledge. Finally, one must not forget that a work which is marked by pretentiousness can be irritating, while a work which is modestly and correctly performed will always be sympathetically received.

Two examples of the different use of colour. The hilly landscape above is shown by the delicacy of tonal variations, while the landscape below, representing the Mediterranean scrub in Sardinia, relies on the brilliance and variety of colours.

On the opposite page, the photograph of a building in São Paolo, Brazil, shows a composition in which the graphic elements and contrasts of light and shade prevail and the basic, uniform colour has a secondary role.

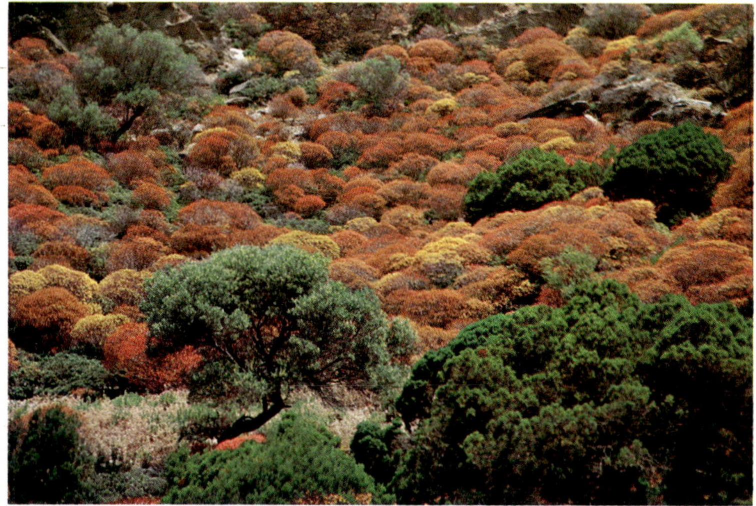

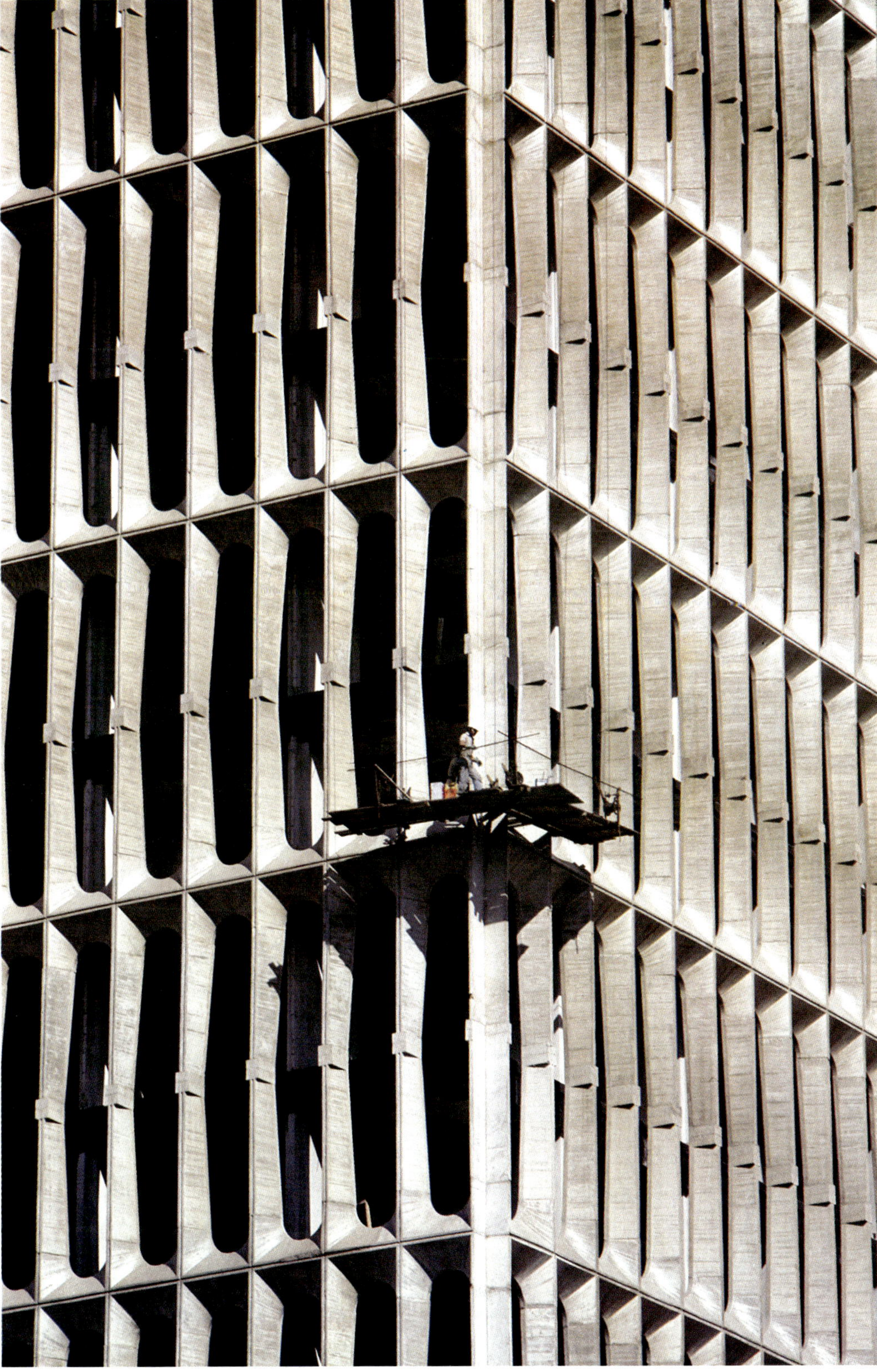

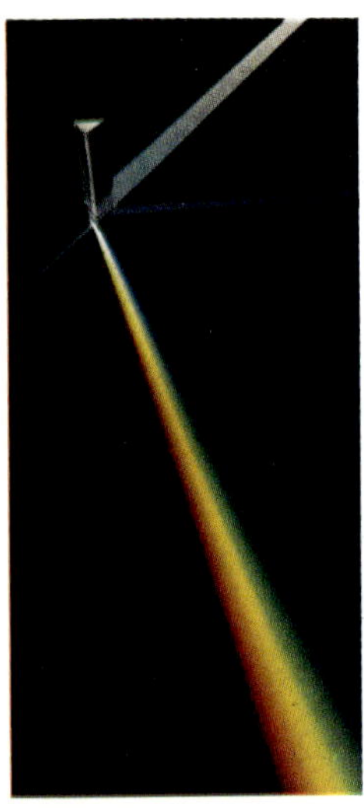

Left, a prism breaks up white sunlight into the basic colours of the rainbow.
Right, the circle of colours shows how they are arranged progressively according to their wavelengths. By putting colours which are diametrically opposed side by side, a colour contrast is produced, while a harmonious effect is obtained by juxtaposing colours belonging to the same arc of the circle.
The main element in the aerial photograph below, is the skilfully framed geometrical motif of the crops. In this case, colour takes second place in the picture.

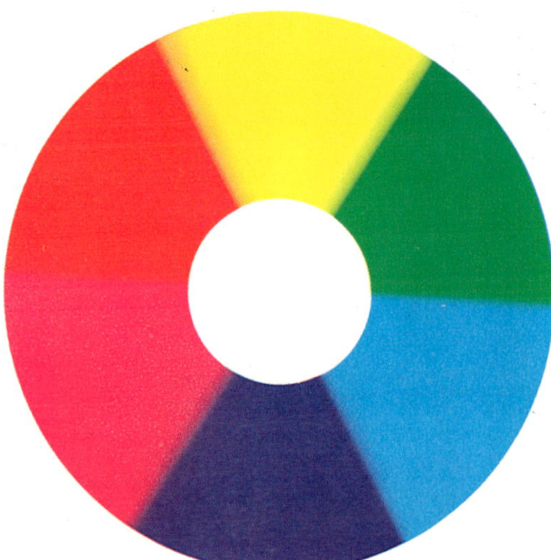

Light

Light is an electromagnetic radiation like radio waves, infrared rays, X-rays, gamma rays, etc. Each of these "beams" of electromagnetic radiation is characterized by a range of wavelengths: from radio waves with wavelengths from kilometers to centimeters and less. Visible light has a wavelength of from 8000 to 4000 Å (Å = angstrom, or $\frac{1}{10}$ of a millionth of a millimeter). The famous colours of the rainbow correspond to wavelengths in this range and are "pure" colours, that is, they are composed exclusively of waves of equal length (for example, red is equal to 8000 Å, violet to 4000 Å and the others come in between). To make a comparison with sound, which is also a wave phenomenon, the equivalent of these "pure" colours is a "pure" sound like that of a flute. All the other colours are mixtures of the pure ones in different proportions. Then how is it that by mixing blue and yellow, green is produced? All three are pure colours and it is physically impossible to obtain one from the other two. And yet we see the colour green! Here is the explanation. We see green, but the light which strikes our eye is still blue and yellow. Only our eye cannot distinguish this mixture, from the pure colours. Why is that? Because our eye has precise limitations in the identification of colours. While our ear can distinguish a very large number of wavelengths, our eye can distinguish only three, that is, it is sensitive to the whole band of visible light but is only capable of analyzing each colour as the sum of three different stimuli coming from three different types of receptor in our eye. The receptors contain special chemical substances which are sensitive to all the visible wavelengths, but above all, to three particular pure colours, of which two are green and one red. It is from the way in which the receptors are stimulated that our eye establishes the presence of the other colours.
The same stimulation can be achieved in many ways, that is, by using different basic colours in different percentages. This is what photography and colour television do, when they use three basic colours, generally red, green and blue. In common usage, the primary

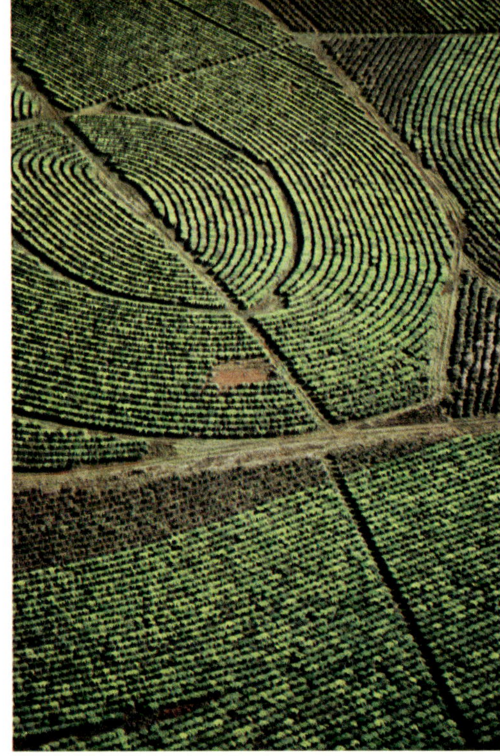

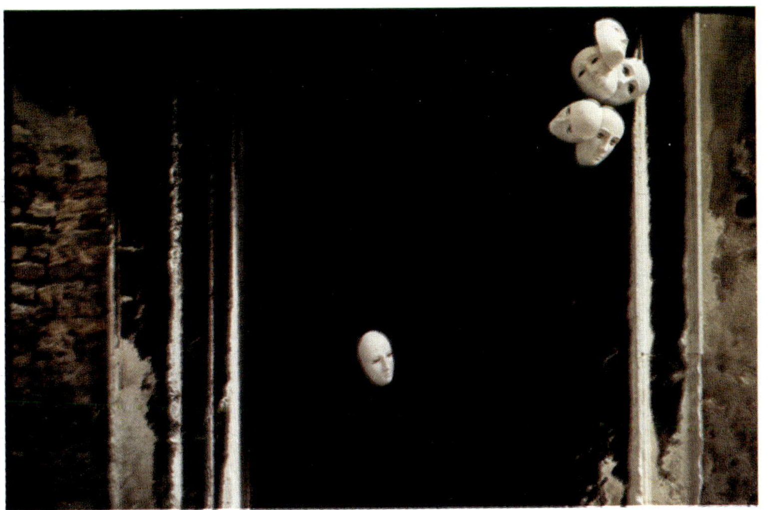

Fulvio Roiter, who took the photograph on the opposite page, based on a geometrical composition, shows in the picture on the left his ability to capture essentially chromatic values by strong contrasts in light. The photograph below left, shows a search for harmony based essentially on chromatic values. However interesting, the walls and disjointed roof would not have been sufficient justification for the photograph if they had not been set off by the blending of colours, which is particularly harmonious here. It shows how chromatic values can be achieved even in a composition devoid of any very lively hints of colour.

The photograph, right, shows the emphasis of colour clashes which, by their very intensity, redeem the relative anonymity of the subject.

colours of light – red, blue and green – are distinguished from those which, when added together, produce white, and when mixed produce all the other colours plus the complementaries – magenta, cyan and yellow – each composed of two primary colours which are complementary to the third (that is, when added to the third, they give white light). Apart from differing in brightness or tone, colours differ in their saturation or intensity. The maximum contrast between colours is obtained when a primary colour is put next to its complementary; but other contrasts can be based on tone, saturation and even the difference between "warm" colours and "cold" ones.

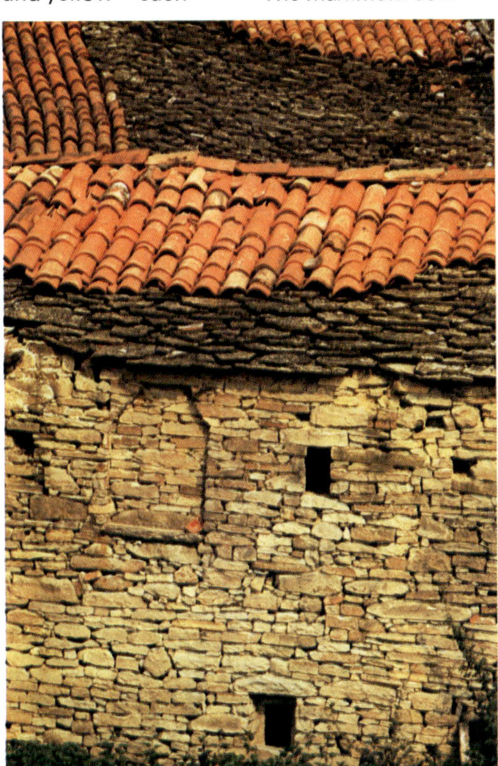

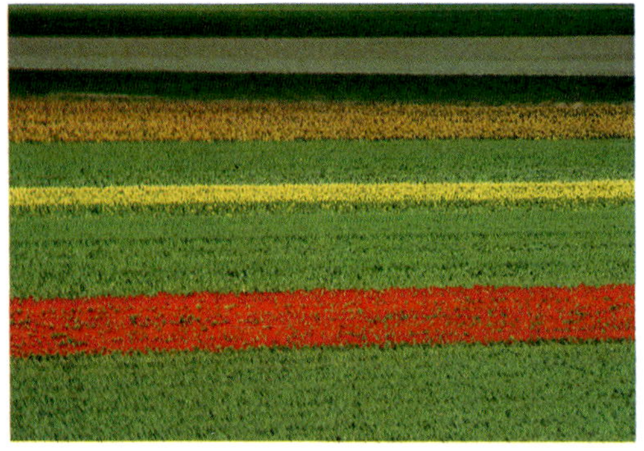

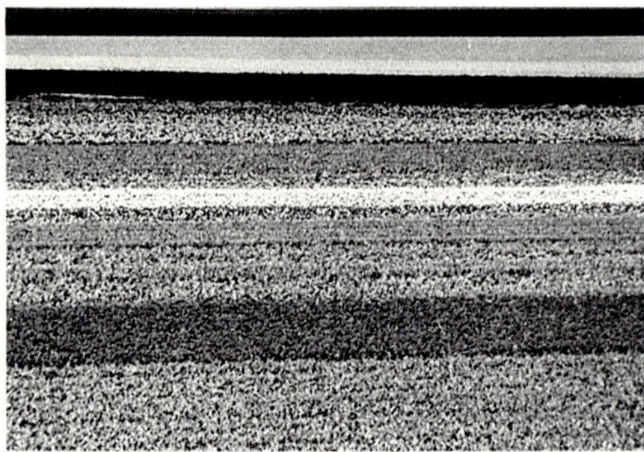

Colour choices

The accentuation of contrasts in colour or black-and-white is one of the effects which is relatively easy to achieve. Greater sensitivity and experience may be required when one is trying to achieve more harmonious juxtapositions, such as subtle ones, both in terms of tone and colour. Subtle colours are not necessarily associated with a foggy atmosphere or uncertain light. They are found in many other situations which, to the unpractised eye, may even seem monotonous and comparatively uninteresting. Even in adverse weather conditions, such as rain or mist, or with landscapes which are basically uniform, one can capture highly expressive and unusual aspects, even ignoring the fact that colours are nearly always accompanied by other compositional motifs: lines; planes; volumes, and the effects are produced by a combination of all these ingredients. Note that the colours in the mind's eye are not sufficient in themselves to produce a good photograph. In excess, they can cause violent clashes, and one must also pay attention to reflecting surfaces, which the inexperienced photographer may not know about and which desaturize colours. The light should also be measured very carefully: overexposed photographs

Above, an interesting comparison between a photograph of flowers planted in strips of different colours, and its translation into black-and-white. The different tones of grey show by their variety and delicacy that chromatic effects can be achieved even in a black-and-white photograph.
Below, the chromatic values of this photograph depend entirely on the softness and delicacy of the transitions in colour, aided by a lack of strong contrasts or sharp outlines.

On the opposite page, two photographs in which the colours are particularly striking.

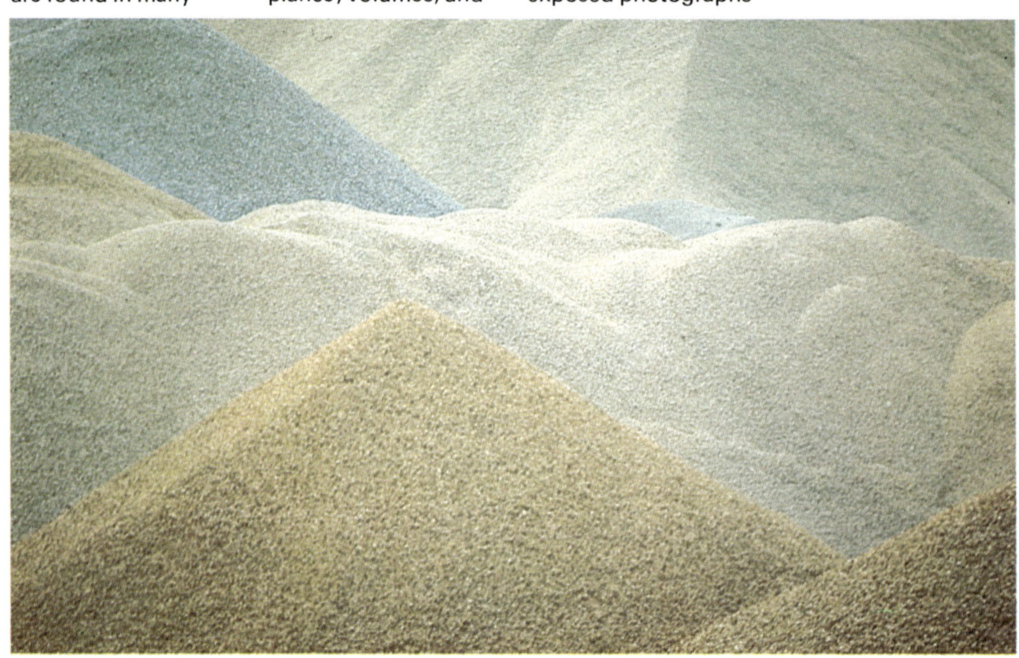

can obviously weaken colours, just as under-exposed ones can introduce totally unexpected greys and blacks. One must, of course, bear in mind the type of film, which may differ in its sensitivity to various colours. Strong colours, which are so sensitive because of their striking effect, can easily cause imbalances and deprive the picture of all meaning.

With landscapes, it is often a good idea to use a telephoto lens, not just to isolate the image one wishes to reproduce, but also because by so doing one can avoid contrasts which seriously upset the overall composition. Excellent photographs can be taken even when there is chromatic dominance – that is, when one colour clearly prevails over all the rest. This dominance can also be achieved artificially by the use of filters and other systems (for example, by taking a photograph through coloured glass or using a film for artificial light in daylight and vice versa). One can obtain a predomination of cold or warm colours and this can help make the atmosphere of the landscape more expressive; for example, by emphasizing the blue in a winter landscape or the yellow or red in a summer landscape. These effects, which are obtained above all by the use of filters, can be such as to change completely the atmosphere of a landscape and make a uniform, grey environment appear to be lit by brilliant sunshine. The case of dominant colours is different, because this does not involve upsetting the whole image but merely accentuating certain elements. It can also be very important in a situation where colours are uniform to pick out a note of colour which may be isolated, or very limited, or very fleeting, but capable of livening up the whole picture. It may be a reflection of sunlight, or a passing figure. It may only be there for an instant, and the skill of the photographer will lie in perceiving and capturing it with the best technical precision.

A very different field Is that of colours which are artificially accentuated for dramatic or simply unusual or surreal effect. These effects can be achieved by using films for false colours, that is, colours which do not correspond to the natural ones, such as infra-red (IR) films, or by using colour filters, above all dual filters, to avoid excessive uniformity or colours can be altered in the darkroom.

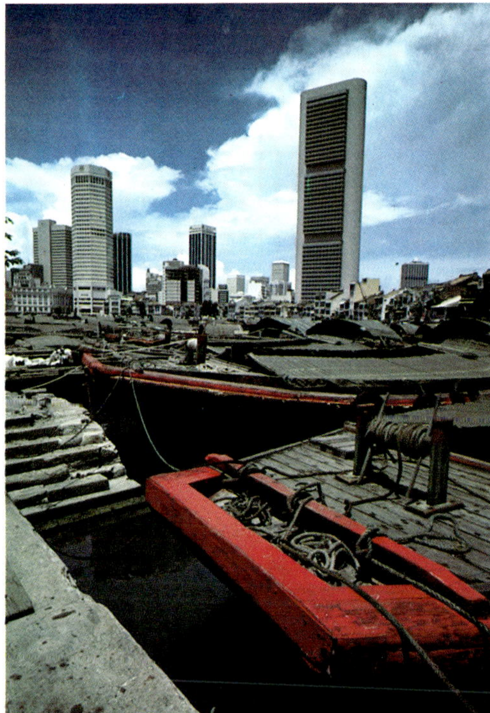

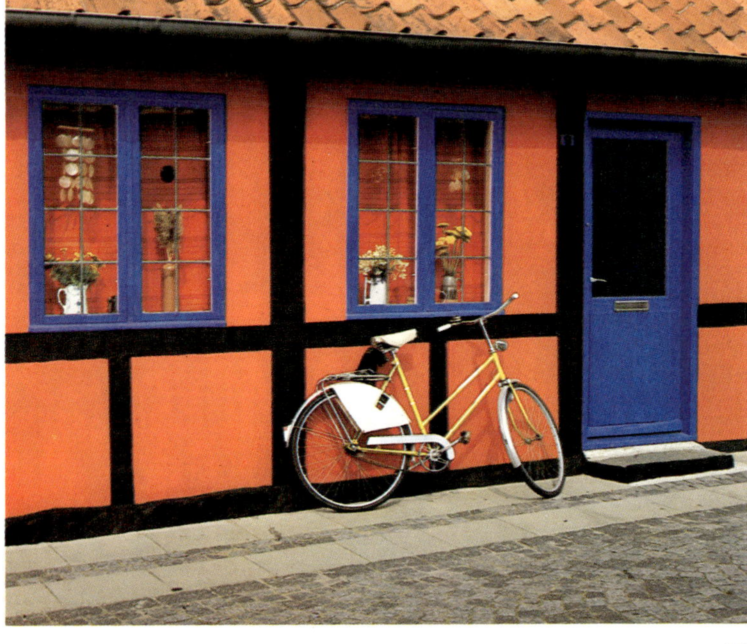

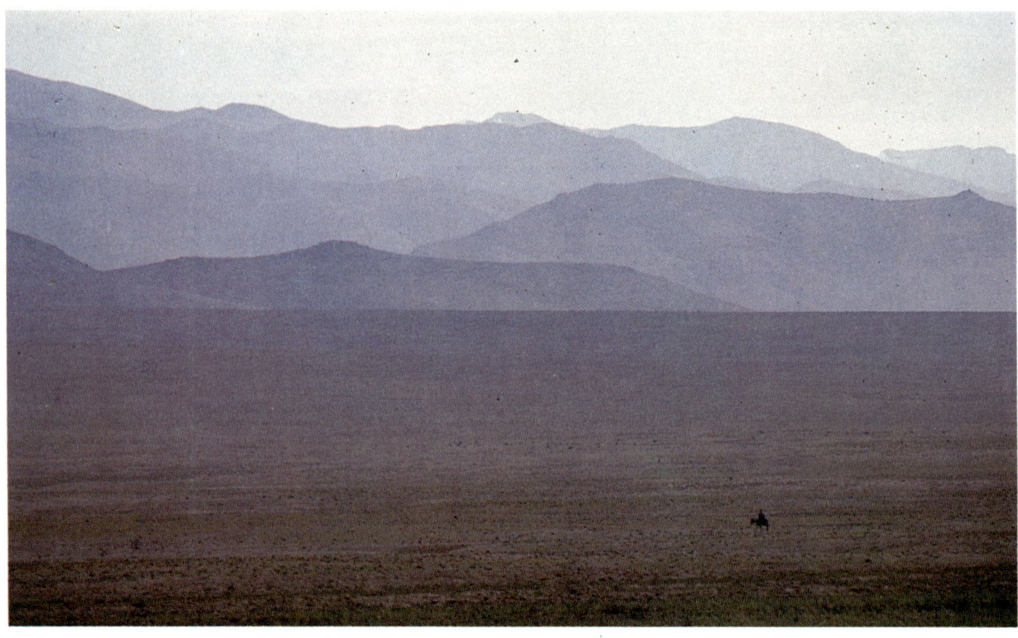

This photograph, by Fulvio Roiter, demonstrates a phenomenon due to the filtration of colours as they pass through the atmosphere; the mountains look blue in colour, varying in intensity according to their distance.

The value of colour

The standardization of our lives, their urbanization, the fact that each of us gives up living in touch with nature, even for long periods, tends to impoverish our colour sensitivity.
For anyone of us walking through a town – or worse still, driving through it – a cursory look is sufficient to provide an awareness of the presence, size and speed of the obstacles and things we come across. The experience is dimensional, rather than chromatic.
Furthermore, the uniform grey of the town is the least likely to fire our visual imaginations. If some coloured object catches our eye, such as a billboard, an unusual-coloured vehicle, or a particular item of clothing, the impression received tends to be purely quantitative, not qualitative, and can be more detrimental than stimulating.
We are surrounded by colours everywhere, often without even noticing them, as anyone can readily establish.
All that need be done, wherever one is, whatever the time of day, even with the white page we are reading, is to abandon our careless glance and observe each of the colours around us a little more attentively, even if they give the impression of being mediocre and lacking in character. They will immediately be enriched before our gaze and assume a fullness and quality hitherto unsuspected.
That is the reason why we are sometimes incredulous at colour photos and think that the result is totally artificial, not just because of the sensitivity of certain films – which is not to be underestimated.
Naturally, artificiality may be inherent in the sensitivity of the films, but the more usual reason for our astonishment at those colours is that the camera has recorded colours which were essentially there, but which we did not see.
We can no longer do without colour. The very diffusion of colour photography, colour films and coloured picture books demonstrates this fact.
But we are less well trained than ever to see colours, to recognize and interpret them. One only need look at a painting by one of the great Impressionists – Manet, Renoir or Monet, for example – to be immediately flooded by an incomparable flow of light and colour.
Our eyes feel gratified and stimulated

On the opposite page, above, a picture by Manet, The Jetty at Boulogne. *This great Impressionist painter synthesized the atmospheric effects in the thick, dark strokes with which he outlined the boats. The dazzling light of the sea, the distance and movement, in fact prevent a more detailed perception, which is subordinated to the overall effect.*
Below, in Spring, *Claude Monet achieves a vivid sense of atmosphere by other means, by breaking down the colours into small touches and mixing them skilfully to convey all the airiness and vibrant light of the landscape.*

by such pictures. They create an atmosphere of joy, giving us a feeling of exhilaration and well-being, which we were unaware was there, just around the corner, waiting to be seized and enjoyed by our senses.

And all this can be achieved through the language of colour, in capturing an atmospherc which is expressed through the softness, sensuality and seduction of colour.

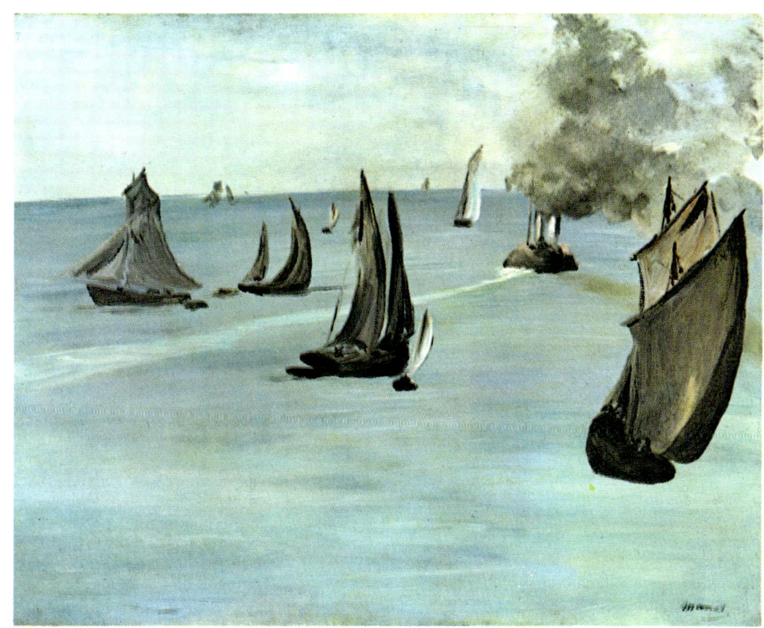

All these things, which seem so accessible in the Impressionists, are also to be found in other painters. They all literally teach us how to see things, not just when we pick up our paintbrush or load our camera, but at any time of day. And after we have assimilated their sensitivity and enriched our experience in their company, it will be much harder for us to fall back into the general run of visual conformism and bad taste by which we are all too often surrounded.

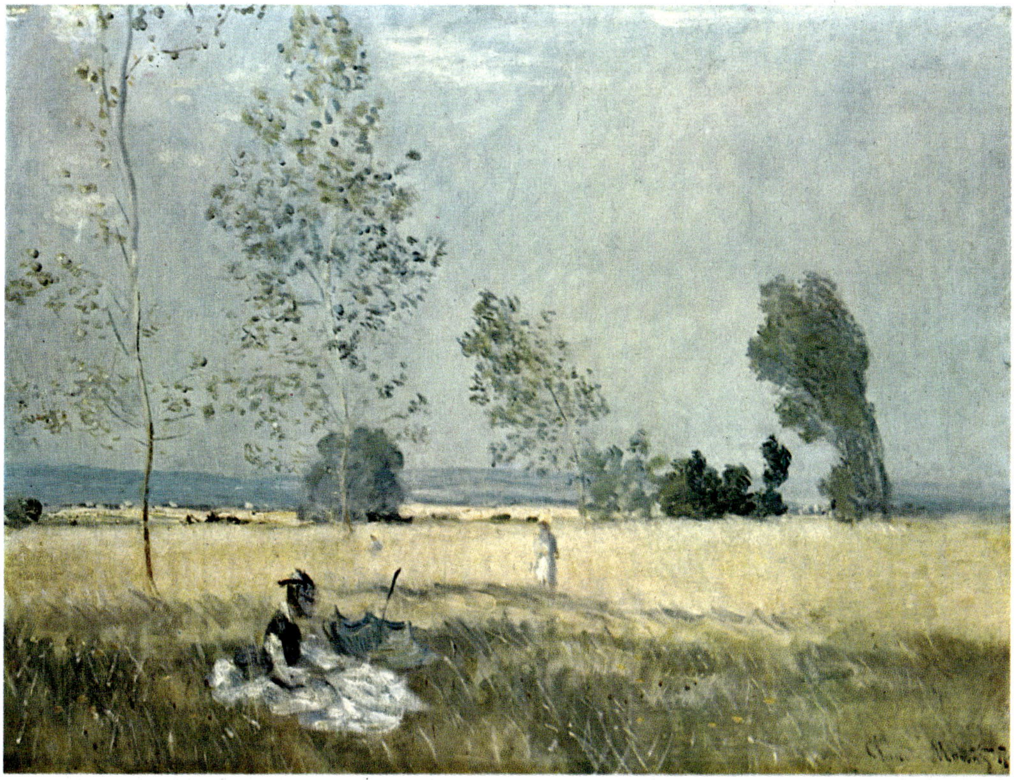

The view

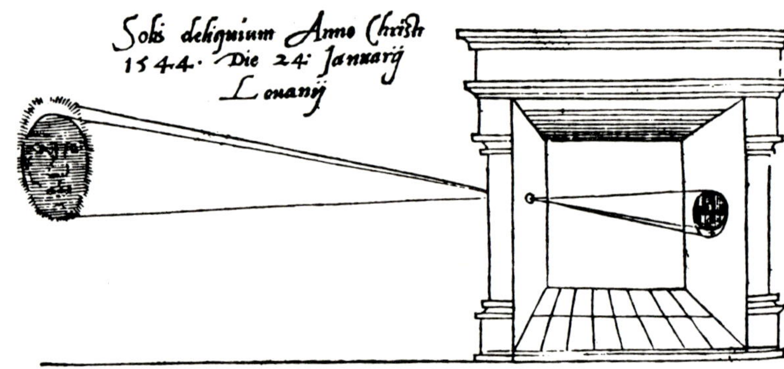

Canaletto, who was active in the eighteenth century in Venice, and for some years also in London, is particularly interesting to us, because he can in fact, be regarded as one of the most "photographic" painters of all time. He was so acutely aware of the problem of accuracy of reproduction, that he made extensive use of the camera obscura, a technical device which was an embryonic form of camera.

The camera obscura uses the phenomenon of the refraction of light rays when they pass through a small hole similar to a camera lens, thereby reflecting an image of the point of departure on the opposite wall. This procedure enabled Canaletto to sketch an outline of his paintings, establishing certain proportions (although this did not prevent him from rectifying the image at the same time) according to the rules of geometrical perspective, which from the Renaissance onwards had never been entirely abandoned, even if, in Venice as elsewhere, they had been replaced at times by more empirical procedures. These rules were still used successfully for scenography and the "sets" of the quadraturists, or scene painters, who specialized in the late seventeenth to eighteenth century in the ornamental construction of large, architectural scenarios, an ideal environment for experiments on spatial effects. Yet Canaletto, one of the most painstaking and diligent of painters, while interested in respecting objective reality, also became one of the most lyrical and

Above, a representation of a camera obscura in a sixteenth-century treatise. This basic instrument was used to advantage by many painters.
Below, a lighting effect on the island of S. Giorgio in Venice. The particular atmospheric conditions after a squall have made an outstanding subject of one of the most familiar views of Venice.

On the opposite page, the effects of the distortion of architectural perspective with a normal, 50 mm lens and the same subject corrected by the use of a perspective-correction (or shift) lens.

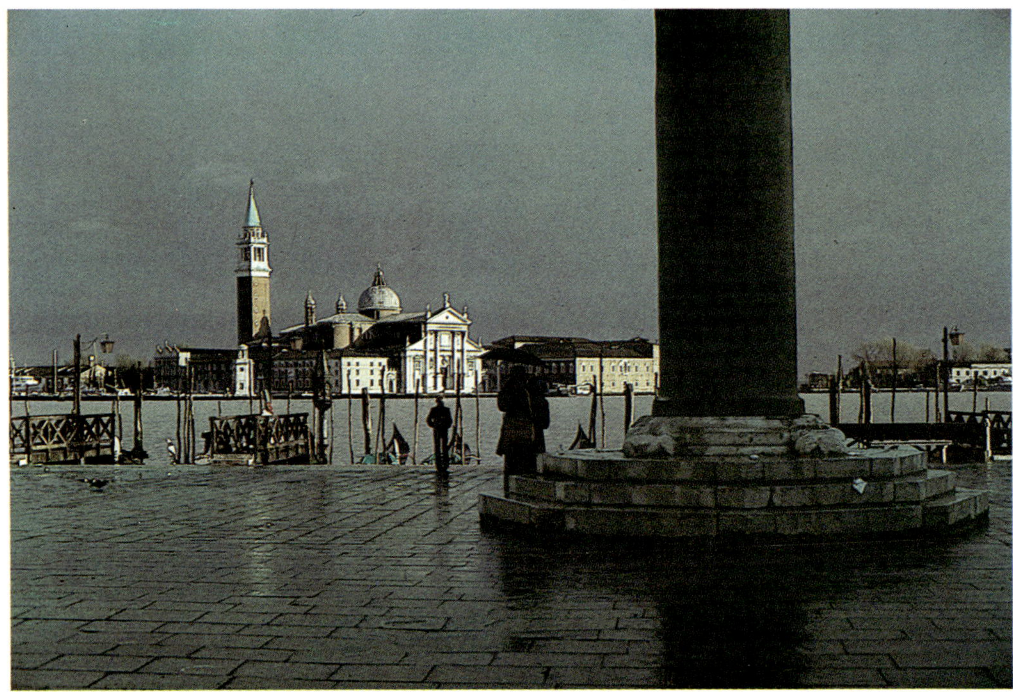

inspired painters, capable of transforming even the most mundane view into a source of wonder, poetry and emotion. This was due to his way of interpreting the objective data, and the harmony he managed to achieve in the reflections of the atmosphere and the variety of his colours. Anyone not fully convinced of the possibilities every artist has of transforming reality, even when he wishes to reproduce it as faithfully as possible, need only study the works of Canaletto, or his nephew Bellotto, who has left us some unforgettable pictures of Venice, Munich, Dresden and Warsaw which are perfectly true to reality but brimming over with his descriptive enthusiasm. The scrupulous realism of Bellotto was confirmed comparatively recently when Warsaw, which had been largely destroyed in the War, was rebuilt. The views of Bellotto provided a valuable reference for reconstructing the buildings.

Canaletto and Bellotto often used something which not all landscape photographers know how to use appropriately – wide-angles. Wide-angle lenses cover a very large field, but distort certain parts of the image and can be risky to use, as they may make the area depicted almost unrecognizable. They can be technically very useful and even give poetic results, but are definitely not recommended, for example, when one wishes to reproduce works of architecture. In this case, photographers are inclined to use them, because they ensure their being able to include the whole of the building even when the focal length is minimal. In this way, one can obtain a complete view of the building in question, but that is not to say that when one goes to see it, the picture will correspond very closely to reality. Canaletto, Bellotto, and other painters of views and landscapes, were able to use the most acrobatic possibilities of perspective solutions because they could correct them with the freedom of means available to them, by retouching lines and colours – something which a mechanical instrument like a camera can only do partially and with greater difficulty. But their example does confirm the interpretational freedom which is available to all.

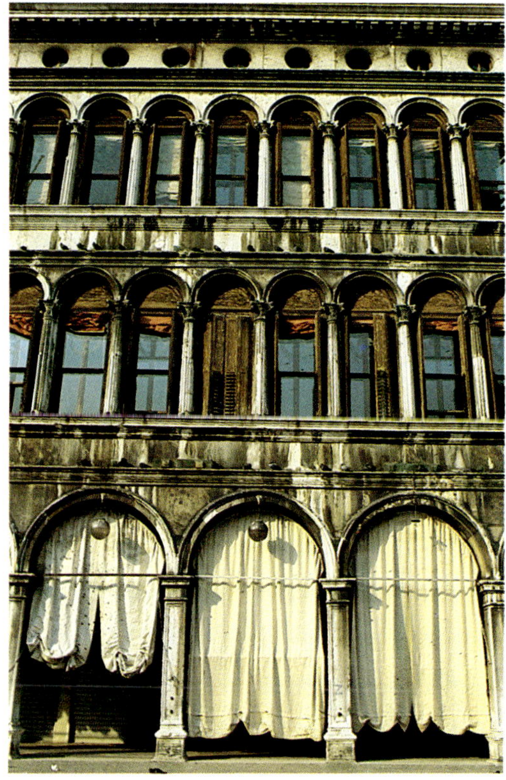

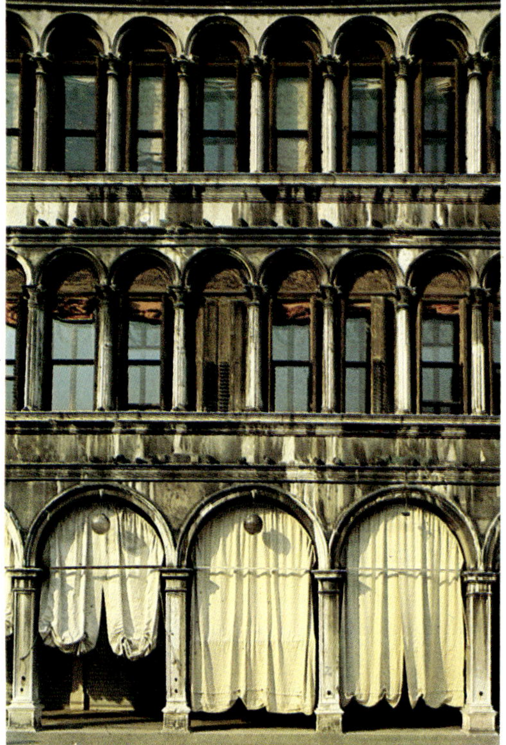

It was, above all, in their time that a way of seeing the landscape was developed which was eminently scenographic. This subsequently influenced many painters of the last century, and from painters it passed to photographers. Despite the time which has elapsed we often imitate, albeit unconsciously, their way of seeing things.

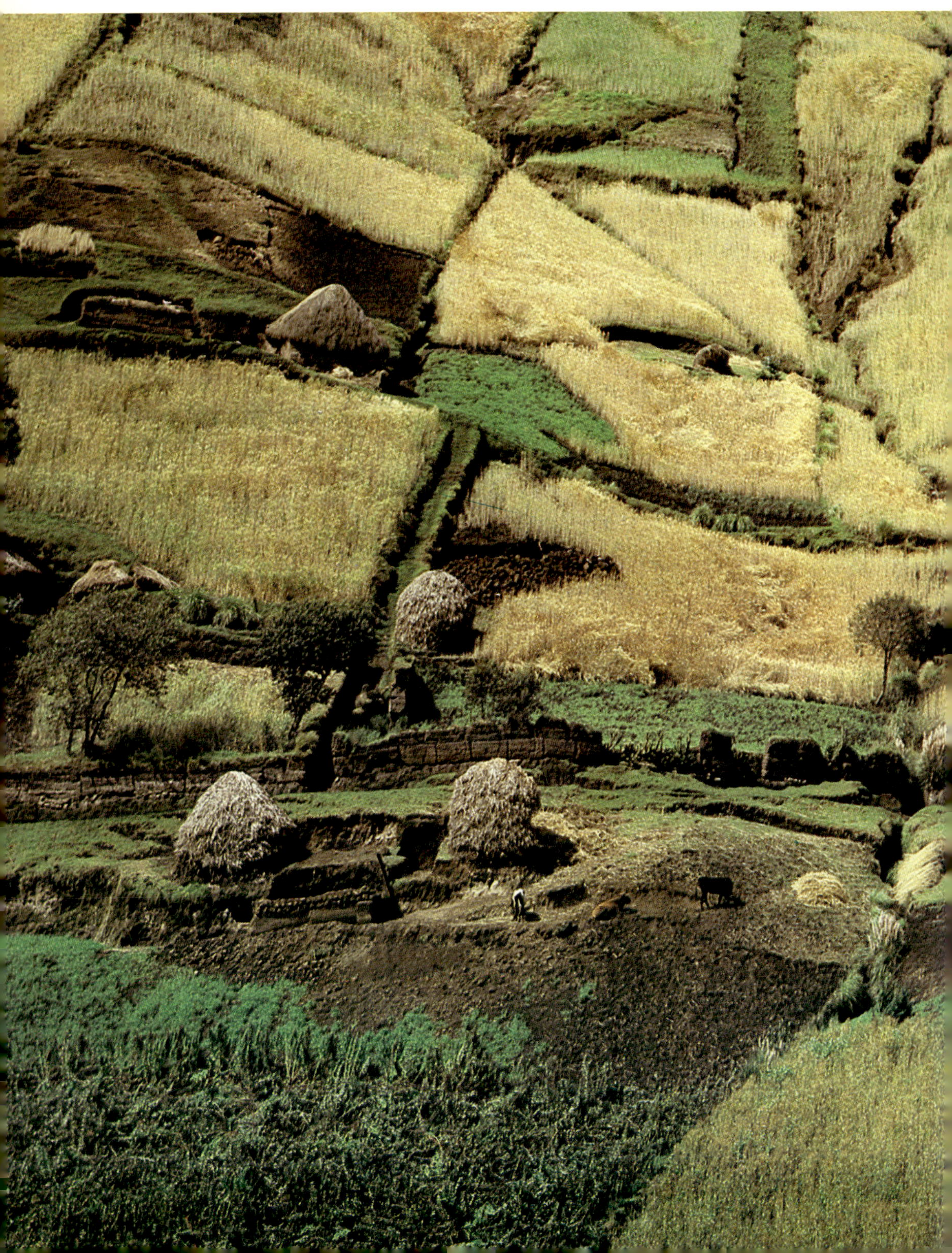

PROBLEMS AND HOW TO OVERCOME THEM

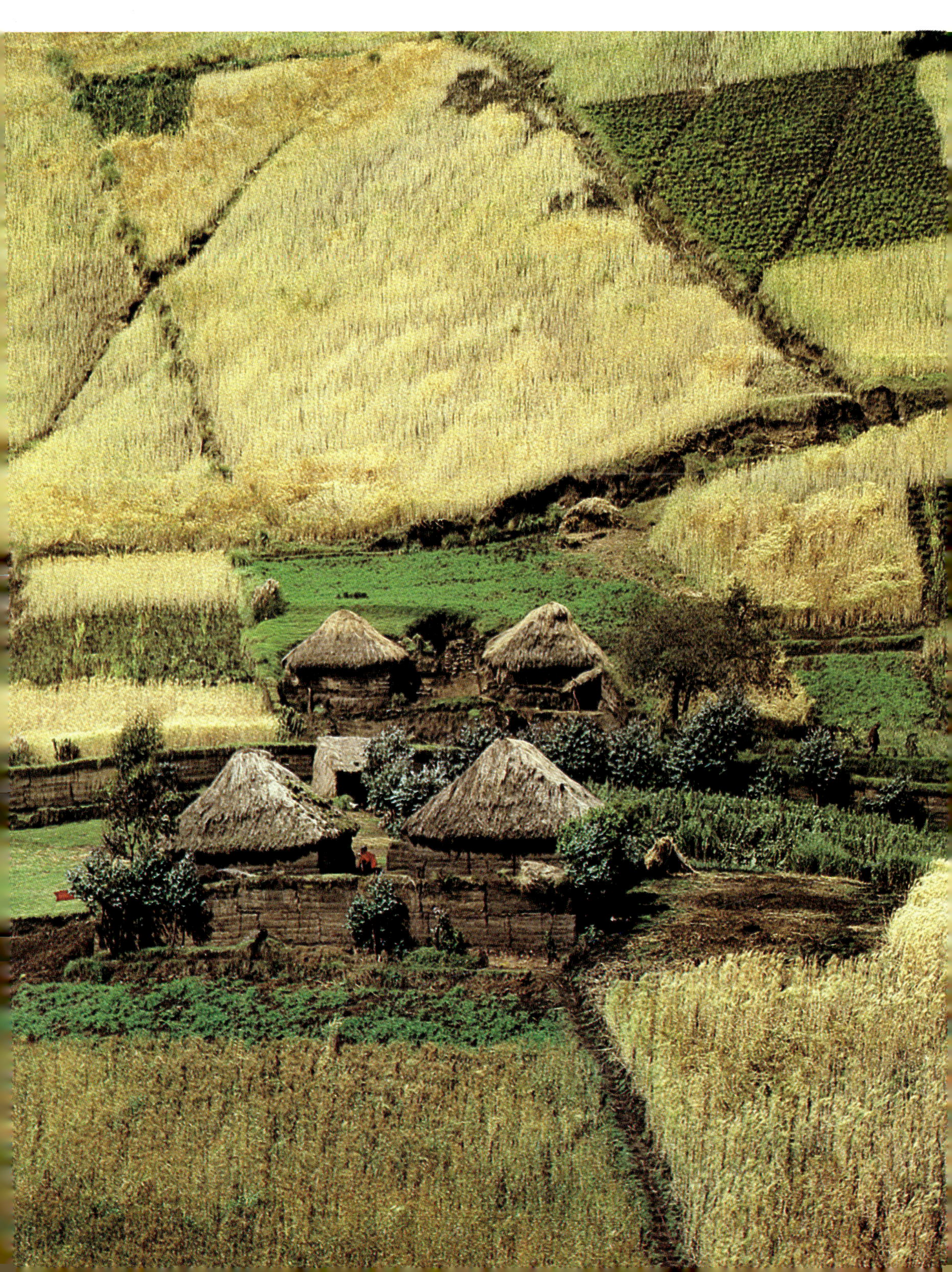

Importance of light

Landscape photography often demands a higher level of technical competence than other types of photography, due to the larger number of elements which nearly always compose it. We have already mentioned space as being peculiar to the landscape and the rendering of space is one of the most complex problems a photographer has to tackle. A person photographing a portrait, or an object, has no problems of space, or very few.
Even a reporter has relatively few spatial problems because, although his pictures involve a greater degree of space than a portrait or an object, for example when he has to photograph players on a football field, a local festival or a road accident, it is nonetheless not the space itself which is of interest, but the action taking place in it.
The landscape photographer is not only required to have a different type of sensitivity and competence from that of photographers in other fields; in the final analysis he also has to undertake more difficult choices, assessments and experiments.
Take, for example, the problem of light. For a reporter even the light can be secondary to his aims, always assuming there is enough of it. Even a portrait photographer has comparatively few problems. Certainly, he must know how to distribute light, to the point where many portraits are done in studios where the photographer can avail himself of a whole armoury of reflectors. The portrait photographer needs to be thoroughly familiar with the problems of light and know how to solve them. But he has a fundamental element in his favour, in that he nearly always has the means of solving these problems. He can construct the light he needs.
This is not so for the landscape photographer, who is not simply concerned with the amount of light. To interpret the scene in the way he has chosen, he needs a particular type of light. He can do absolutely nothing to acquire it, therefore only two options are open to him: to wait for the right moment, putting off taking the picture or else to change the meaning

Below, the homogeneity and intensity of the light are played up in this landscape by Franco Fontana, taken in brilliant sunshine. The emphasis on clarity of line and colour in the composition gives it an almost abstract character.

On the opposite page, above, the effect of light on a skyscraper, in a photograph by Vautier de Nanxe. In this case, the strong contrast in lighting dramatizes the image, giving it an unreal atmosphere, which is partly due to the exceptional nature of the phenomenon. The view of the lagoon in the photograph below relies entirely on the subtle tones of the mist in which it is immersed. All the outlines are vague and the areas of sky and water tend to be confused. Only the image of the boat in the center introduces a sharper note, contrasting with the indeterminateness of the rest of the composition.

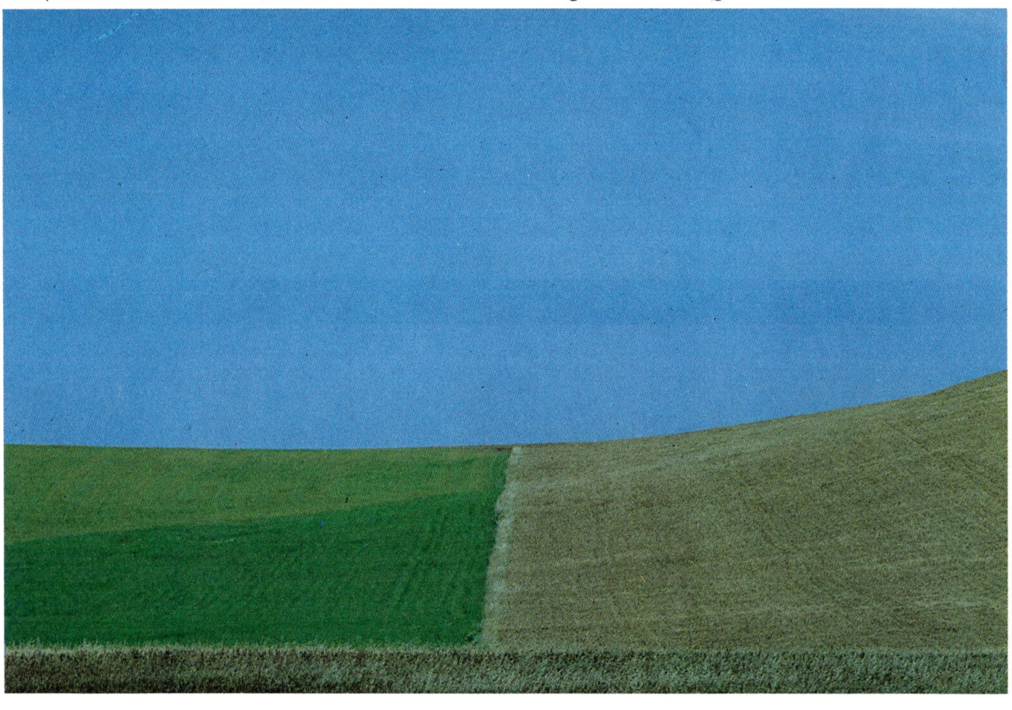

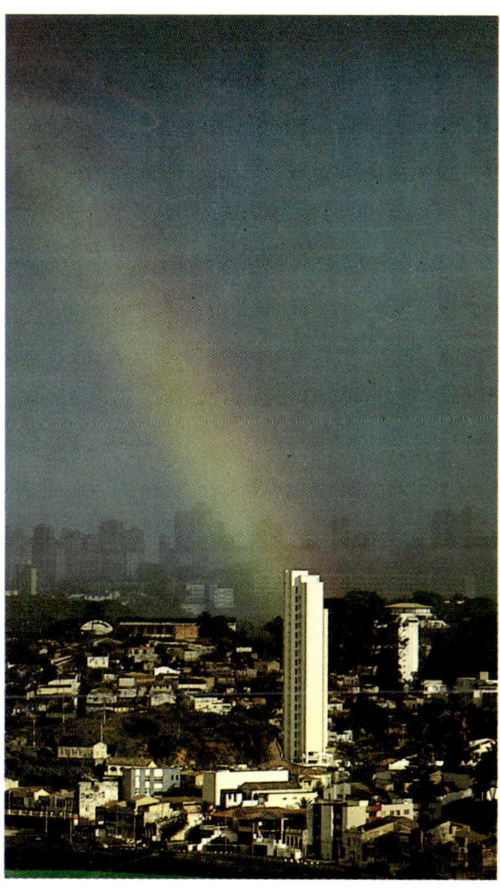

of his photograph completely, always assuming that this is possible. Admittedly, a mountain landscape can be beautiful even on a wet or foggy day, but photographs taken under such circumstances will certainly not be the same as those taken on a sunny day. Thus the photographer needs particularly sound intuition, experience and technical know-how to remedy the differences in light and also know how to make the most of its characteristics, given that light is a fundamental element for showing the size and quality of space. Space, this basic element, the very essence of the landscape, glories in light. Light is the raw material which fills it. The reproduction of a landscape can be based on a detail from it, a particular frame of a mountain, a tree, a piece of architecture; but these elements will only reveal a landscape if immersed in a space, which is part of the space by which they are surrounded. The great landscape painters all understood the enormous importance of this dimension, where they did not actually turn to landscape painting because of it. Space often relies on vast horizons, the unlimited expanse of the sky even when something rises up to obscure our view. Even when space is hidden from view, provided its presence is suggested to us, it draws us into a dimension which delivers us from the limited and the temporary, projecting us towards the infinite or the eternal.

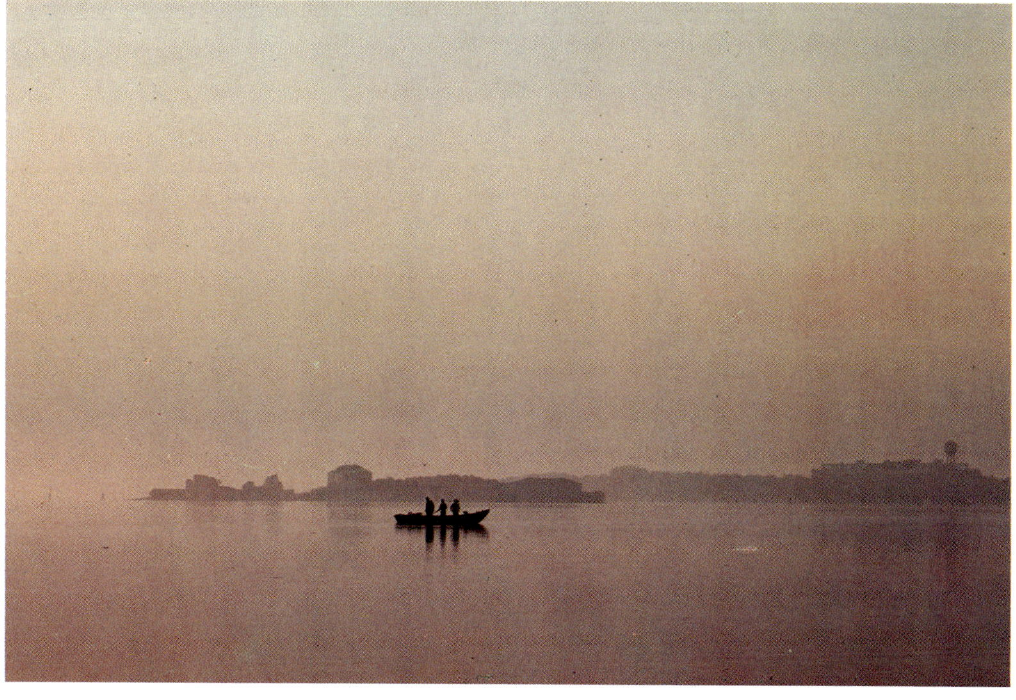

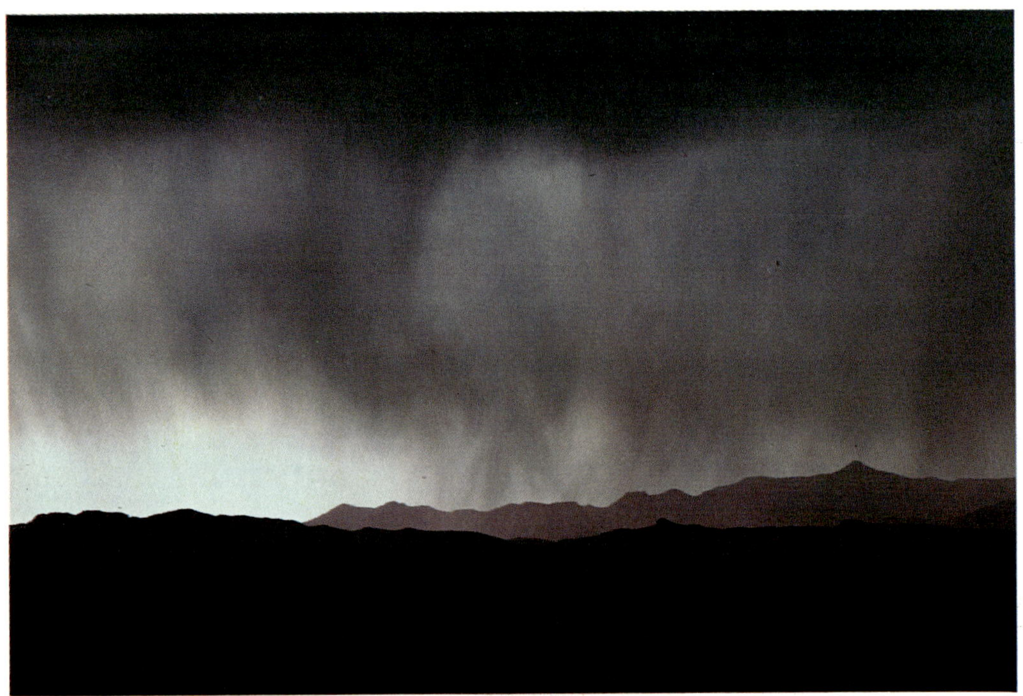

Black-and-white and colour

One cannot say that oil painting on an easel is better, in absolute terms, than engraving. Oil painting certainly offers a range of possibilities which cannot be obtained with engraving, and has been represented by very great artists; but even engraving has its merits and the masterpieces produced by Dürer or Goya using this technique, are in no way inferior to their paintings. Often, in fact, these engravings have qualities of their own, which would not have been achieved in a painting.

Black-and-white photography differs from colour only from a technical point of view and equivalent results can be achieved by both means, even if some photographers will prefer black-and-white and others colour. Likewise, some themes will be more suited to a rendering in black-and-white and others better interpreted by colour.

If the choice between black-and-white and colour has more to do with artistic than technical considerations, similarly, within these categories the photographer will know how to choose each time between the desirability of emphasizing the strength of colours and their autonomy, or blending them; creating a geometrical, linear type of photograph, or a tonal one. The photograph will depend on the objective data, the stimulus, the pretext offered by reality and the temperament of the photographer.

In this, as in very many other cases, it will be impossible to lay down hard and fast rules. Like every other category of artists, every photographer, above all every great photographer, has his own rules in which he believes implicitly. This is his strength and also his limitation. His strength, because it helps him to be coherent and express himself with immediacy and assurance; his limitation when he is inclined to judge the works of others by his own yardstick.

Artists are often bad judges, precisely because of the exclusive nature of their principles and sensitivity. Therefore the beginner must be very wary of making

Fulvio Roiter has succeeded here in capturing with particular sensitivity the effects of sheets of rain during a storm in the mountains. Note how the photographer has relied on spatial dimensions pure and simple and the most elementary effects of light and colour, eliminating every detail of the landscape.

On the opposite page, Giuliano Cappelli in his Cypresses in the Castelfiorentino Countryside *also eliminates all superfluous references and entrusts the meaning of the photograph to the great expanse of the sky, illuminated by the light of dusk and barely etched and enlivened at the top by the profile of the moon and at the bottom by the sequence of cypresses, whose denser tones form a vivid contrast with the vastness of the space above them. While the previous photograph is rendered in tonal mixtures which seem to reveal the exuberance and vitality of the atmosphere, here, balance is achieved by a subtle distribution of outlines.*

SCALE OF COLOUR TEMPERATURES

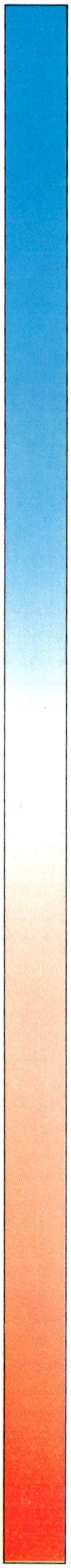

K	Light source out-of-doors	Light source indoors
18000	snow, water, blue sky	
6000	extensive shadows, blue sky	
5800	average daylight, central latitudes	electronic flash
5600		
5400	sunlight at midday	blue bulb flash cube
5200		
5000	average daylight northern hemisphere	
4800		"daylight" fluorescent tubes
4600		
4400		
4200	sunlight in early morning, late afternoon, or at sunset	
4000		"warm white light" fluorescent tubes
3800		flash with white bulb
3600		
3400		photoflood lamps
3200		photographic lamps (pearl argon)
3000		
2800		150–200 W bulb
2600		40–60 W bulb
2400		25 W bulb
2200		
1930		candle light

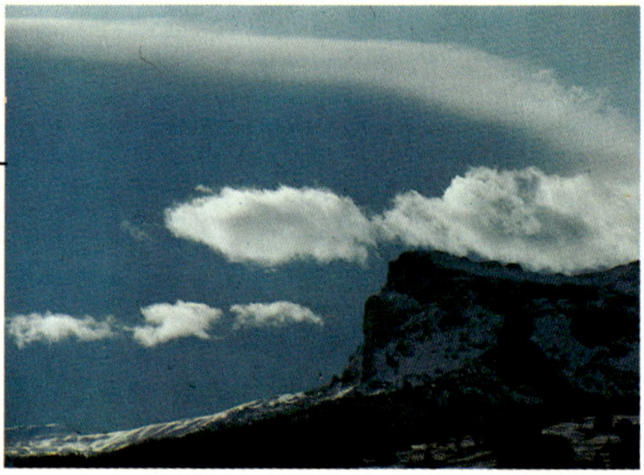

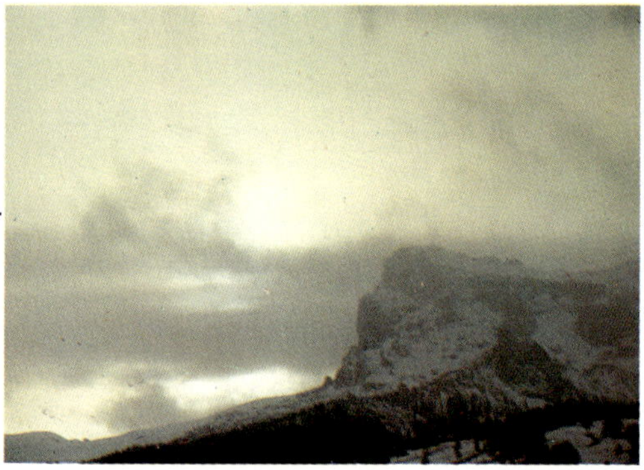

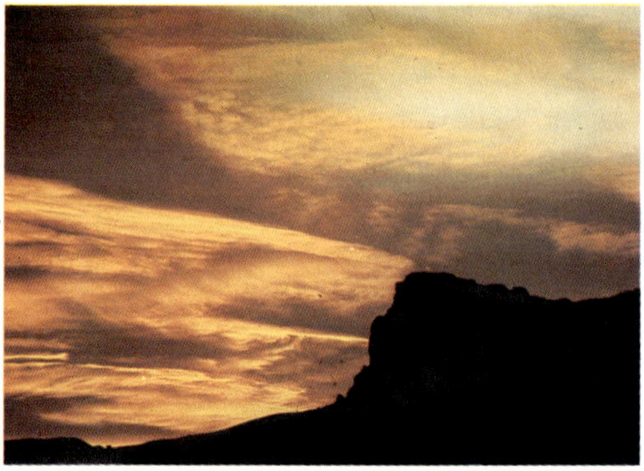

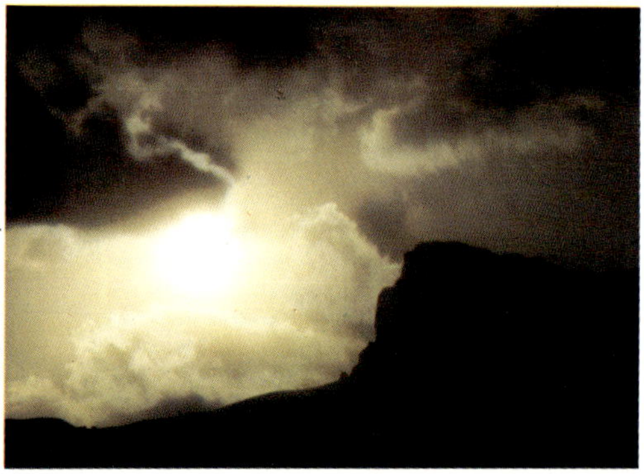

Left, the sky can be the subject of an incredible variety of spectacles in a single day, each with its own type of composition, lighting, movement and colour blends. Naturally some places, such as mountains, can be a theater of exceptionally varied and intense effects, due to the particular atmosphere which characterizes them. It will be up to the photographer to interpret these natural elements in such a way as to emphasize a scene or characterize a state of mind.

Even artificial light at night, as in the photograph below, can have its magic. The streets of a city, the façades of a building, can form the backcloth for fascinating revelations.

unilateral choices of model straight away and must experiment with different types.
The distinction between warm and cold colours is a purely conventional one, based on a few elementary psychological sensations which colours normally produce: red as evocative of fire, blue of night and ice, yellow of the sun, etc. But beware. These are purely conventions because the coldness or warmness of a colour is only revealed in its context and one can have cold reds and yellows and warm blues. Normally, however, within a given context, a predominance of such colours can accentuate a warm or cold effect.
A very different matter is the temperature of colours, by which the colour content of light is indicated. This content, and hence the colour temperature, is expressed in degrees Kelvin (K). Most light sources have a typical colour temperature which can be shown in suitable tables.
The classification is based on the fact that a heated object emits electro-magnetic radiations, starting from infra-red rays, going towards a light which contains a high percentage of red, and progressing, as the temperature rises, to a white light tending to blue. Most light sources are based on heating and are therefore easily classifiable. But other types of lighting such as neon or the light from the sky can be included in this classification with a fair degree of accuracy, despite being due to different phenomena. The two most important temperatures are those of daylight, around 5500°K, and tungsten light, from 3200–3400°K, because these are the ones most frequently encountered (tungsten light is the type produced by ordinary light bulbs).
It is useful to know the colour temperatures in order to make the necessary adjustments to variations in colour which our eye adapts to involuntarily, unlike film.
Finally, you should always remember that the colour temperature refers to the quality of the light, not the colours themselves.

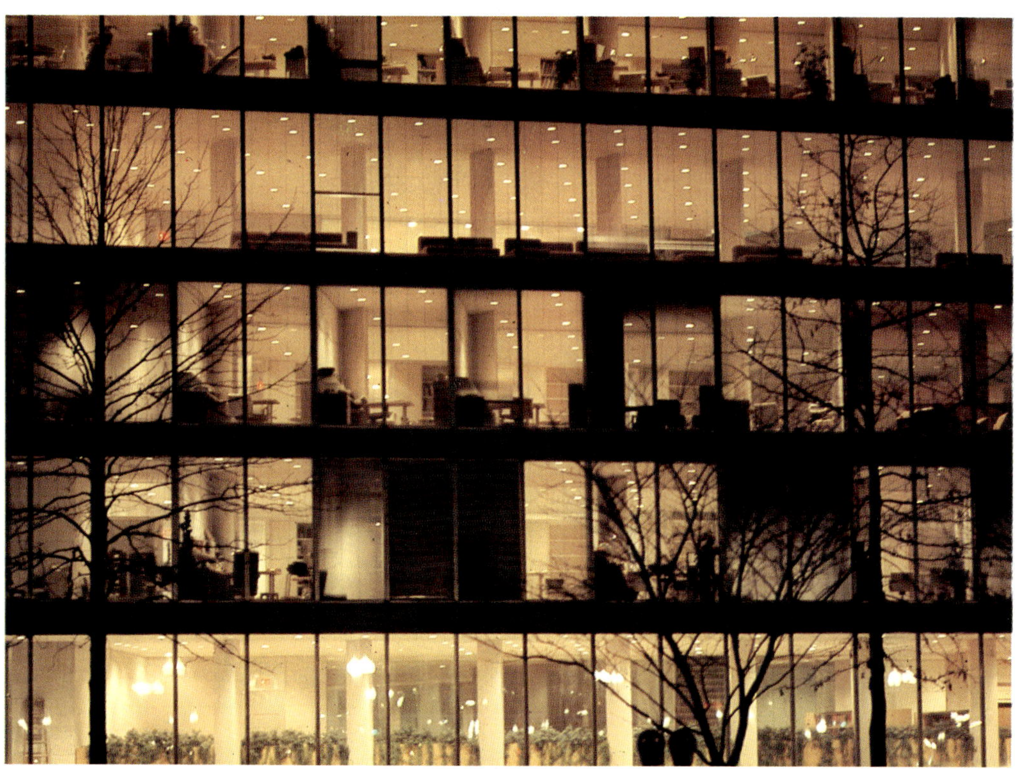

The camera

The remarks in these pages may be sufficient to understand the type of preparation landscape photography demands, if one is not to be content with run-of-the-mill results. But it would be wrong to think that all the top photographers in this field use particularly sophisticated equipment. Certainly, they can, and are, sometimes obliged to do so, but much more often than one thinks their excellent results are achieved without anything mysterious or complicated being adopted.

Very often when the layman sees a particularly good photograph, feeling it to be far beyond his capabilities, he tends to assume that heaven knows what technical devices, cameras, lenses, filters or special films have been used. Therefore, instead of concentrating on sensitizing his eye and gaining a thorough command of basic technique he often turns straight to the difficult techniques, and goes in search of strange and costly equipment.

But highly original photographs – and by original we mean photographs that are executed skilfully and with a personal touch and not just particularly unusual pictures – are often produced using very elementary techniques. Experience shows that their value and significance depends much more on the eye of the photographer, his

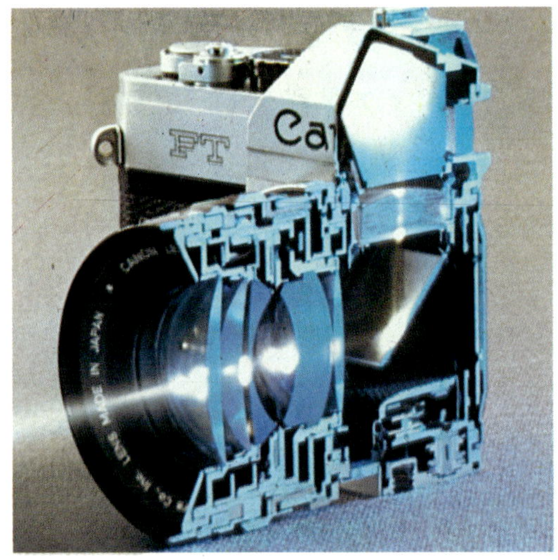

mode of framing, of emphasizing motifs, lights and colours, than on the technical means available to him. Very often this also applies to those special photographs which are out-of-the-ordinary and closely linked to the inventiveness and possibly the eccentricity of the photographer and which, a moment ago, we were wishing to exclude. But we wished to exclude them above all to stress the idea that originality depends first and foremost on the interpretational force of a photograph

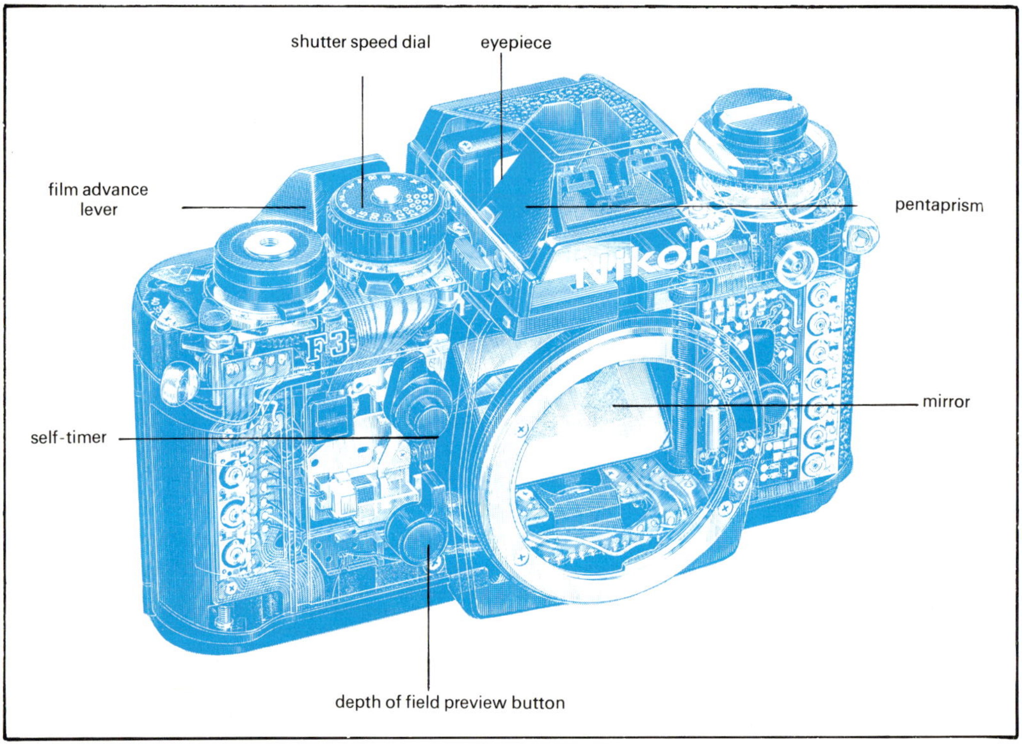

On the opposite page, above, cross-section of the Canon FT QL. The lower part shows the single-lens reflex camera system, which enables one to see in the viewfinder the exact image which will be on the film. The mirror is raised automatically at the moment of shutter release.
Below, a high technology camera, the Nikon F3.

The drawing on the right shows the basic elements of an incorporated electronic system in a modern camera. Below, an example of the extraordinary variety of accessories available for the most varied uses with high quality cameras.

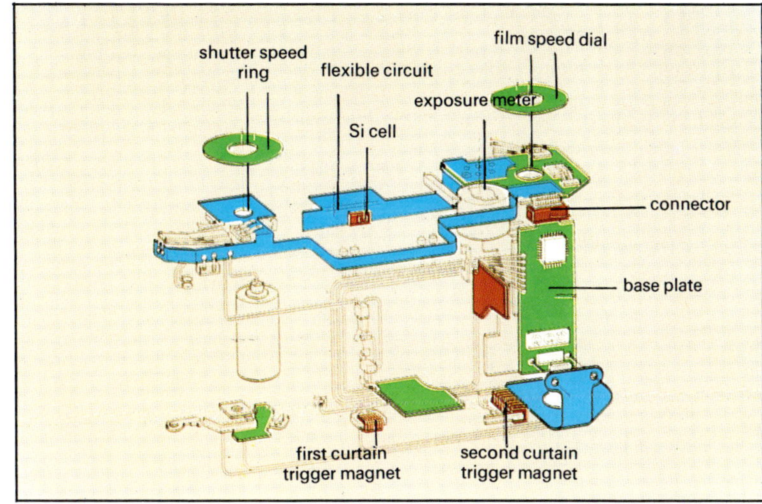

rather than its eccentricity. Since even eccentric, novel, surprising photographs are possible and perfectly legitimate and can also be excellent, we will note that these too depend more often than not on the inventive power of the photographer rather than the use of any very rare instruments. This should be of some comfort to the layman who can thus feel that he is starting out on an equal footing with the top photographers, even if his store of technical equipment and know-how is elementary. But it should also make him aware of how necessary it is to sharpen his sensitivity, train his eye – in short, acquire the type of first-hand experience which is not bought in shops and which is the only means in the final analysis of developing his personality

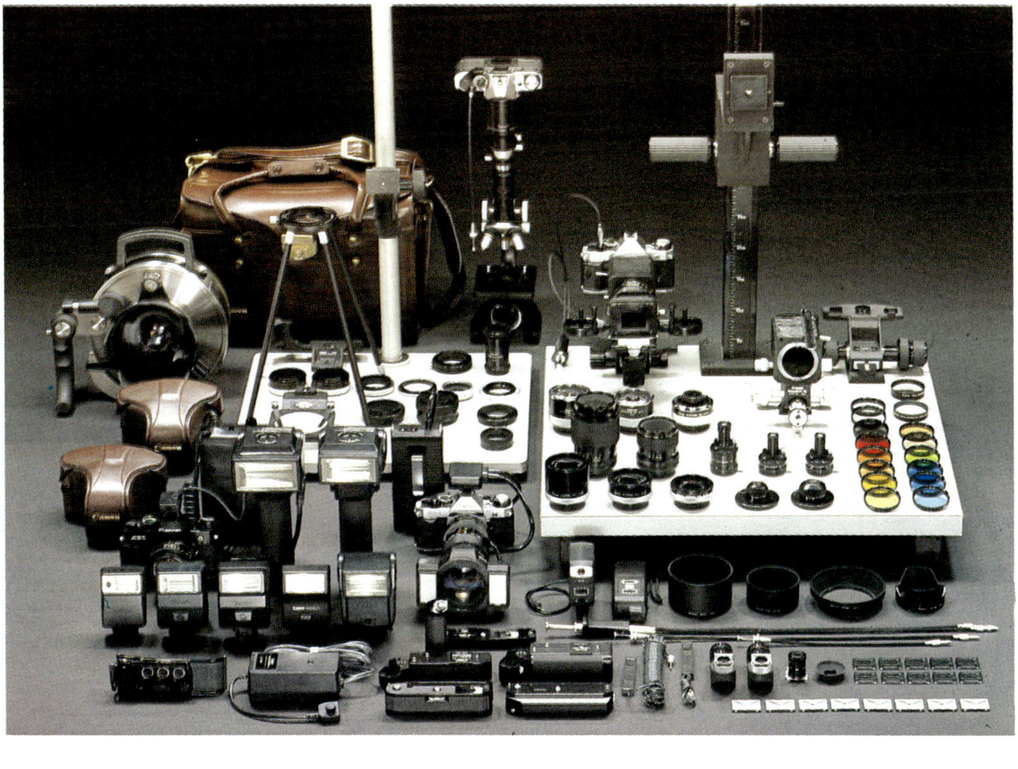

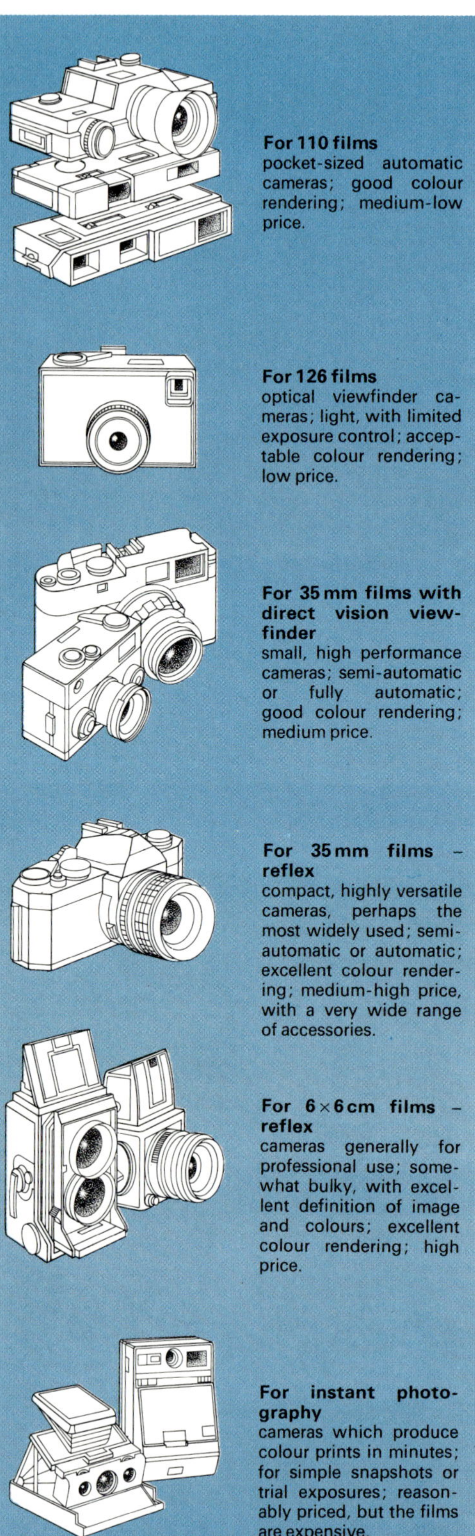

or, to stay on the subject, his originality. Although a discussion on cameras is of a general nature and concerns all types of photography, it is worth repeating here with particular regard to landscape photography.
Cameras can be classified under various categories (size, cost, mechanics, uses, etc.). A fairly common subdivision for the most widely-used types is shown in the drawing on the left and is based on the size of the film and other factors.

Left, types of camera currently on the market, arranged according to their film format and type of viewfinder.
The drawing below illustrates parallax error.

On the opposite page, left, in reflex cameras, focusing of the image is facilitated by the presence of a split-image rangefinder and microprism collar, which shows correct focusing by both image clarity and vertical alignment.
Right, some examples of interchangeable focusing screens for 35 mm reflexes, to improve focusing or for other special uses.

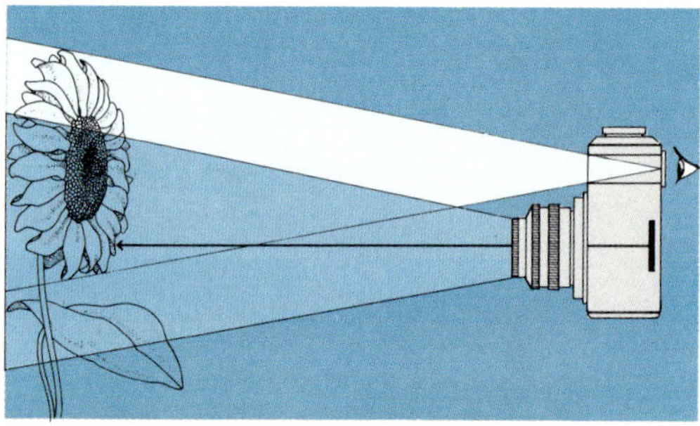

The first category consists of cameras which use type 110 16 mm films: the pocket cameras. The great improvements made to films, and mechanical refinements, permit comparatively good results nowadays which have contributed a great deal to the popularity of this type of camera. But its chief advantage is its extremely small size and light weight. Its very simplicity of operation precludes the type of performance a good landscape photograph requires, although it should be remembered that a very important factor in the quality of a camera is the quality of the lens, which can be independent of its size.
A second category is made up of 126 cameras which use square, 35 mm negatives. As in the case of pocket cameras, these have a fixed focus lens and only one exposure time and they are therefore too simple to offer very high performance.
Next come the types of camera which use normal 35 mm film and are equipped with a direct vision viewfinder. These are simple, economical cameras, but they generally have fixed focus lenses and the

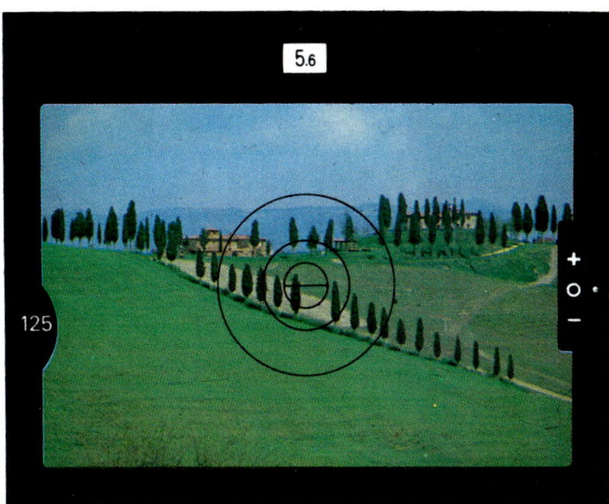

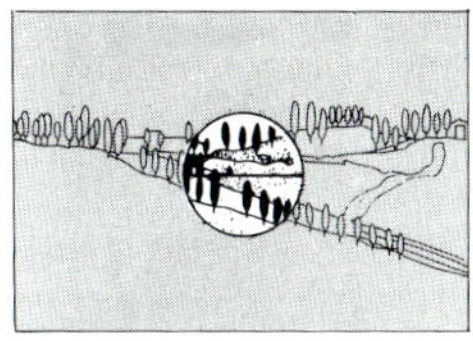

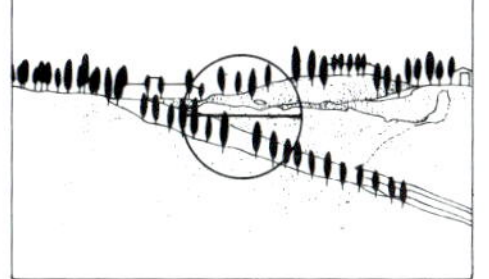

variations in exposure time and aperture are very limited, as is their light-gathering power. Therefore they cannot be used in dim light. Another limitation is what is known as parallax error, or the fact that the image seen in the finder is shifted in relation to the one actually framed by the taking lens. These cameras in fact use a direct vision finder in which the framing is done through a separate window from the taking lens, while in the reflex finder, which we shall be discussing below, the frame is viewed through the taking lens. Even the performance of this type of machine is therefore somewhat limited.

Next we have the SLR (Single Lens Reflex) 35 mm cameras, which are the most versatile, and those with the most advanced automation. They are characterized by the fact that the image is viewed through the taking lens, which avoids any parallax error. They are heavier and more expensive, have a very wide range of accessories, and despite their small size permit an exceptional variety of uses with excellent results, even for landscape photography.

Another category consists of reflexes which use 6 × 6 film (with 6 × 7 and 4.5 × 6 variants). They are somewhat heavier and one of their advantages is the larger format of the film.

Last come the instamatic cameras, much valued for specific purposes, but a lot less recommended for serious photography.

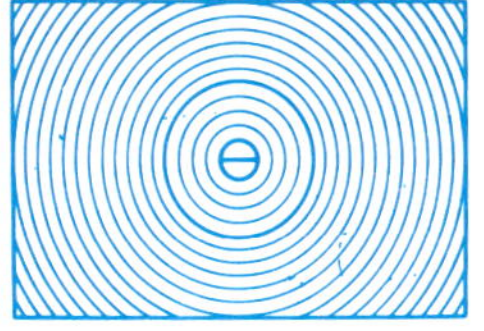

Ground glass with Fresnel lens and condenser lens; for general use; the horizontal split image rangefinder facilitates focusing.

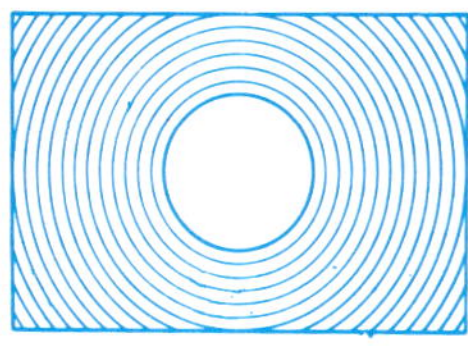

Ground glass with Fresnel lens and condenser and a finely ground area in the center; it is most useful for very long, slow telephoto lenses.

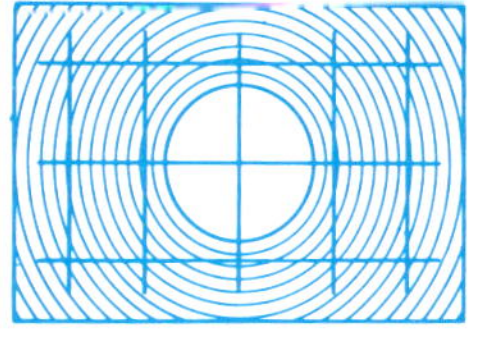

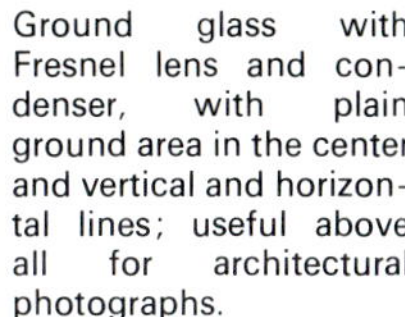

Ground glass with Fresnel lens and condenser, with plain ground area in the center and vertical and horizontal lines; useful above all for architectural photographs.

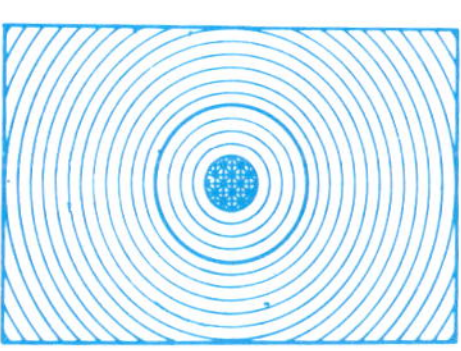

Ground glass with Fresnel lens and condenser and a microprism grid in the center; for general use; it is the simplest to use.

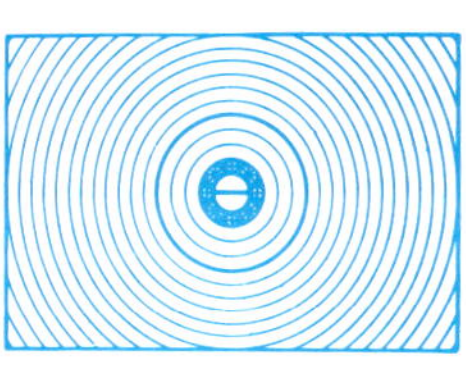

Similar to the foregoing, it has a horizontal split image rangefinder in the center which facilitates focusing; for general use.

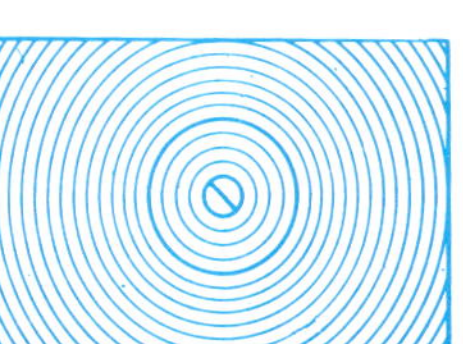

Ground glass with Fresnel lens and condenser, with split image rangefinder angled at 45°; it permits focusing of horizontal lines as well.

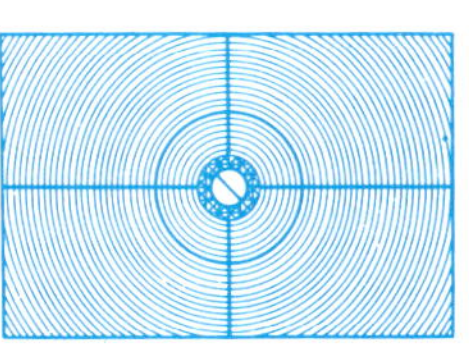

Ground glass with Fresnel and condenser, with split image rangefinder angled at 45° surrounded by a microprism collar; two orthogonal lines guarantee widespread use of this screen.

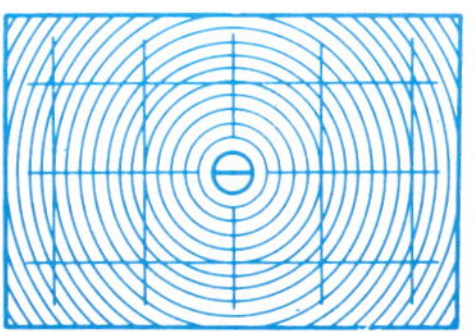

Ground glass with Fresnel lens and condenser, with split image rangefinder and vertical and horizontal lines for controlling the verticality of the frame; useful for wide-angles.

Exposure and exposure meters

Some photographers are naturally fast at their job; others slow. But in both cases, their confidence is the fruit of experience. The beginner should not be discouraged by their seeming infallibility and after having discarded his hundredth photograph – not taken in haphazard fashion, but alas with every intention of doing something good, he should not think he has chosen too difficult an art, for which he was unaware that he had no ability whatsoever. Practice, patience and tenacity are required. To avoid anxiety and enjoy your work, and therefore make the most of your apprenticeship, you are strongly advised to progress by gradual stages and start by learning how to use the camera in the simplest way. It is a good idea, in short, to learn the "correct" way of doing things before anything else. The pursuit of originality at all costs can be counterproductive, partly because it distracts you from simpler compositions which are, in fact, the best way of learning how to calculate simultaneously all those technical factors which are the backbone of all photographic experience. Fortunately, a vast store of technical knowledge is not needed for a photograph to be correct. You only have to set the right aperture with the right focus; use the right exposure time with the right film. Many of these things can be calculated mechanically. For example, the instructions on films give their sensitivity and the relative ratios between the aperture and exposure time.
If focusing is a basic operation, measuring the light is no less important. The photographer can vary it by altering the exposure time and aperture to achieve the necessary effect, either with a long and limited exposure, or a short and powerful one. In this way, he can obtain radically different results. But first of all, he needs to know what exposure to use. For an ordinary photograph, it can be sufficient, though highly approximate, to judge by eye. But for greater accuracy, you will need to use the special instruments for measuring light called exposure meters.
In most cases nowadays, the exposure meter is built into the camera and the light passing through the lens is measured by one or more photoelectric cells (TTL – Through the Lens reading). This system has made it necessary to produce smaller and smaller cells.

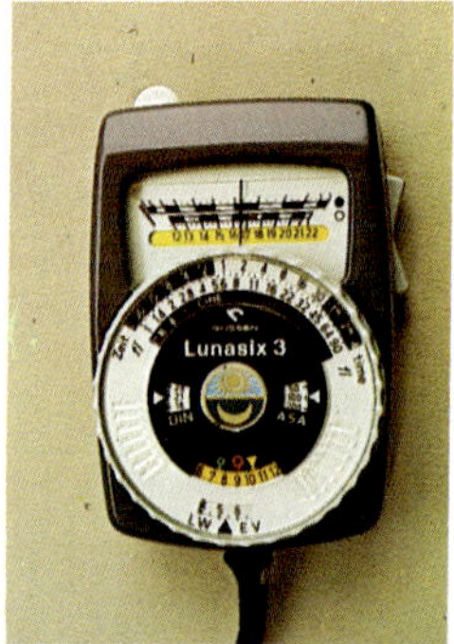

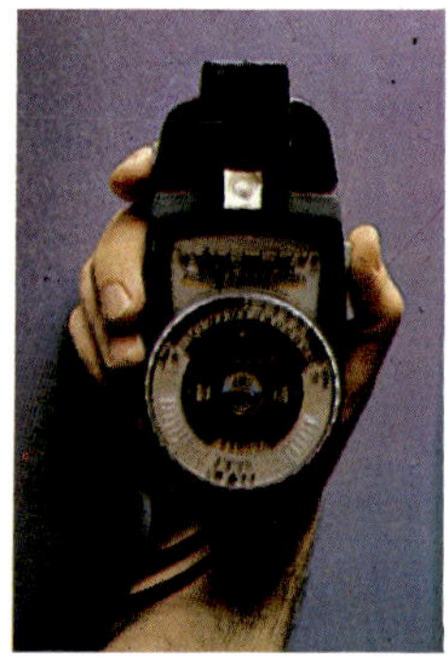

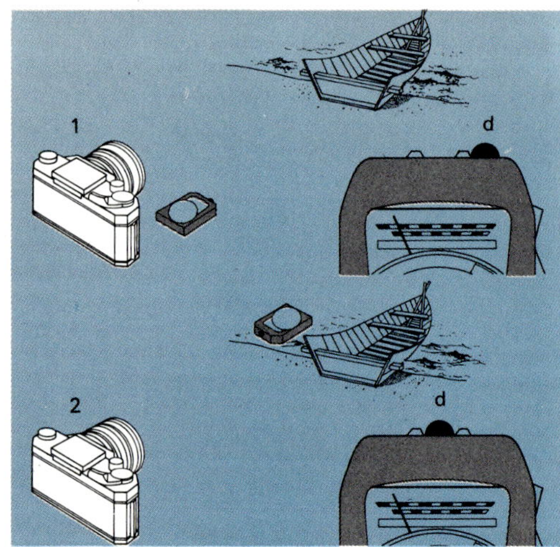

Measuring the intensity of the light is vital to the success of a photograph. Instruments called exposure meters are used for this purpose.
Above, diagram of phases of exposure sequence. 1) the light rays coming through the lens are reflected on to the exposure meter (e) and the viewfinder by two mirrors (m); 2) pressing the shutter release button stops down the diaphragm and causes the mirrors to flip up; 3) the shutter exposes the film; 4) the mirrors fall back, the diaphragm is reopened and the initial situation is restored.

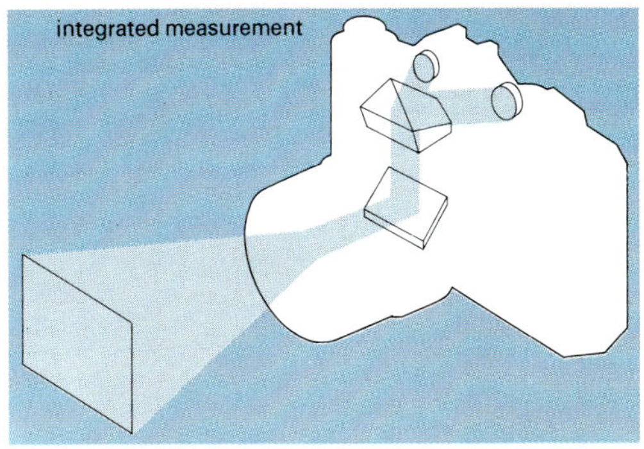

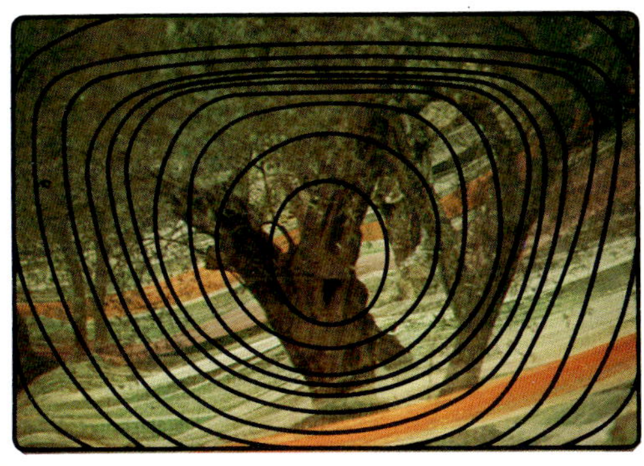

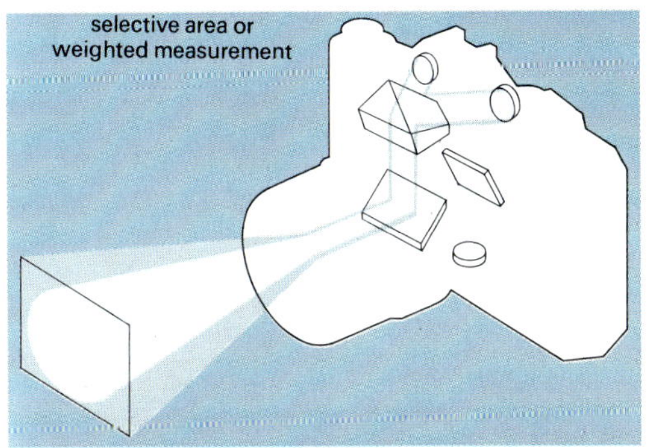

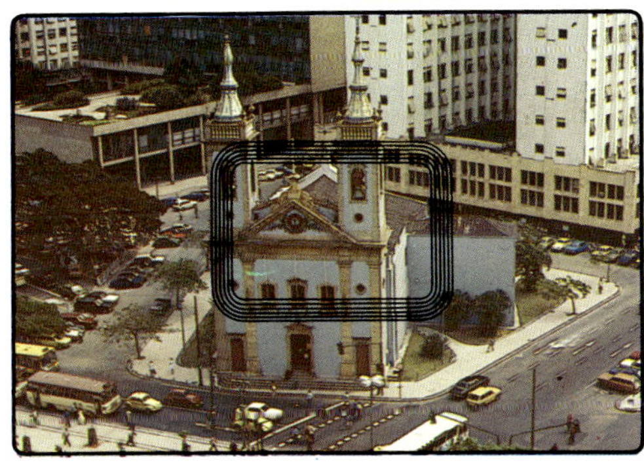

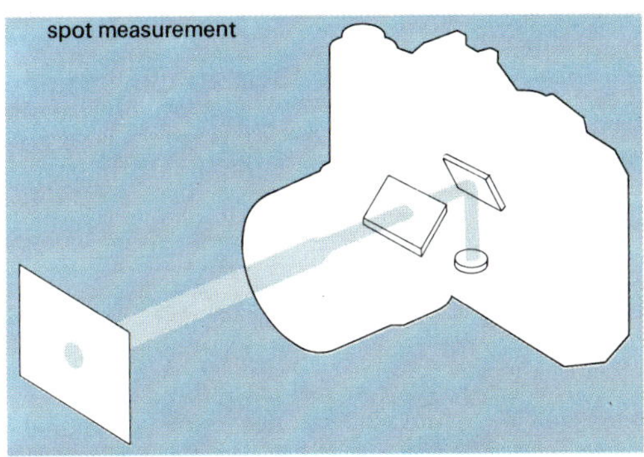

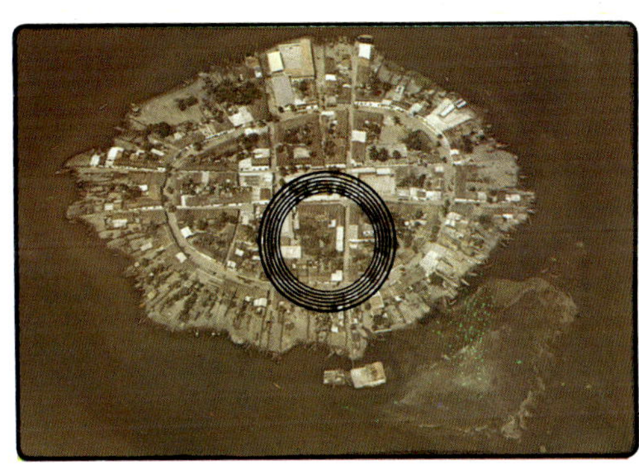

On the opposite page, the Lunasix 3 manual exposure meter by Gossen (left) and the same exposure meter with a tele device (right). Below, the two ways of taking a light reading with a manual exposure meter. 1) Reflected light reading: the exposure meter is turned towards the subject to be photographed according to the axis of the lens and the diffuser (d) is shifted to the right. 2) Incident light reading: having shifted the diffuser (d), the exposure meter is turned to measure the light entering the lens.
The commonest type of incorporated exposure meter is the TTL (through the lens) type. A very important problem which must be taken into account is that the lighting of the subject may be uneven, sometimes very markedly so. One type of meter measures the average intensity over the whole area of the image viewed, but giving more weight to the central part. This is the integrated light meter. Spot exposure meters are used when there is a strong contrast between the subject and background, and they select the light in the part of interest. Weighted or selective area metering is a compromise between the two.

GaAsP (gallium, arsenic, phosphorus) cells are now used which are highly sensitive and balanced for colour.
TTL exposure meters vary too, according to the area they measure. Some take an integrated reading which gives the average brightness although with greater sensitivity in the central part of the image; or a spot reading which gives the exact exposure only for the central part of the frame; while the weighted or selective area reading is a compromise between the other two.
Manually-operated exposure meters are useful even if there is a built-in exposure meter, as they permit a much more accurate reading. The most popular type today are CdS (cadmium sulphide) meters whose performance is excellent, even in unstable lighting conditions.

Diaphragm and shutter: depth of field

Another typical aspect of landscape photography is the very large number of details it often has to include. Particularly when a photograph is more descriptive than evocative, that is, when the description of an environment is more important than its interpretation, or when the latter relies on the number, variety or vivacity of details, then it goes without saying that the photograph must be accurate in every respect. This is where the difficult problem arises of giving the same definition, or at least the same weight, to details distributed at different depths and with different colours and brightness levels. Sometimes – when, for example, the frame includes strong contrasts in light and shade and it is obvious that the same definition cannot be achieved in both parts, certain obstacles can even be insuperable and you therefore have to resort to technical expedients or radically different frames to solve the problem.

It is relatively easy to photograph near planes or set the focus at infinity. But when you need to show up both near and distant details you often have to resort to complex and delicate solutions. These problems are multiplied with cameras which have a limited focal length, as in the case of most portables.

To return for a

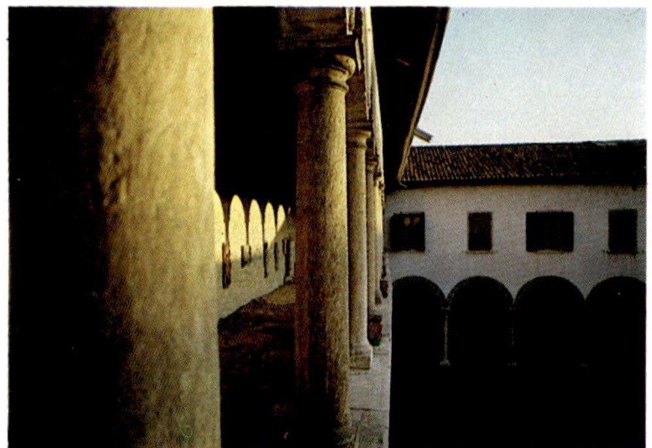

wide-angle with diaphragm stopped right down

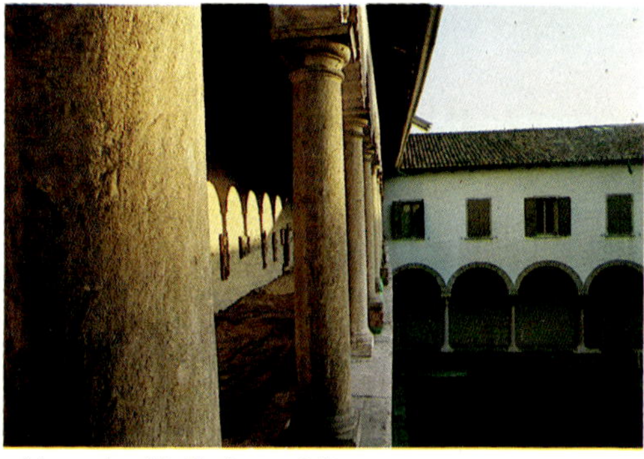

wide-angle with diaphragm fully open

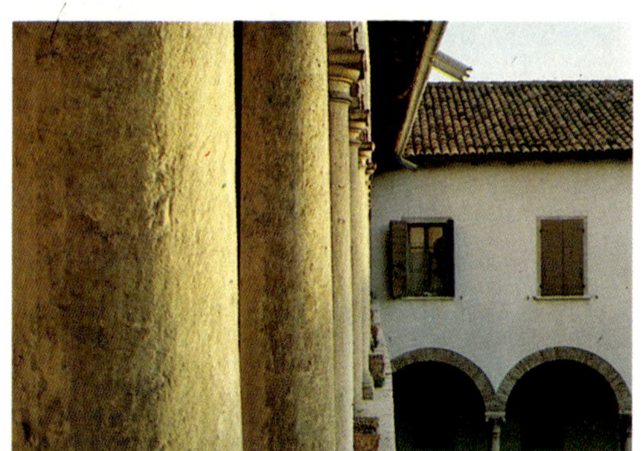

normal lens with diaphragm stopped right down

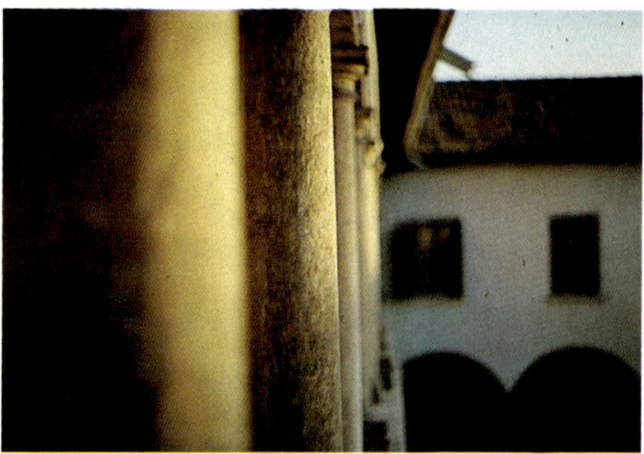

normal lens with diaphragm fully open

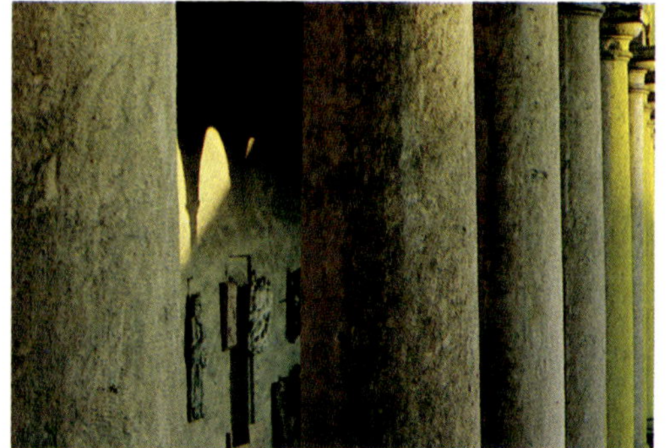

telephoto lens with diaphragm stopped right down

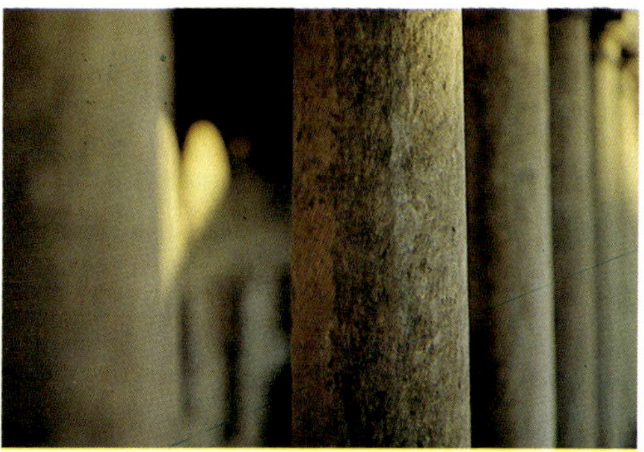

telephoto with diaphragm fully open

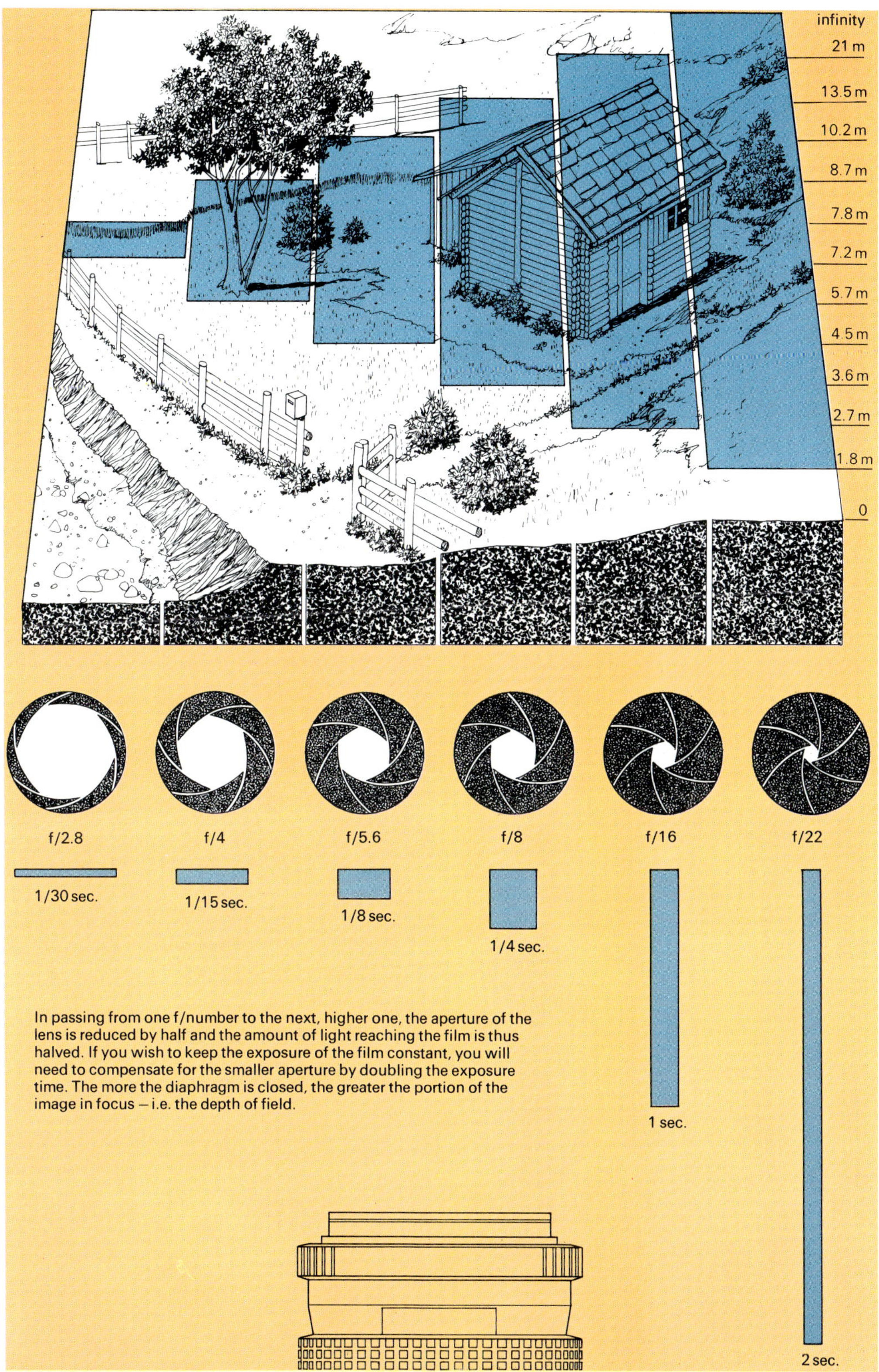

In passing from one f/number to the next, higher one, the aperture of the lens is reduced by half and the amount of light reaching the film is thus halved. If you wish to keep the exposure of the film constant, you will need to compensate for the smaller aperture by doubling the exposure time. The more the diaphragm is closed, the greater the portion of the image in focus – i.e. the depth of field.

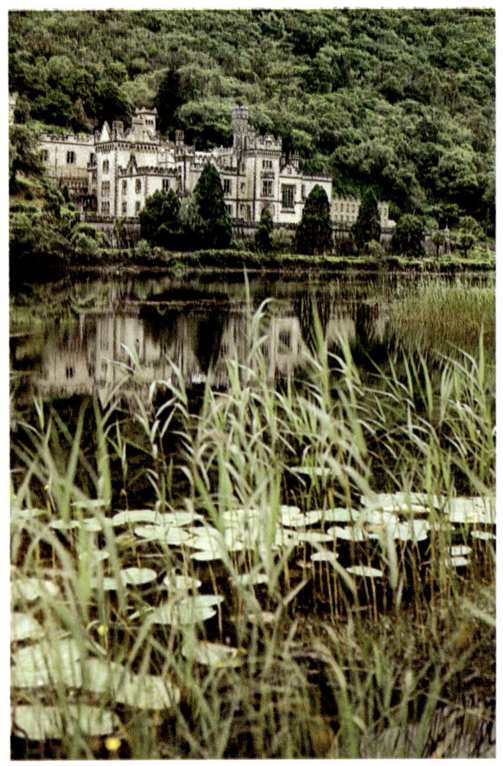

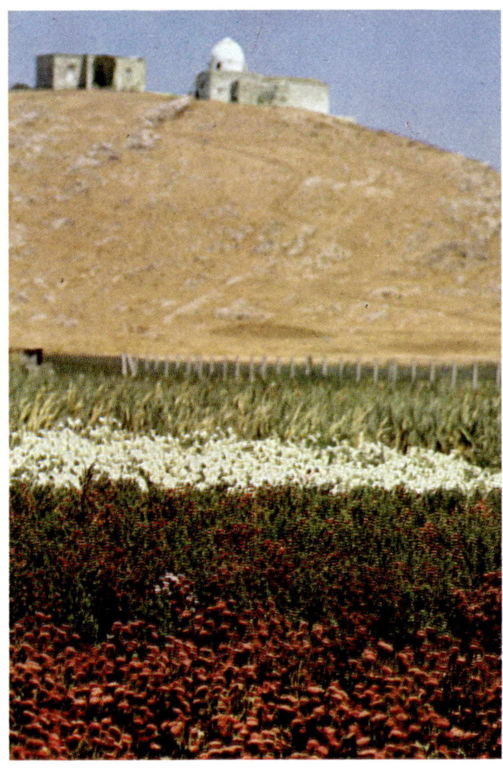

moment to the three basic operations of photography: the exposure time, diaphragm aperture and focus. As you will know, there is a precise relationship between the exposure time and aperture. For a given light, each variation in exposure time is automatically matched by a variation in the aperture. As the exposure time and diaphragm aperture directly influence the illumination of the film, clearly if the exposure time is increased, the aperture can be reduced, and vice versa. The exposure time is particularly important in landscape photography, where, in many cases, it might not seem to be so important. For example, where there are parts in movement (the waves of the sea, or a waterfall, or the effects of wind, or moving figures or objects).

Thus far, the problem seems to be limited to a choice of definition or the desirability of sharpening or blurring certain details. But as every photographer knows, the aperture of the lens is, in turn, directly related to the depth of field. And in a landscape photograph, depth of field is all-important.

The depth of field indicates the space within which objects look sharp at a given lens aperture.

In some very simple cameras the problem of depth of field does not exist, because the lenses permit simultaneous focusing of both foreground and infinity. These lenses are very small and therefore cost little. But their obvious flexibility is inversely proportional to their efficiency. They are a compromise and as such, can only offer limited, though respectable, results. If you wish to take good photographs with good lenses, the problem of depth of field is fundamental.

The depth of field is related to the focal length of the lens. The longer this is, the shorter the depth of field. Furthermore, the depth of field of the lens increases as its aperture is reduced and this is why, by stopping down the diaphragm, you obtain greater depth of field.

A recurring problem in landscape photography is focusing when the distance between foreground and background makes it impossible to include both in the same depth of field. Clearly, focusing on the nearest planes can blur the more distant ones and vice versa. The photographer therefore has to choose.

In the photograph on the left, the view of the castle was given prominence, in the belief that blurring of the plants in the foreground could fit in with the mobility of the water; while in the photograph on the right, the situation is reversed, given the greater anonymity of the background.
On the opposite page, the blurring of the photograph above is completely absorbed by the character of the flowers, which are seen as variegated masses of colour, while in the photograph below, the photographer has achieved an extraordinary balance between the near and distant parts.

The depths of field are nearly always marked on camera lenses.
Just as a fixed progression of exposure times has been established, expressed in seconds according to the scale: 1, 1/2, 1/4, 1/8, 1/15, 1/30, 1/60, 1/125, 1/250, 1/500 in which each speed is about half the preceding one, similarly, indication of the diaphragm apertures has been standardized, with the result that the amount of light passing through the lens is reduced by half for each f/number.
Accordingly, you have the scale f/1, f/1.4, f/2, f/2.8, f/4, f/5.6, f/8, f/11, f/16, f/22, f/32, f/45, f/64.
The f/number is given by the ratio of the focal length to the useful diameter of the lens. An interesting point is that different lenses set at identical f/numbers always let through the same amount of light and therefore generally require identical exposure times.
The problem of focusing different planes at once can in some cases only be solved by choosing a particularly meaningful area, putting it reasonably in focus and trying to limit the damage caused by blurring of the planes which are excluded, by preventing their forming a vital part of the composition, or by avoiding their including significant details which would immediately draw attention to the lack of definition of the image. Or you can try choosing between the near and distant planes, focusing on one or the other as appropriate. You can also try restricting the view of the landscape, assuming the aims of the photograph permit this, by arranging for a suitably emphasized detail to convey the most significant parts of the whole.
In some cases the problem does not exist, for example, when the planes are all sufficiently distant, or the diaphragm can be stopped down sufficiently.

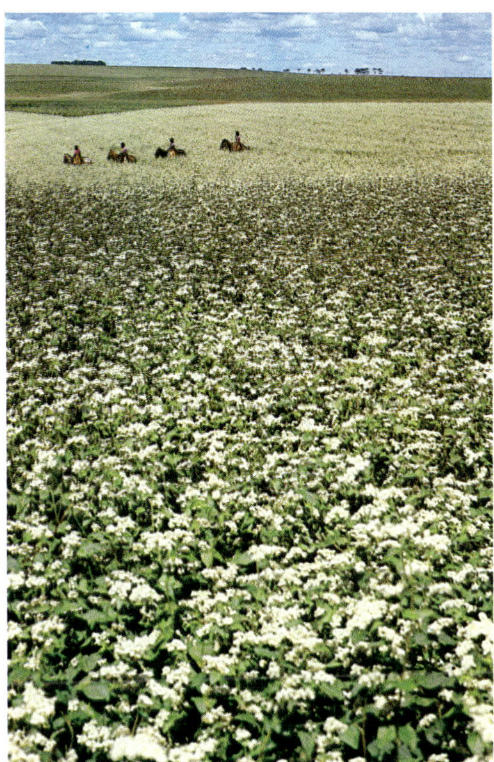

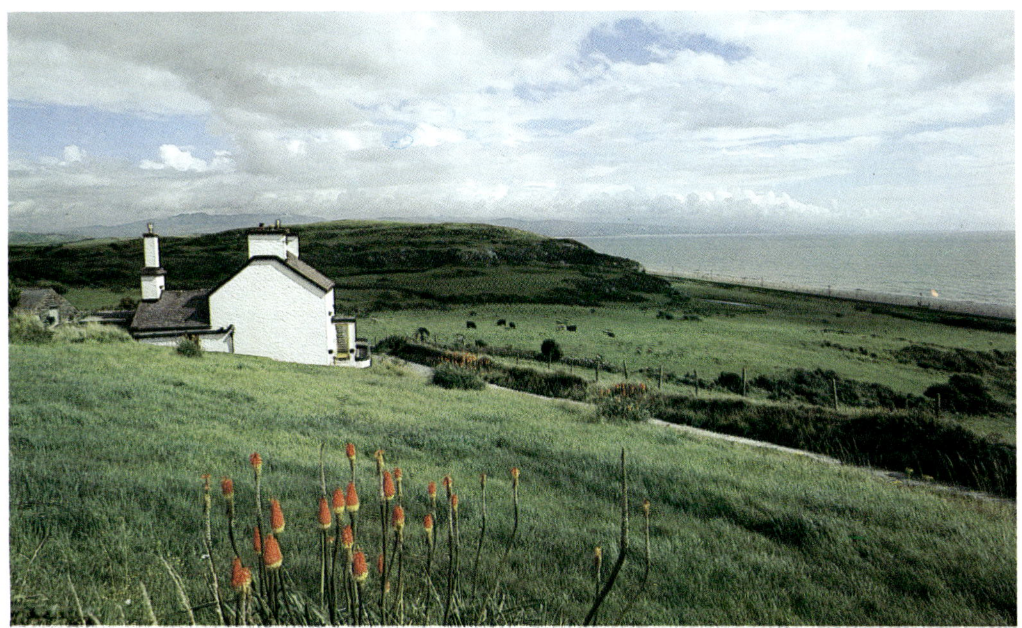

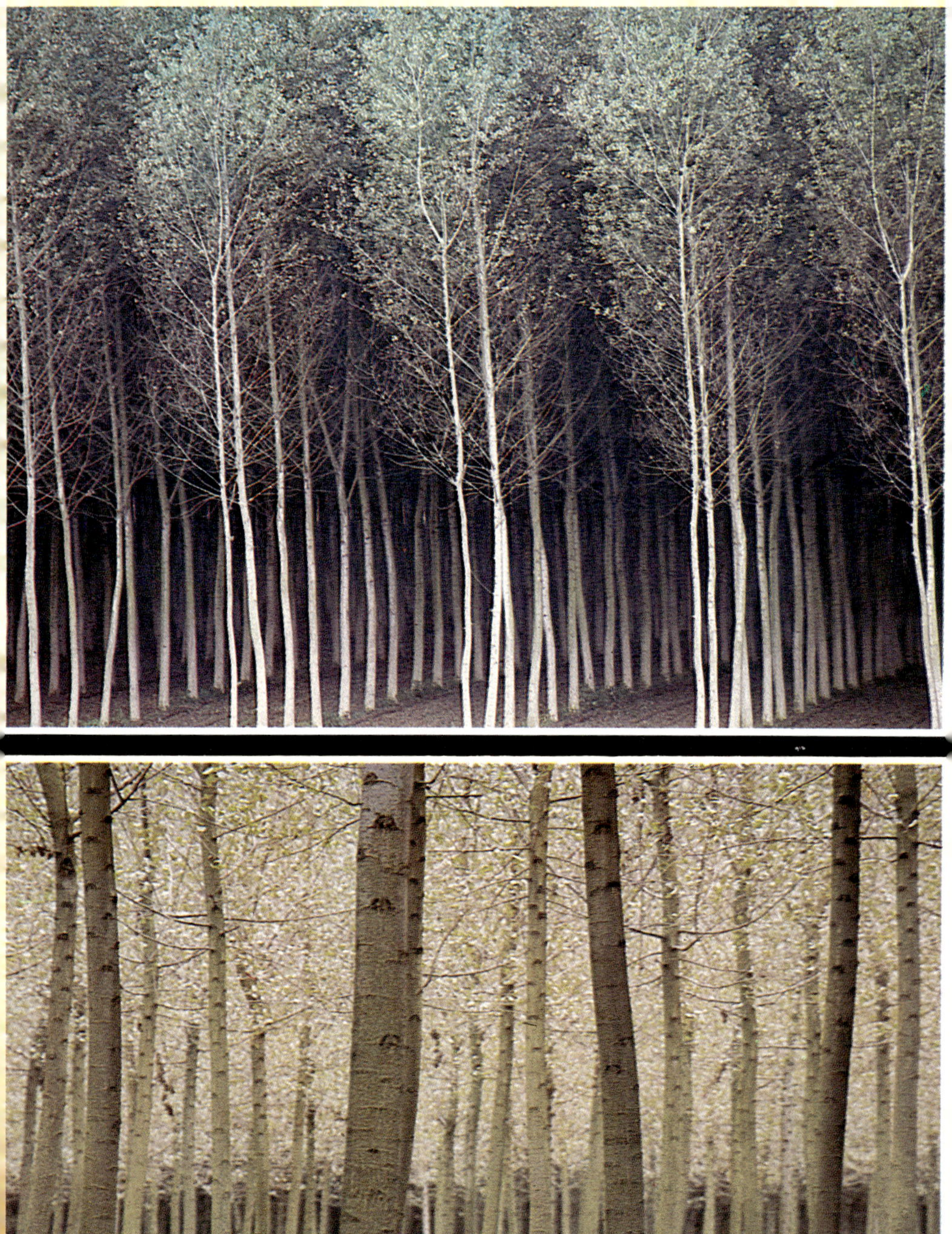

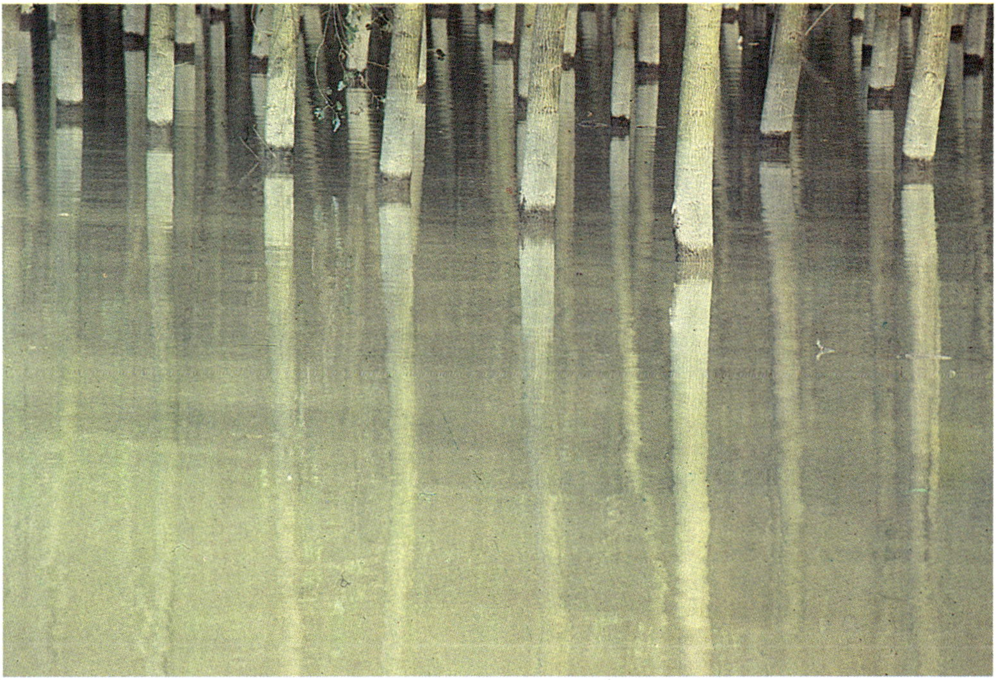

These pictures taken in a poplar grove are further proof of the opportunities available to an attentive photographer, even in a seemingly monotonous environment. In the pictures opposite he captures the linear, geometrical, almost abstract rhythm according to which the plants are arranged; then dwells on the contrast between the airy imprecision of the leaves and the firm, clear outline of the trunks. Above and below he shows up the liquid surface, both to discover chromatic values in the deep fluid harmonies of the water, to reveal the mobility of the reflections, and to contrast the thin, transparent notes with the more solid notion of the tree-trunks. Note the use of continually changing angles of perspective and depths of field. One moment, the pictures are based on linear sequences; the next, on planes of light. All these photographs were taken with normal equipment, without the use of any special technical devices.

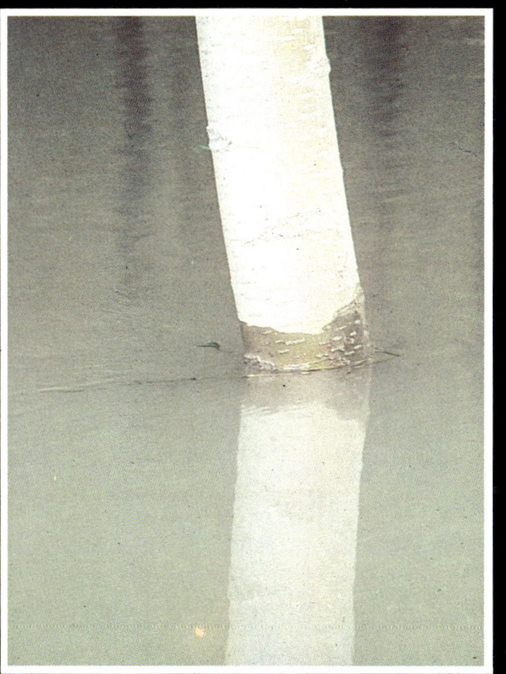

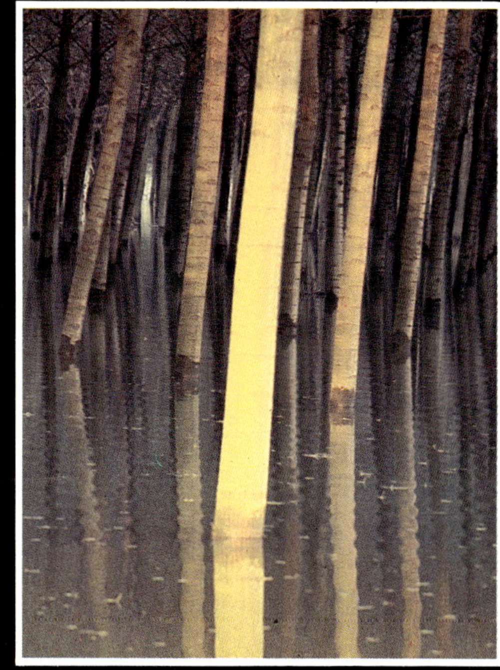

Lenses

A camera lens is composed of a system of convergent elements, at times very different in structure and therefore highly complex, through which light passes to expose the film. All lenses have a focal length which is measured in mm and corresponds to the distance between the lens itself and the spot at which the points of light converge inside the camera, when the focus is set at infinity. The simplest type consists of a convergent lens. All lenses have an angle of view corresponding to their field of vision and a precise speed. They are the fruit of various compromises between different needs which, apart from the focal length, angle of view and speed, take account of the degree of contrast one wishes to achieve and correction of aberrations. There is no such thing as a perfect lens: all lenses have qualities and defects.

The number of elements used is necessary to correct aberrations. At least three are needed. But their number is not proportional to the efficiency of the lens – the quality of the lens elements counts more than their number.

Lenses are generally divided into three categories, based on their focal length: normal, wide-angle and telephoto. A lens whose focal length is approximately equal to the diagonal of the

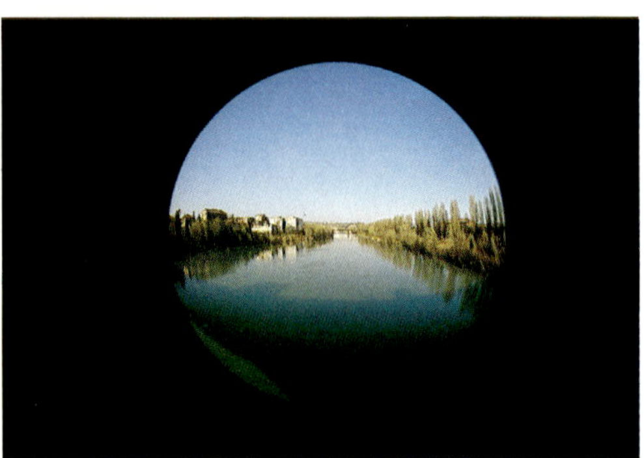

fish-eye

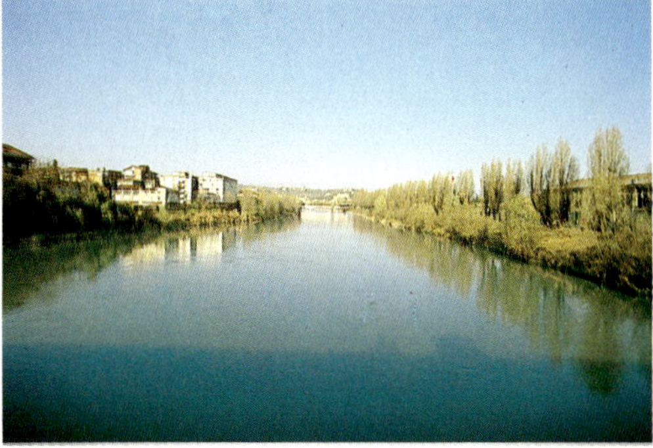

20 mm

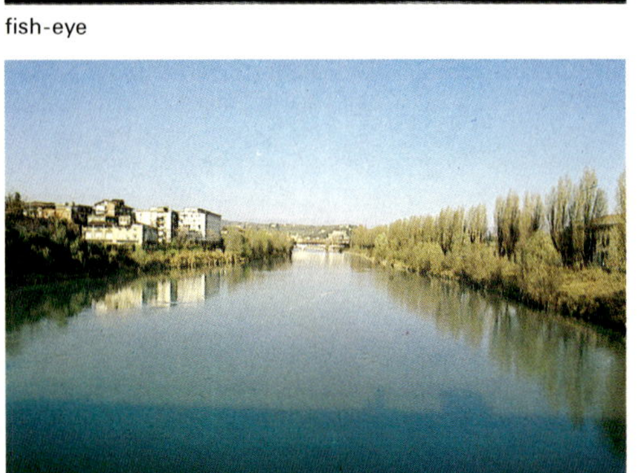

24 mm

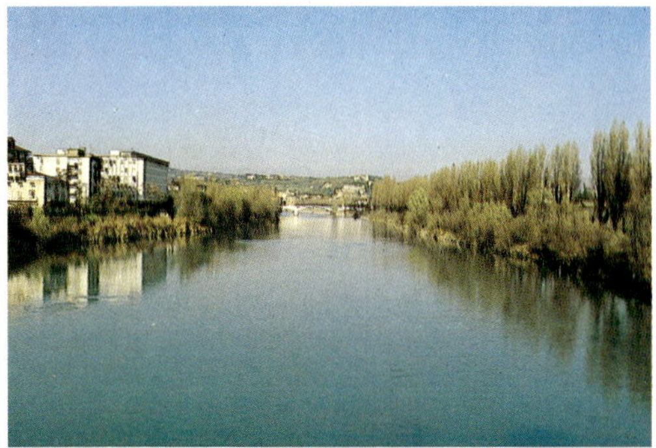

35 mm

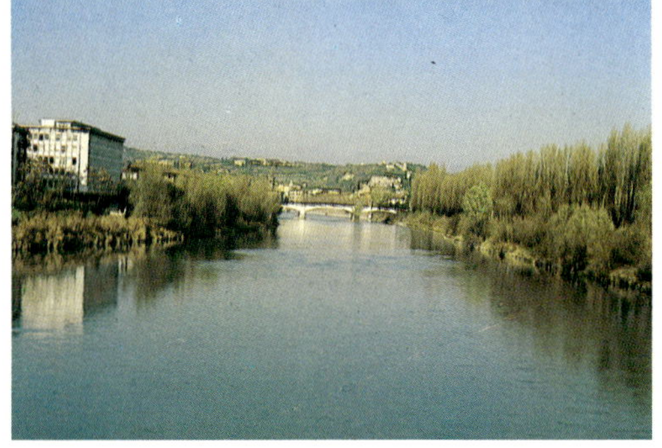

50 mm

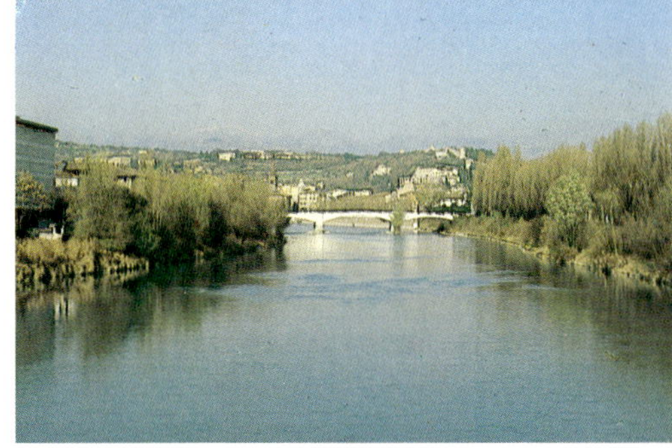

70 mm

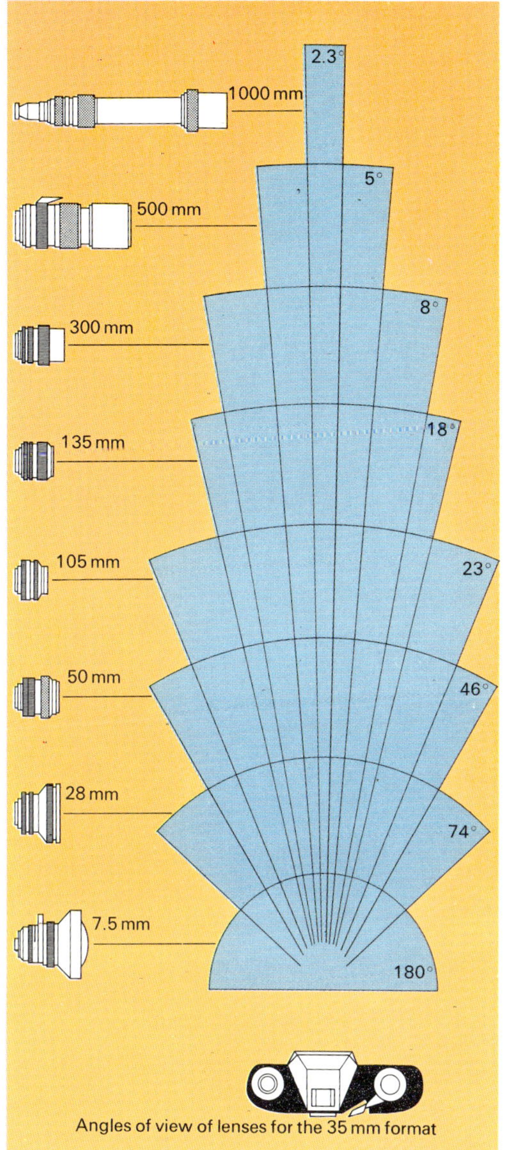

Angles of view of lenses for the 35 mm format

film format it uses is called normal. For example, for a 24 × 36 mm film, a 50–55 mm lens is normal, or standard; while for a 6 × 6 cm film, a 90 mm lens will be normal. Below this measurement, a lens can be classified as a wide-angle, and above it as a telephoto.
Lenses for normal optics generally have an angle of view of about 45–55°. But to be defined as a true wide-angle, a lens should have an angle of view of over 70°. Similarly, the angle of view of a telephoto should not exceed 35°, if it is genuinely to be considered as such.
The wide-angle lens is very useful for landscape photography. Above all in built-up

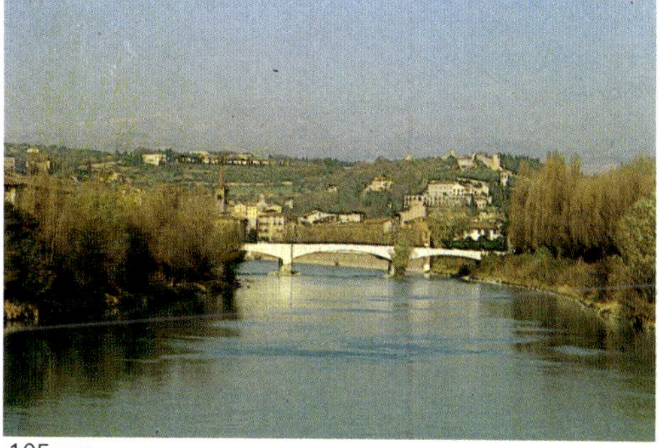
105 mm

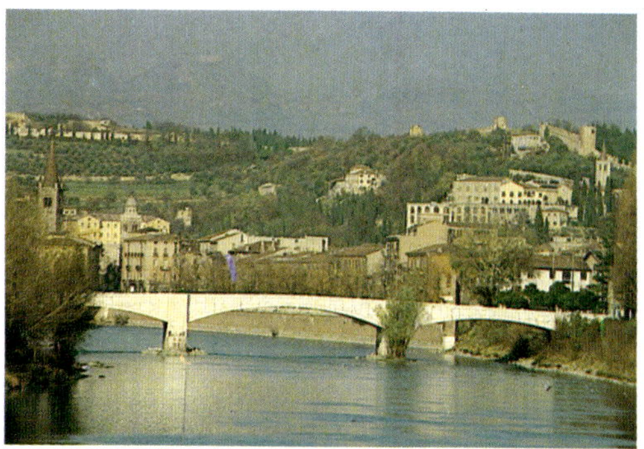
210 mm

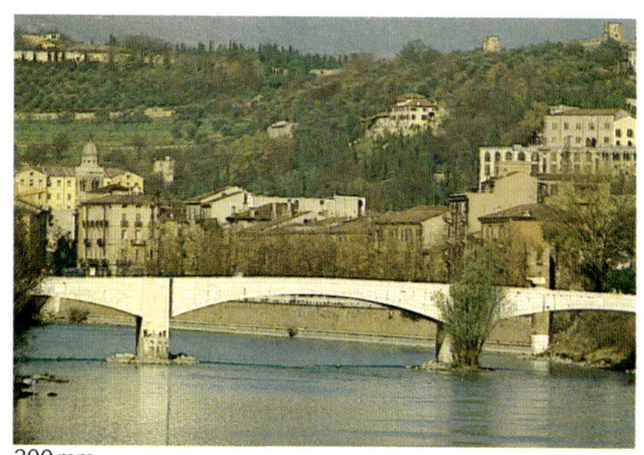
300 mm

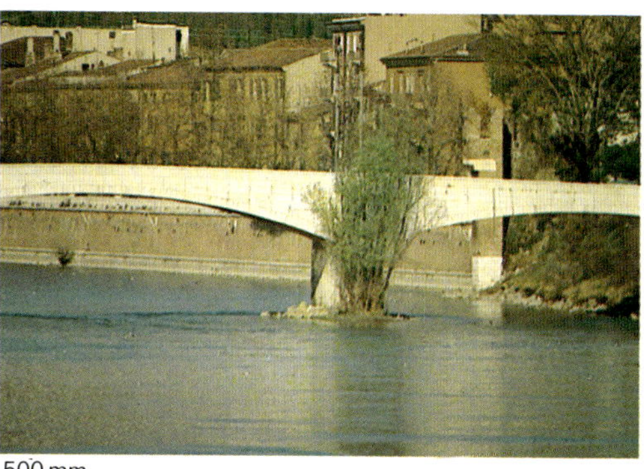
500 mm

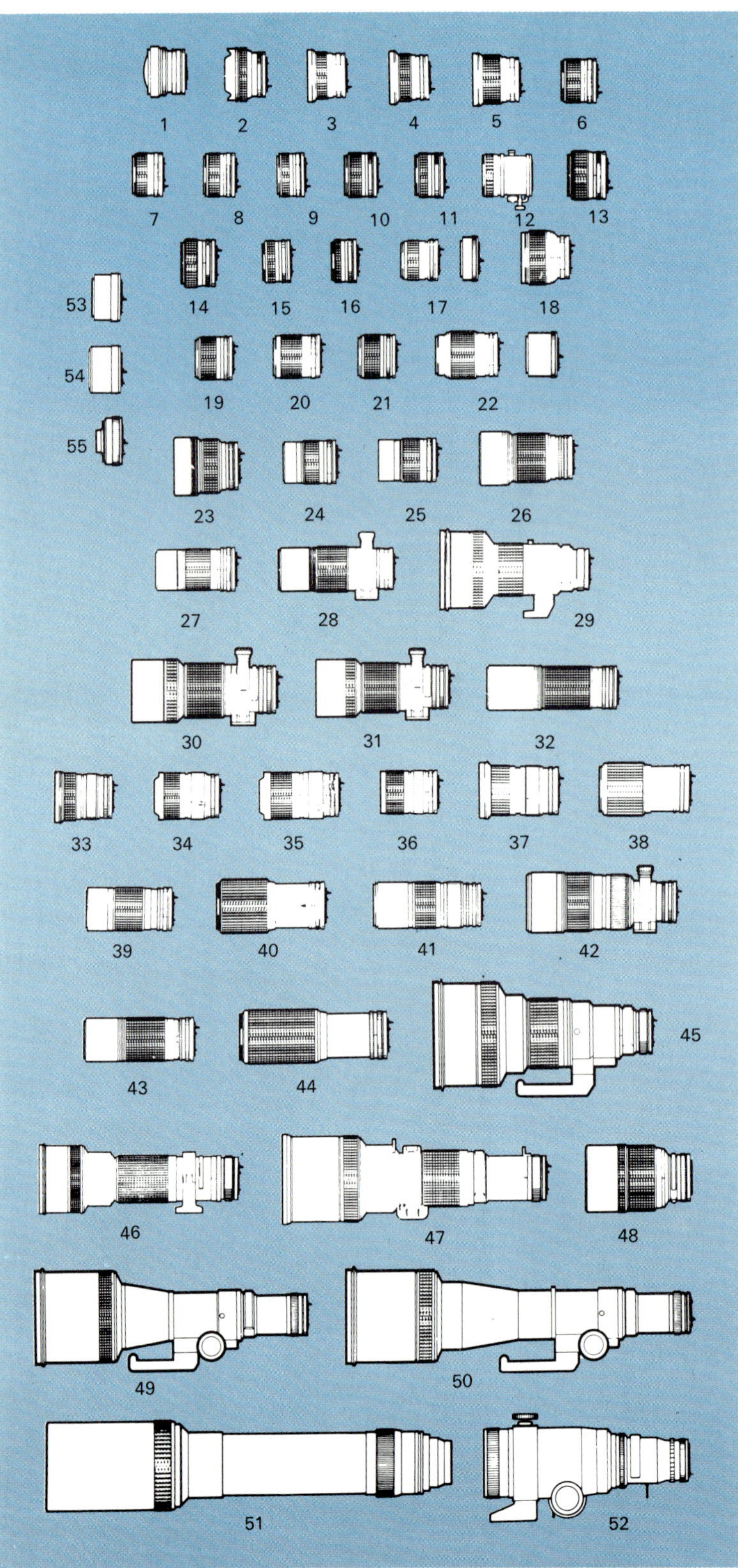

Left, an example of the imposing variety of lenses on the market; their maximum aperture is indicated together with their focal length.
1) 7.5 mm f/5.6 fish-eye;
2) 15 mm f/2.8 fish-eye;
3) 17 mm f/4;
4) 20 mm f/2.8;
5) 24 mm f/1.4;
6) 24 mm f/2;
7) 24 mm f/2.8;
8) 28 mm f/2;
9) 28 mm f/2.8;
10) 35 mm f/2;
11) 35 mm f/2.8;
12) 35 mm f/2.8 TS S.S.C.;
13) 50 mm f/1.2;
14) 50 mm f/1.2;
15) 50 mm f/1.4;
16) 50 mm f/1.8;
17) 50 mm f/3.5 macro with extension tube 25-U;
18) 85 mm f/1.2;
19) 85 mm f/1.8;
20) 100 mm f/2;
21) 100 mm f/2.8;
22) 100 mm f/4 macro with extension tube 50-U;
23) 135 mm f/2;
24) 135 mm f/2.8;
25) 135 mm f/3.5;
26) 200 mm f/2.8;
27) 200 mm f/4;
28) 200 mm f/4 macro;
29) 300 mm f/2.8;
30) 300 mm f/4;
31) 300 mm f/4;
32) 300 mm f/5.6;
33) 24–35 mm f/3.5;
34) 28–50 mm f/3.5;
35) 35–70 mm f/2.8–3.5;
36) 35–70 mm f/4;
37) 35–105 mm f/3.5;
38) 50–135 mm f/3.5;
39) 70–150 mm f/4.5;
40) 70–210 mm f/4;
41) 80–200 mm f/4;
42) 85–300 mm f/4.5;
43) 100–200 mm f/5.6;
44) 100–300 mm f/5.6;
45) 400 mm f/2.8;
46) 400 mm f/4.5;
47) 500 mm f/4.5;
48) 500mm f/8 new reflex;
49) 600 mm f/4.5;
50) 800 mm f/5.6;
51) 1200 mm f/11 S.S.C.;
52) focusing adapter;
53) 2x-A teleconverter;
54) 1.2x-B teleconverter;
55) 1.4x-A teleconverter.

On the opposite page, general view of a corner of Manhattan between Fifth Street and Park Avenue. Right, a detail of the same frame, taken with a telephoto lens.

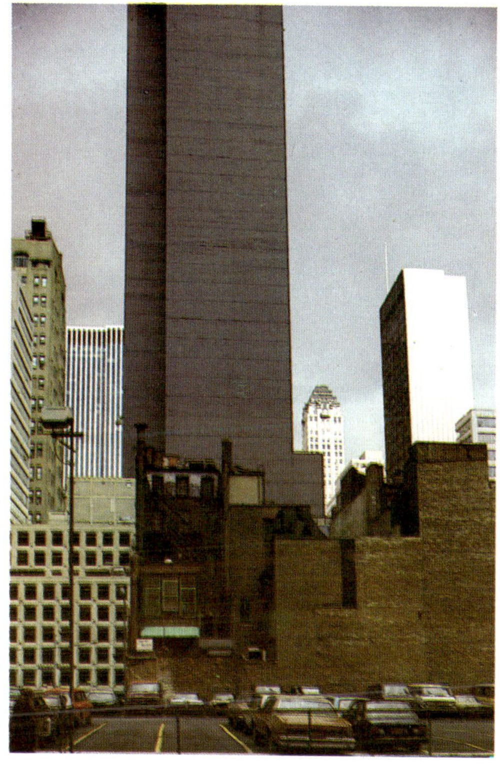

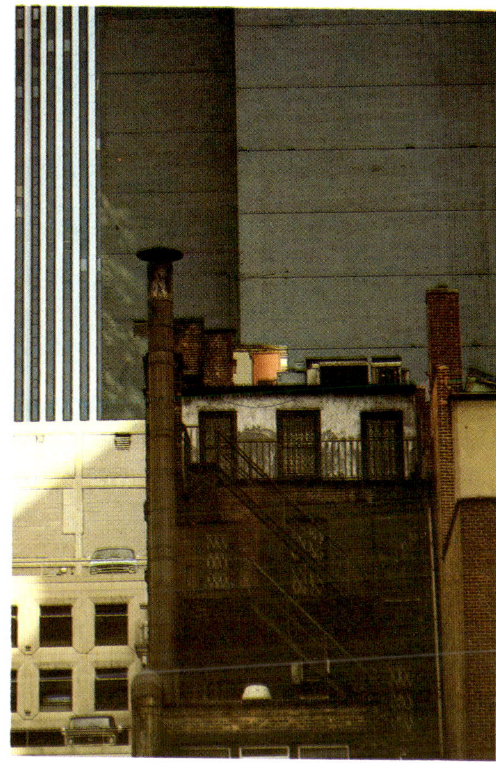

areas, where there may not be room to back away enough for perspective, the wide-angle can be invaluable.
But bear in mind that it deforms the image, introducing very different spatial relationships from those perceived by the human eye, by increasing, for example, the apparent distance between foreground and background. It also tends to curve objects at the edges of its field of vision and exaggerates the phenomenon of the convergence of lines of perspective. The distortion of the image is increased as the focal length is decreased and reaches extremes in the wide-angle lenses called fish-eyes. Lenses of this type have a very broad angle of view, of as much as 180°, and create a curvature of all lines of the picture, both vertical and horizontal. Since other things being equal, the depth of field is inversely proportional to the focal length of the lens, wide-angles are the most suitable for homogeneous focusing even of planes which are very far apart. The depth of field of wide-angles can be further increased by closing the diaphragm, but remember the alteration in real dimensions which wide-angles cause.
At the opposite extreme, the telephoto has a very restricted angle of view and also a much more limited depth of field. A shortcoming of the telephoto lens, therefore, is that it does not permit homogeneous focusing and therefore flattens the image. But the latter will be described in far greater detail and will tolerate much greater enlargement. Furthermore, telephotos enable you to isolate the image you wish to take and can remedy certain inherent limitations of small format cameras like the very widely used reflexes. If you think of all the difficulties the photographer who devotes himself to very large spaces often has to grapple with, in an effort to avoid elements which would spoil the picture, such as telegraph wires, lampposts, parked cars, moving people, etc., you will appreciate what a relief it can be for him to isolate the image by using a telephoto. The telephoto lens also offers another considerable advantage for small format cameras of limited focal length. By shooting from a fair distance, you can keep the film parallel or almost to the object to be photographed, avoiding those shots in which the camera is tilted upwards, causing a sharp convergence of lines of perspective which so much detracts from the quality of the image.
Large format cameras have corrective devices, rising front and shift movements, and lines can also be straightened out during printing, but

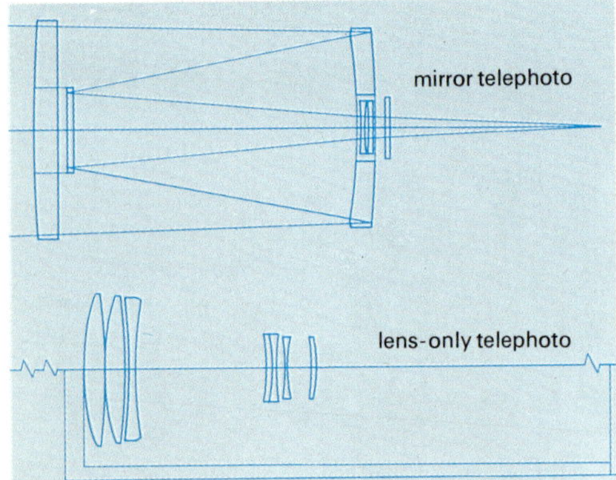

using a telephoto certainly provides the most immediate solution.

The fish-eye lens is only one of the special types included in the very wide range of accessories manufactured above all for reflex cameras. Macro lenses, for example, enable you to photograph an object at much closer range than allowed by standard lenses (all lenses have a minimum focusing distance which is the greater the longer the focal length). Although the very purpose of a macro lens might seem to exclude it from landscape photography, do not forget that a landscape can also be evoked by a detail and therefore even close-up shots can be useful, although an exception.

We mentioned above the need to shift the axis of the lens in order to correct the problem of converging verticals (a very serious problem, particularly in architectural photography). Shift lenses are also made for this purpose, fitted with a jointed mount which permits variation of the focal plane in order to restore the original lines of perspective.

A very important group of telephotos are mirror lenses, which despite having a very long focal length, for example 500 mm, are compact and lightweight. Their limitation is that they have a fixed aperture. As they have no diaphragm, grey neutral density filters are used with them. These are the lenses which create a distinctive, ringed effect in blurred areas.

Together with conventional lens-only (or refracting) telephotos, mirror (or reflecting) models are available. These are based on the same principle as reflecting telescopes and are lighter and more compact than the lens-only variety. But they can not be stopped down and therefore reproduce blurred parts of the image as a mass of circles (as in the photograph below).

The photograph on the opposite page shows a typical effect obtained with a (lens-only) telephoto. The disproportion between the magnified sun and the belfry which creates a particularly unreal effect, is due to the fact that the belfry is a very long way away from the camera and being far off, looks very small compared with the sun, whose size is not affected by distance. In all images with telephotos, the more distant planes can look enormously enlarged, creating effects which are totally unpredictable to the casual observer.

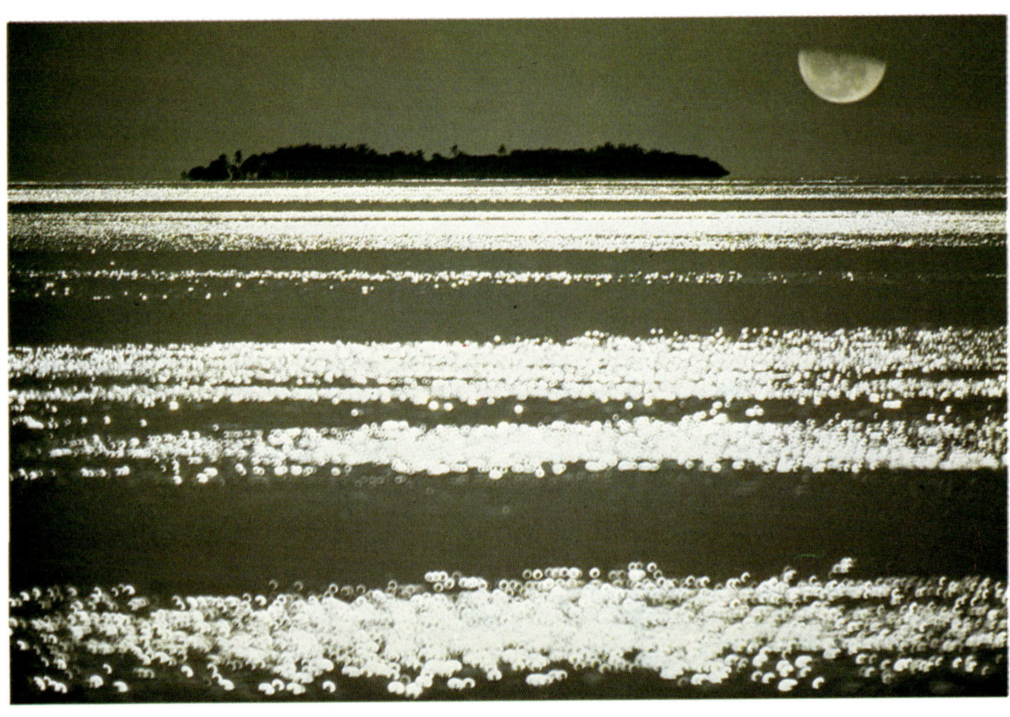

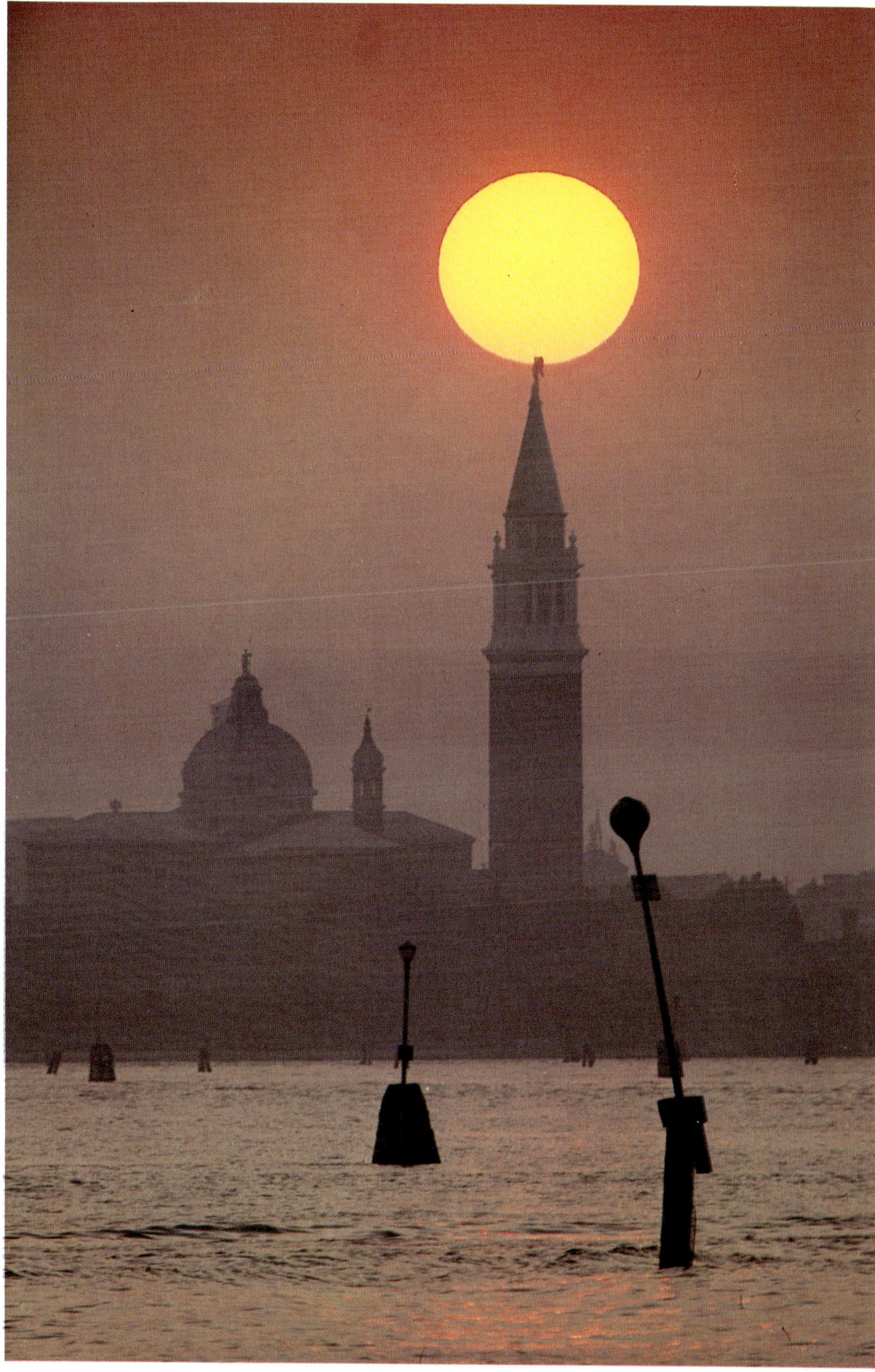

Flash

It might seem absurd to talk about flash in a manual on landscape photography, given that the opportunities for using it will be very few and far between. But there are occasions when small-scale landscapes are photographed – for example, urban, architectural and others – when the need can arise to lighten up a detail in the foreground and flash can be useful.
Nowadays, electronic flash units are available which are synchronized with the camera and have very short recharging times, plus, of course, the traditional combustible flash bulbs. A basic problem when using flash is that is is impossible to establish the exposure in the normal way, as it does not emit a continuous light. But the exposure can be calculated if you know the power of irradiation which is indicated by a number (GN) on the flash unit, referring to a film speed of 100 ASA and related to the distance of the subject. Remember that the intensity of the flashlight falls off according to the inverse square law of distance.
Flash is a valuable and sometimes irreplaceable means of taking photos which would otherwise be impossible, or improving them. But it must be used within these precise limits and should not be abused. Where possible, it is much better to resort to longer exposure times or the use of reflectors, because flash generally creates a totally false play of shadows, altering them so profoundly that they lose sharpness and flatten the image. Furthermore, the very strong light can create reflections which are also unpredictable and artificial.

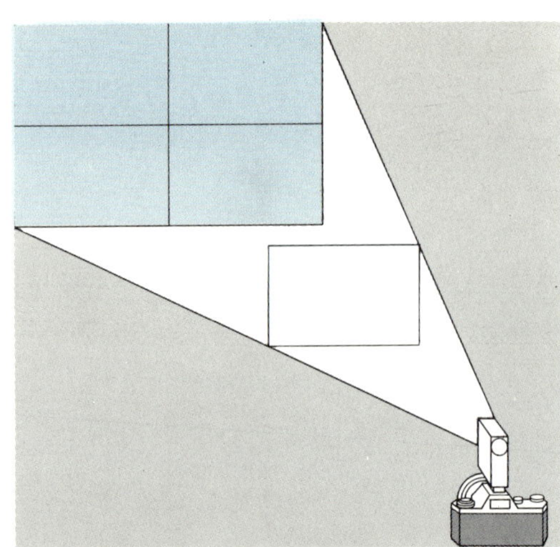

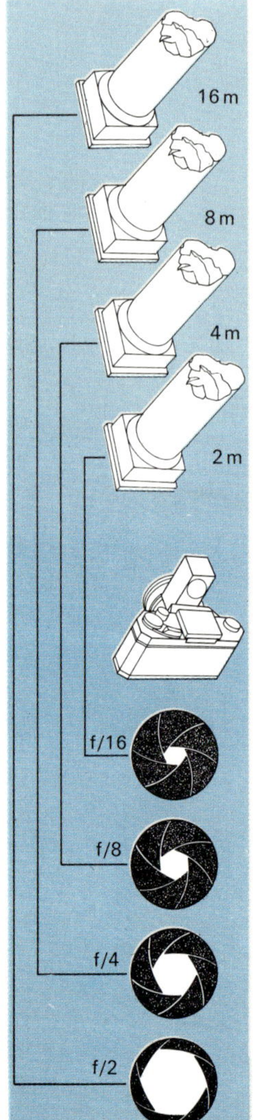

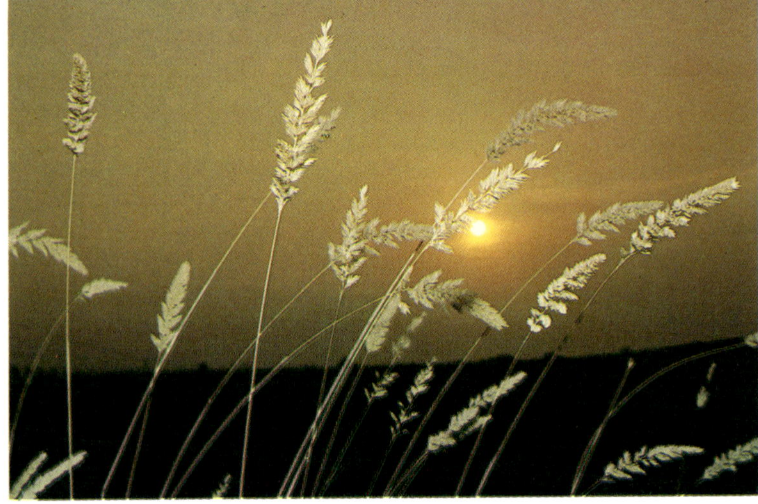

The drawing top right illustrates the inverse square law: if you double the distance between the light source and the subject, intensity of the incident light is reduced to a quarter.
Left: if the distance between subject and flash is increased, the aperture will be increased accordingly. The photograph above shows an infrequent occasion on which flash is used.

On the opposite page: the waterfall was photographed, on the left with a film for daylight, and on the right with a film for artificial light. Below, full-size reproduction of the most commonly used film formats.

Films

Films consist of a transparent support on to which the sensitive emulsion is spread. This is composed of a gelatinous solution in which grains of silver bromide are suspended. It is through the silver bromide that the images are formed, because it reacts to light and undergoes a transformation which is chemically consolidated in the developing bath. The coarser the grain – that is the clumps of grains of silver bromide – the more sensitive the film, or the less light is needed for it to react. Obviously therefore, this type of film will be preferable where there is a shortage of light. In compensation, the finer the grain and therefore the slower or less sensitive the film, the more detailed the image will be. Therefore where one can, it is advisable to use a low-speed film even in dim light, making up for the loss of sensitivity by longer exposure times. Obviously, this is only possible in certain circumstances, for example, where one does not have to photograph moving objects. But in the case of landscapes, the opportunities will be more frequent than elsewhere. You will also need to use suitable equipment and in particular, a fixed support which for that matter is always recommended for successful photography. The result will be a much sharper photograph, much more useful for enlargements.

The sensitivity or speed of a film is normally measured according to two scales: ASA (American Standards Association) and DIN (Deutsche Industrie Norm). While the DIN system is based on a logarithmic scale, the ASA one is directly proportional to the sensitivity of the film. Practically speaking, a 100 ASA film is twice as sensitive as a 50 ASA film, while a DIN film doubles its sensitivity every three numbers – that is, a 27 DIN film is twice as sensitive as a 24 DIN one. The ASA method is normally used, but conversion tables are available.

Naturally, films are also distinguished by their format. They are sold in rolls which have a given number of exposures. Many small format films, the ones most widely used, are also sold in more economical

COMPARATIVE TABLE OF FILM SPEEDS

ASA	6	12	25	50	100	200	400	800	1600	3200	6400
DIN	9	12	15	18	21	24	27	30	33	36	39

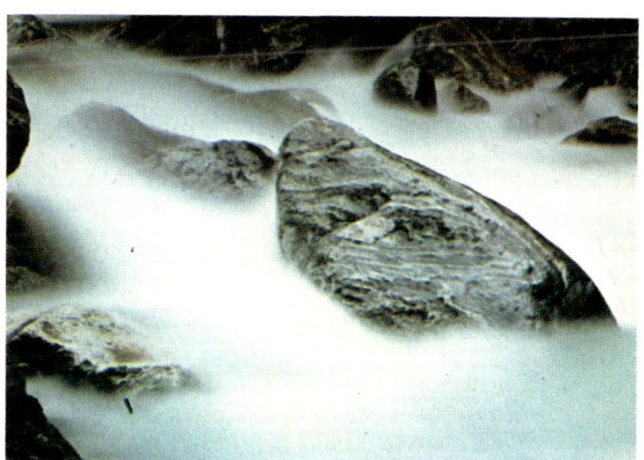

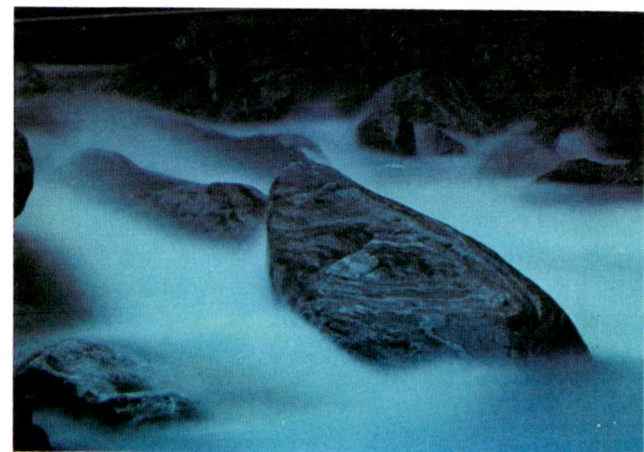

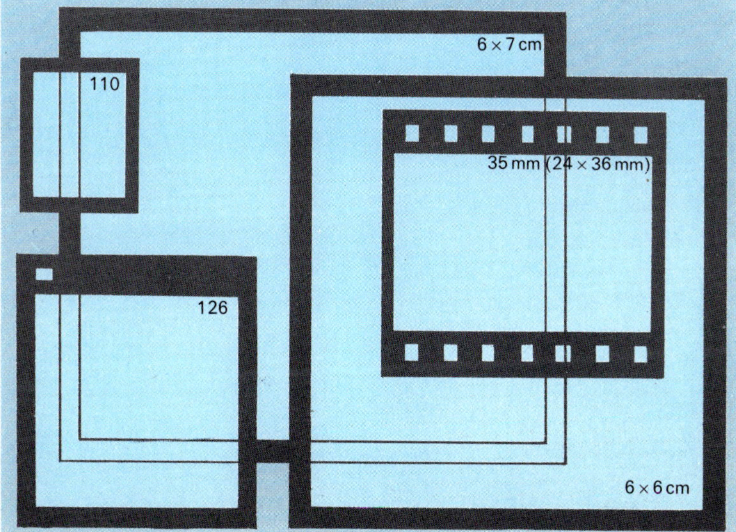

strips, usually 15 meters long.

One advantage of large-format cameras is the greater size of the sensitive film, which permits reproduction of details and allows excellent enlargements to be obtained proportional to their size. If you have a big enough film, even just the details of it can be enlarged, thereby enabling you to correct the photograph by trimming off parts which spoil it, but which could not be avoided.

A similar though opposite solution can be adopted with small format cameras – by fitting a telephoto. In this case, the trimming is not done afterwards, during printing, but before, by circumscribing what you wish to photograph. One of the reasons for the success of telephotos is not just their ability to bring distant objects closer, but also the fact that you can "clean up" the picture, leaving out any undesirable elements on near planes.

To return to small format cameras, which are the type most widely used today, the improvements made even to 24 × 36 films are such that they can be manufactured with so fine a grain, even for colour, as to permit incredible enlargements. Obviously, in these cases the photographs must be technically perfect.

Even the fact that you can choose a horizontal or vertical frame with the 24 × 36

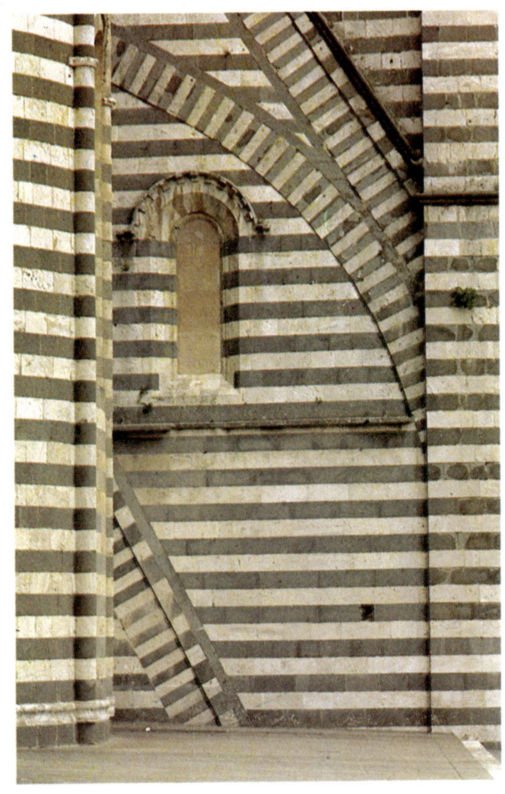

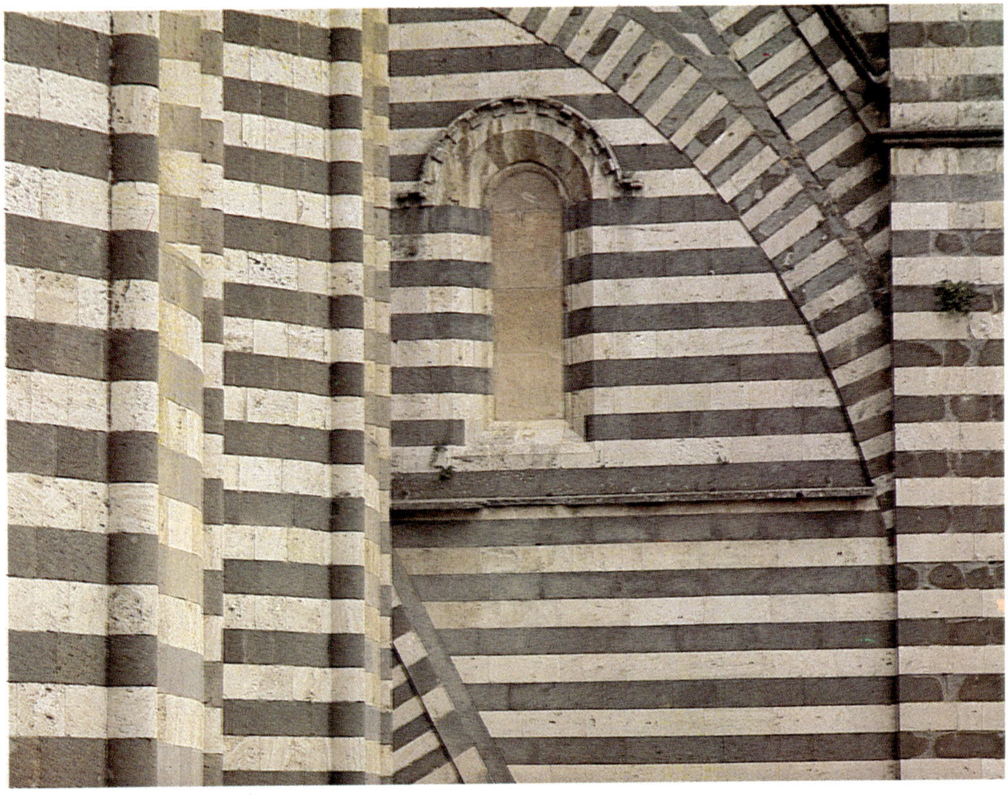

On the opposite page, above, detail of Orvieto cathedral, taken from a vertical colour photograph, 24 × 36. A further enlargement has been taken from this (below) without the definition of the image suffering in the least. This goes to show that the degree of technical perfection of even small format films is such nowadays that they can tolerate considerable enlargement.
Both photographs are functional: the first in giving a general idea of the decoration of the walls; the second, in offering a more analytical view of their structure.

The photographs on this page, taken at the same twilight hour, show two different ways of using the 24 × 36 format: vertically and horizontally.
Both photographs are effective. The first gives a better idea of the depth of the market, while the second is more suitable for showing the movement of people.

format is generally sufficient to cover the different types of presentation a photographer always needs and which, of course, are a lot less problematic with large format cameras, where the frame can be chosen and adapted at the actual printing stage.
To overcome this very problem and allow the photographer the greatest possible relative freedom, intermediate format cameras have also been produced, such as the square 60 × 60 made famous by the Rolleiflex series. This format, being much larger than the 24 × 36, allows the frame to be adapted to all uses and can of course be trimmed later as desired. But this system of reducing and correcting the photograph during printing is not favoured by all photographers. It can be very useful and is sometimes necessary, but it also delays completion of the picture.

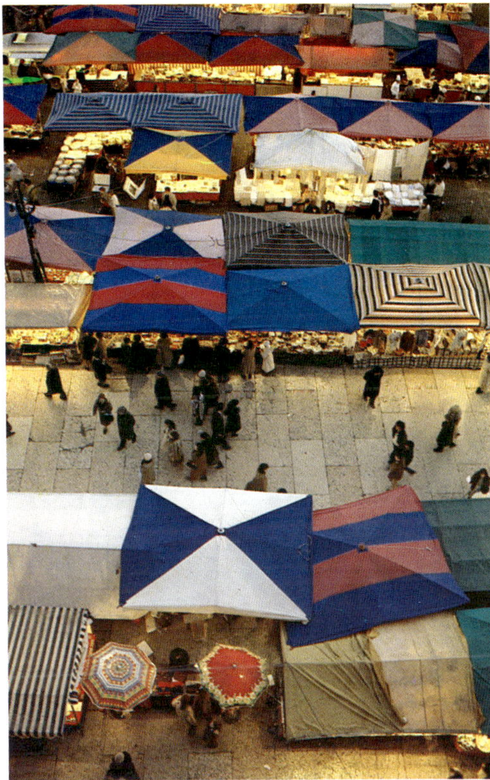

In these cases the photographer should be able to foresee the results from the frame presented to him by the lens.
But the eye of the photographer often tends to identify with his camera lens. The thing which most distinguishes the beginner from the expert is not just the greater technical skill of the latter, or a greater interpretational capacity in a general sense, but the ability to visualize the results of the photograph at the moment the frame is chosen.
For this reason, it is always very difficult and unwise to trim photographs taken by skilled photographers.
However odd it may seem, many good photographers prefer black-and-white to colour. We can in fact remember the polemics which accompanied the transition from black-and-white films to colour, and one must admit

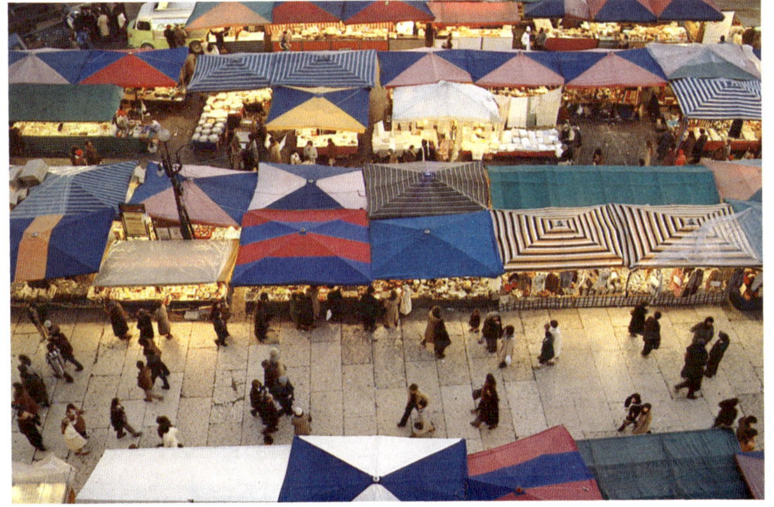

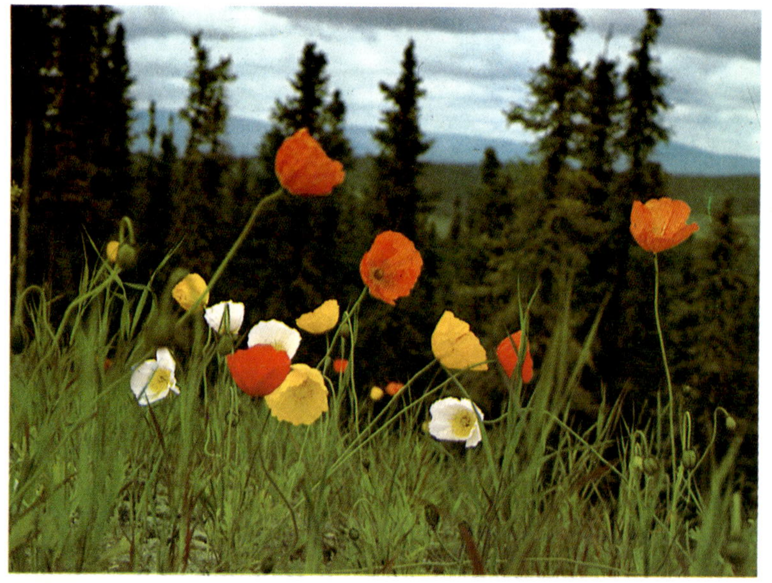

that many of the greatest screen masterpieces are in black-and-white. Many photographers prefer black-and-white on account of the greater interpretational freedom it allows. The play of forms, which is always extremely important in photography, as in every other type of figurative work, and is based on lines, surfaces and rhythms, can be more clearly shown in black-and-white, while these contrasts often dissolve in colour. A colour photograph is generally

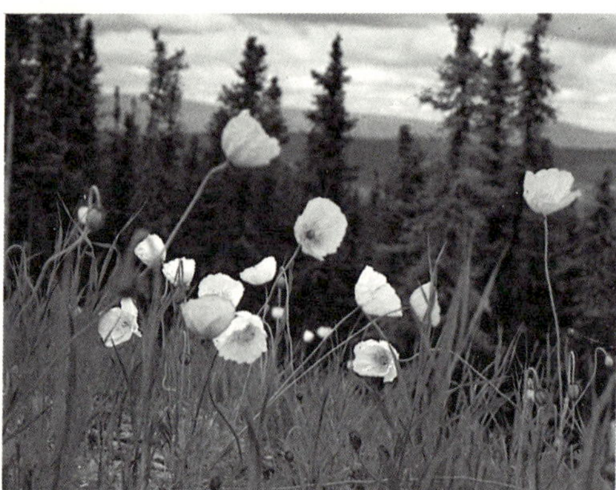

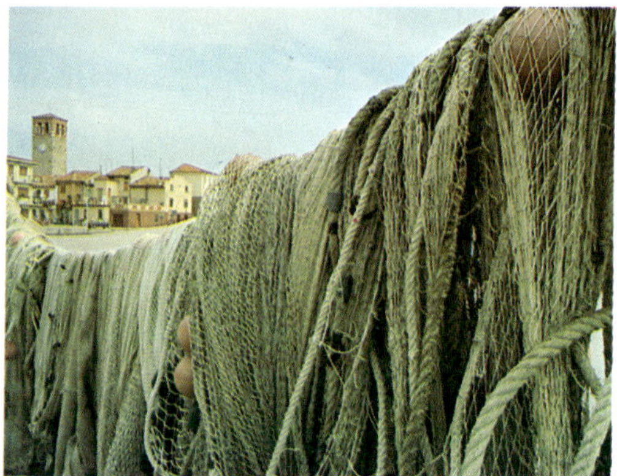

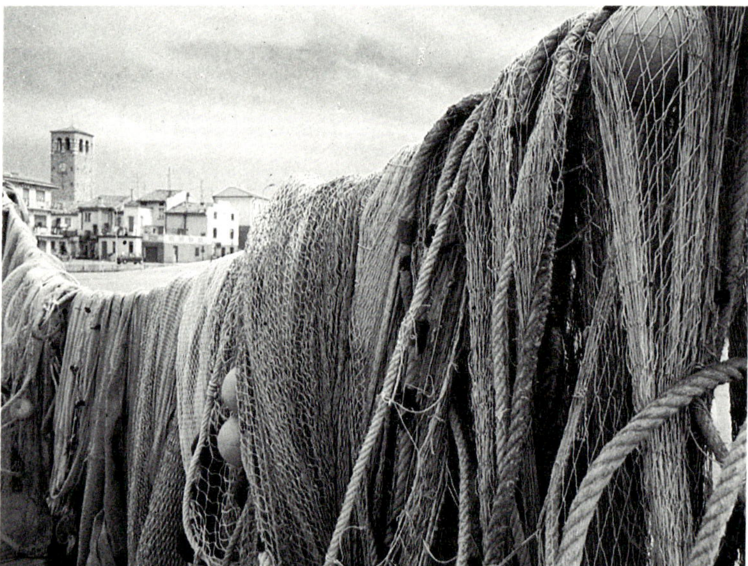

On this page we have two different examples of the appropriateness of using black-and-white or colour. In the first case, colour is necessary to show the brilliant tints of the flowers, while in the second, the uniform tint of the rope is shown much better in black-and-white.

On the opposite page, the photograph of a southern environment with its chalky colours, would seem best suited to a rendering in black-and-white. But the note of red in the child's clothes is sufficient to liven up the whole picture and make colour indispensable.

regarded as being easier, because it is already pleasing in itself. But with black-and-white, the photographer can sometimes achieve a sharper image and can also more easily superimpose his own abstract interpretation on the objective image, partly because black-and-white is in itself an abstraction from reality.

Naturally, we do not wish to establish a scale of values between the two here. For that matter, such a thing would be impossible. We merely wish to emphasize the different opportunities they offer, but without forgetting that technical improvements, above all to films, have helped spread the use of colour even to the most exacting photographers. It is possible that colour photography, which is increasingly popular and now widely used for book illustrations, will relegate black-and-white to a more limited, virtuoso and consciously aesthetic sphere. But the two types will certainly continue to coexist, just as drawing and engraving have continued to exist alongside oil painting.

In the specific case of landscapes, black-and-white and colour photographs observe many common rules, but they are also at variance from a technical point of view, above all as far as the rendering of the light and sensitivity of the film are concerned. Obviously, some filters whose purpose it is to emphasize or play down the presence of a colour in the atmosphere, are quite useless in a black-and-white photograph, and likewise other filters which are useful for black-and-white, are totally irrelevant to a colour photograph.

But the eye of the photographer also changes in one or the other case and his way of observing and recomposing reality within the frame is different. Some landscapes will seem better suited to black-and-white photography. For example, those in which there is a shortage of colour and shapes and clear-cut lines prevail, as in certain landscapes of the deep south where the sun's rays are very intense, or certain snow scenes. Other landscapes, which have a wealth of different colours and shades, such as a garden in bloom, or woods in autumn, would lose a great deal and could even look flat if rendered in black-and-white. But when all is said and done, despite these objective situations, the decision whether to use one or other technique will always depend on the preference of the photographer. Nonetheless, we believe that experimenting with black-and-white can be a very useful exercise for the beginner.

The question of colour is extremely important when applied to the particular field of

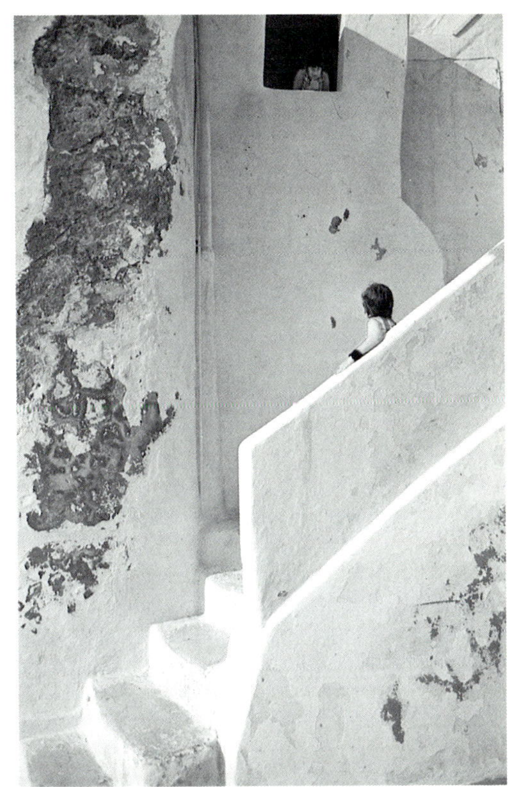

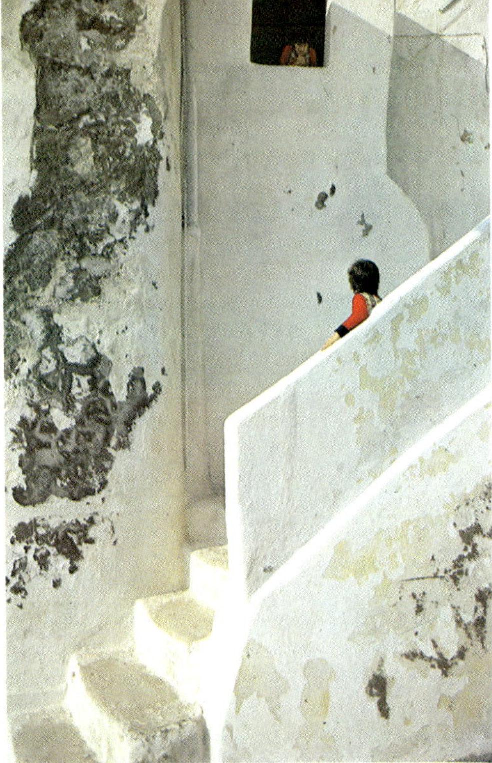

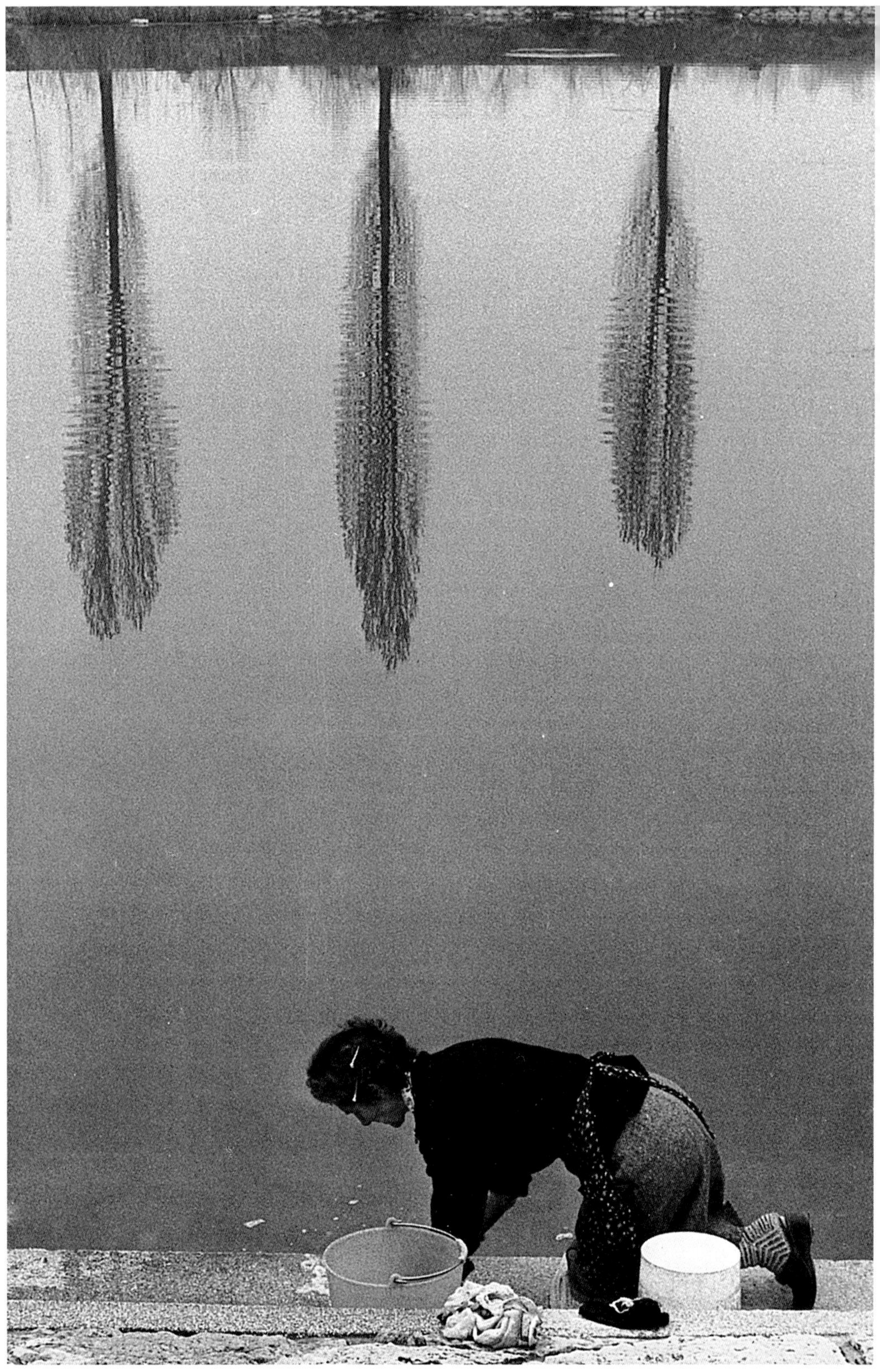

These pages show three black-and-white photographs with considerable expressive force, which would probably be dispersed with the use of colour.
The first, with three poplars mirrored in a river, is based on the strong contrast of a part of the liquid surface with the profile of the trees and a segment of the opposite bank with the profile of the woman. Black-and-white is indispensable to emphasize this contrast to the maximum extent.
Right, the profile of the streetlamp and outline of the bench owe their effect to a similar contrast.
Below, this interpretation of St. Mark's in Venice at high water is expressed through a strong chiaroscuro effect, which is also most effective in black-and-white.

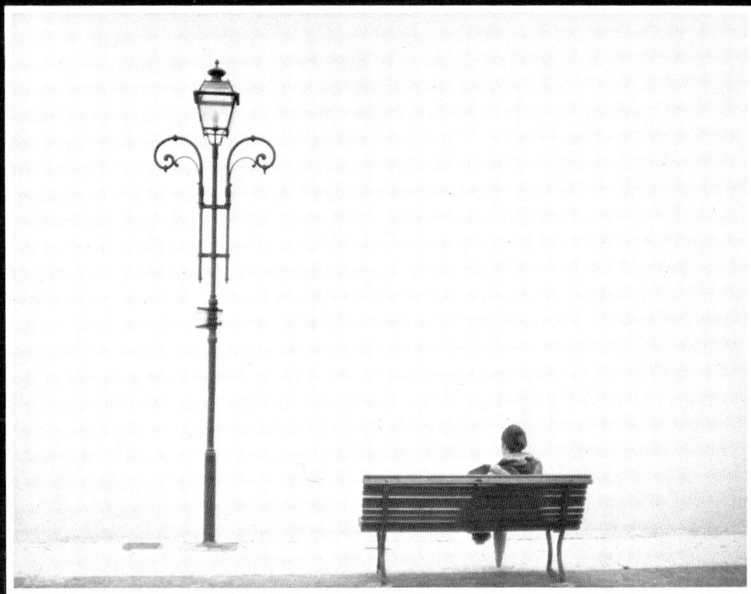

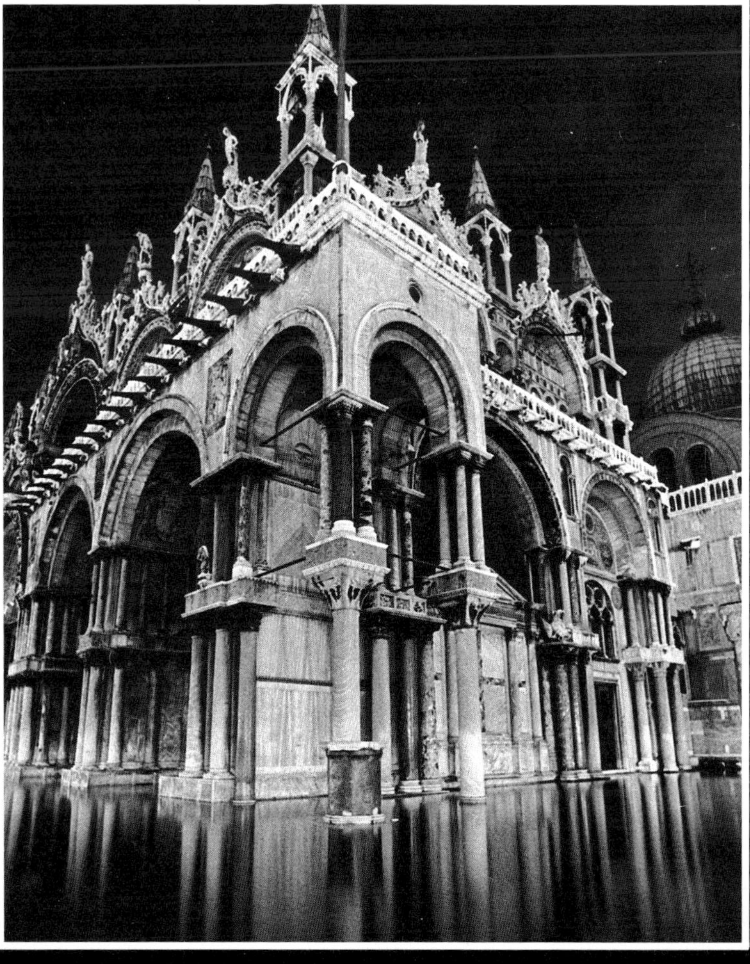

landscape photography. Even for black-and-white, of course, because, as we shall be seeing later on, this must also take account of colours. Not to mention the fact that black and white, with all their intermediate tones of grey, are also colours.
To some people, black-and-white photography will seem *a priori* less rich than colour. But artistic values are independent of the technique one uses. Were this not so, the invention of the camera, for example, ought *de facto* to have done away with painting, but we all know that painters have often achieved far greater results than those obtained by the photographers who have taken up their themes.

Filters

There is an old argument about the use of filters. For some, they are the secret of every good photograph; for others, they are almost superfluous. In fact, it all depends on their use. There are circumstances in which they can be useful and even necessary; others in which they are of no interest whatsoever.
Filters are used for both black-and-white and colour. It may seem odd that they should be used in the first case, but a moment's reflection can demonstrate their purpose.

The black-and-white films sold today are panchromatic, that is, sensitive to all colours, which are rendered in particular tones of grey. But it can happen that two colours which are different, but of equal intensity, give rise to the same tone of grey which not only prevents one distinguishing them, but can also cause imbalances in the photographic rendering compared with the real composition. To remedy this coloured filters can be applied, which can select colours by letting through only the colour of the filter and blocking the

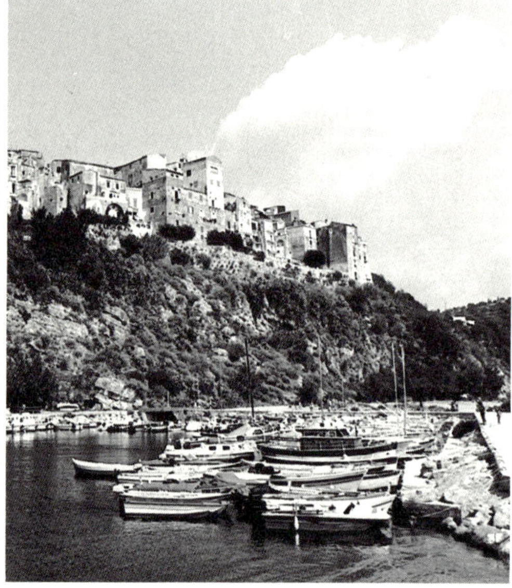

no filters

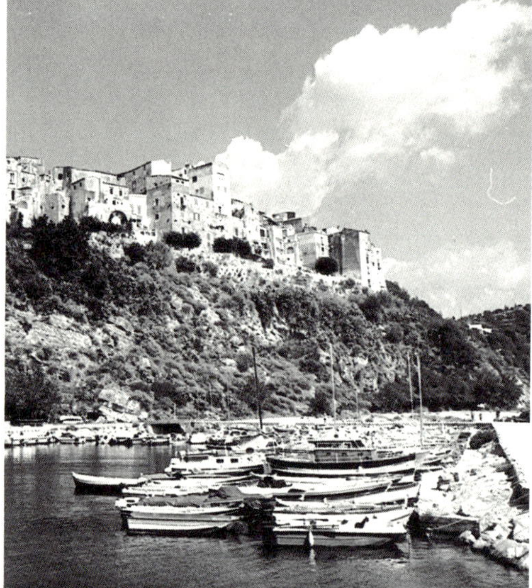

yellow filter

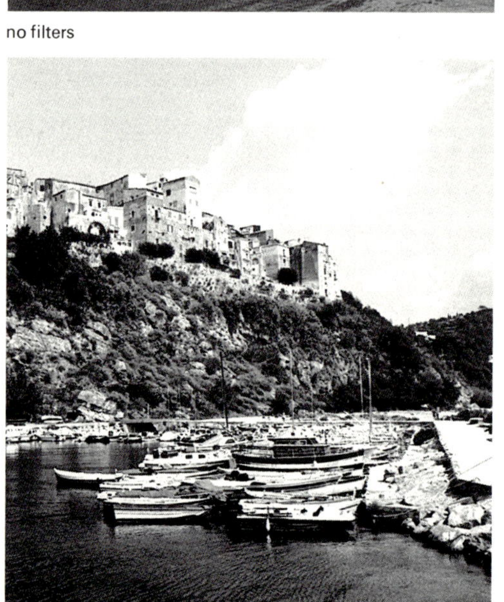

blue filter

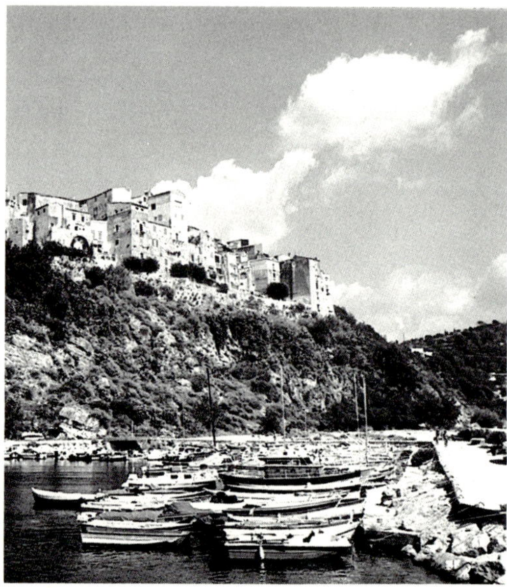

green filter

Sperlonga, in the province of Latina, was chosen for a series of experiments in the use of filters. These examples have a purely demonstrative value. The filters used were, in order: normal, yellow, blue, and green; and on this page, starting from the top: orange, red, and red plus polarizer.
It is important for the photographer to know of the existence of these filters, which can be used to achieve various effects. Using them calls for particular experience, which can only be acquired through practice, even if, as these photographs show, they are very simple to adopt.

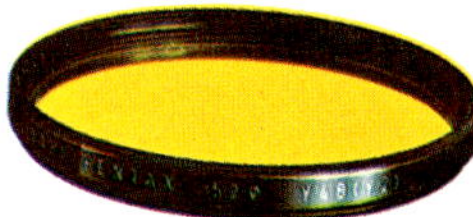

yellow filter

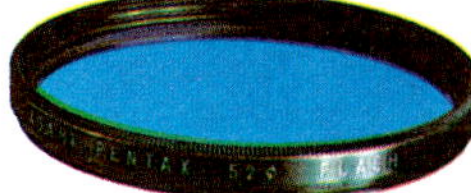

blue filter

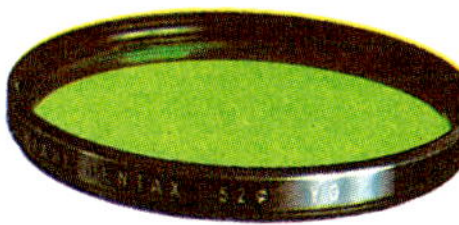

green filter

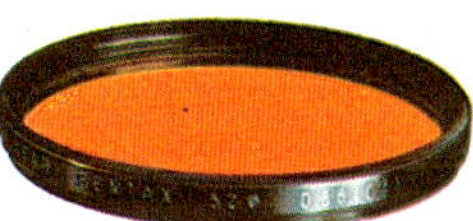

orange filter

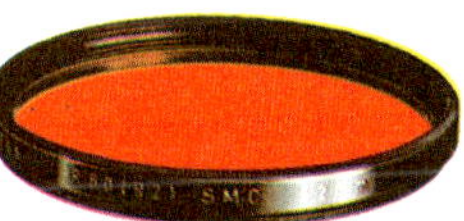

red filter

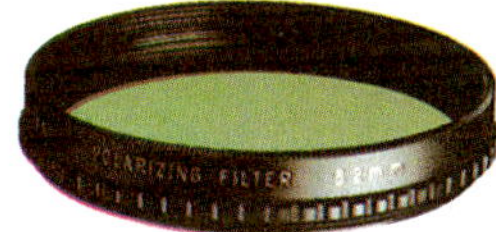

polarizing filter

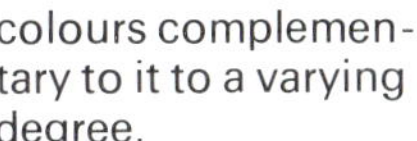

colours complementary to it to a varying degree.
For example, a red filter will let through all the colours close to red, but will reject green and blue, and it is the same with filters for the other basic colours.
The yellow filter is widely used to modify the strength of the sun. Indeed, many photographers recommend leaving it on the lens at all times. A major obstacle always encountered on bright days, even when not excessively so, is in fact, the rendering of the sky. It exercises an undoubted fascination, but its light is invariably too powerful, and sufficient to dazzle the rest of the picture. Apart from using a yellow filter it can be necessary to limit the area of sky in the picture, by lowering the lens on to other details. Or wait for the sky to fill up with clouds which, although they in turn can be very bright, will always be less dazzling than the blue.

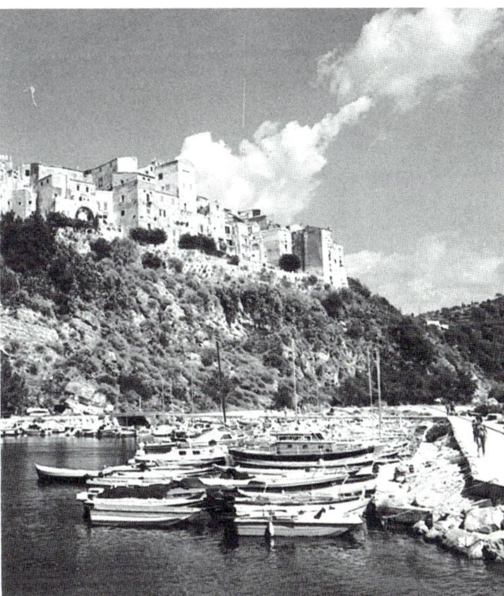

orange filter

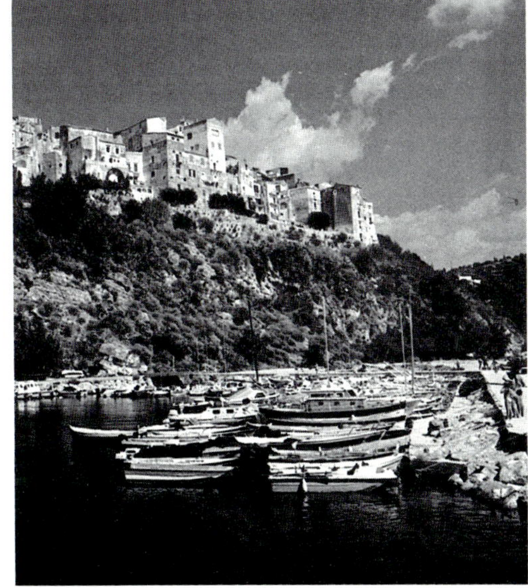

red filter

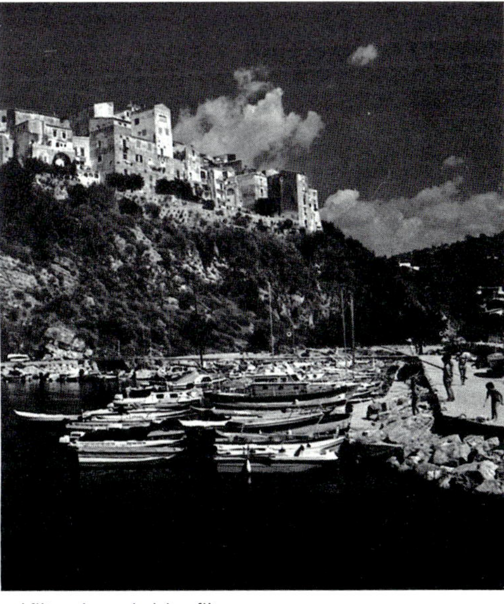

red filter plus polarizing filter

Subject	Effect desired	Filter recommended	Increase in f/stops
blue sky	natural	yellow	1
	dark	deep yellow	1½
	spectacular	red	3
	almost black	deep red	4
	nocturnal effect	red and polarizer	5
seascapes with blue sky	natural	yellow	1
	dark water	deep yellow	1½
sunsets	natural	none	—
	brighter	yellow or red	1–3
distant landscapes	increased haze for atmospheric effect	deep blue	2½
	natural	yellow	1
	reduction of haze	deep yellow	1½
	marked reduction of haze	red	3
near foliage	natural	yellow	1
	light	green	2½
portraits out-of-doors against sky	natural	yellow	1
flowers and foliage	natural	yellow	1–2
leafy plants	lighter to show up detail	green	2½
brick buildings, wood, textiles, sand, snow, etc. in sunlight and with a blue sky	natural	yellow	1
	better rendering of texture	orange	2½

Apart from distinguishing colours, filters are also used to reinforce them. If you want a given colour to show up particularly well and above all to be lighter and brighter, you will have to use a filter of that colour. If, on the other hand, you wish to darken it, you will need to use a filter of a complementary colour.

Filters can clarify or fog the image and special tables can guide you through their use. You will thus find that noticeable changes can be made to the real data, for example, turning a blue sky almost black by using a deep red filter, making a sunset brighter with a yellow or red filter, increasing the haze of a distant landscape with a deep blue filter or conversely, reducing the haze with a deep yellow filter. You can also increase the definition of a landscape in brilliant sunshine and with a blue sky, by using an orange filter. All filters have the effect of attenuating the light and you will therefore need to use a larger diaphragm aperture, according to the ratios shown in the table above.

"Correction" filters are available which serve to adjust films for use in anomalous conditions (for example, when reflectors are used with daylight films, etc.).

Some photographers rarely use filters or confine their use to the most elementary effects, even in colour photographs – which are the ones which normally lend themselves best to this technical aid – and yet they still obtain excellent results. Nonetheless, a knowledge of all the properties of filters would seem to be a necessary part of any photographer's stock-in-trade.

The drawing below shows the theoretical action of five coloured filters.

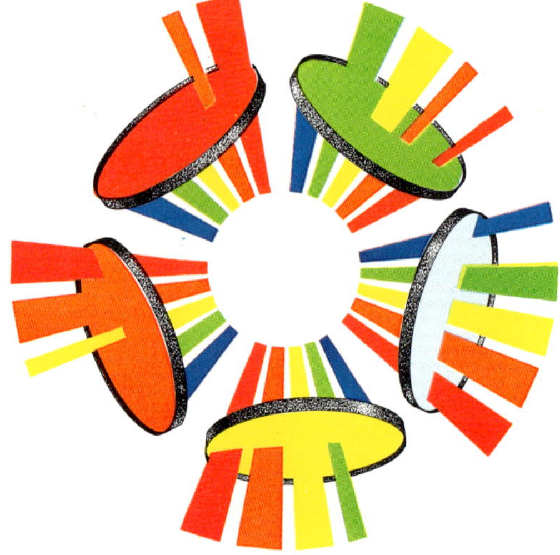

Polarizing filters

A very different type from the ones listed so far is the polarizing filter. When normal light is propagated in one direction, it oscillates on all planes passing through that direction. The glass of the polarizing filter is capable of blocking light oscillating on a single plane.

As reflected light is a polarized light (that is, it oscillates on a single plane), by blocking this plane you also block the reflection. Polarizing filters have a swivelling device for locating the polarizing plane to be eliminated. This system, which can be variously applied in the scientific field, can also be useful in landscape photography. It can be important, for example, in eliminating the reflections from a liquid surface such as the sea, a lake or pond, when one's aim is to show up the bed of the sea or lake and the reflections prevent one from doing so. Sometimes one also wishes to eliminate the reflections to enhance the colour of a sea or lake, which will look more homogeneous and interesting (from a certain point of view) through a polarizing filter, with more saturated colours, even if polarization of the light tends to lower the general brightness level. In any case, polarizing filters can be useful in the presence of strongly reflective surfaces other than water – for example, snow, window panes or some backlit scenes, etc.

They are not for general use and are indispensable in only a few cases.

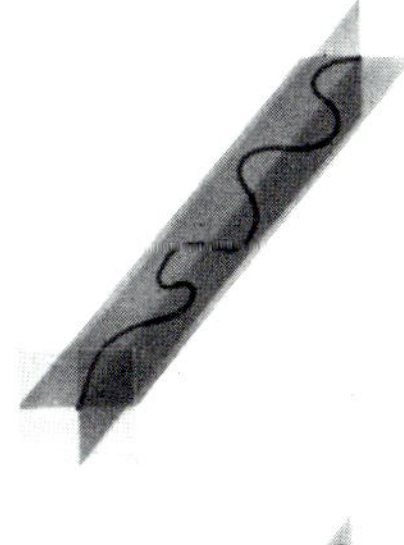

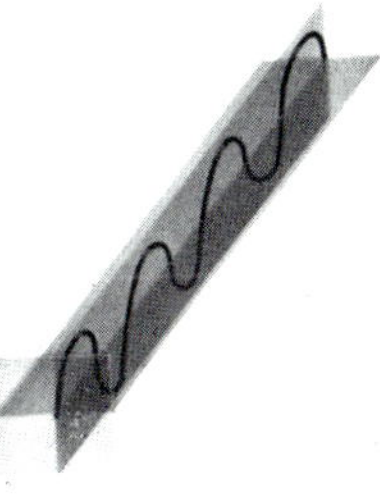

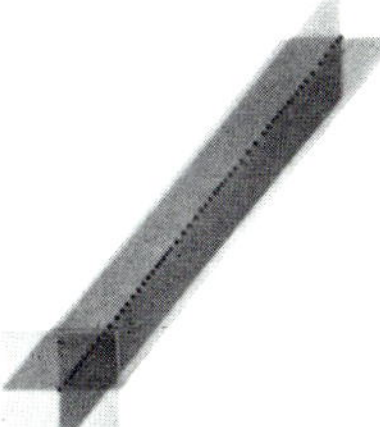

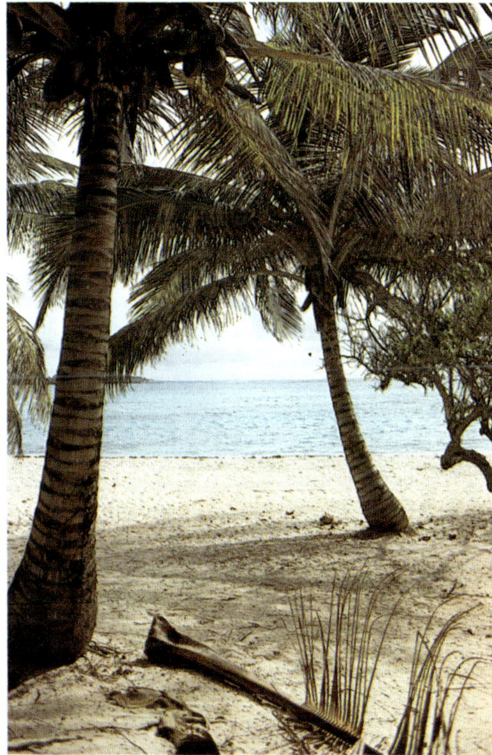

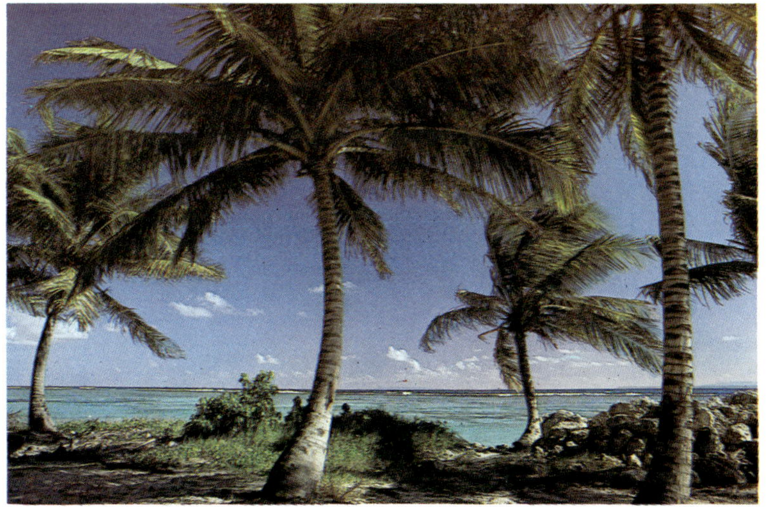

A polarizing filter lets through light waves oriented in one direction only and absorbs and therefore neutralizes the rest. The drawing above left shows three different types of propagation: at the top, that of normal light waves; in the center, that of polarized light waves, which move on a single plane; and at the bottom, a longitudinal, non-luminous type of propagation. These two photographs show a landscape in Guadeloupe, above, without a polarizing filter, and left, with one.

Filters for colour

Just as there are occasions when you need to use filters for black-and-white, they can be useful for colour. Apart from specific applications, which elude generalization, their purpose is to accentuate certain colours, create monochrome photographs or harmonize certain normal photographs in which the presence of violently conflicting colours can create imbalances within a given context.
As always, the use of colour filters will depend on one's aims. Special filters are available for producing equally special effects, such as the spot or anular filters, which have a clear area in the center and a coloured surround. There are graduated filters which are coloured over one half only, and in which the transition from clear to coloured area is gradual. Spot filters can also be graduated. These filters are of particular interest for landscapes, even if they can only be used very infrequently. There are also dual colour filters which can be rotated to vary the colour effect to the top, the bottom, or the side. Finally, different filters can be used together – i.e. both coloured and special effects. All this comes under the heading of highly sophisticated photographic operations which are perfectly legitimate in theory and can even be valuable in prac-

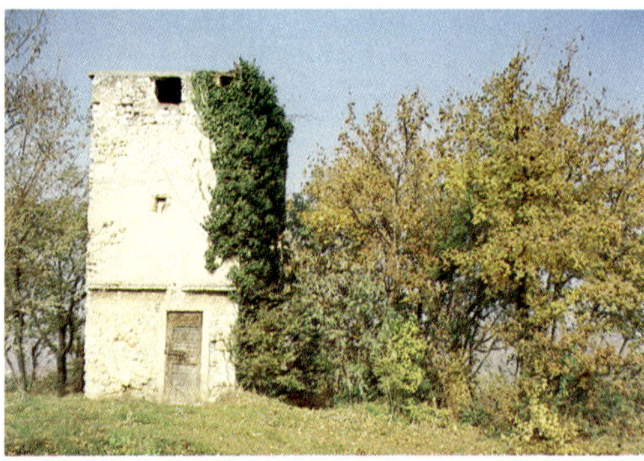

no filters

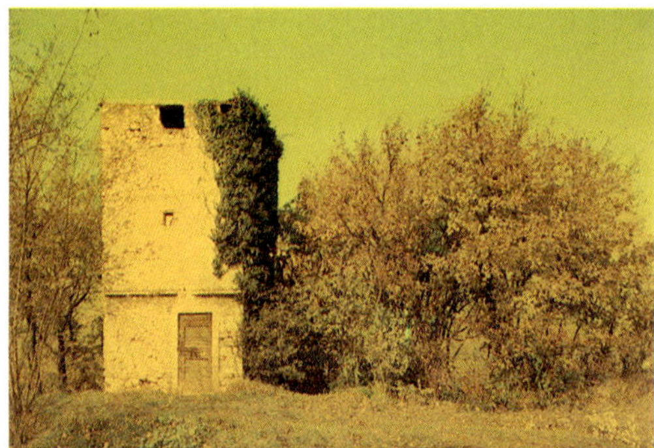

yellow filters

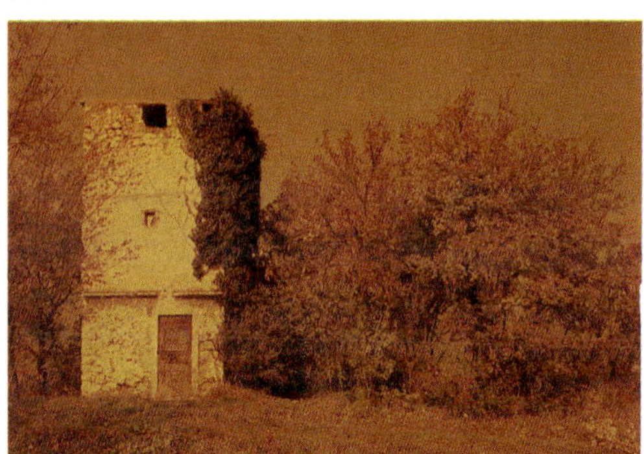

orange filter

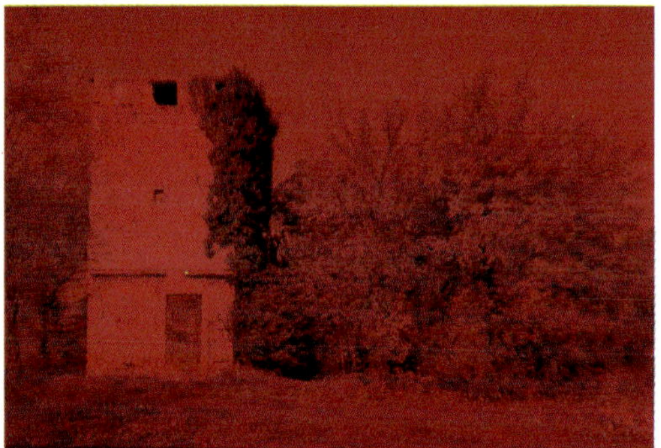

red filter

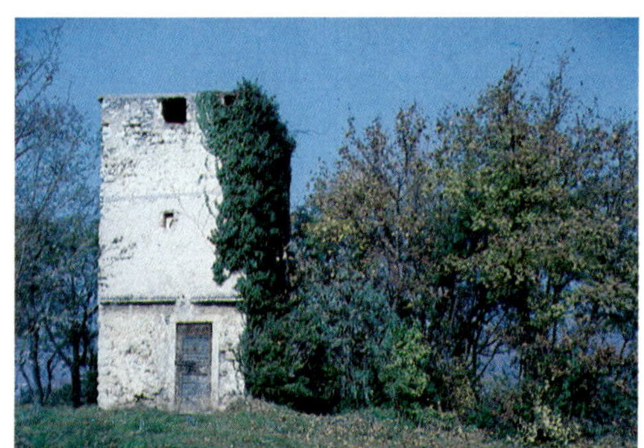

blue filter

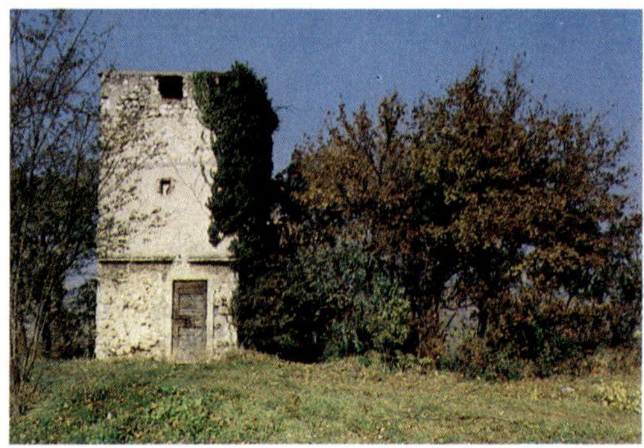

graduated blue filter

tice, but which absolutely cannot constitute a rule and can, on the contrary, be counterproductive for someone not knowing how to use them with skill and a thorough knowledge of his own aims and equipment. Unless the photographer is seeking to achieve particularly artificial results he will probably make very sparing use of filters and will prefer the ones with milder effects, remembering that all filters reduce the intensity of the light, even if the paler ones do so to an almost imperceptible degree.

A polarizing filter used with colour has more or less the same effect as a yellow filter with black-and-white; and can increase the density of the sky, showing up cloud. For a uniform reduction in light intensity, neutral grey filters can also be used (for example, with mirror telephotos where the aperture cannot be varied).

Then there are UV or ultraviolet filters, which are virtually transparent but block an excess of ultraviolet rays. These are particularly useful in situations where such radiations are abundant, when the air is very pure, as in the mountains or by the sea, and they can prevent a blue fog over the image and a loss of definition.

An area in which the latest technology has indulged its whims is that of filters for effects by light refraction. The commonest are the following.

The *cross screen*, a

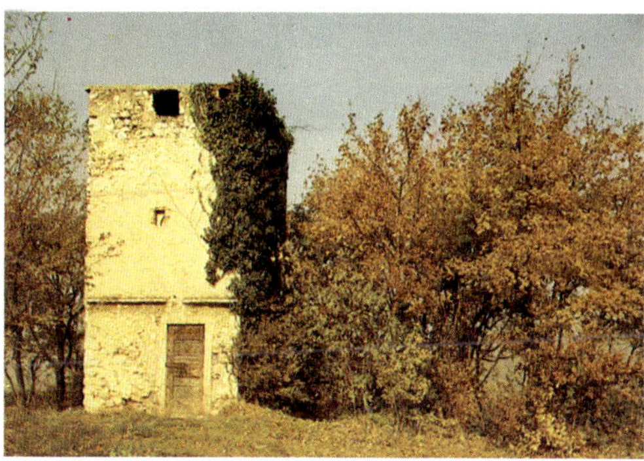
amber filter

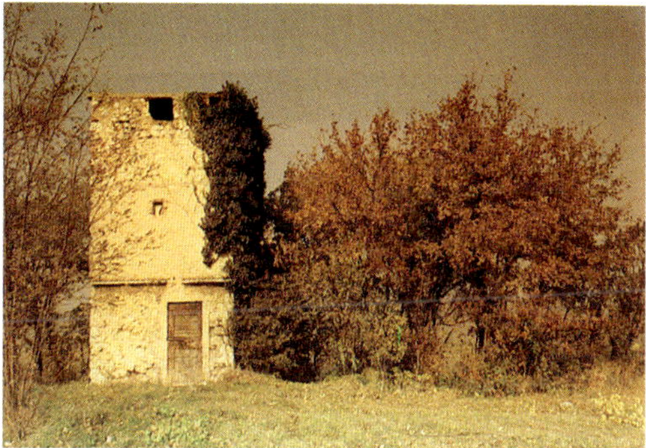
graduated amber filter

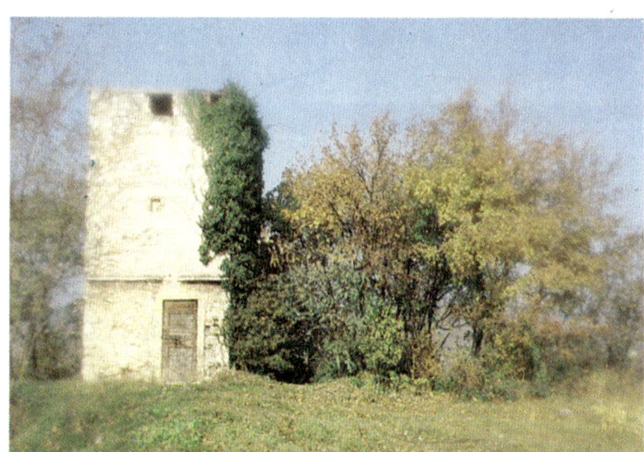
weak soft focus spot filter

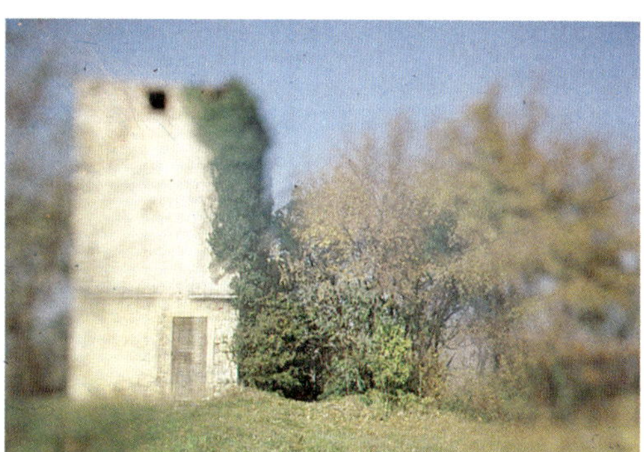
strong soft focus spot filter

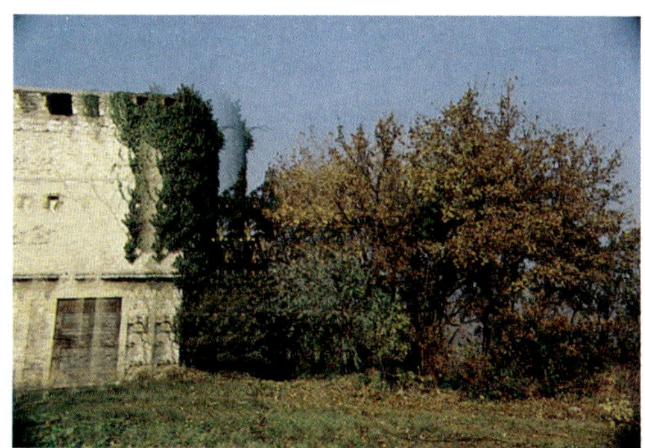
prismatic filter

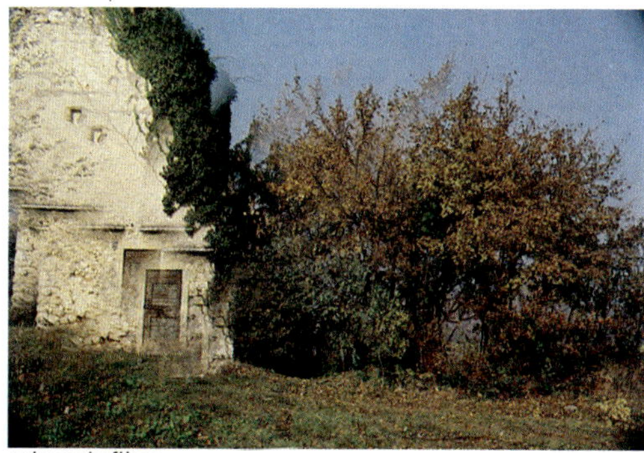
prismatic filter

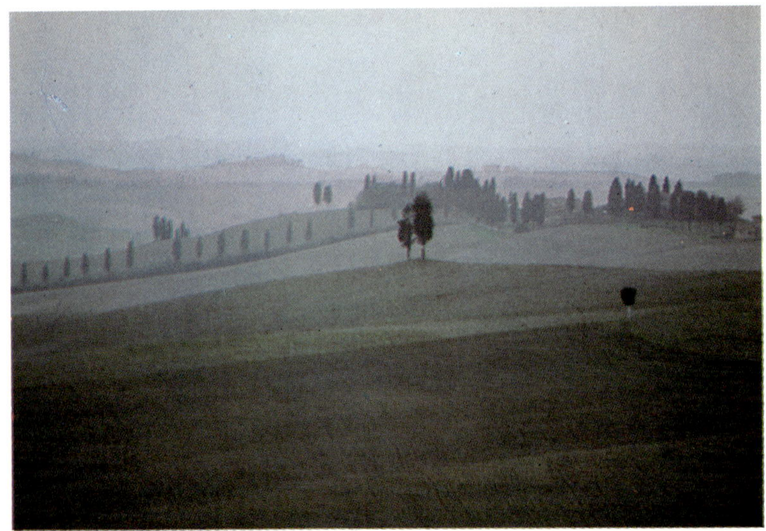

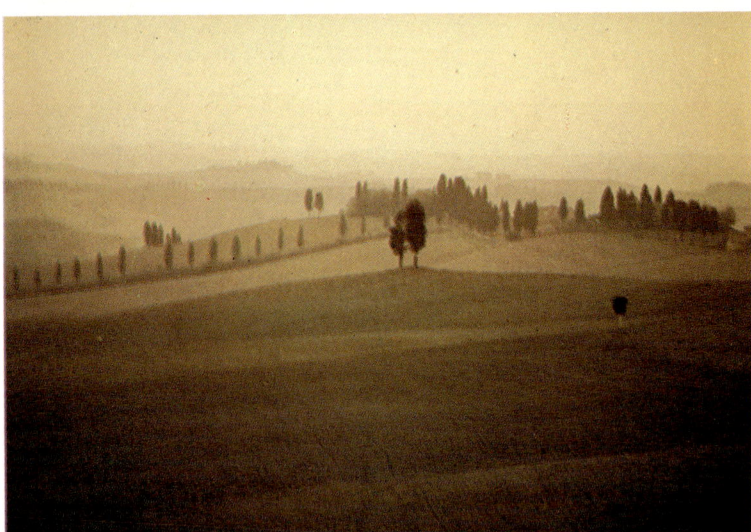

The photograph at the top shows a Tuscan landscape near Mucigliani (Siena) and was taken after sunset without using any filters.
In the center we see the same landscape, photographed at the same time of day, but this time using a pale orange (A29) filter of the Cokin series. The impression of the time of day is completely reversed and the light seems to take on the joyful radiance of dawn.
The photograph below left shows a view of Stockholm on a grey day, but use of a graduated grey filter, by darkening the top part of the sky, has created a totally artificial storm effect – which dramatizes the otherwise monotonous view of the city. Similarly, in the photograph on the right, the use of a graduated yellow filter has created an effect of sunlight and fine weather.

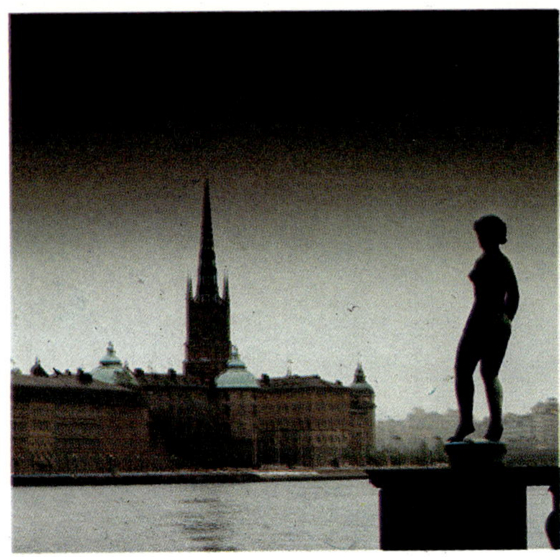

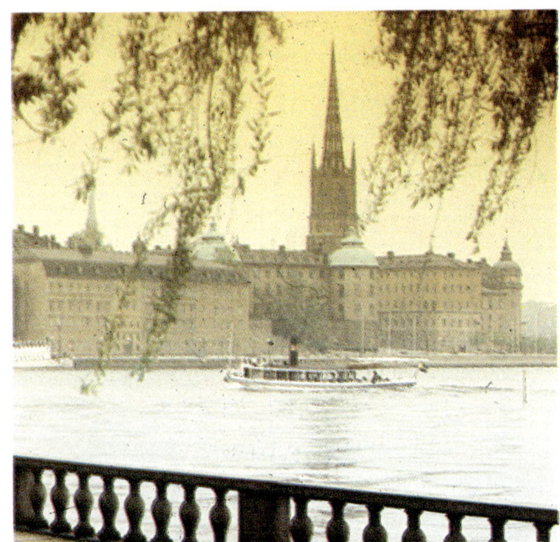

In the photograph on the right, the use of a blue filter, producing a typically nocturnal effect, has emphasized the abstract character of these skyscrapers in Brasilia, giving a nobler, more solitary tone to their imposing mass. A graduated red filter, below, has emphasized the character of the ground on which Brasilia rises. We do not consider that these devices have much improved the artistic and expressive tone of these pictures, but one can see that such methods can greatly alter the real data and can therefore be useful in increasing the interpretational freedom of the photographer. What must be avoided is their indiscriminate use. The newcomer is often fascinated by them and may even use them for the sheer eccentricity of their results. Overestimating them can be detrimental, in that it can distract one from looking for more authentic values.

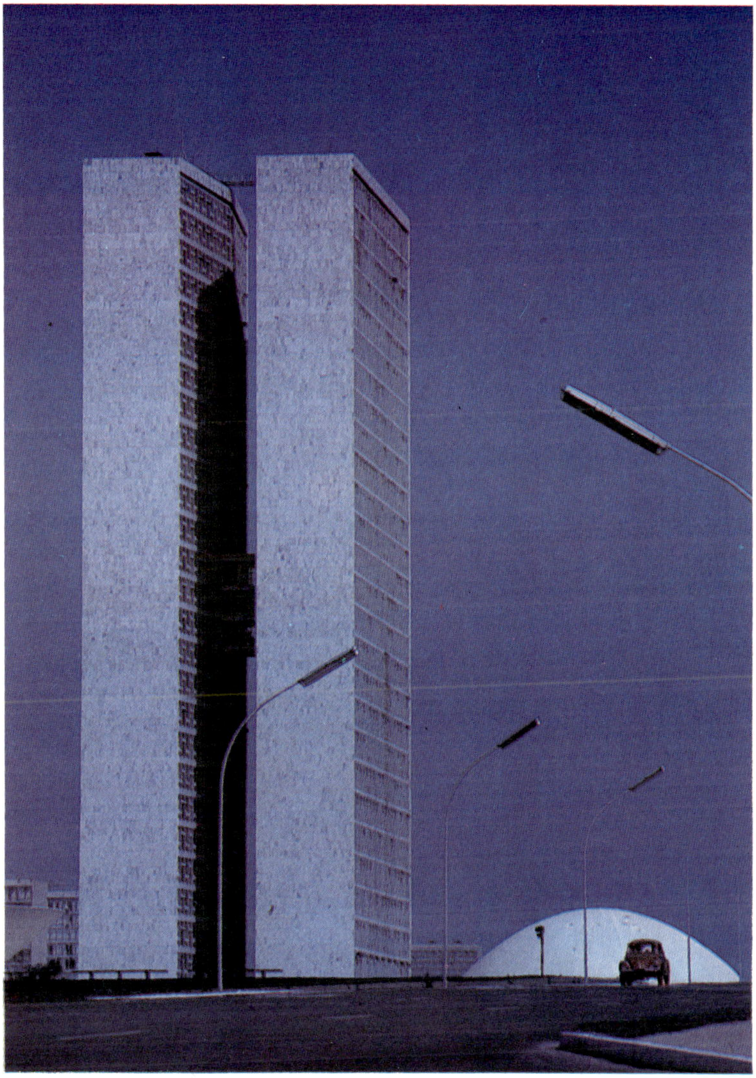

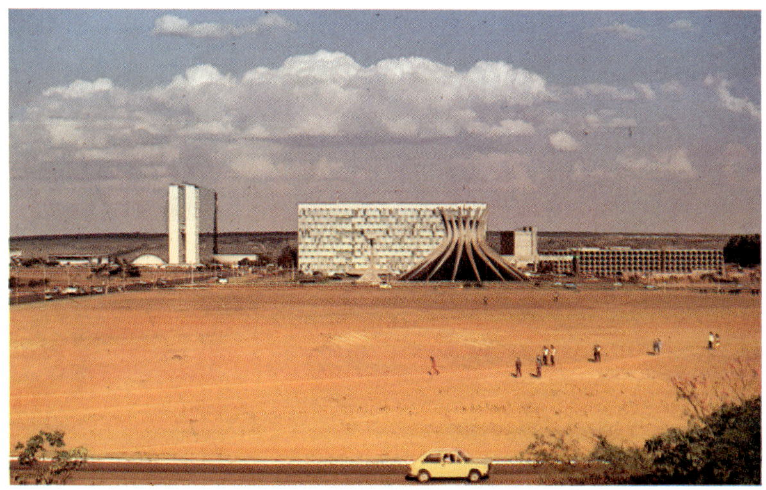

It cannot be said too often that the sophisticated use of photographic devices is not essential to the success of pictures and many photographers have produced masterpieces without using any artifice. But it is also true that in specific cases certain technical devices can be extremely useful to the photographer, who may even be obliged to use them.

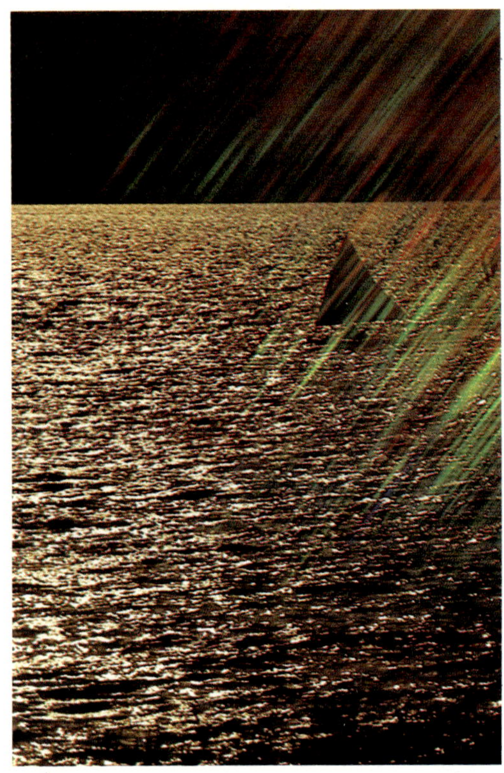

lattice of incised lines which intersect perpendicularly to each other, producing a star with four or more points in places corresponding to a light source or brilliant reflection. The *snow cross*, which has a different type of lattice, which causes brilliant signs like asterisks to be sent out from the brightest spots. The *multi-image* and *multi-image colour* lenses, which multiply the subject in the photograph; the *center lens*, which creates an image which is very sharp in the center and softened and diffuse on the outside; the *split field lens*, which enables you to bring both very near planes and infinity into focus at the same time; the *chromostar* series, in which an ordinary polarizing filter and a coloured polarizing filter are combined with a type which enables you to vary the density of a colour by rotating the polarizing mount, and another which enables you to pass from one colour to another through the whole range of intermediate colours, and so on. An expert photographer can even use combinations of these filters, obtaining results which are pleasing, but also very hard to achieve.

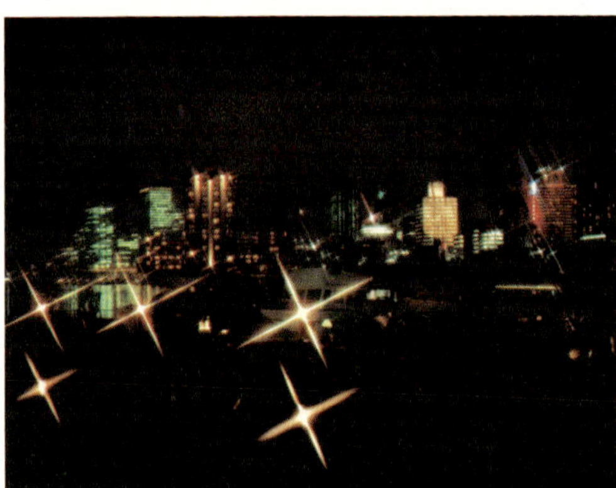

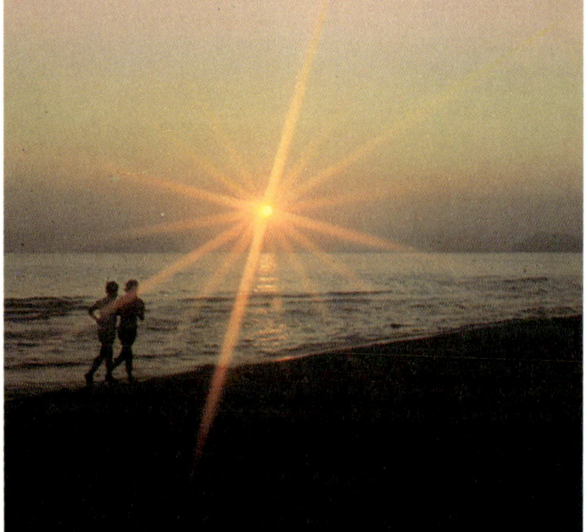

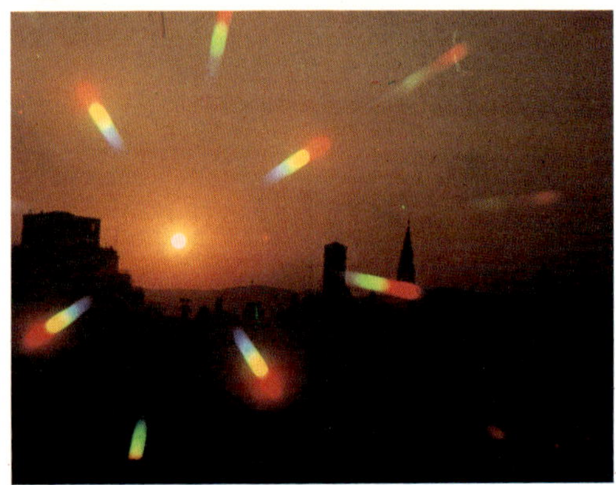

Top left, Lake Garda viewed from Sirmione through a diffraction filter which is responsible for the effect of golden rays crossing the image.
Center, Montreal seen through a cross screen. The cross screen is a fairly common type of filter for creating star effects by breaking up light sources and their reflections.

Below, sunset in Vienna photographed with a snow cross. Instead of forming stars, the snow cross forms rays like asterisks.
Above, sunset over the sea, photographed with a cross screen.

Left, a sea view with clouds taken through a blue-red polarizing filter. This has changed not only the natural colours, but also the contrast, which has been dramatically emphasized. Naturally, in the hands of a great photographer, these techniques can be put to very positive use, but if adopted as ends in themselves, they are comparable to rhetorical formulae in literature, which can consist of words without any real content. As such, they can be more tiresome than entertaining.
Technique alone never produces any results and it is an illusion to think that owning sophisticated equipment is enough to create better photographs.

Below, Lake Pusiano (Como) seen through the coloured facets of the multicolour filter. It is a clear example of the multiple and often incredible effects which can be obtained using special filters.
The multicolour consists of six sections which filter different colours. The multiplication of images which is obtained with multi-image filters, which always has a fantastic and surreal character, can be effective, for example, for advertising purposes, where the unusual, startling and even paradoxical nature of the image can be the thing most sought after. Obviously, in referring to advertising, we do not just mean billboards, but every other type from the advertisements appearing in magazines to book covers or packaging.
Novelty has undoubtedly played an important role in this field hitherto, and the possibilities are endless.

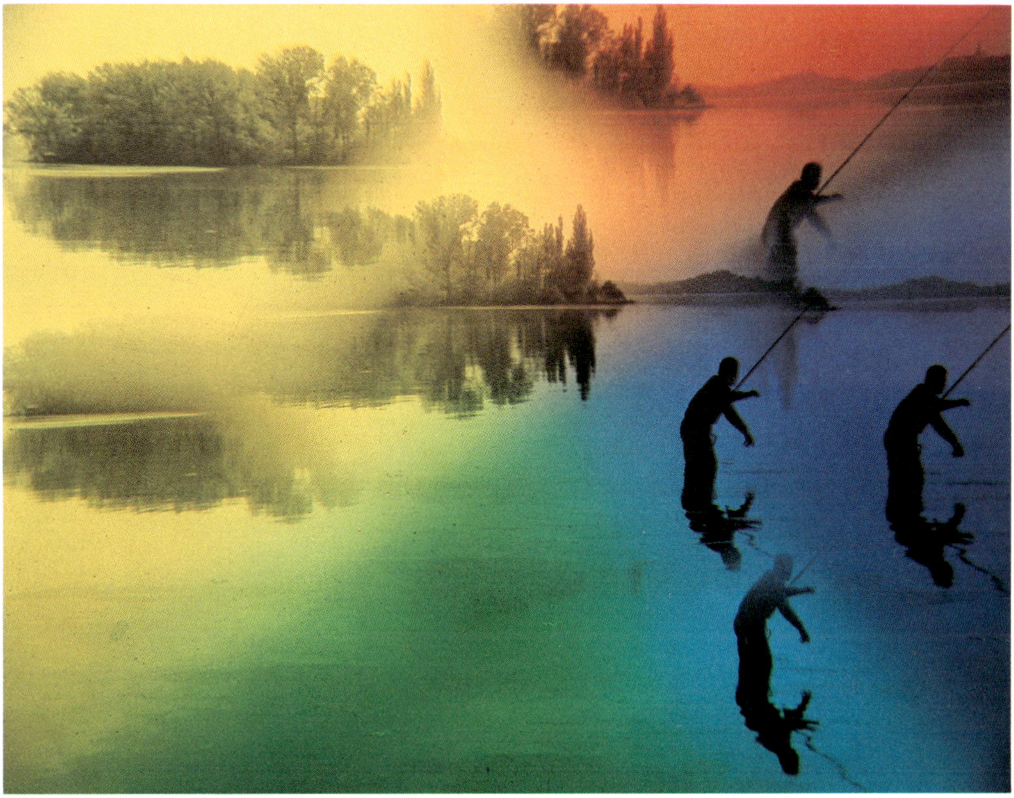

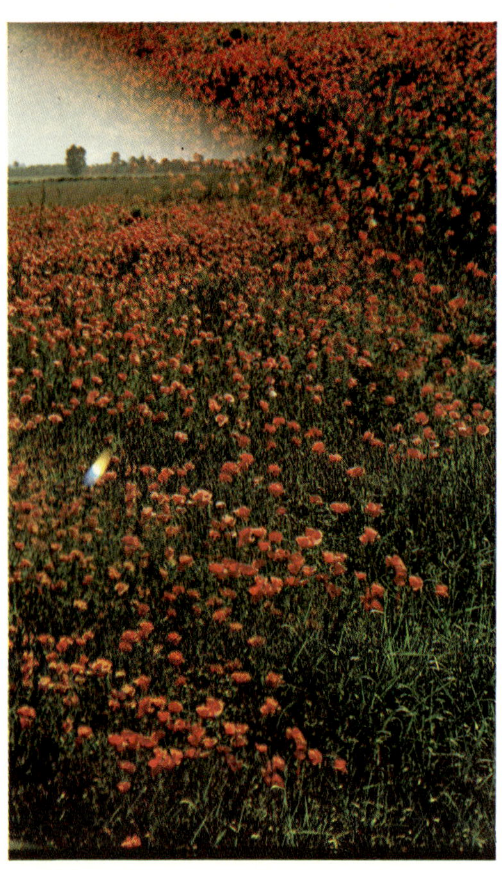

Left, red poppies taken with a split-field lens. This is a filter which enables both a very near foreground and infinity to be focused in the same frame. Like other filters exemplified on these pages, it forms part of the range of optical accessories which have come on the market in recent years, opening up new horizons for the photographer who knows how to use them intelligently.
Below, parallel images of Venice taken with a multi-image filter in very dim light. The multi-image and multi-image colour filters reproduce the same image several times over (from 3 to 6), either parallel or in volleys.

On the facing page, a photograph taken in Russia with a multi-image filter, in very low light. When using particularly sophisticated filters, you also need to take account of the focal length of the lens. These special filters are normally designed for use with a 50 mm lens for the 24 × 36 format and an 80 mm lens for the 6 × 6 format. Therefore it is best to keep to a normal focal length when using them. This does not prevent your using them in special circumstances for particular effects. But only considerable experience of these techniques and a thorough knowledge of the basic principles of photography can enable you to use them appropriately.
Clever photographers can get away with using different filters simultaneously, achieving highly original results which at one time would only have been conceivable using special processes in the darkroom. When these filters are applied to telephotos, softer results are obtained, while the opposite is the case with wide-angles.

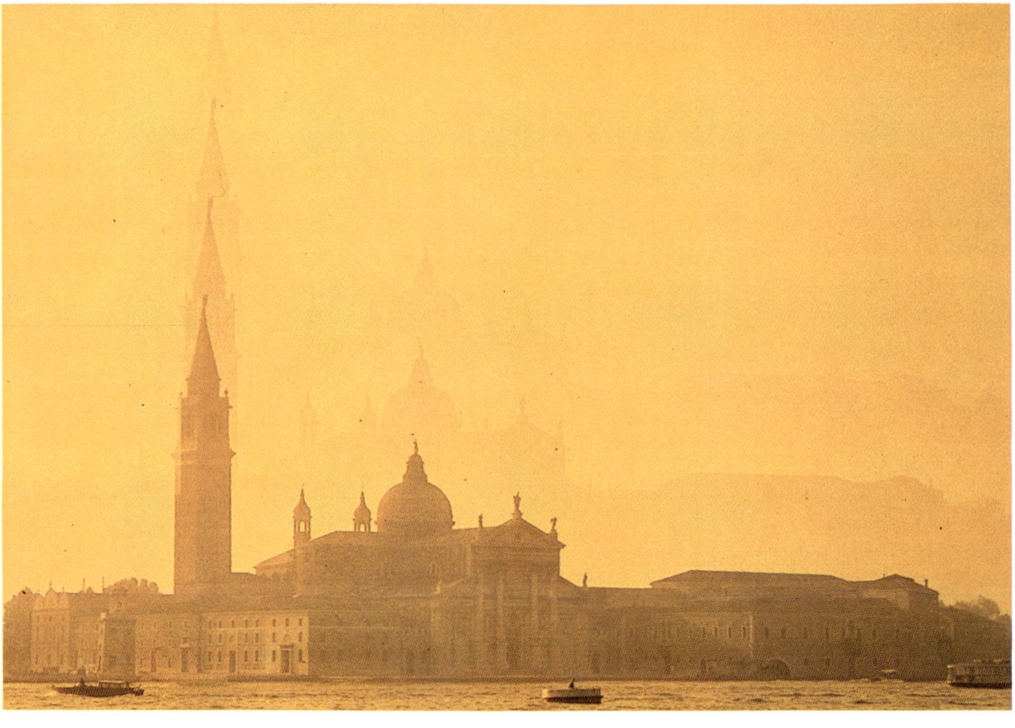

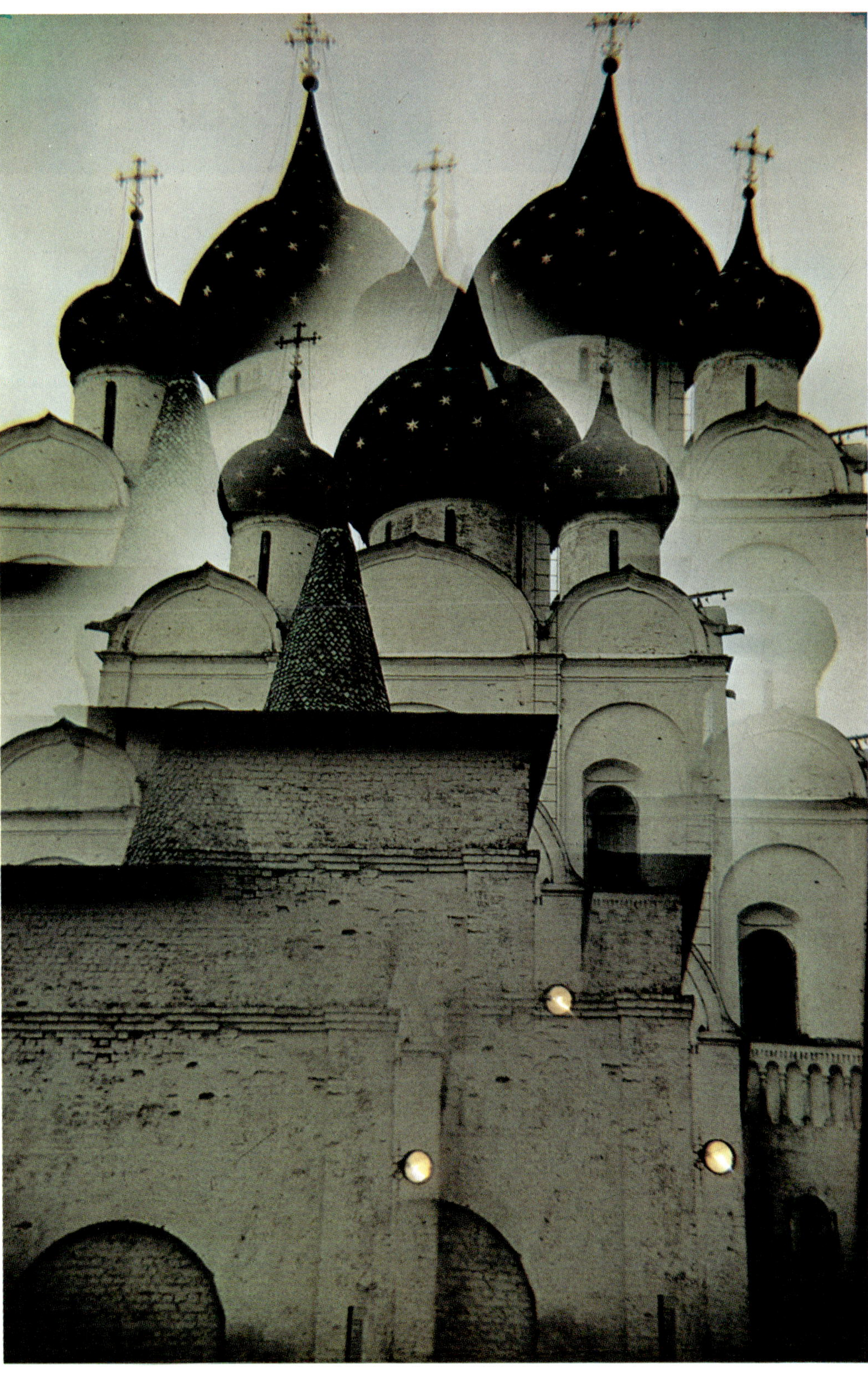

Special effects

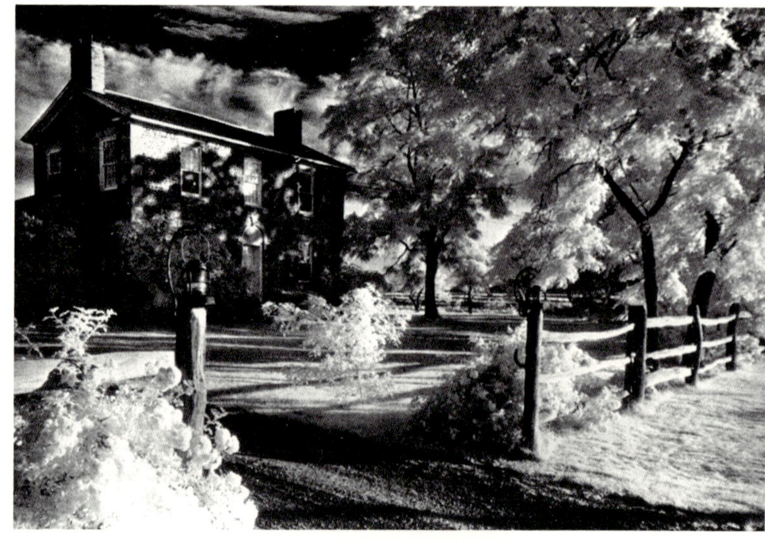

Infra-red films must also be included in the virtually unlimited field of special effects. These capture wavelengths – and therefore colours – which are not perceived by the human eye and which can give the photograph a totally unexpected and sometimes even surreal character. For that matter, even normal films can be more sensitive than our eye in perceiving certain colours – such as the blue reflected by rain water on a sunless day. The development and printing processes naturally offer unlimited scope for the production of all sorts of effects. All types of transformation are possible in the darkroom, although obviously, there is no guarantee that they will give pleasing effects. A system which can be of particular interest to landscape photography is reticulation, which consists of subjecting the film to treatment while it is still soft. As we have said, a black-and-white film is made up of grains of silver bromide suspended in a gelatin emulsion which, in turn, is spread over a plastic support. When the emulsion is damp it is also very soft, and this is why a fixer is used to harden it. But if, instead of using the fixer at that moment, strong variations in temperature are produced, the gelatin will consolidate unevenly, creating a "crazed"

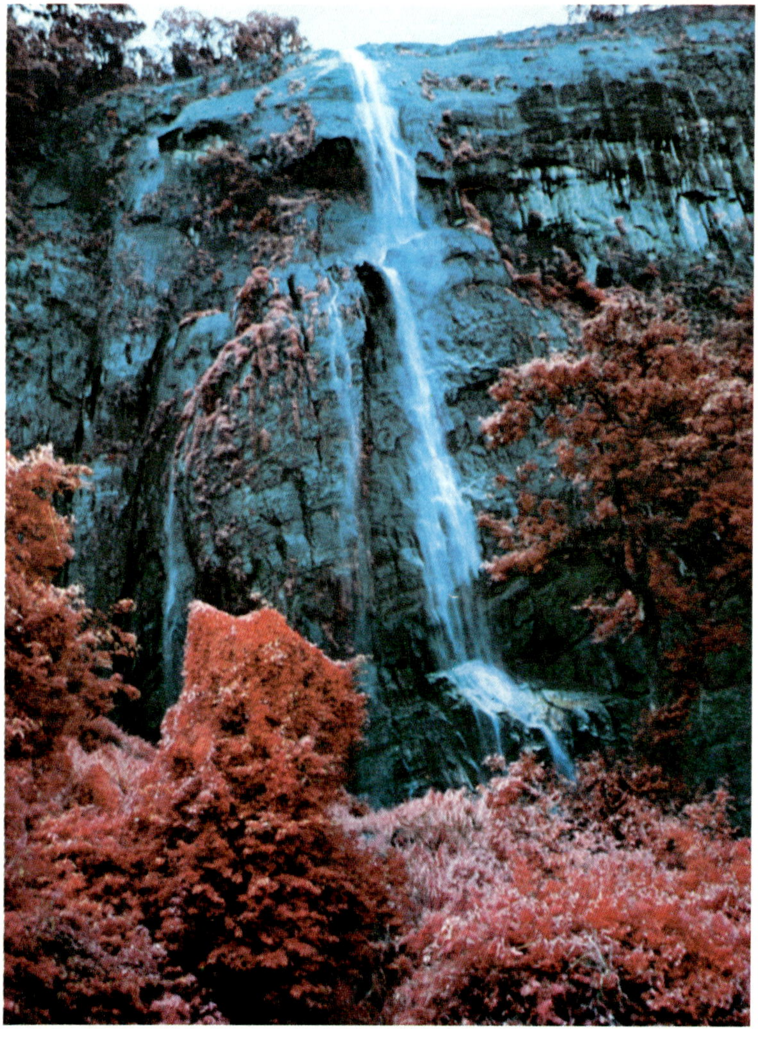

Films are available which can capture effects invisible to the human eye. This is the case with infra-red films which record invisible, infra-red rays, together with normal, visible ones, producing unusual photographs.

On the opposite page, above, a black-and-white infra-red photograph: Cobblestone House, Avon (New York).
Below, the foliage framing this waterfall on the island of Sri Lanka looks red when reproduced by infra-red film, because the chlorophyl in plants is capable of reflecting infra-red rays to a large extent.
Other effects — of unlimited range — can be achieved in the darkroom.
The photograph top right shows a picture of a forest obtained by "reticulation," a process which is applied while the emulsion is still soft.
Below, a "high contrast" image obtained by using films of that name.

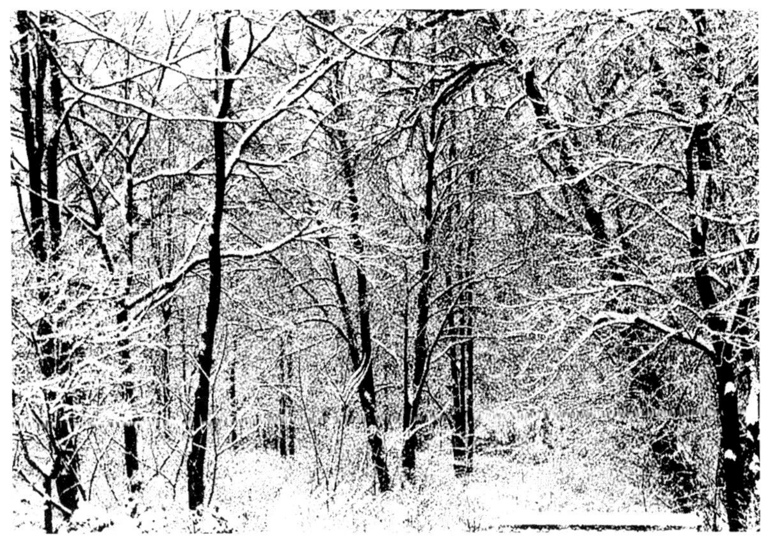

relief known as reticulation.
The results of this process are always unpredictable, therefore it is advisable to develop the film normally first and then take a copy of the print, on which you can experiment without the risk of perhaps spoiling a good photograph.
In a normal film, reticulation can be a nuisance, but when it is caused deliberately it can be used for various effects which will vary according to the intensity and duration of the changes in temperature produced.
Another area of intervention is that of high contrast effects, which are produced by taking virtually normal photographs in black-and-white with high contrast films, which produce pictures with no intermediate tones.
A high contrast print can then be used to develop other techniques such as tone separation, which consists of separating out the normal tones of a photograph into distinct colours. The operation is also known as posterization, because it is particularly effective for producing posters with very garish, abstract colours.
Another popular system is toning, which consists of transforming black-and-white films into colour (and vice versa), by choosing a basic colour which can, however, be given varying degrees of intensity. The result will be monochrome pictures which can be an effective way of livening up old photographs, or emphasizing certain results.
Blue toning, for example, is used to create nocturnal or wintry effects with snow and ice and for seascapes. Similarly, sulphur toning mixed

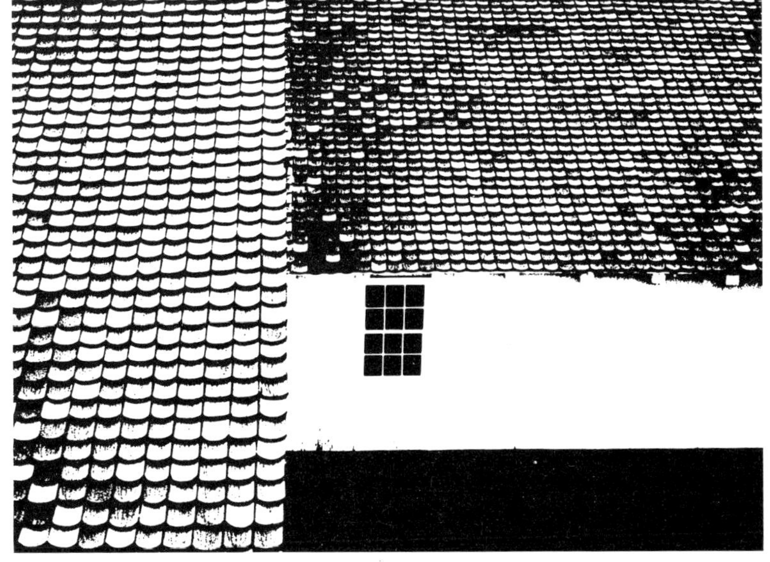

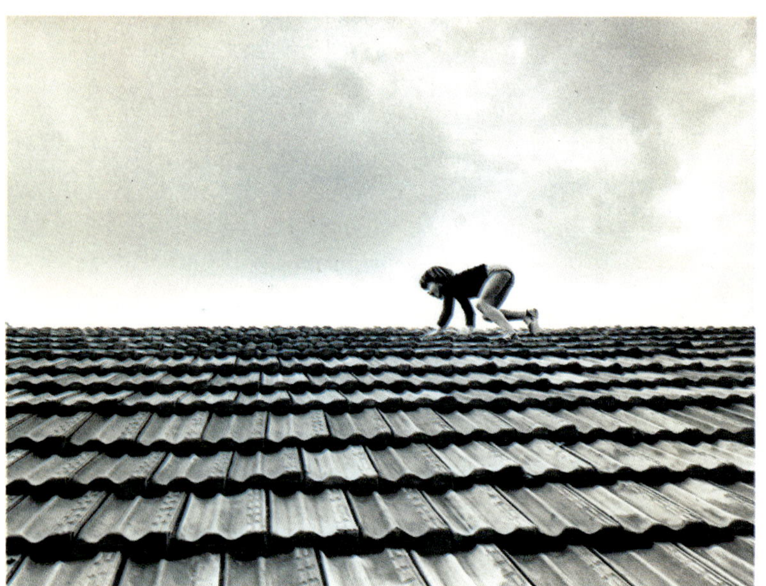

Left, an example of toning in blue, that is, an effect created by immersing a normal black-and-white print in a special bath.
Below, an example of partial toning in sepia, achieved by shielding part of the print during the toning operation.

On the opposite page, above, an example of the Sabbatier effect, which consists of forcing colours. This is done during development by re-exposing the film or print paper to light.
Below, an example of solarization is obtained by extreme overexposure in the order of 1,000 times the amount of light needed, which causes an inversion of the image. It is very difficult to achieve with modern films, which resist inversion, but the results are very similar to those of the more commonly used Sabbatier effect.

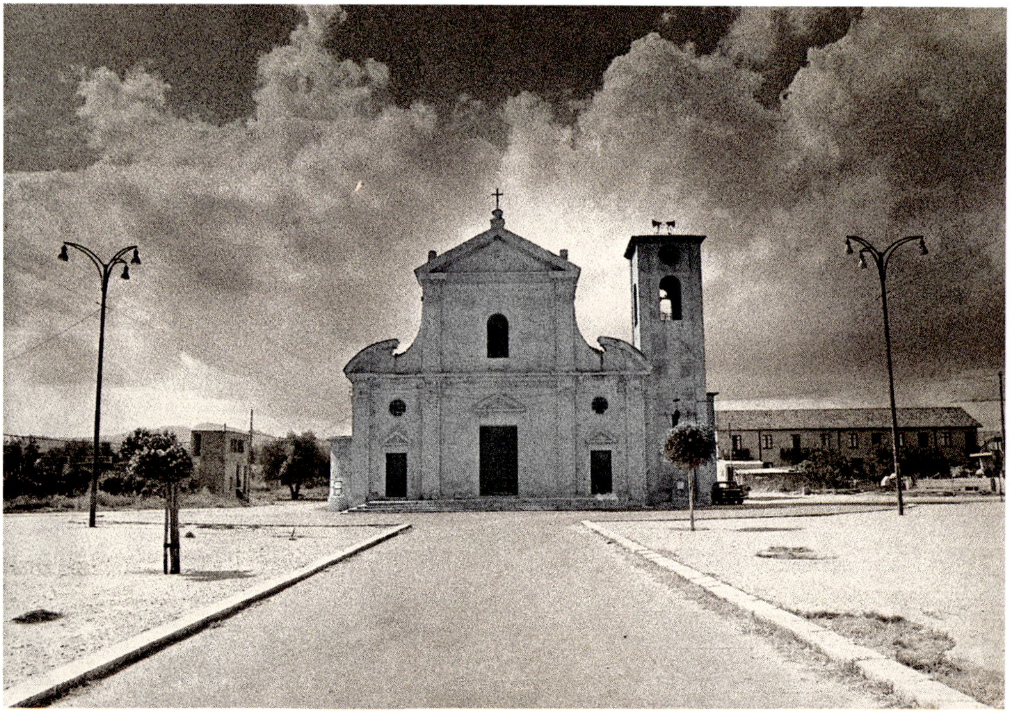

with gold is particularly suitable for showing the red of sunsets and fire, while a warm brown toning can give a sensation of sun. A solarization effect is obtained by greatly accentuated exposure of the film, in the order of 1,000 times the normal exposure time. In these cases, the image is reversed, with the result that both negative and positive are produced on the film and print simultaneously. The Sabbatier effect is very similar to solarization, but this is obtained by re-exposing the film during development. The Sabbatier effect can be produced on both films and paper, although it is preferable to use film. It consists

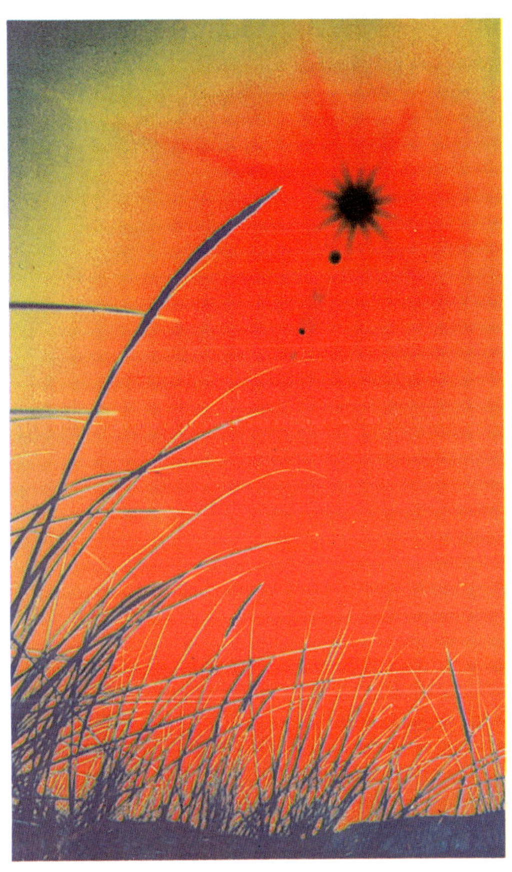

of creating certain marked effects which give the image a fantastic character. It is distinguished from solarization by the presence of an edging in the areas where light and shade are contrasted. When the photograph is printed, this edging looks like a dark surround to the main picture. The strength and duration of the re-exposure and the duration of development after re-exposure determine the results of the Sabbatier effect, for which the companies supplying the necessary materials generally offer full advice.

The Sabbatier effect is particularly good in colour, as it can create entirely new, unreal colours.

Different colour filters can also be applied to the light source during re-exposure, thus providing a very wide range of colour choices – always assuming, of course, that the photographer is acting for a precise purpose and not just from a taste for the eccentric.

The series of effects obtainable in the darkroom continues, of course, with montage photography, the masking of certain parts, corrections, tidying up operations and all the techniques which constitute the stock-in-trade of anyone who is an expert in this field.

To these must be added the techniques of retouching and colouring, which can be applied to both prints and transparencies and for which a vast assortment of materials is available. Results are also

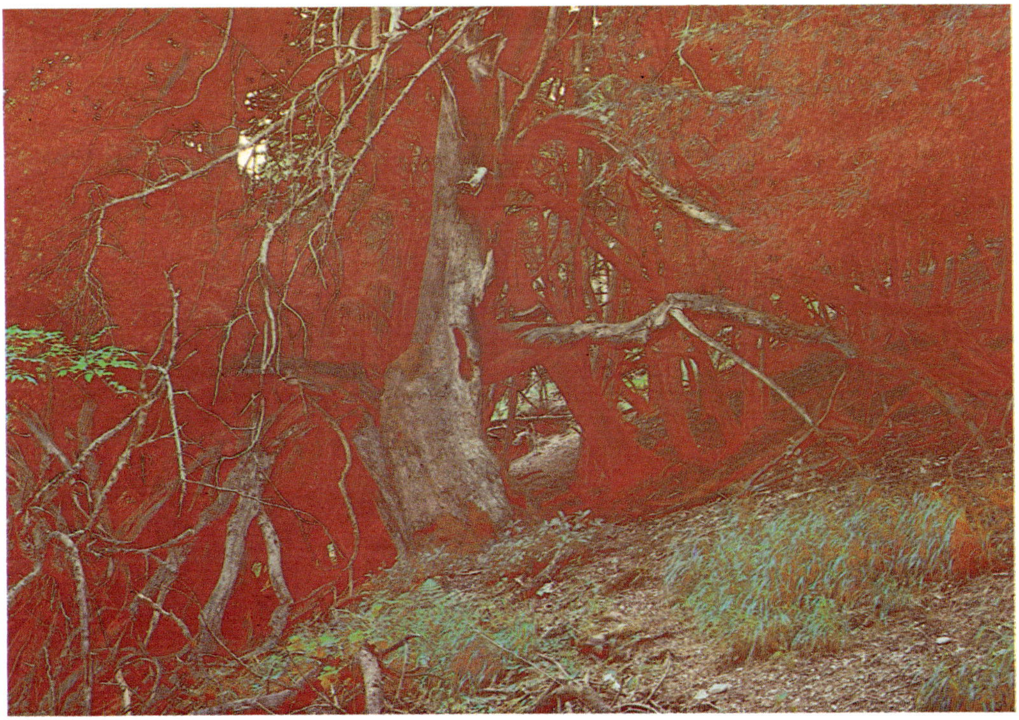

Left, top and center, the same photograph, taken from the original black-and white negative and after toning and colouring. Apart from toning, black-and white can be given coloured effects by retouching or colouring the print, using various means and materials manufactured for the purpose.
Darkroom techniques are widely used by the photographic industry. A knowledge of these procedures can be very useful and at times invaluable, but they are not absolutely necessary to the photographer. Some very good photographers rely entirely on tried and trusted techniques for development and printing.
Below, a wholly exceptional type of landscape, if one can call it so: a surreal landscape created with the aid of a model. Compositions of this kind, which can easily overlap into the field of pop art and other contemporary artistic movements, lend themselves to countless variations.

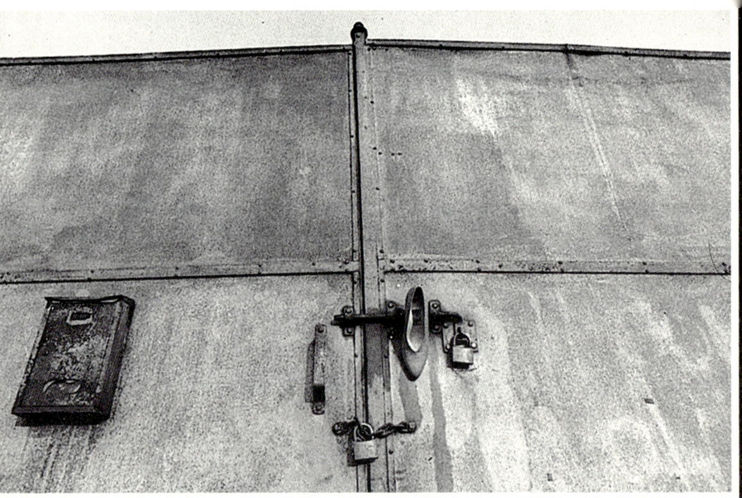

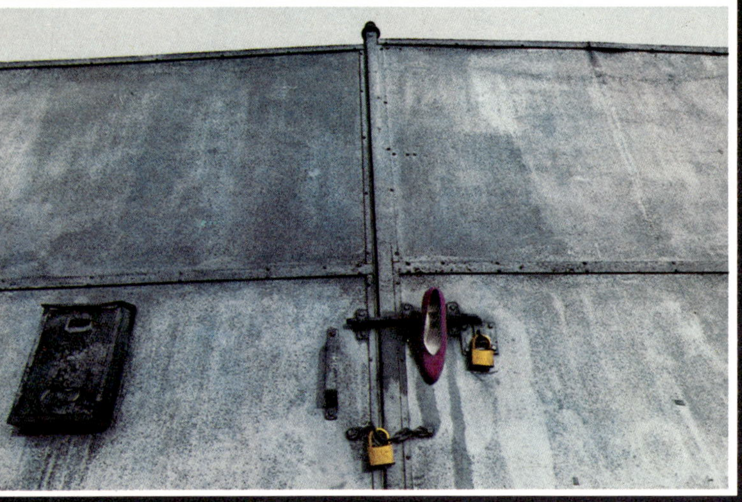

obtained by sticking coloured tissue paper on top of the print. In short, the ways of influencing the picture are unlimited, partly because the various techniques can be combined in different ways. Experimenting with them will be interesting and worthwhile provided one does not expect outstanding results immediately. In view of this, anyone wishing to try out these techniques is advised to use inexpensive, surplus material

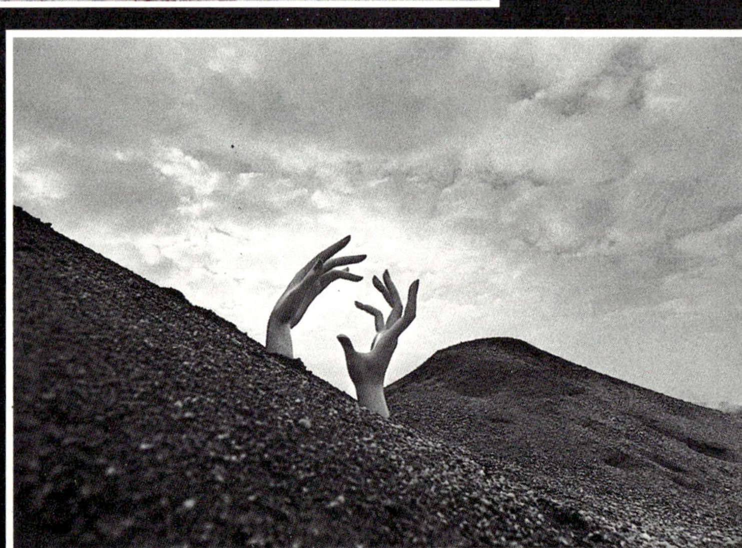

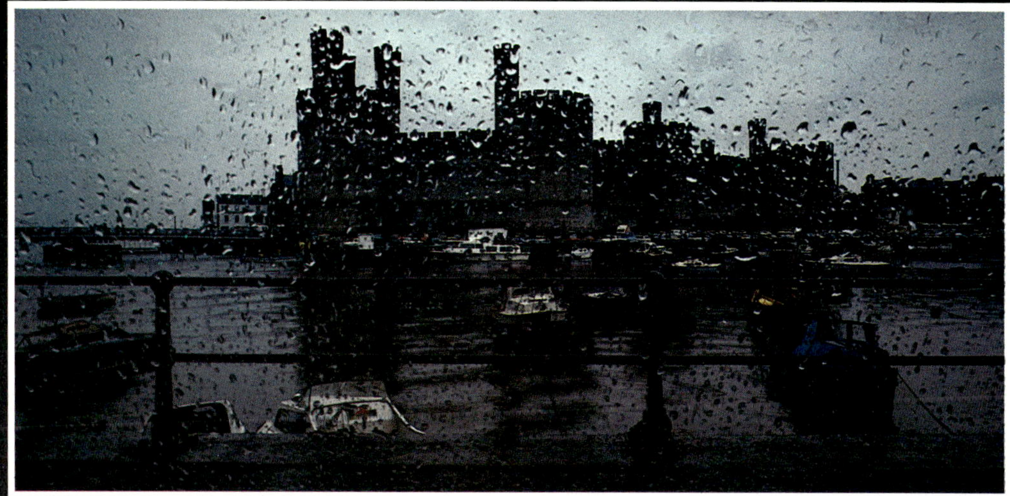

However strong the attractions of darkroom technique may be, the photographer often prefers to trust to the inspiration of the moment for the invention of special effects. This is the case with the view above of Caernarvon Castle in the county of Gwynedd, Wales, seen through a wet windscreen. Note how effectively the photograph interprets the particular atmosphere of this landscape.

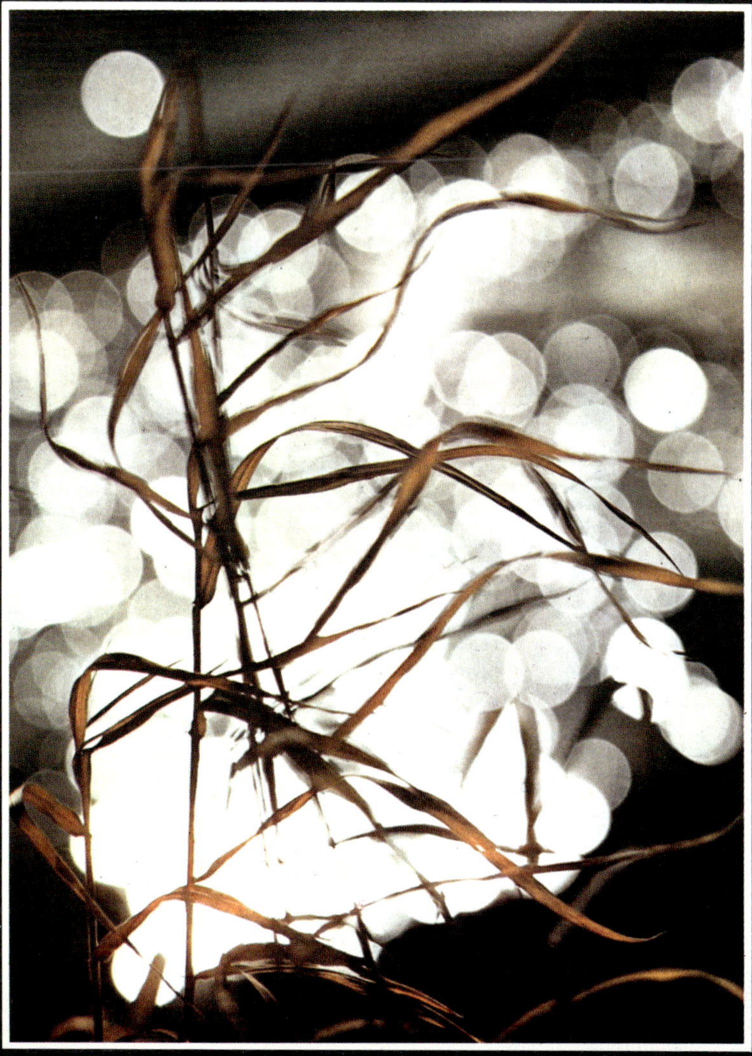

Right, a photograph of blades of grass taken at very close range. The subject has assumed fantastic connotations, emphasized by the multiplication of circles of light which are none other than very blurred light sources. The fanciful character of the image is such that it is quite unimportant to know the nature of the main light source.

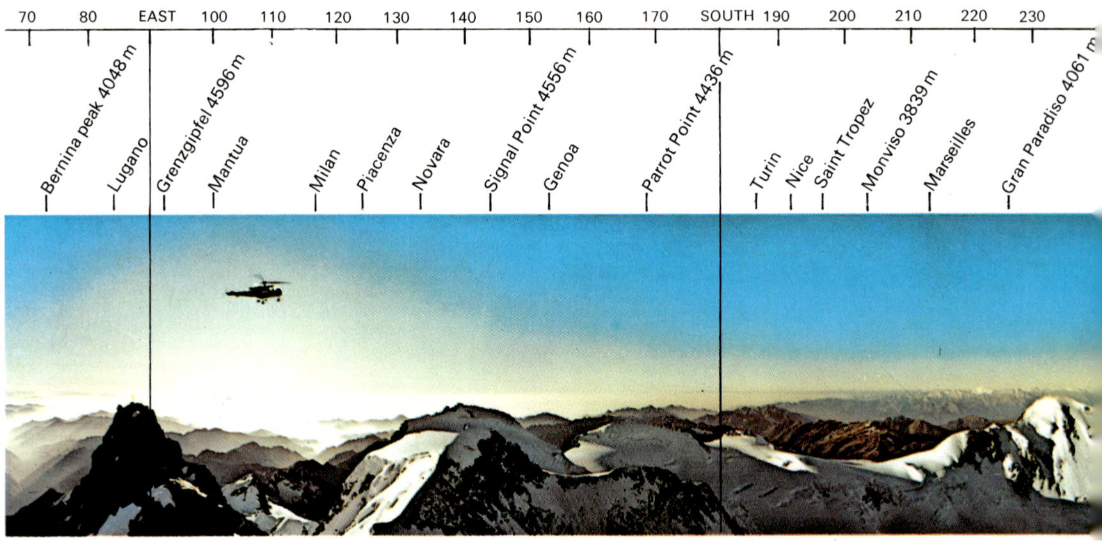

Two special wide-angles

To embrace the entire circumference of the horizon in a single image is an ambition which only the photographer can satisfy, because only technical devices can permit a 360° view. In this way, photographs can be obtained which embrace the immense panorama which can be enjoyed from a mountain peak. But even without resorting to these global solutions, it can be interesting to achieve a greatly expanded breadth of vision, greater than that perceived by the human eye.

Cameras for aerial photography do this. They are known as continuous cameras in which the film is advanced at a constant speed and a rotating prism is applied to the front of the lens and synchronized with the film, so the image gradually unfurls on to the film.

Naturally, there is also a mechanism to compensate for the movement of the aircraft. The resulting photographs are curved.

Also adopted, with similar results, are 15–16 mm fish-eye lenses. These have an angle of view of 180° and can completely cover a 24 × 36 film.

Two examples of panoramic photographs. The one above embraces the 360° of the horizon and was taken from Dufour Point on Monte Rosa with a special set of three cameras, each with an angle of view of 120°. A helicopter was used to shield them from the sun. Below, a view of New York harbour, taken with a model F415A rotating prism camera, which can embrace a 180° angle of view.

Right, the Japanese Horizontal camera for panoramic photos in which the film is laid on a curved surface.

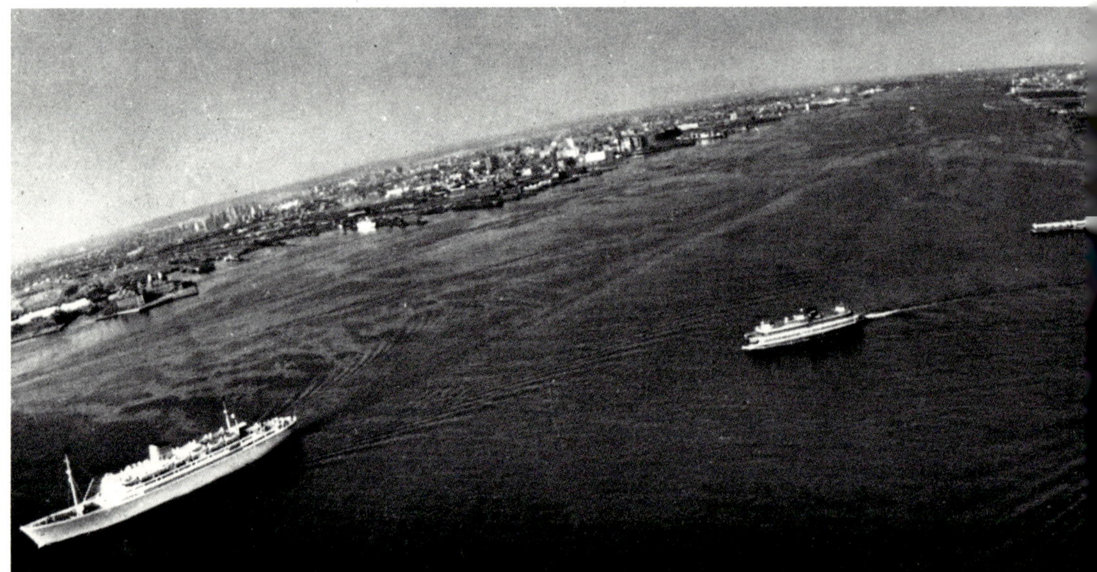

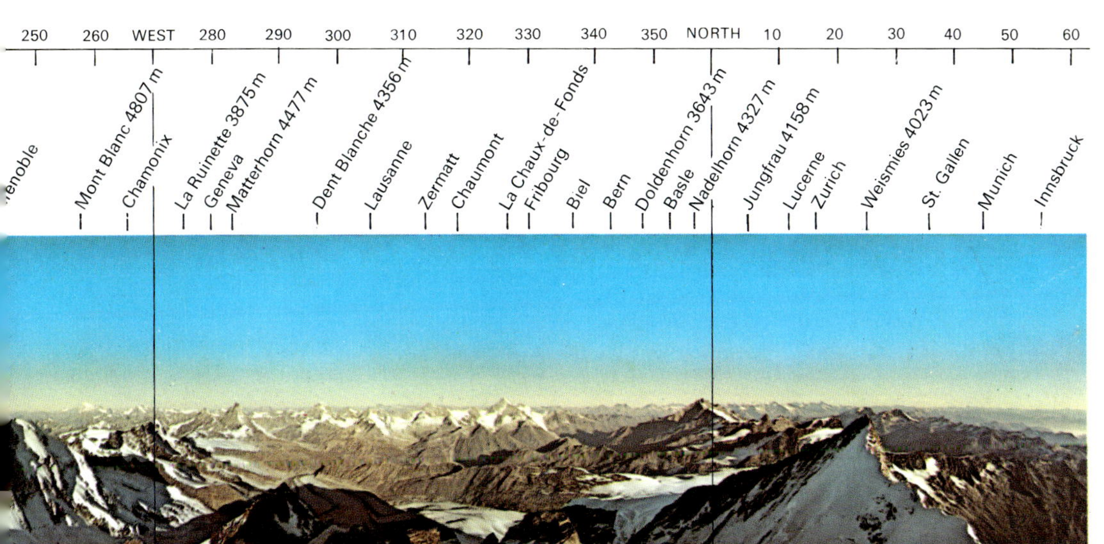

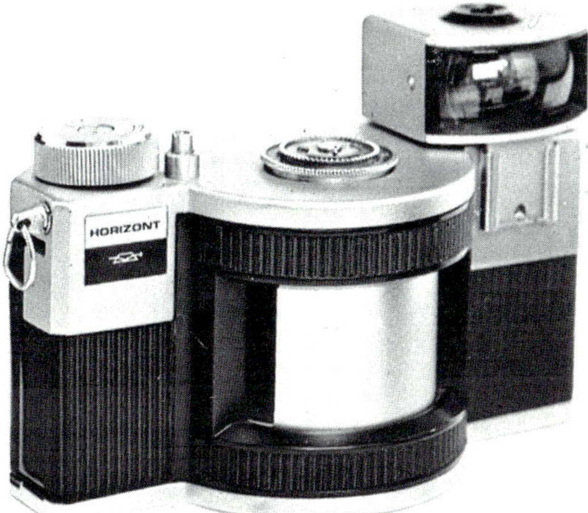

They are expensive, but not prohibitive. Rotating cameras are also made, which can fit a 360° image into a single frame. Montage is, of course, often used to obtain these effects, that is, the joining together of several photographs taken simultaneously, looking towards adjoining angles. One such example is a very famous photograph put together by the Swiss, Emil Schulthers, from three photographs taken simultaneously by three cameras from the top of Monte Rosa. Taking them was a daring and ingenious feat. The photographer had himself lowered on to the summit of the mountain, together with his equipment, by a helicopter which then hovered at a pre-established point to prevent the light of the sun striking the lens.

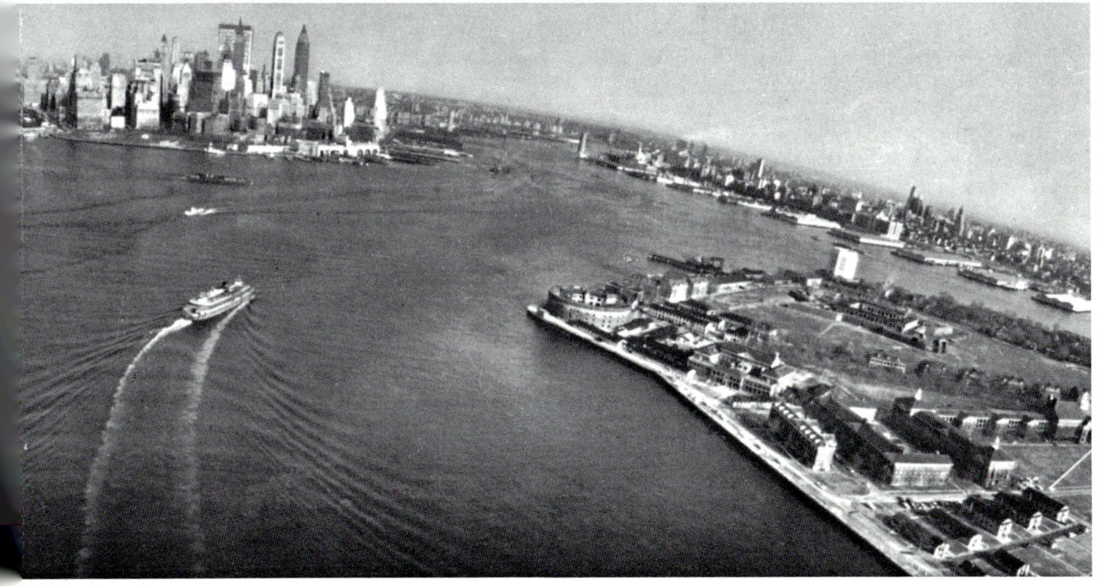

The aestheticism of nature

No landscape is unworthy of being photographed. No seasons or days, however inclement, are without a beauty of their own, or deserve to be dismissed. Naturally, subjectivity has a very large part to play in the choice of theme, and an infinite variety of occasions, interests and affinities enter into such choices. Some people feel more at ease in the fullness of summer months; some like the changing tones of autumn or feel better able to express themselves on a wet or wintry day. Nor need our preferences of today necessarily be those of tomorrow. In some periods, according to the way we feel, we prefer certain colours or environments, just as we prefer to read some books rather than others, listen to certain music or cultivate certain friendships.
We can be consistent even through very different experiences and the events of a lifetime can lead us through quite different spiritual seasons.
Some of us are more easily influenced by what we encounter at different periods; others instinctively reluctant or slow to change our tastes and habits.
The number of different cases is infinite, as is our subjectivity. But this does not prevent the reality about us from making its own choice of stimuli, not just through our culture or social relations, but also, and often to a considerable extent, in terms of the objective reality of nature. In other words, natural environments, no less than things and people, can stimulate us in a given direction. Even if every creation is always subjective, even if every interpretation of natural reality depends in the final analysis on ourselves, there is no denying that nature, in its objective form, has an effect on us. A foggy landscape can lead to romatic reflection, a sunny landscape to a sense of exhilaration, a sunset to memories of the past, a moonlit night to dreaming. This is what Rosario Assunto, in a very beautiful book entitled *Estetica del paesaggio* (The aesthetics of landscape), calls the "aestheticism of nature."
In short, nature is full of occasions and stimuli which can in themselves direct us towards certain aesthetic emotions. These will of course be entirely our own, but would probably never have existed if they had not been triggered off by references which are wholly external to us.
The fact is that there are landscapes which are capable of creating more or less strong impressions on us, and above all of different kinds.
We repeat once again that the force of these impressions depends to a large extent on us,

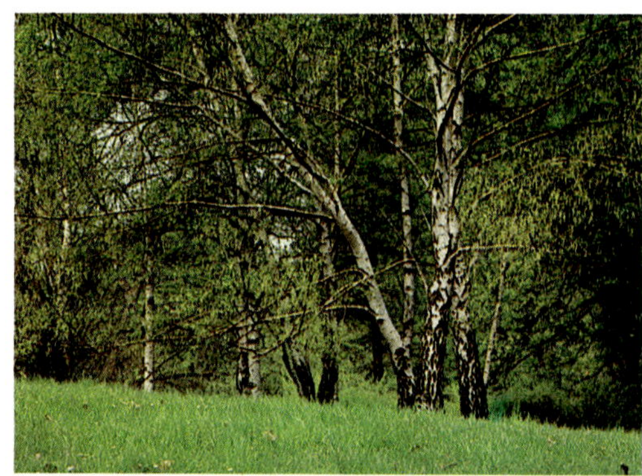

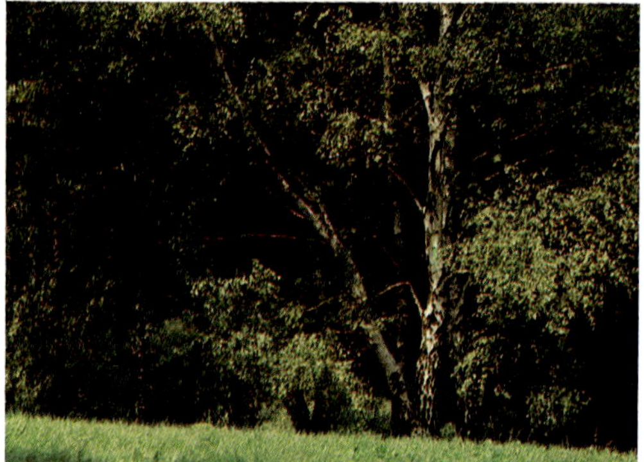

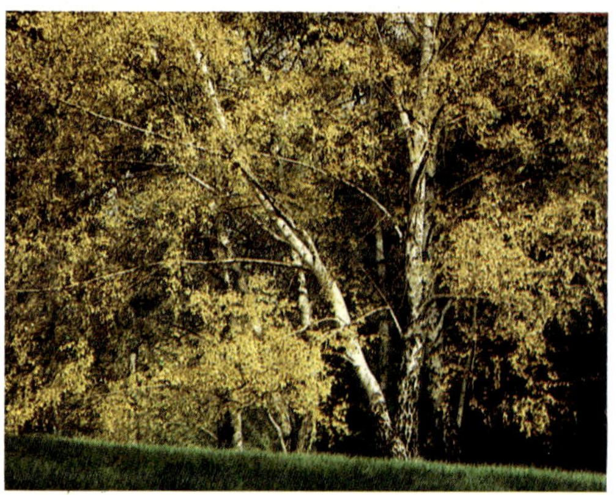

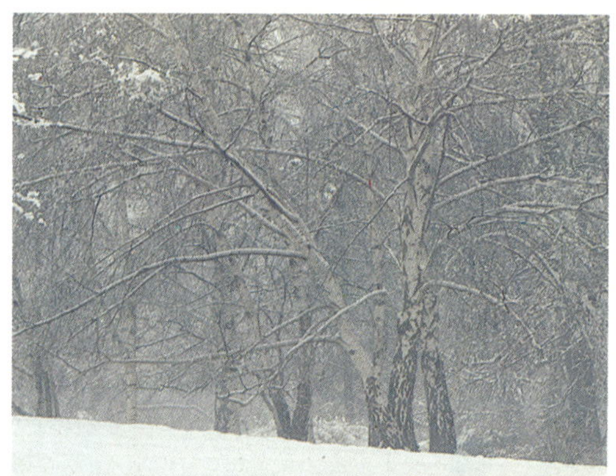

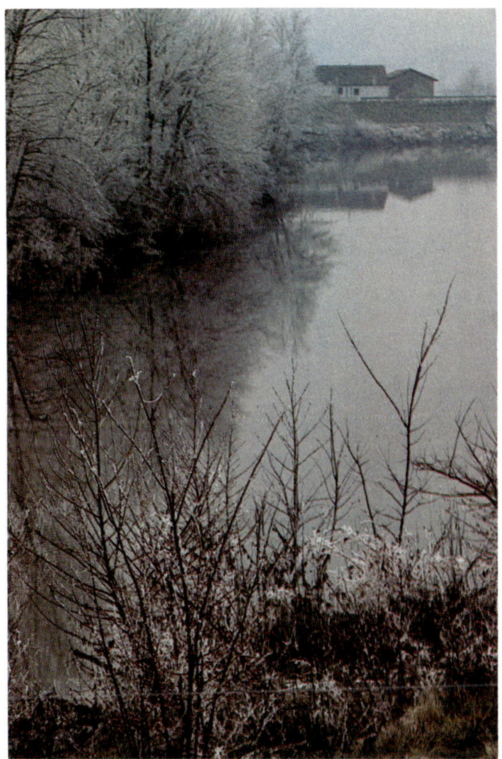
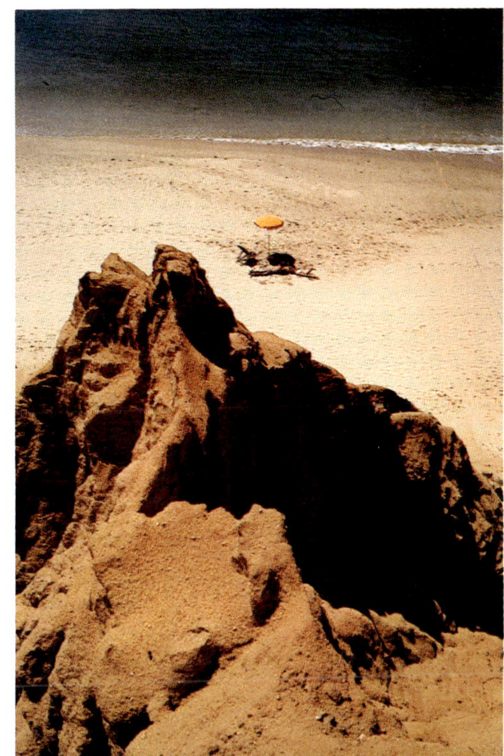

On the opposite page, a classic and inexhaustible repertoire for the landscape photographer: the evolution of the seasons; the same tree photographed in spring, summer, autumn and winter. There is no limit to the inspiration of nature.

Above, two diametrically opposed pictures taken by the same photographer, Fulvio Roiter. On the one hand, the sense of winter, the prevalence of cold tints and the graphic effects of the trees covered with frost; on the other, the triumph of the sun and summer, symbolically expressed by the immobility of the rocks and resplendent colours, and the limitless expanse of the beach and sea.
Right, another type of landscape, taken by Giorgio Lotti, the subject of which is the sky on a moonlit night. The evocative power of the image is due to the fortuitous nature of the composition and the purity of the light.

on our sensitivity. The same landscape at the same season, with the same light, can even generate contradictory feelings, depending on the memories and expectations it arouses in us. Thus a certain type of landscape need not necessarily only give rise to a certain type of emotion. The fullness of a summer landscape, which can easily arouse a sense of joyful communion with nature, can also suggest a sense of isolation and oppression to a wounded soul, who is thus disturbed by the euphoric atmosphere of that season.
The calm waters of a lake at dusk need not necessarily arouse a sense of melancholy. Some may find the strength to smooth the

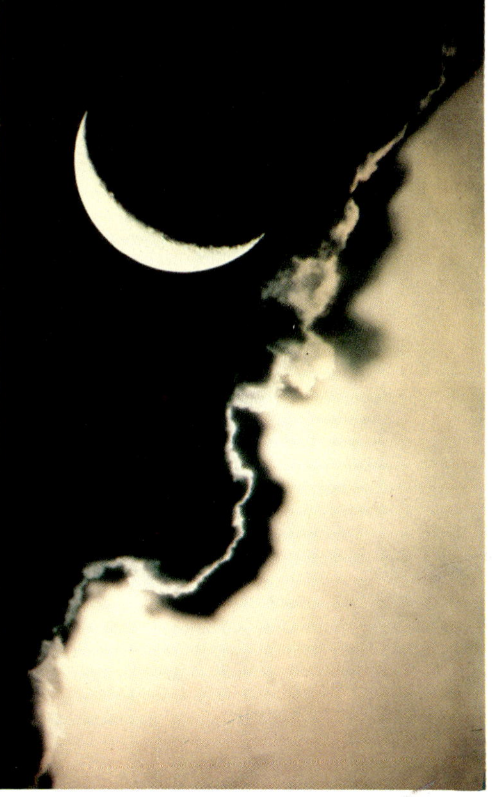

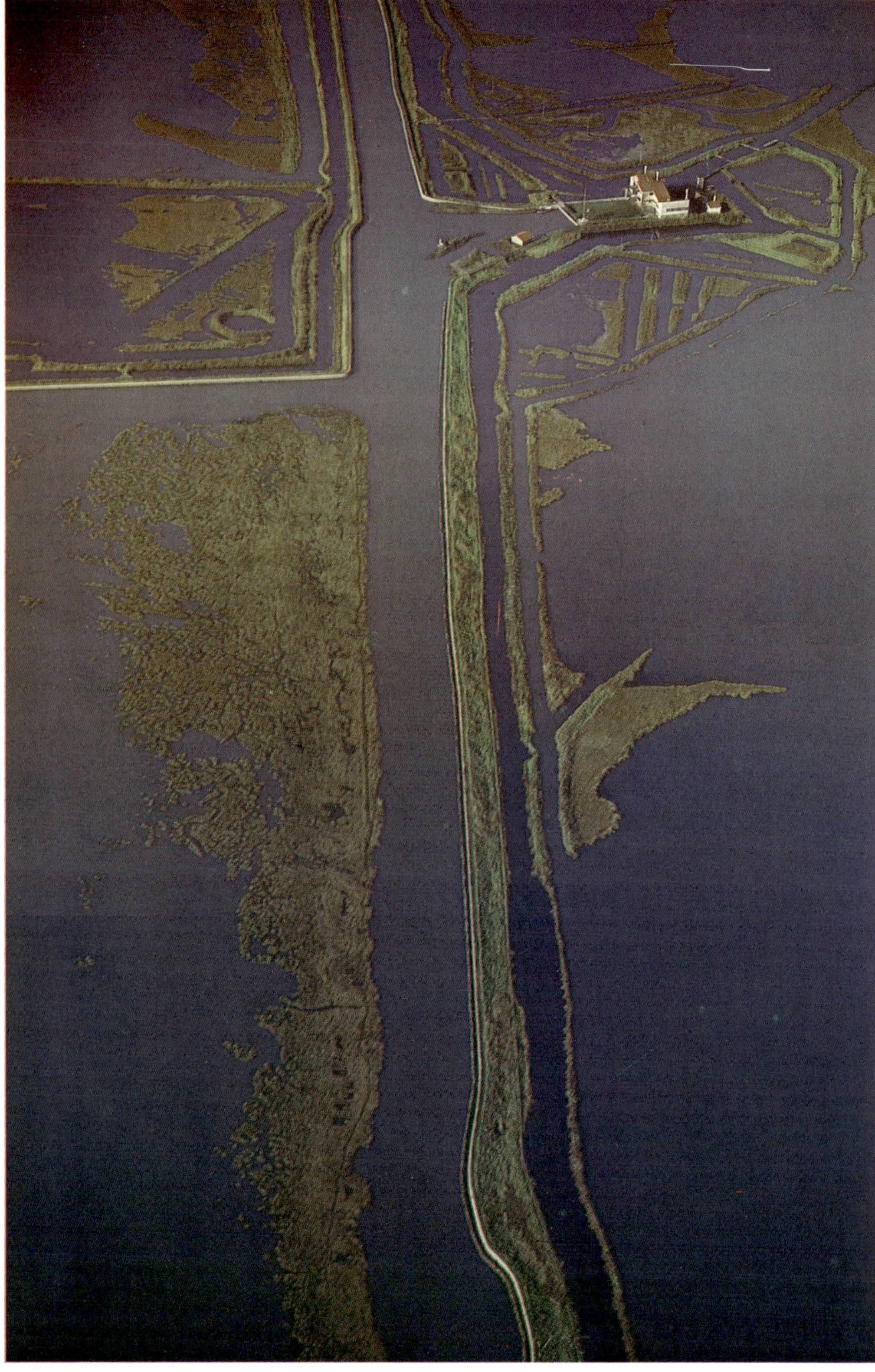

In the photograph on the opposite page, showing a lagoon characterized by the presence of canals, embankments, a few roads and isolated houses, the photographer has succeeded in giving us a clear view of elements barely emerging from the water and the uncertain profile of the alluvial deposits.

The picture below brings us back to the presence of man, which can prevail over the natural elements, given that the two bathing huts with their stereometric order, are the things which define the setting of this beach.

troubled waters of their spirit in that secluded calm and face up to the future with greater confidence. Should an isolated house on a mountainside in winter give a sense of solitude and human frailty against the forces of nature, or conjure up visions of a fireside and the tranquillity and confidence of man, master

The photograph on the right shows a landscape characterized by the effects of wind, shown not only by the direction of the fronds and fraying of the clouds, but by the undulation of the very tall, almost threadlike trunks of the palm trees, like highly sensitive needles responding to changing atmospheric conditions. Taken on the beach at Salvador de Bahia in Brazil.

of himself before the universe? Each of these responses can be perfectly legitimate. But what cannot be denied is that each of these forms of landscape has its own intrinsic structure, similar to the forms of life itself. Mountains, countryside, seas, lakes, spring, winter, windy days, noon, evening, everything which can appear before our eyes in the infinite variety of the world, has its own structure, composition, and organic unity.

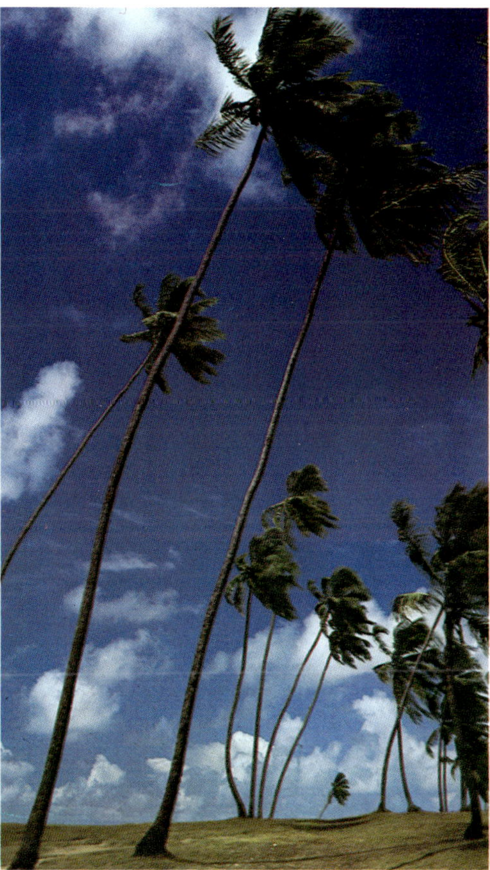

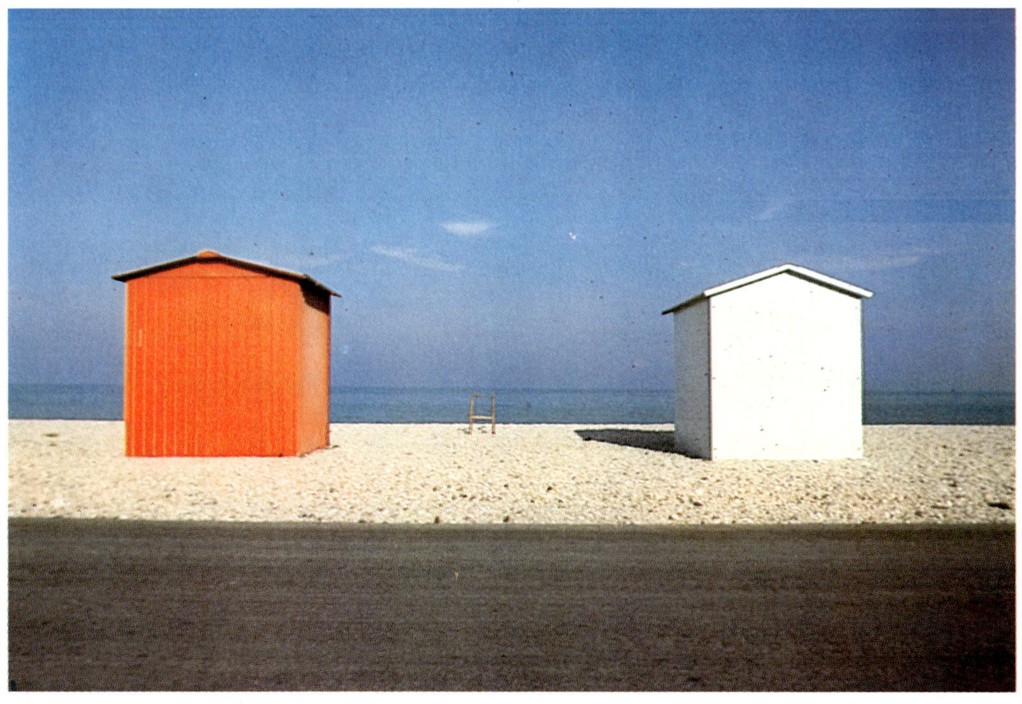

How to photograph the sea

As we have said, the material dimensions of a landscape are very important, but they are only one of the things which go to make up the landscape. In the case of a seascape it will be interesting not only to note the breadth of the horizon, but also the movement of the waves, the composition of the sky, light refraction, the presence or otherwise of wind, some boats, or the rapid flight of birds. This in the case of the open sea, but in the case of a beach or cove the forms and

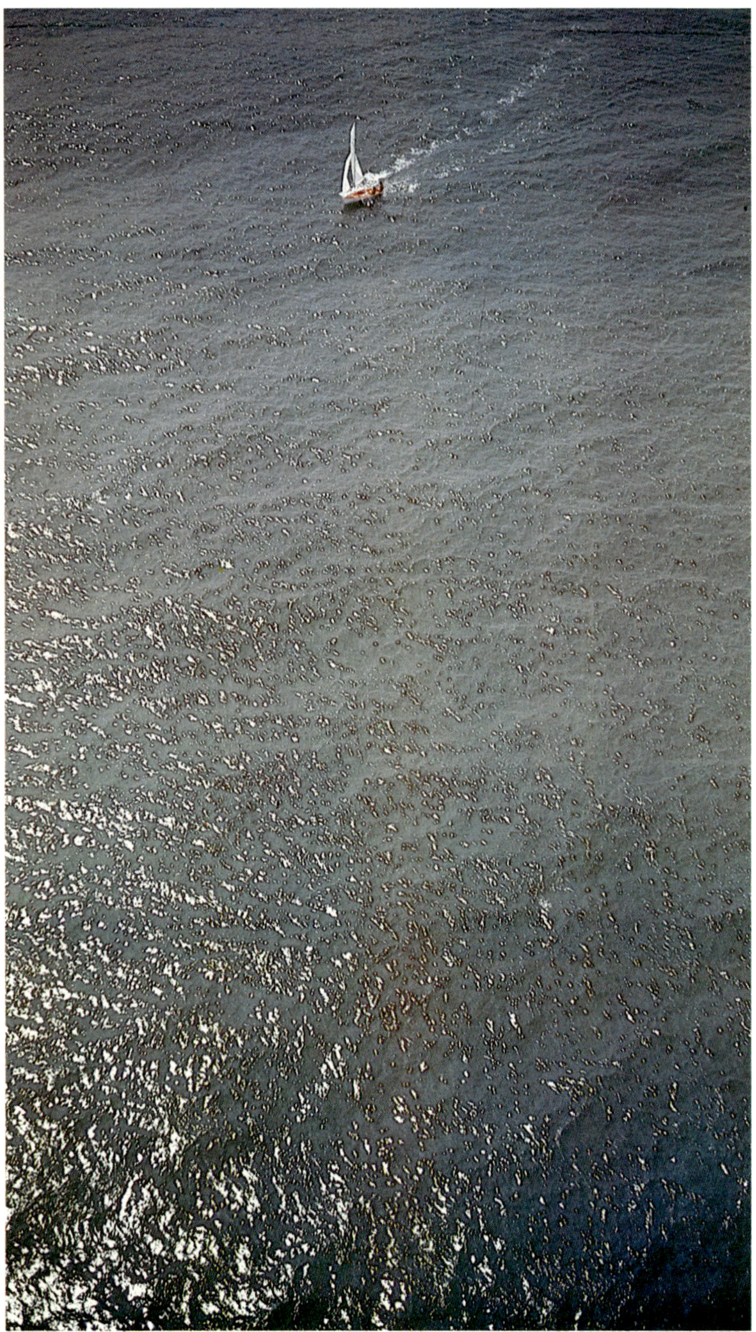

Here we have three of the infinite number of possible interpretations of the sea, each a classic of its kind. The first, taken by Fulvio Roiter, shows us some of the basic elements of a seascape: its immensity; its brilliance; its vibrant movement. While the ripple of the waves and sparkle of the reflections fully convey the last two aspects, note how the sense of space is given, by the height from which the photograph is taken and the material dimensions it embraces, and by the presence of the boat, which provides a very valuable term of reference. The profile of the sailing boat barely interrupts the enormous expanse of water through which it is ploughing, and is visible in the top part of the picture, where the waves are smaller.

The top photograph on the opposite page evokes the particular atmosphere of a fishing environment rather than the immensity of the sea.
There is no physical human presence, but this is implicit in the fish lined up to dry, which form a dynamic contrast with the rocks.
The photograph below does not show the sea, but its presence is suggested by the sandy surface of a beach studded with minute irregularities – tiny pebbles casting long shadows in the low sun, which emphasize the smooth, homogeneous nature of the ground, over which the undertow from the tide seems to have passed shortly before. A composition with an infinite number of similar details, indistinctly arranged, just like the surface of the sea, which has a great wealth of features, but is at the same time undefined and limitless. The photographer has sensed this relationship, at a moment when the light was singularly appropriate.

quality of the sand, the outline of the hills of mountains, the types of vegetation, the presence or otherwise of figures and objects, will be important motifs. If the sea is viewed from a jetty, any number of details will go to make up the scene and determine its atmosphere: the human activity taking place in that port; the various types of equipment used. Even the immensity of a seascape can be better understood from a partial view seen, for example, in relation to a beacon, a rock, or the masts of a boat, rather than a panorama of the open sea. In these cases, much of the effect of the photograph depends on the contrast in values: the finite versus the infinite; dark versus light; immobility versus movement.
Some of the most

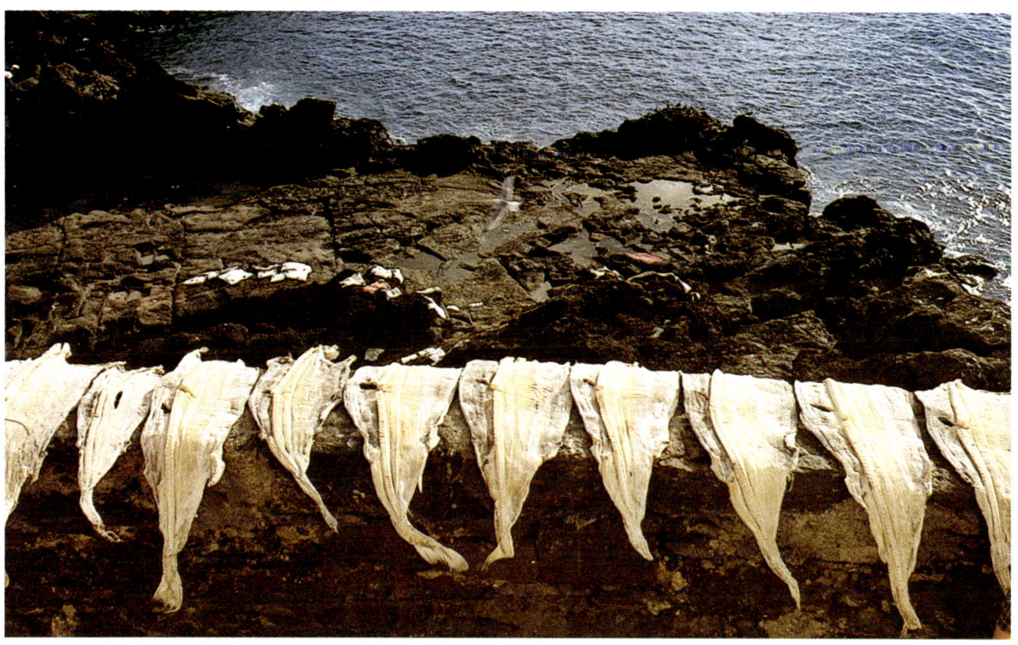

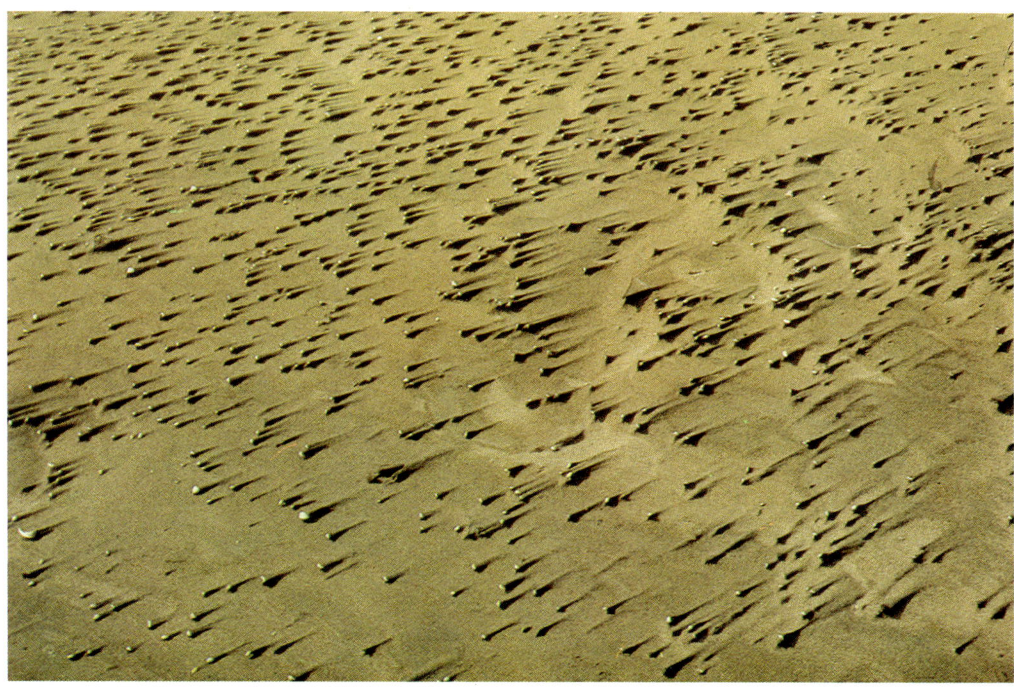

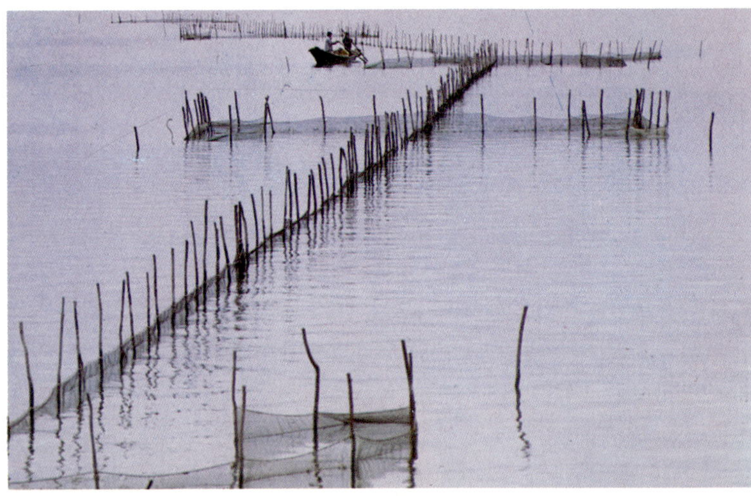

Choice of a detail can often be an enormous help, even when photographing the sea. A detail can even give a better idea of size than an overall view.
Left, by concentrating on a few details, Fulvio Roiter has reconstructed a typical scene in the fish hatcheries of the lagoon. The monotonous diagonal lines of posts holding the nets and the presence of a boat in the distance give an idea of the calm of this stretch of water and its size.

interesting aspects of pictures of the sea are the variety of reflections on the water, the movement of the waves and composition of the clouds which are often present in the marine space.
Reflections will be particularly well emphasized by taking photographs wholly or partially against the light, or even with side lighting. A constant danger with photographs taken on the seashore or from a boat of some kind is overexposure.
Therefore, it can be a good idea to use a yellow filter for black-and-white or an ultraviolet filter for colour.
The movement of the waves can be photographed to emphasize any spray or convey the general vitality of the scene by using very fast, or relatively slow, shutter speeds.
A speed of 1/500 second is the best for fixing every ripple, as if the wave had suddenly been frozen as it broke. A speed of 1/125 can show the tension of the wave itself, while at slower speeds such as 1/15, the water loses all transparency and the blurring of details will give a better idea of the continuity of movement of the sea's surface.
Obviously, colour can play a very important part in photographing the sea. You need only think of the incredible variety of light in a single day. Even the angle of the sun, first high in the sky then low on the horizon, can help show the unevenness of the beach and the waves to particular effect.
Added to this is the infinite variety of cloud compositions, the size and shape of which will vary on each occasion. A point which can easily be forgotten is that the camera must be protected very carefully from both the salt water in the atmosphere and the sand on the beach.

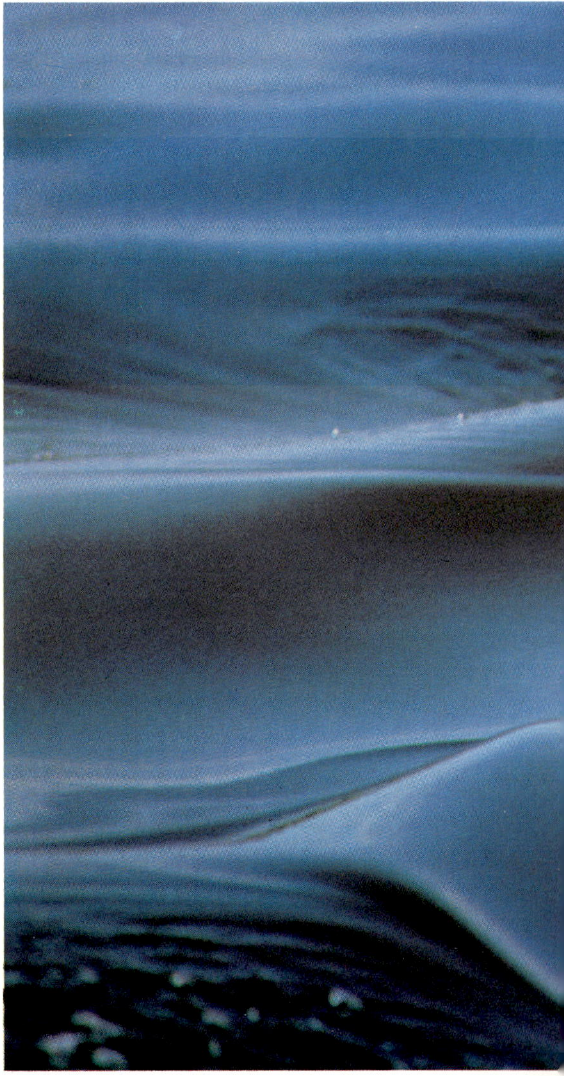

Right, here, the detail of a coloured sail and section of jetty are sufficient to show the protection of a small harbour, the activity taking place in it and the ease of access to the open sea, which envelopes the scene in its light.
Below, a masterpiece by Lotti, a reproduction of an infinitesimal portion of the undulating surface, which seems to convey all the extent and depth of the sea, set off by the radiance of the light.

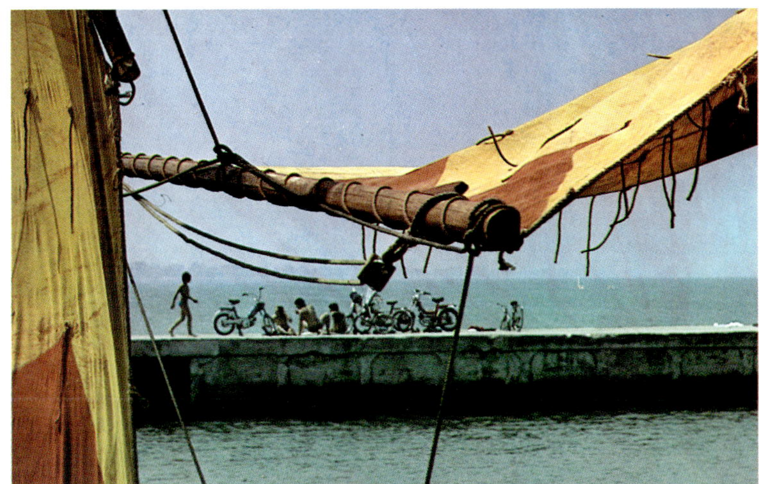

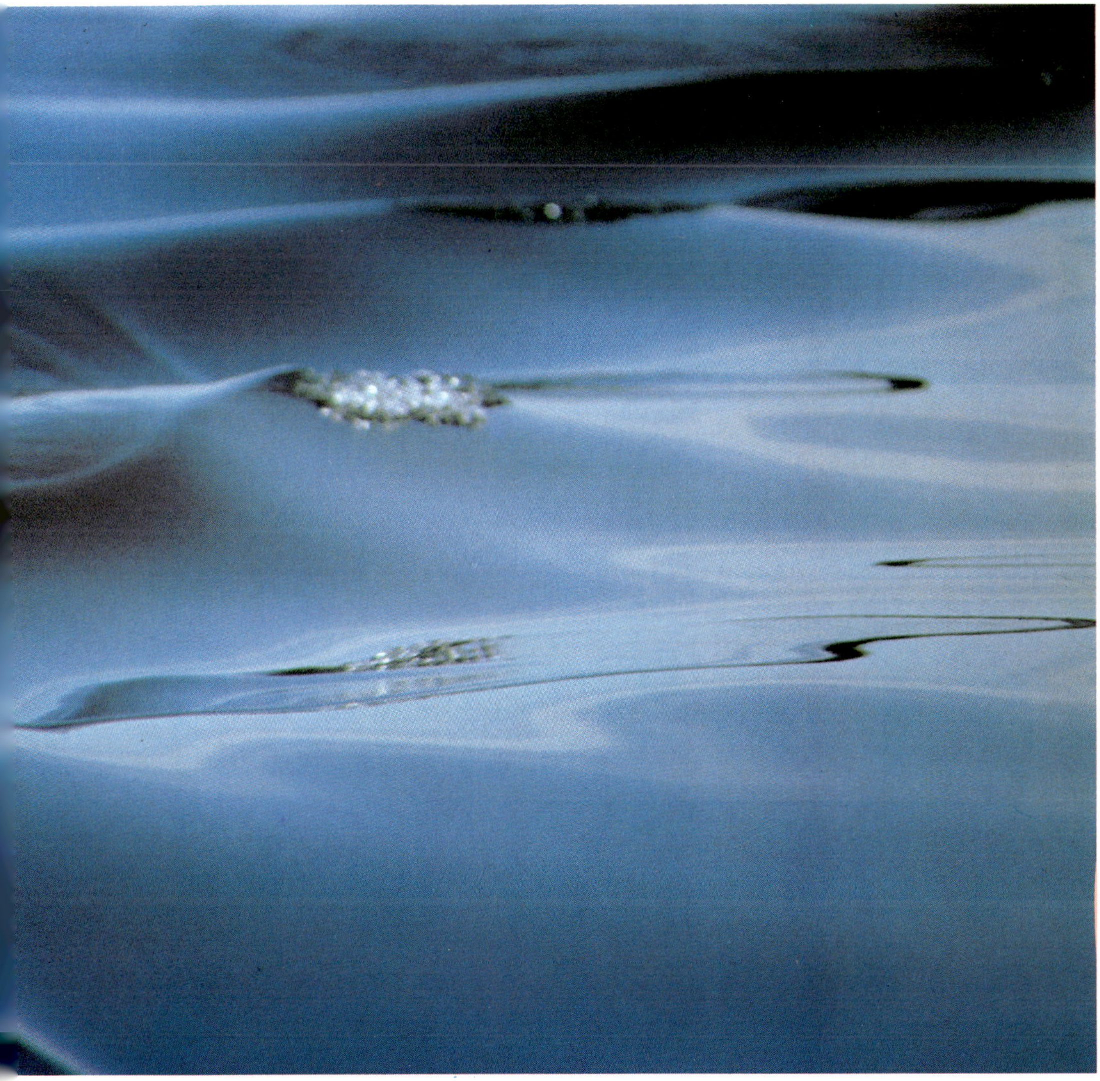

How to photograph inland waters

Sometimes the waters of the sea are still and look the same as the protected, inland waters of lakes and canals. But the thing which most distinguishes inland waters, apart from their calm surface, is the character of the banks surrounding them, which are less subject to the assault of the waves and therefore have a far greater variety of vegetation and man-made features extending to the water's edge.

This is very important if you consider that one of the basic characteristics of calm waters is their ability to mirror what is before them. The symmetry of a landscape reflected in water is a source of endless fascination to the photographer. It can be rendered by an exact duplication of the real landscape in a motionless surface, or reproduce the wave motion of the spread of concentric circles formed when the surface is disturbed by a falling object – the movement of an oar, for example, or simply a stone thrown into the water.

If the photograph is taken against the light, the quiver of the water will be accompanied by a slight sparkle of reflections, capable of enriching all the details mirrored on the surface.

Calm water often looks uninviting, like a rather dark, monotonous mass. Therefore, the environment reflected in these waters, which are a lot less lively than sea water when they are still, is very important as is everything which can be fitted into a frame of both the shore and water. Or you can wait for a light breeze to ruffle the surface, or again create movement artificially which, even if very slight, can still be interesting.

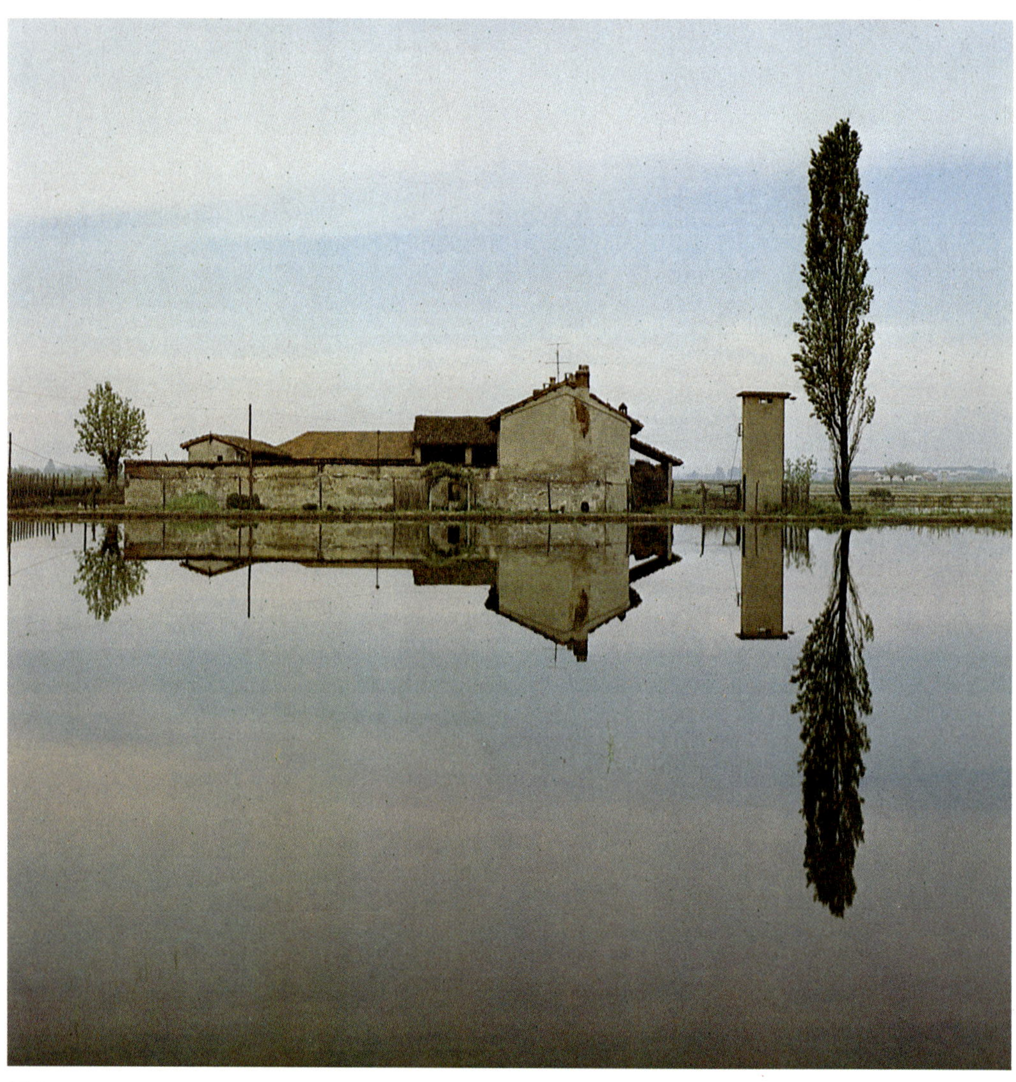

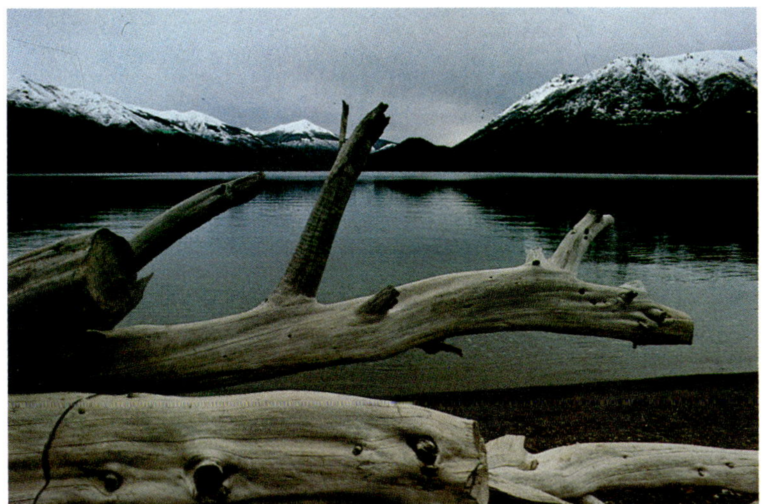

As when photographing the sea, photographs against the light can be particularly effective because it is in this position that reflections are created.
But inland waters need not always be interpreted in a melancholy fashion. The same applies to these as to all landscape photographs: nature can predispose a certain state of mind, a certain interpretation. But the exact opposite can occur, enabling

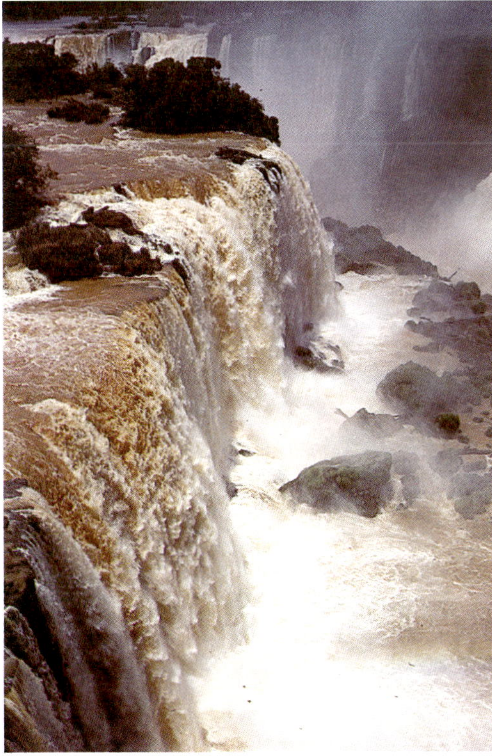

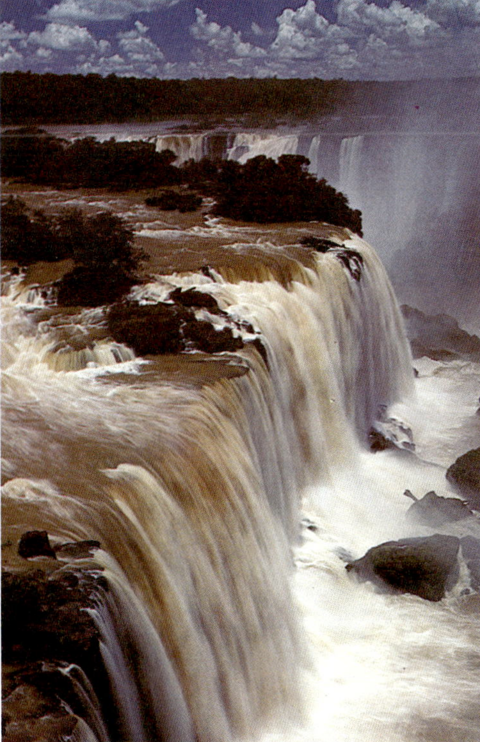

Sheltered waters can provide other solutions, as in the photograph on the opposite page, where the clarity of the reflected part shows the absolute immobility of the surface.

Above, the photographer has played on the contrast between an equally motionless surface and the irregularity of the treetrunks.
Below, the Iguaçu Falls in Brazil: here we have two different ways of rendering the movement of water, first freezing the foam, second, emphasizing its speed, by using different exposure times.

the photographer to produce, for example, an image bursting with vitality out of a small, completely motionless pond.
The mention of ponds brings to mind other themes apart from those characterized by very broad views of lakes and rivers: torrents and streams, in which the liveliness and transparency of the water can be particularly interesting; swimming pools, fountains and city canals.

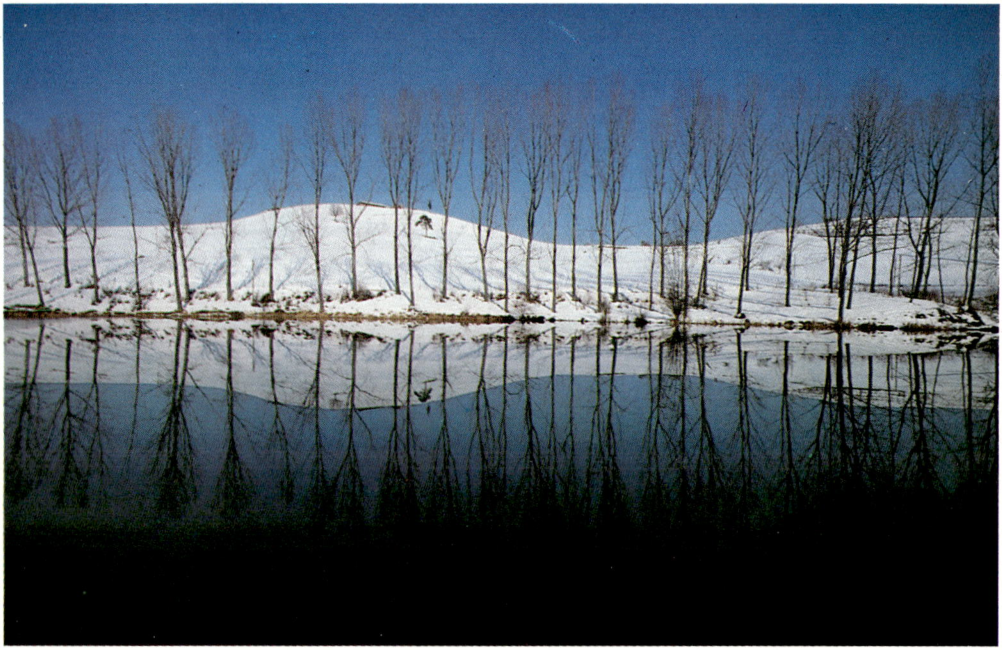

Here are two photographs which interpret these worlds of calm waters in profoundly different ways, but both using rhythmic sequences.
Above, Fontana has emphasized the sense of frequency of the trees not just by taking them in a horizontal frame, but by "duplicating" them, so to speak, in their reflection in the water. The optical horizon is exactly half-way up, underlining the reflective qualities and equivalence of the two parts. The top one, dominated by the sky; the bottom one, extending into the water, introducing light values and a sense of equivalent indeterminacy and fluidity which makes the surrounding atmosphere still more rarified.
Below, de Biasi has captured the parallelism of the wave motion, which is extremely regular, but carries on its surface indistinct colours and reflections of the natural surroundings.

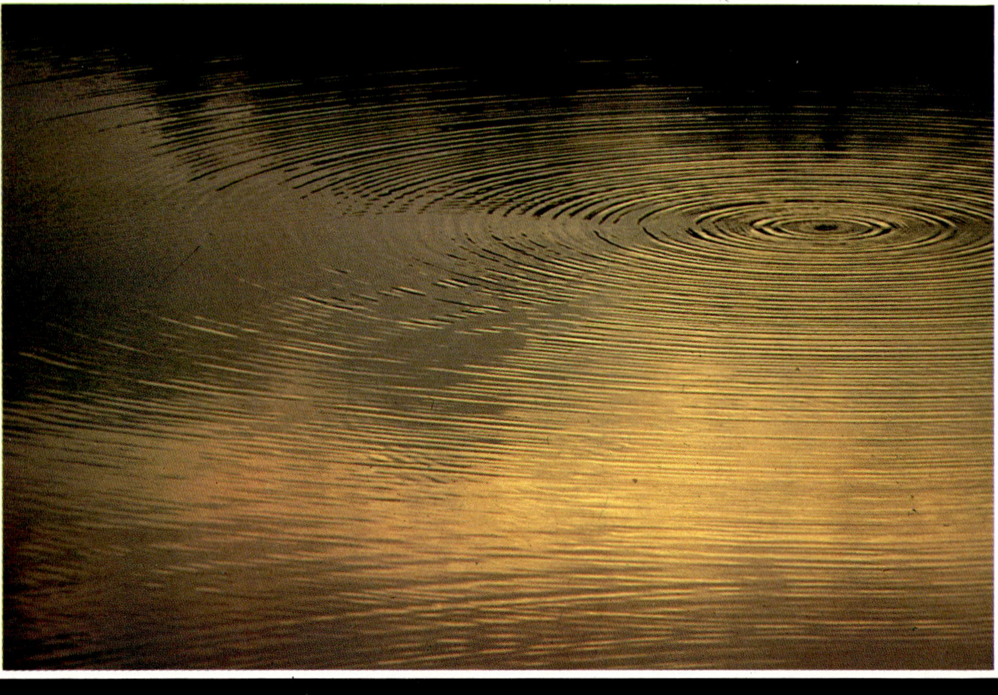

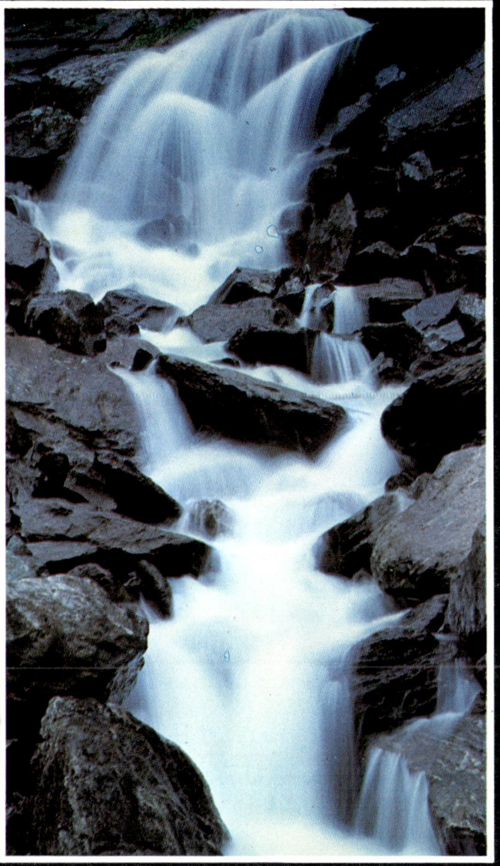

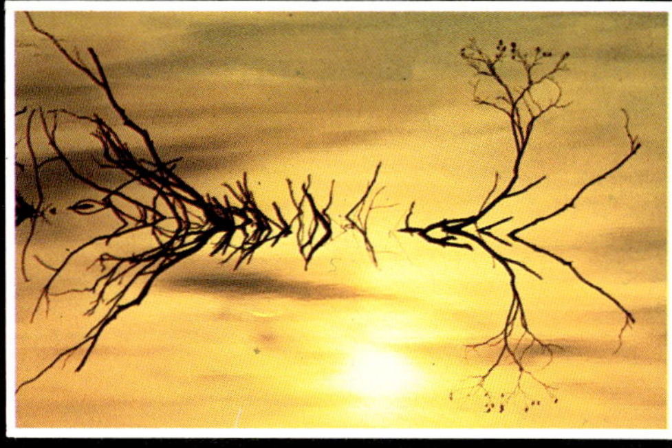

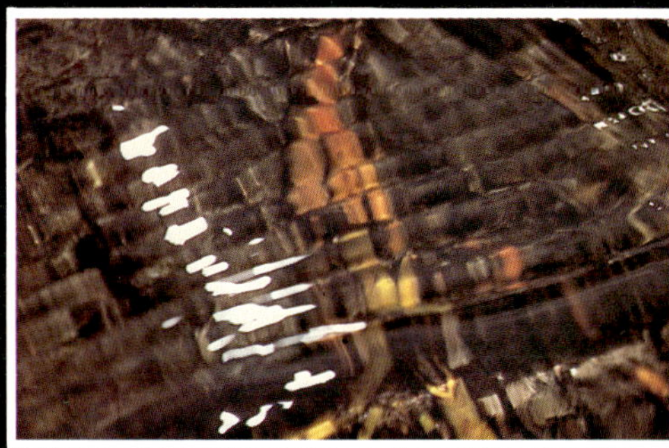

The photograph top left, taken with a blue filter, captures the epic, monumental movement of a waterfall. At the opposite extreme, the photograph top right owes its beauty to the emergence of a shrub, whose profile is redrawn in the golden reflection. The one above reveals the marvellous transparency of a mountain stream. Below is a view of the broad, uniformly-coloured surfaces of the lagoon fish hatcheries.

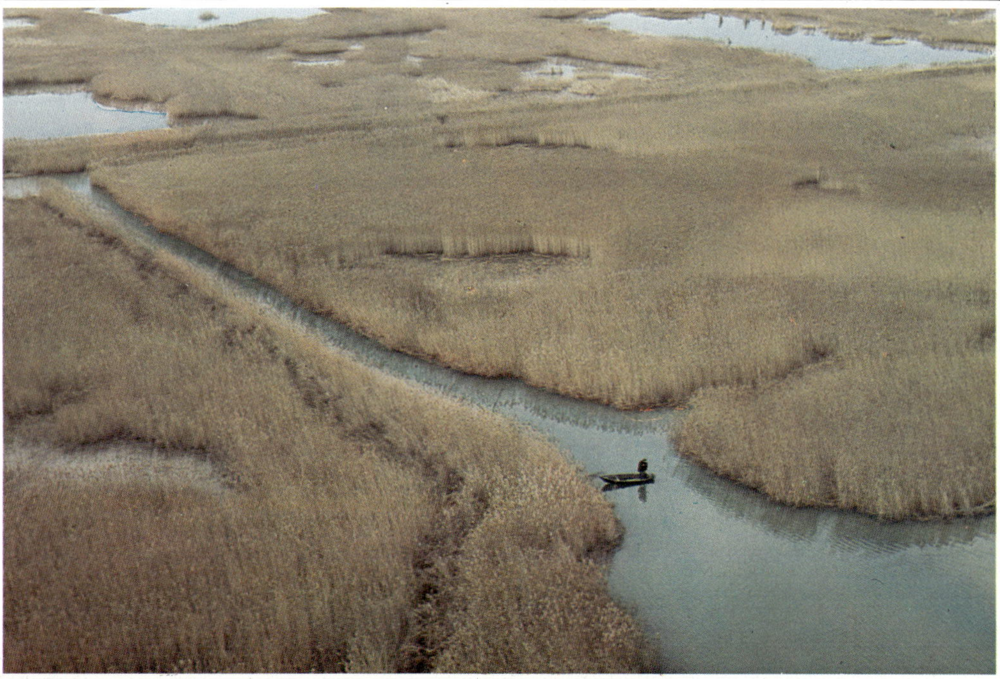

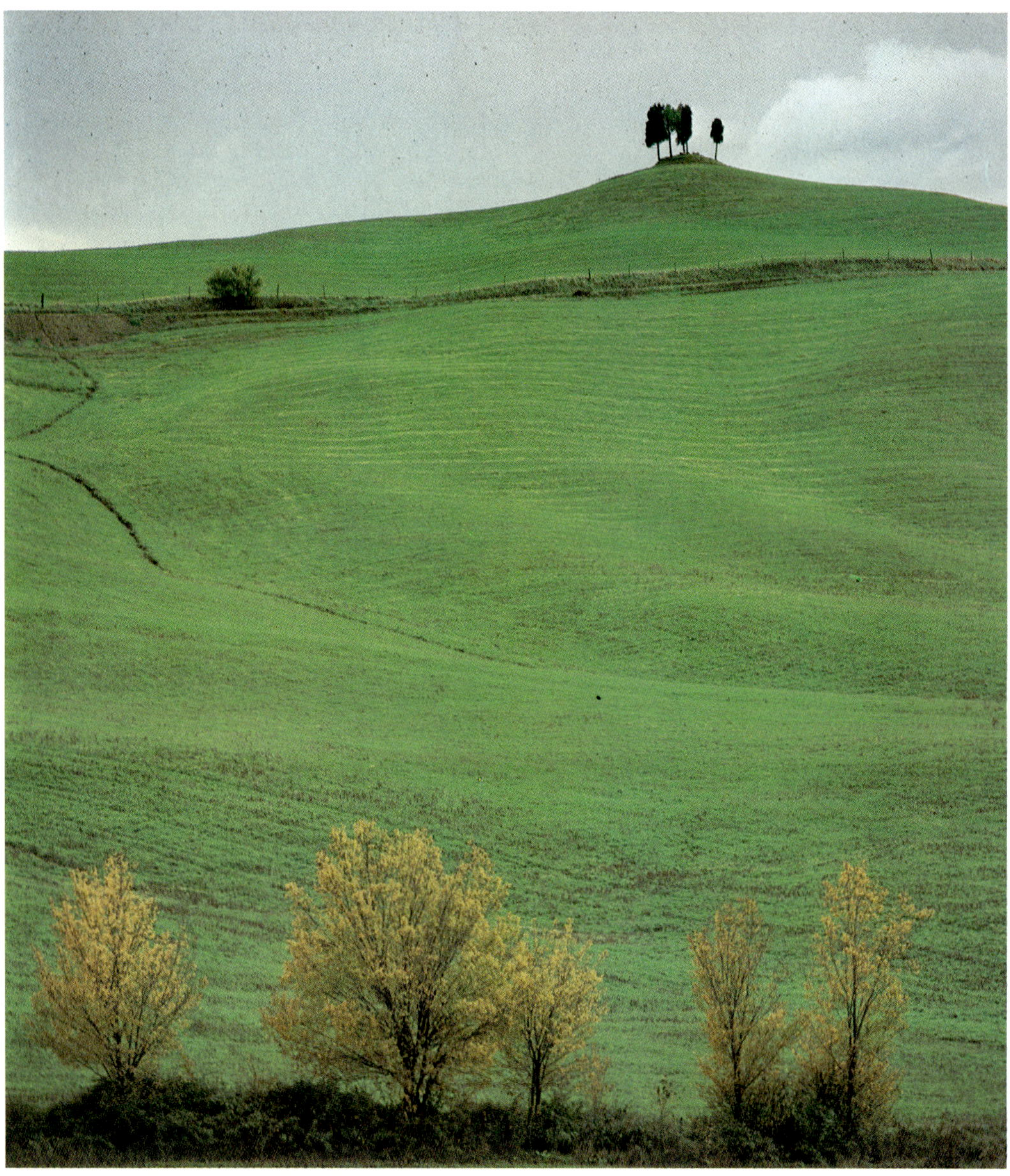

How to photograph the countryside

The sea, mountains or lakes might appear to offer the best choice of opportunities for taking good photographs. But this is a very superficial, though common, view because it only takes account of the emotions some sea or mountain environments can arouse, above all because they are unusual and highly distinctive. The quality of a photograph is not measured by the subject matter, but by its execution. And the value of any natural environment depends on how it is interpreted.
Certainly the sea, or mountains, can greatly stir the imagination, but this can even be counterproductive because the ease with which some subjects can be made to look interesting can distract us from a more considered technical effort. We should test our sensitivity and creative capacity on the normal, not the exceptional, and nothing is more normal from this point of view than a rural landscape.
The countryside involves the work of man, the cultivation of the fields, and as such is mainly concerned with planes and hills – two environments, particularly the first, which might seem unable to offer us particularly original themes, due both to the scarcity of large theatrical "props" in lowlands and the relative monotony of

These pictures show us three ways of photographing the rural environment, which can be no less rich or original a subject than other landscapes.
In the photograph on the opposite page by Cappelli, reproducing the hilly scenery of Tuscany near Colle Val d'Elsa, the dominant green colour, which is often such a problem to photographers, has been given a vital role in the composition.

The subtle graphic motifs of the photograph on the right by Cavallero, showing a flower plantation in Liguria, reappear in geometric form in an aerial photograph by Roiter below.

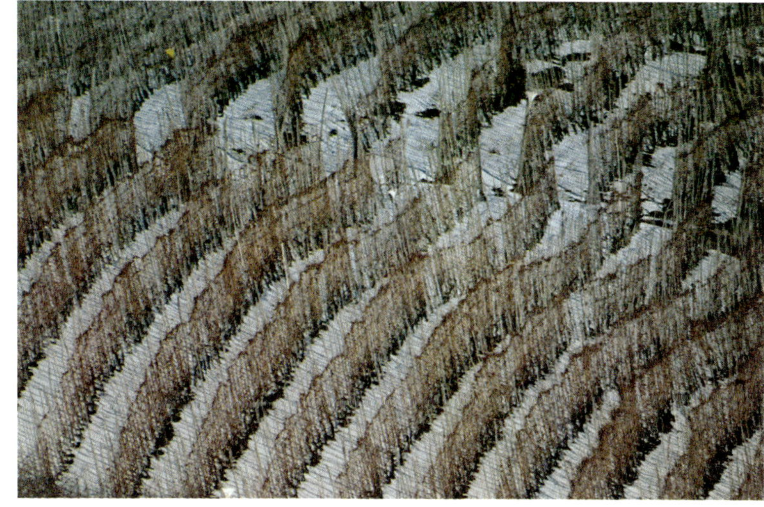

profiles in hills. How wrong this impression can be is demonstrated by the landscape painting of the past, in which Italian, English and Dutch lowlands and hills served as a model for any number of masterpieces. Cultivated countryside, both flat and hilly, has the advantage of combining a geometric order, due to the rational intervention of man, with the spontaneity of nature. The predominance of one or other of these elements varies with the seasons, so that the compositional rhythms and chromatic values are for ever changing. Furthermore, the countryside has a particular human equilibrium, in which the themes of work, traditions and the intimacy of the family are often present, not to mention other elements which characterize it from an historical point of view, to which we shall be returning later. The countryside contains an infinite number of details: farmhouses, implements, animals, flowers, trees, walls and hedges, not to mention the major elements which characterize any type of landscape: horizons, which are particularly vast here, scenic clouds, the play of light and shade at different times of day and, of course, the things which make every piece of country-

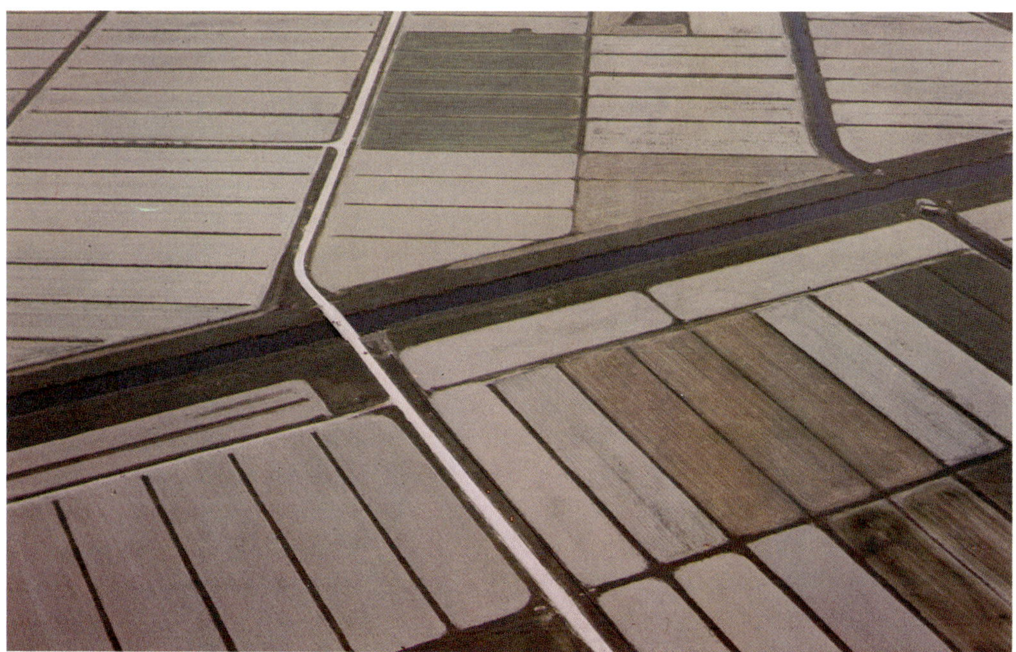

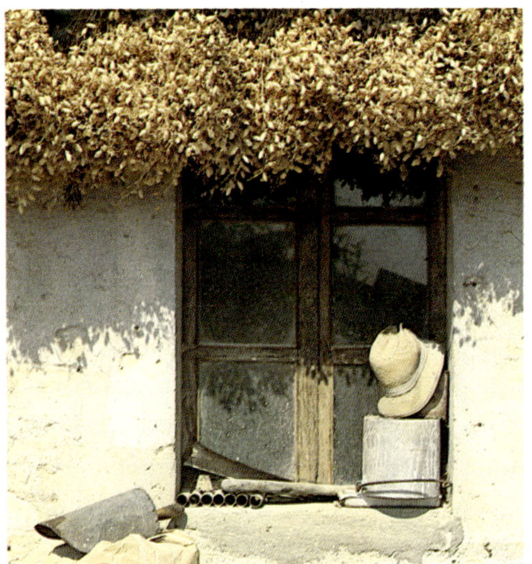

side, hill and plain unique.
Precisely because they often look anonymous and unrelated to any known or easily definable panorama, country landscapes lend themselves to free representation, depending more on an interpretation of the atmosphere of an environment than its description.
This does not prevent even overall views from being possible and effective, remembering that hilly scenery is particularly full of movement and offers broad, panoramic views. And even on plains you only need rise up above them slightly, on to a belfry or even the upper floor of a cottage, for the surrounding area to assume staggering proportions, with particularly grandiose horizons.
The countryside is capable of striking every poetic chord within us, the serene and intimate notes, as well as the solemn and dramatic ones.

This photograph by Gian Paolo Cavallero carries evocation of a landscape to the limit. Strictly speaking, it has virtually nothing of the landscape, being a detail of a country cottage, almost a still life. Yet everything combines to recreate the environment, its frugality, the simple life that takes place there.
The photograph below, however, despite embracing a relatively large area of countryside near Salzburg, appears to be more interested in capturing the almost abstract geometric motif of the two intersecting roads than in revealing the surrounding atmosphere.

On the opposite page, the terraced slopes of the Shansi heights: an excellent documentation of a subject which is in itself very clearly defined.

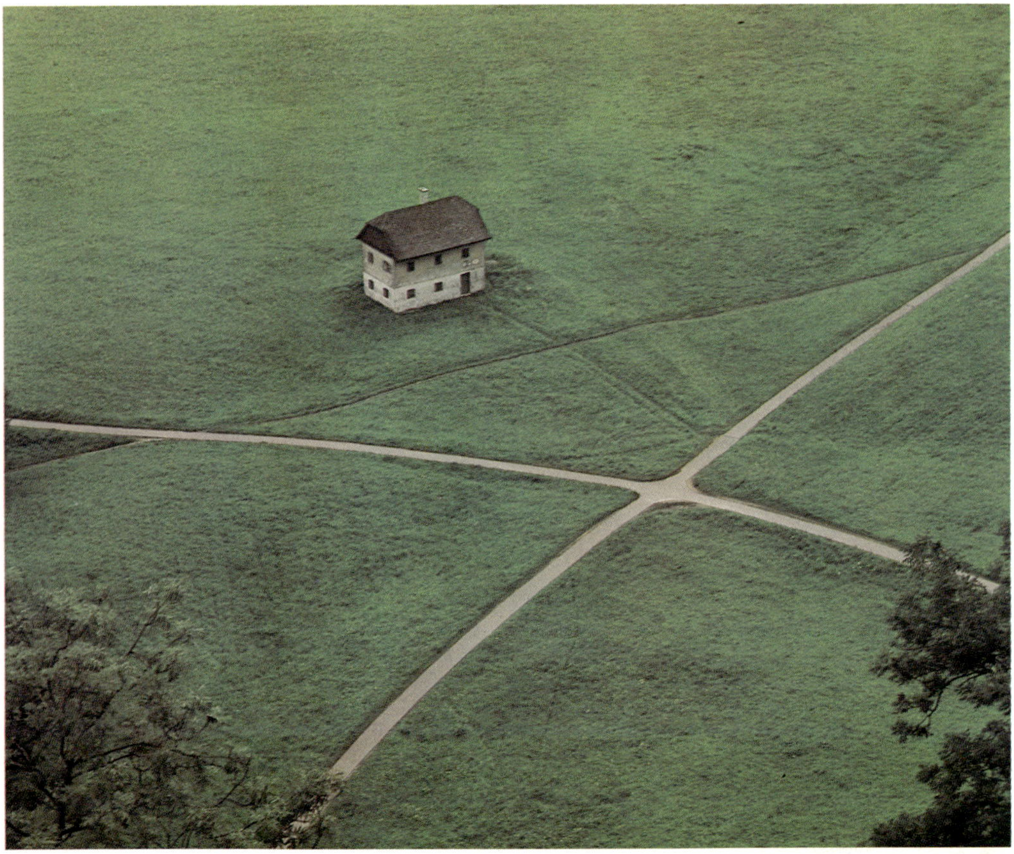

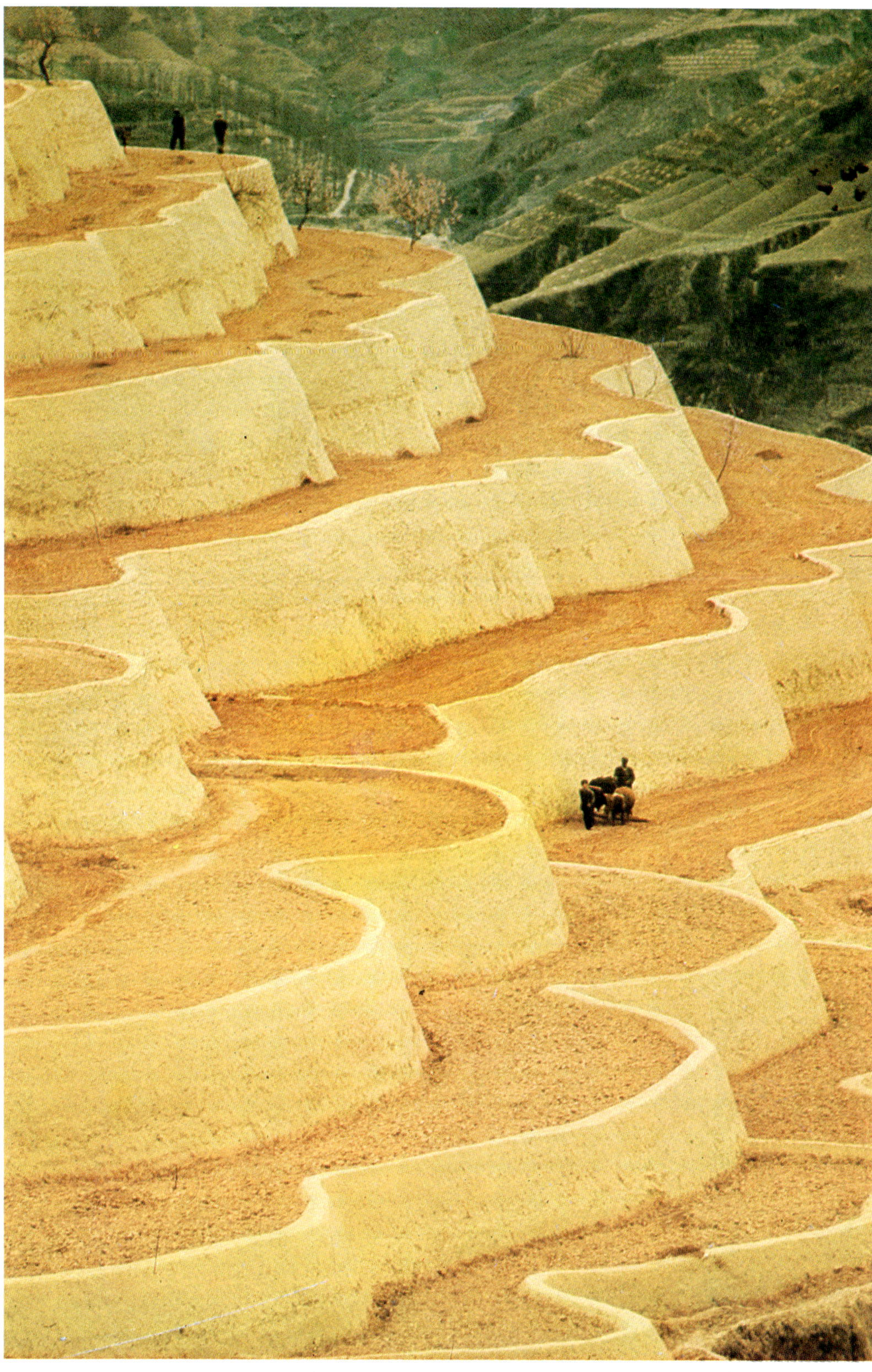

How to photograph the desert

The desert, with its aridity, monotony and monochrome tones, might seem little suited to photography, inasmuch as it rejects all forms of life. The desert regions of the earth vary a great deal in their configuration: sometimes they are flat, sometimes mountainous, sometimes they consist of bare rock, or great oceans of sand. In any case, they appear to be dominated by a few, unfailing attributes: the feeling of immensity, often of desolation, and the abstract, elementary nature of their shapes. All this can be complicated and enriched when these elements of the desert proper meet or are combined with others, above all if the desert adjoins less arid regions, or is interrupted by an oasis, or where human presence is included in the desert, perhaps by chance, as if bound up in an age-old symbiosis.

The photographer will need to take account of a few obvious material factors: the torrid heat during the day and the effect this can have on equipment (especially films); the intense light, because sand and rock surfaces reflect the sun and atmospheric light and therefore pose similar problems to those

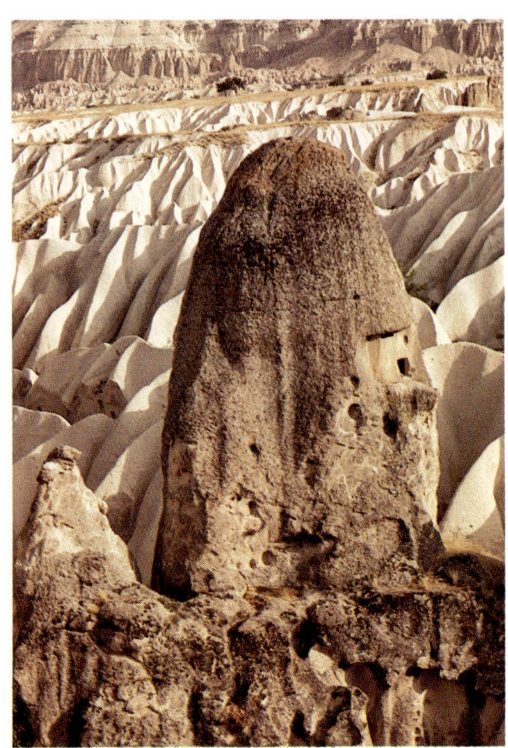

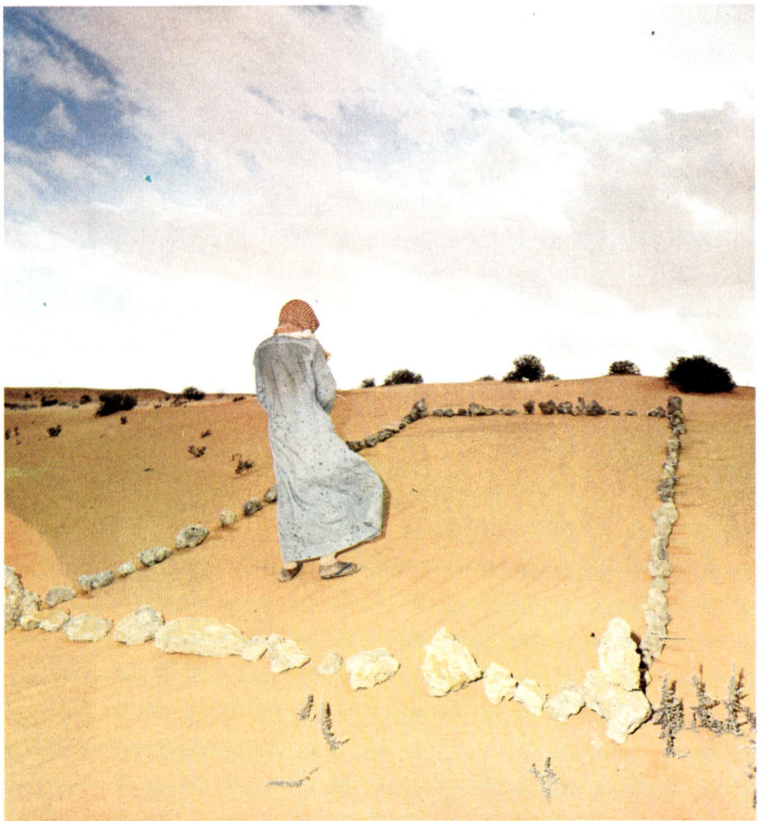

Four very different images of desert regions. Above, the photographer has chosen to reproduce the objective geological features of the area, emphasizing the extraordinary relief of the landscape, whereas the photograph on the left is almost wholly dominated by the human figure and its evocative significance. Note the insistence on the almost flat profile of the figure, contrasted with the geometrical perspective of the stones, surrounded in turn by an unbounded space, with the result that the composition assumes the clear order of certain Symbolist paintings of the early twentieth century.

On the opposite page: above, the rudimentary geometry of the village suggests the proximity of the desert; below, a magnificent illustration of sand dunes, barely interrupted by the contrast with a passing flock at the base of the picture.

encountered when photographing snow or some seascapes. Finally, in sand deserts, the ability of the sand itself to penetrate objects can cause irreparable damage to camera mechanisms, lenses and films.

As the climate in deserts is very stable, the only objective variations to the landscape are those caused by light, by its direction and the height of the sun above the horizon. The photographer has a very wide range of choices from this point of view and can emphasize or play down the chiaroscuro rhythms, which can assume a decisive role in the composition.

Desert landscapes are particularly suited to the type of abstract creation which for that matter any photographer of imagination can always produce, even out of less distinctive environments. But, as we said, the morphology of the desert is diverse and even in the most difficult situations, no natural creations are not or cannot be related to man, and the presence of the human element, whether direct or indirect, will always be highly effective.

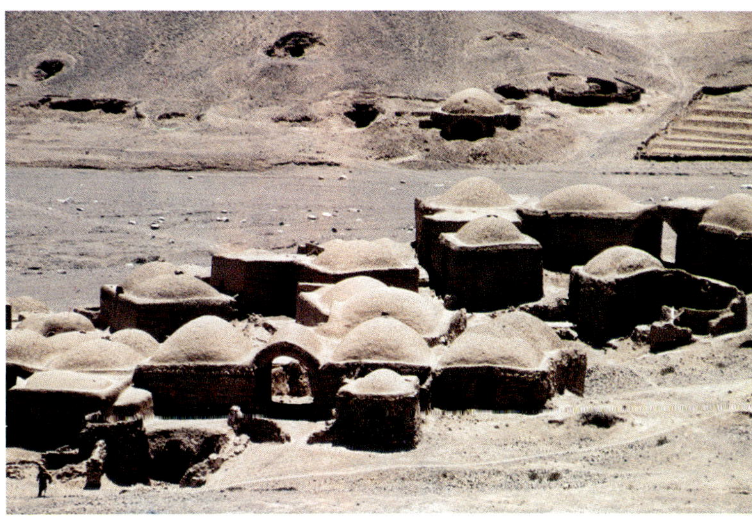

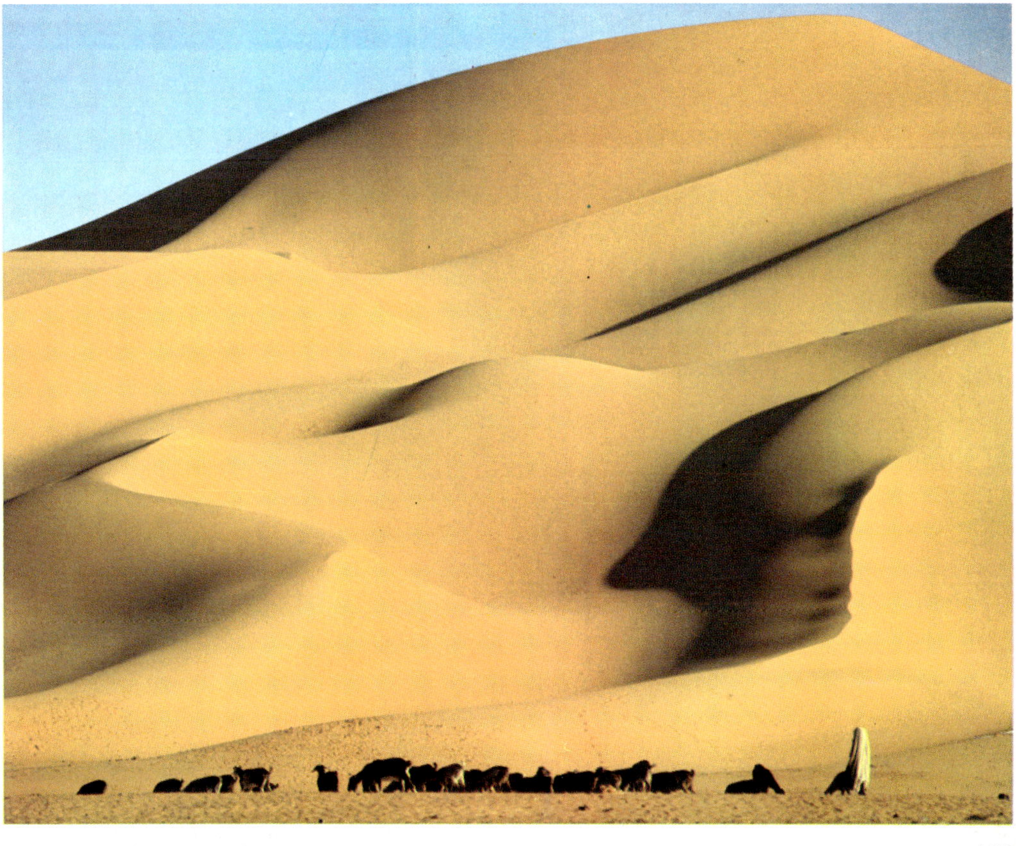

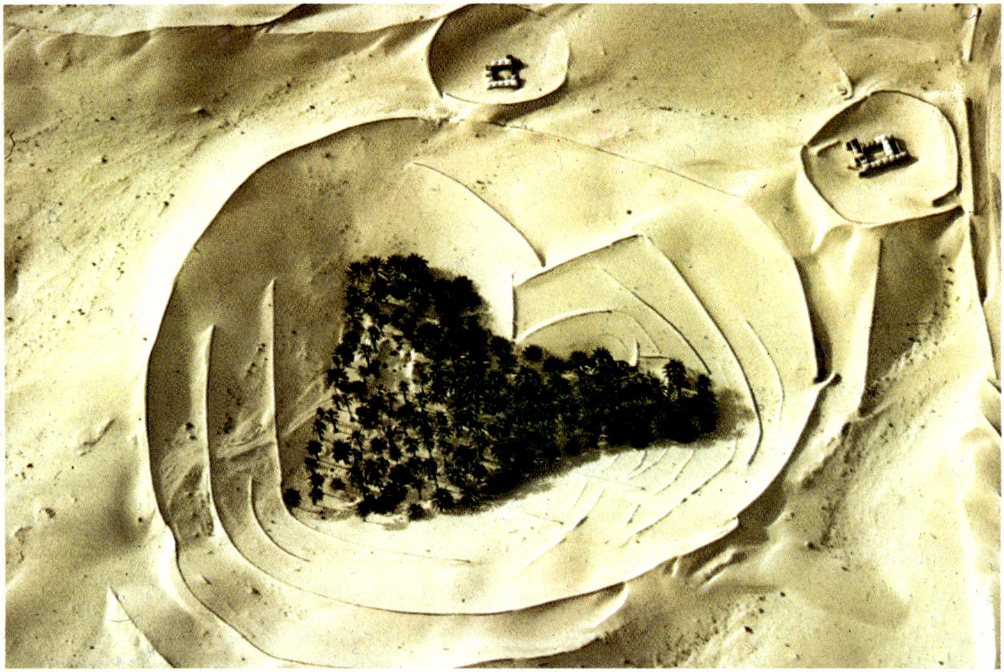

Aerial photographs make particularly good abstract compositions, obviously all the more so in the case of desert regions. The two photographs on this page, however, also do a magnificent job of describing the subject, and represent two very interesting pieces of scientific evidence. The photograph above shows an oasis in the desert; the one below, the effects of a migrant dune which has engulfed a road. The first shows us with extreme clarity the exceptional nature of the phenomenon caused by the emergence of a spring of water, and at the same time portrays the entire scene with jewel-like precision.

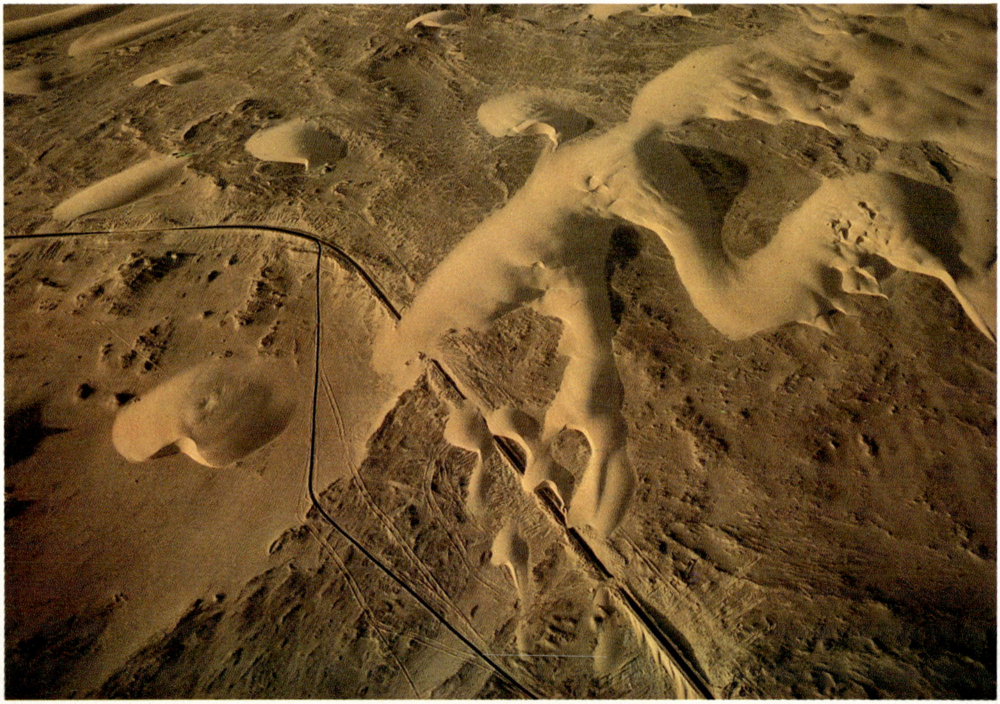

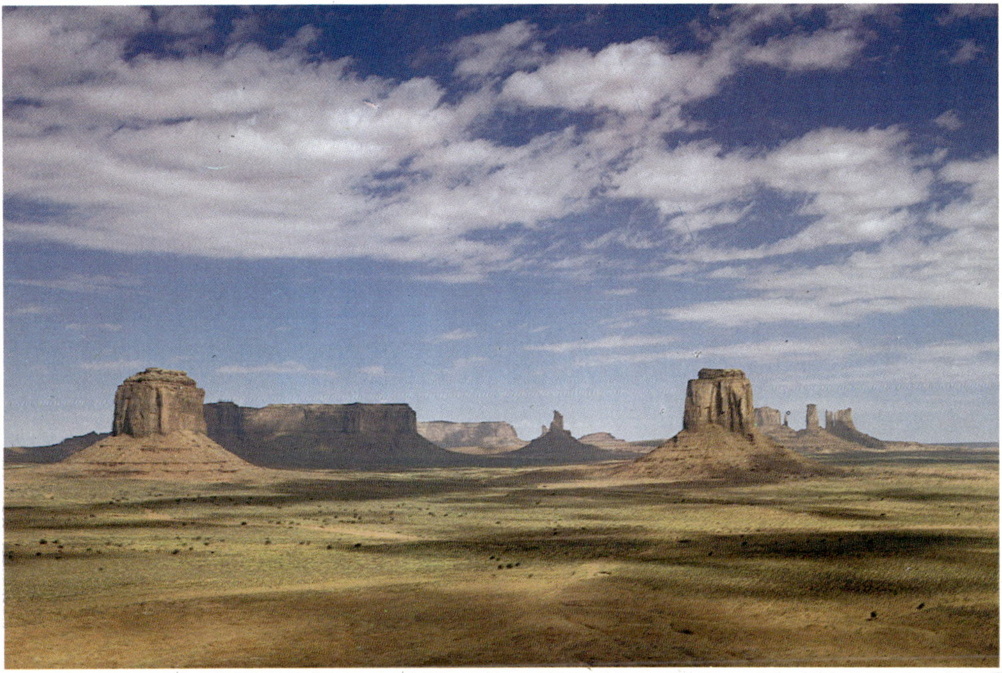

The vivid contrasts, the balance of the composition, the acutely subtle analysis, make us overlook any other factors the environment might have suggested to us, everything relying on the extreme transparency of form, and at the same time, the magical character of the scene.
The other photograph also has a documentary value and is very skilfully framed, to show us the movement of the dune both in its continuity and in its spread across the thin, highly regular, opposing outline of the road – a sure sign of human intervention.

On this page: we could not omit a view of Monument Valley, Arizona, one of the most famous desert landscapes, due both to the exceptional nature of the geological phenomenon which composes it and the fact that it is based on a panorama which is now a classic feature of Westerns.
In this respect, Monument Valley has now become an historic landscape, in which the natural elements and historical associations are combined, imposing certain types of image which make it recognizable, like so many other famous places.
These photographs are often the hardest to take, because the places have become so stereotyped in our memories, that they have to reproduce "exactly right," so that the picture is instantly recognizable.
In these photographs, conventionality is a necessary attribute and the photographer therefore has far less freedom than in other cases. St. Peter's Square in Rome, like Monument Valley or the Three Peaks of Lavaredo, must, of course, appear as they are, but a clever photographer can always bring even the most overworked subjects to life.
The photograph on the right relies for its effect on the contrast between the plant and the sandy ground, covered in furrows from the wind, human footprints and the marks produced by the waving of the long, dry leaves.

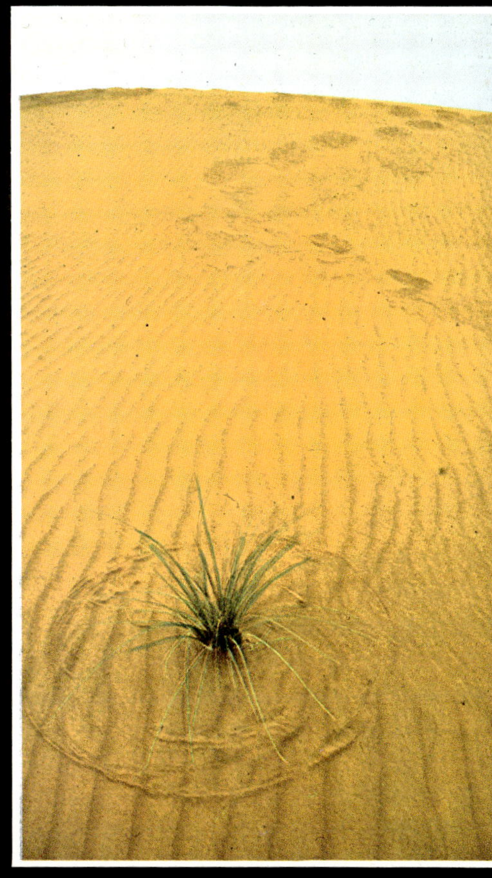

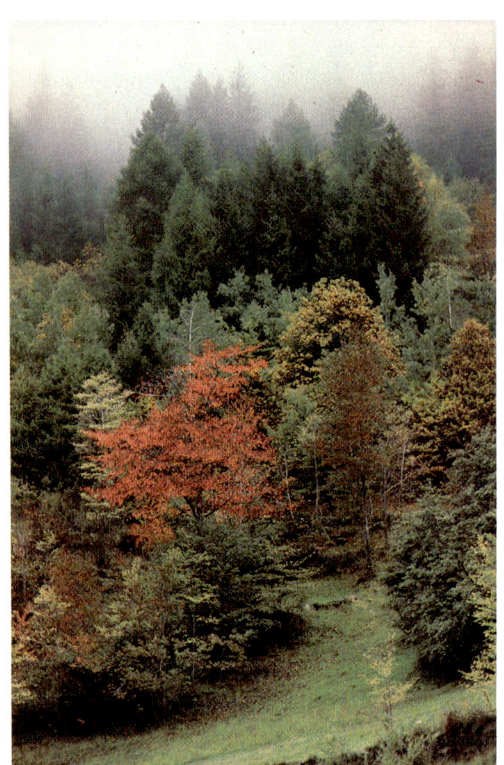

How to photograph woods and forests

Expert photographers know what difficult subjects trees and forests are, above all in summer, when the vegetation is more luxuriant. During the winter it can be interesting to capture the linear motifs of the bare branches of a tree, and the effects that snow, ice and hoarfrost can produce on them. In spring, blossom time makes a fascinating subject. The trees are still quite bare; their foliage is light. In autumn, we have the other spectacle of the forest lighting up with multiple tones of red and yellow. While in summer, the colours are much more homogeneous and essentially uniform and monotonous and a predominance of green can deprive the composition of life and depth. Furthermore, the leafy branches of a tree are often in movement; this poses the problem of whether to fix the details with a very short exposure time or give the image a more impressionistic character, with a very long exposure time, making them appear as broad, indistinct masses. Other problems concern the undergrowth, or the very details of the wood, which often show a strong contrast of light and shade, making it difficult to find the right

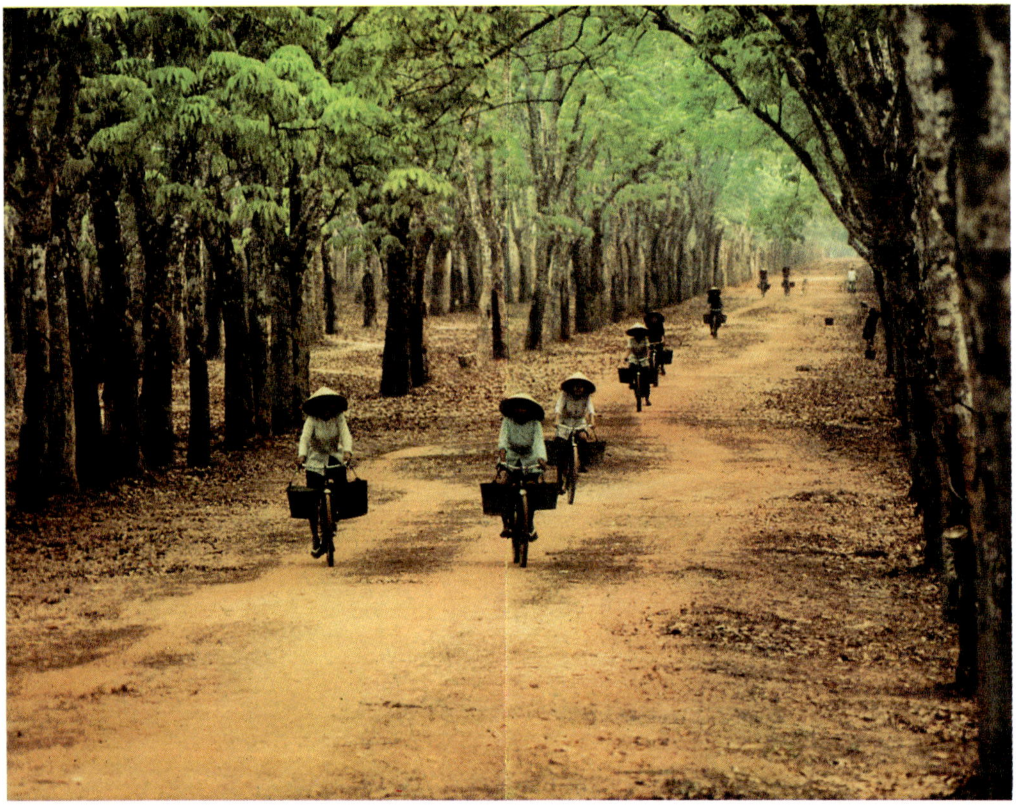

Some notable solutions to the difficult problem of photographing woods and trees.
On the opposite page, above, a wood in autumn, in which the image is enriched by the variety of colours and the difference in light creates graduated planes, giving a sense of great, airy spaces.
The photograph below shows a road inside a forest in Vietnam. Here, the very obvious green colour cast does not upset the picture; on the contrary, it serves to convey the particular atmosphere of the wood.

Right, this photograph has chosen a level foreground dominated by a tree, while the one below relies on the very vivid contrast between the green masses of the trees and the structure of the convent, whose clear geometry forms a perfect balance with the shapelessness of the dense vegetation surrounding it.

balance of aperture, etc. For this reason, many photographers prefer slightly cloudy weather which avoids such contrasts.
In any case, photography of woods is one activity which most betrays the expectations of the beginner, who is generally struck by the richness of the vegetation and does not realize that what will be translated by the camera is in fact quite foreign to such emotions. You therefore need to know how to frame the image to include distinct planes of light or emergent colours, linear motifs or significant details in such a way as to introduce the sense of space uniformity of colour tends to cancel.

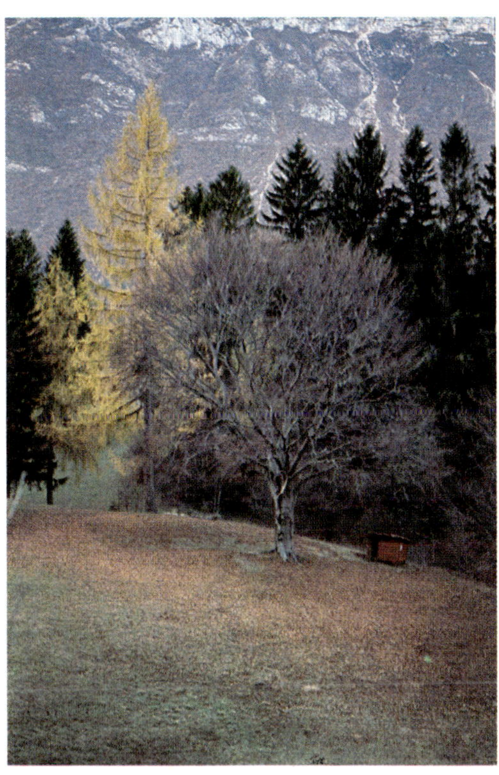

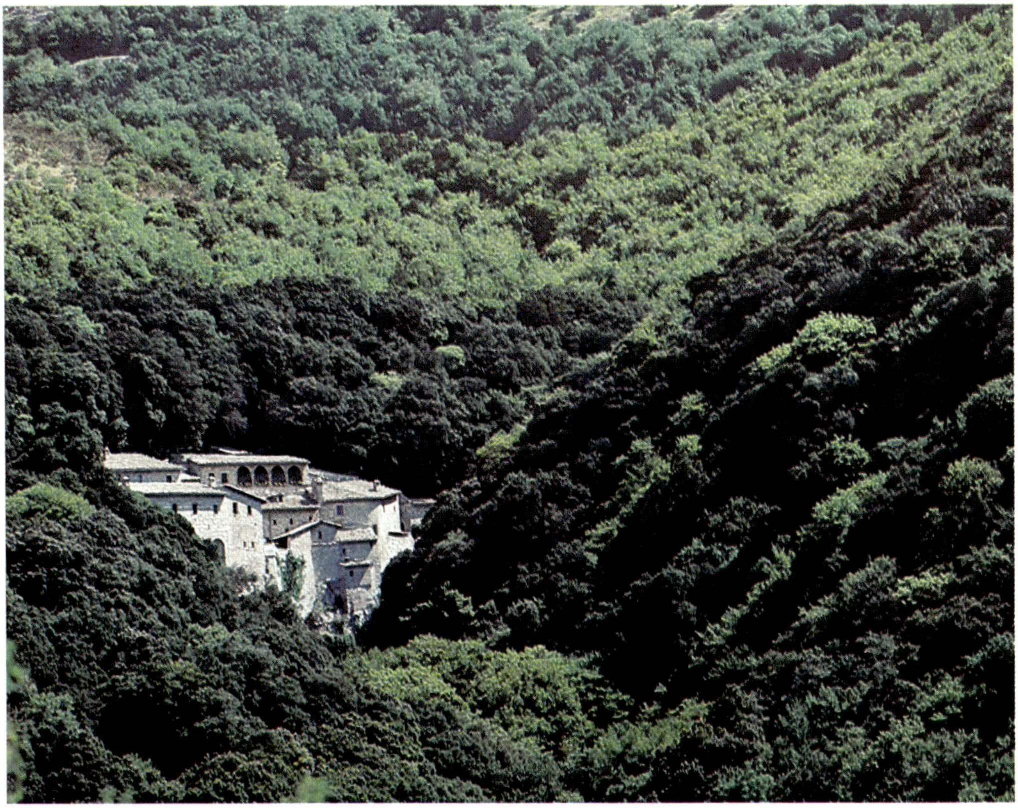

How to take photographs at high altitude

A mountain is one of the subjects most conditioned by variations in light, because the contrast between the parts in light and those in shadow can be intense – sufficient to blot out even very important details in the shade. The most favourable light would appear to be side lighting, or almost that, because frontal lighting tends to flatten the image by reducing the extent and depth of shadows, whilst backlighting cancels details and deadens the parts in shadow.
For good results

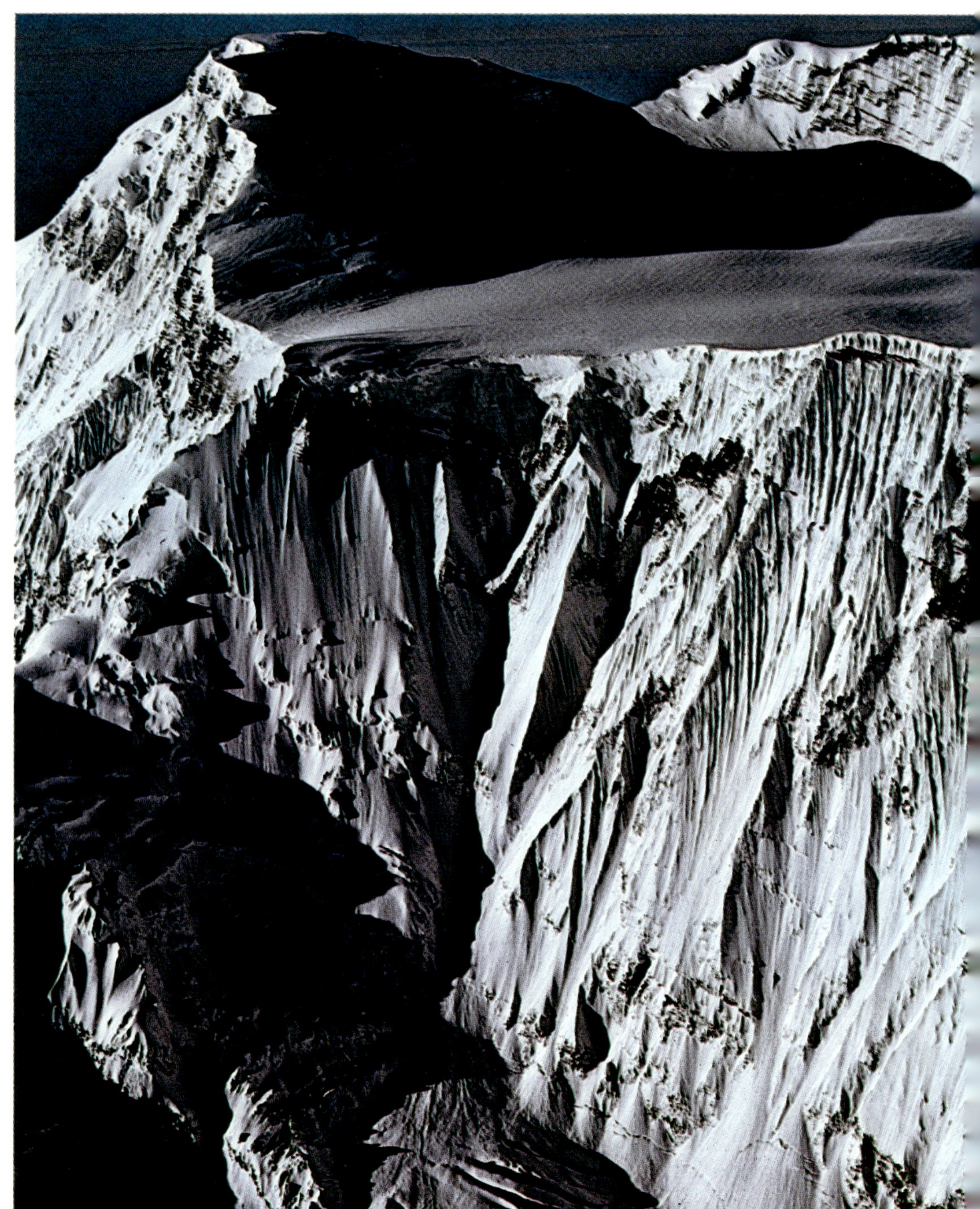

This magnificent photograph of the north face of Lamjung Himal in the Himalayas, is taken in the best light (low side lighting) for showing up the structure of the rock face. The contrast between light and shade is highly expressive.

in the mountains, you often have to be prepared to wait for the right moment. The north face of a mountain will always be a difficult subject. You will therefore have to wait for the sky to cloud over or resort to one of the techniques which expert photographers know how to use with backlighting, to mitigate the ill effects and if possible make them interesting. Another particular problem, at high altitude, is that the light of the sky is extremely

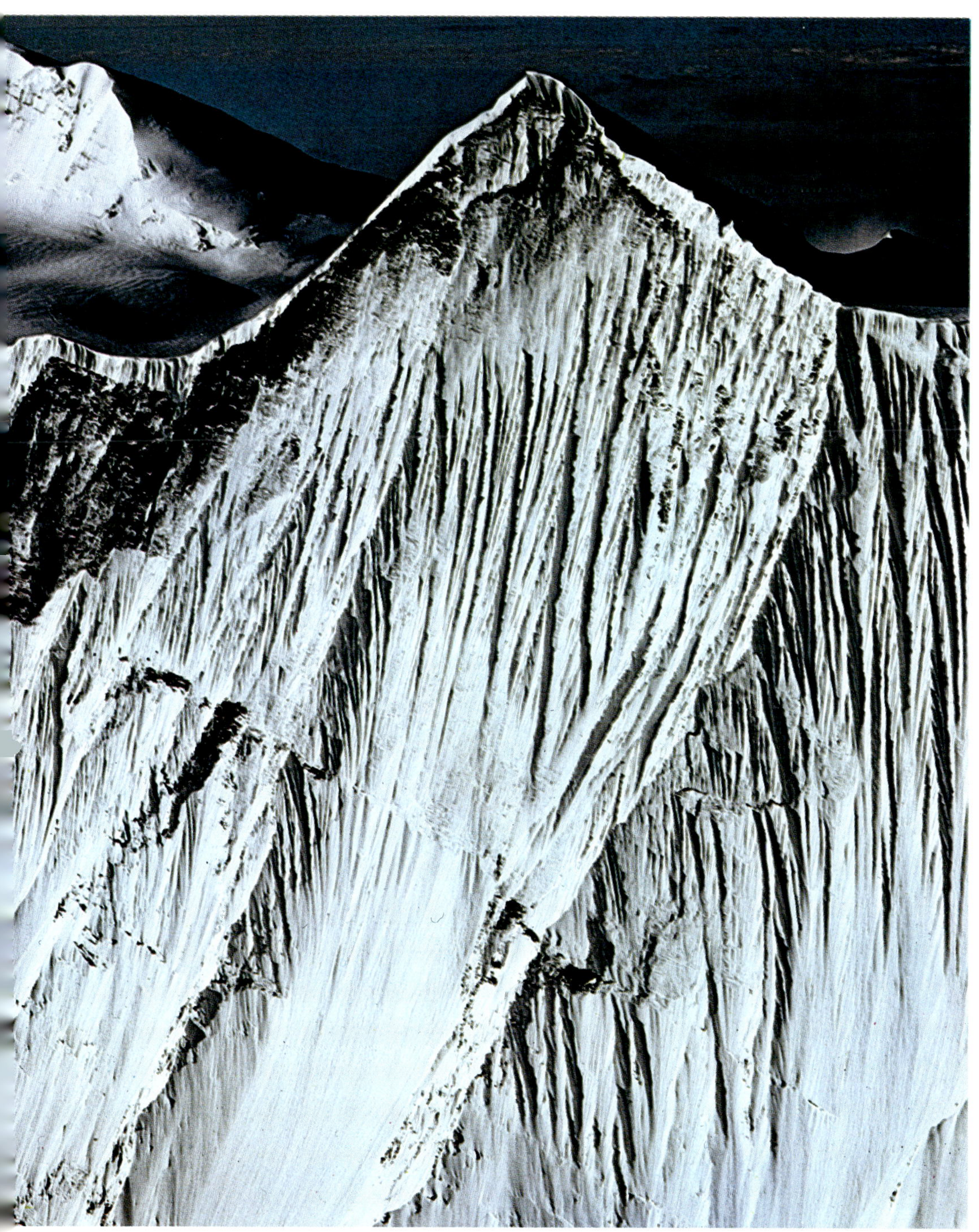

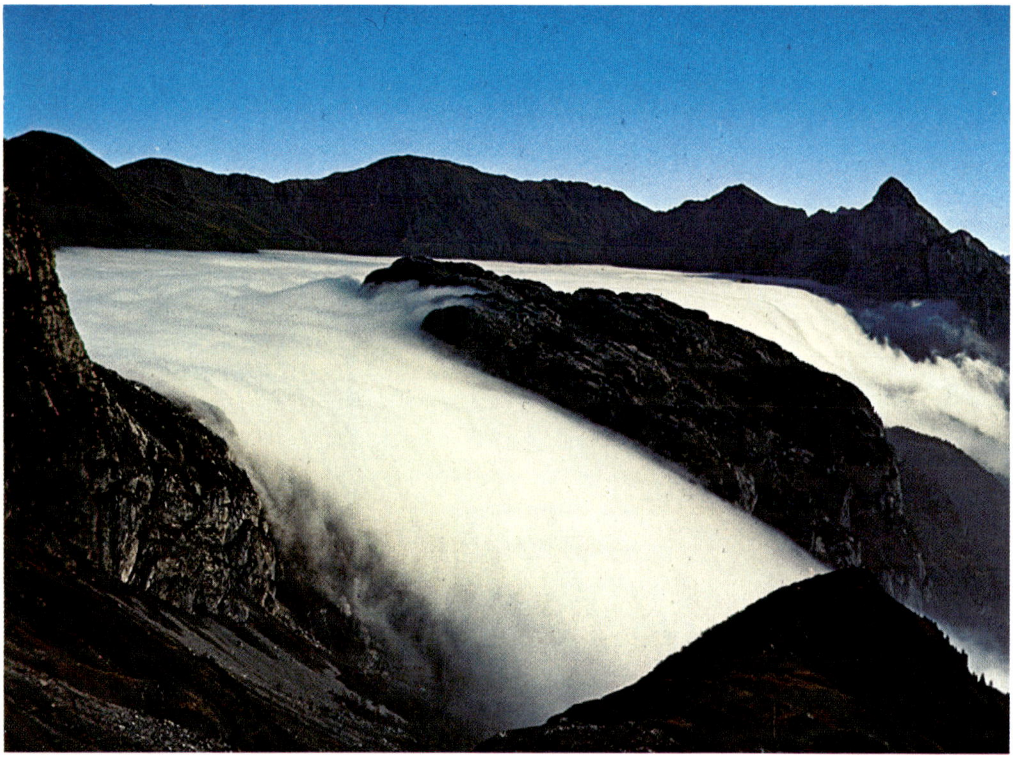

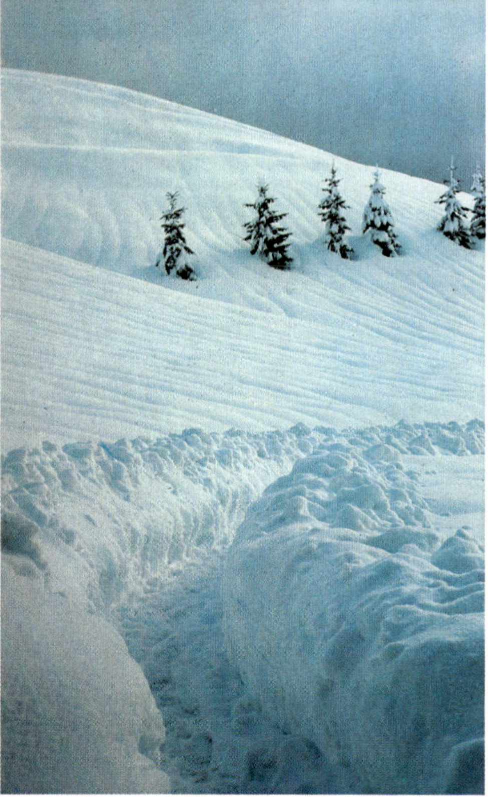

powerful.
Inexperienced photographers, in particular, can be attracted by that brilliance, that intense blue, and be unaware not only that it can easily overexpose their films, but also upset the colour balance and the entire composition, because the result will be, not a vibrant atmosphere of exhilarating depth, but a colourless, shapeless, flat surface. For this reason, many photographers try to exclude the sky as far as possible from their photographs of mountains, or at any rate to limit its extent, and others normally make use of filters to soften or polarize the light. Partial views can often give a better idea of overall grandeur.

The photograph above is an outstanding illustration of a phenomenon which is not uncommon in the mountains: the formation of fog at high altitude. The sea of cloud appears to be rolling down the mountainside like a gigantic waterfall.
Left, a typical winter landscape with the classic blue colour cast of snow scenes. The skilful variation in depth of the planes is interesting here.

On the opposite page, above, the incredible effects of great masses of snow, above which the threadlike track of the cable car winds its way.
Right, a typical effect of snow on trees in the countryside, but here the colour contrast of the persimmon fruit lends particular brightness to this winter composition.

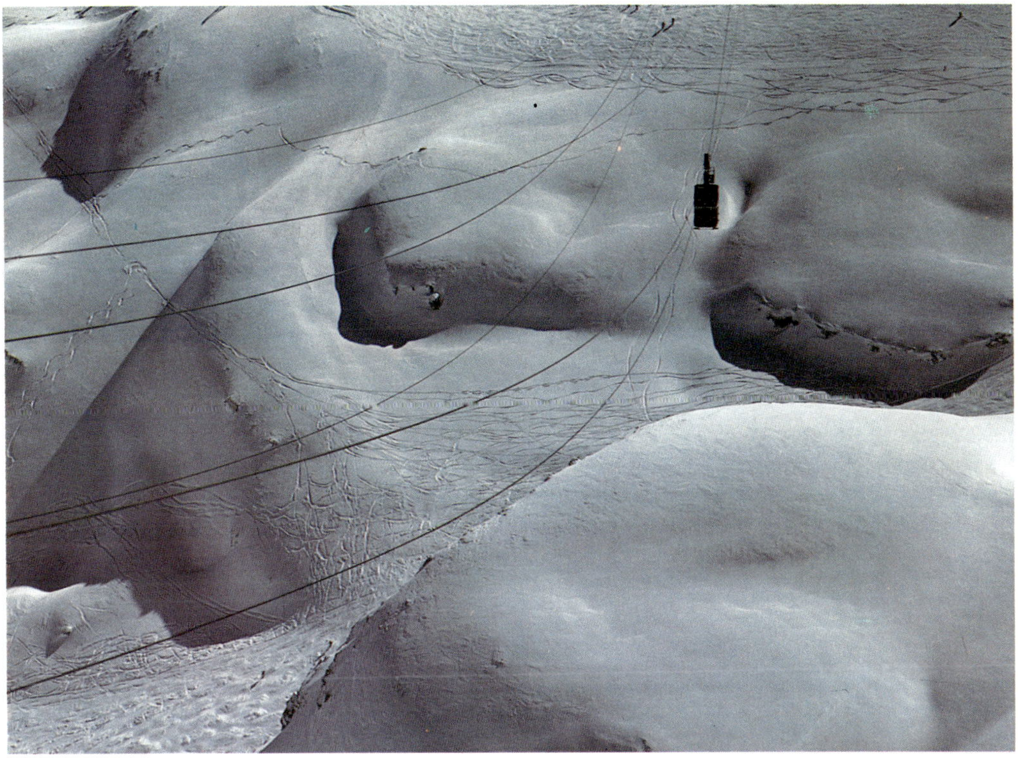

How to photograph snow and ice

Winter is the most fantastic, the most unreal of seasons, the one which reduces nature to elementary shapes. For this reason, winter landscapes lend themselves to interpretation in black-and-white, which can emphasize the skeletal structure of the plants and the clearcut, almost inlaid effects of light and shade. The biggest problem the photographer has to face is the enormous difference in light intensity caused by reflections from snow, which aggravates all contrasts between the parts in light and those in shadow, creating all the difficulties already mentioned, for example, in connection with photographs by the sea or with backlighting.
Even the extreme brilliance of the light from the sky must be borne in mind, above all for photographs at high altitude and corrected with filters of various kinds or by reducing the areas of sky.
Black-and-white, therefore, can be very effective for snow scenes, due both to the clarity of the composition and the fact that it can simplify colours by reducing them to the basic tints of black and white, with a limited range of greys. But even if the landscape tends to be monochrome, colour photographs can give excellent results, particularly if, apart from the contrast of light and shade, some

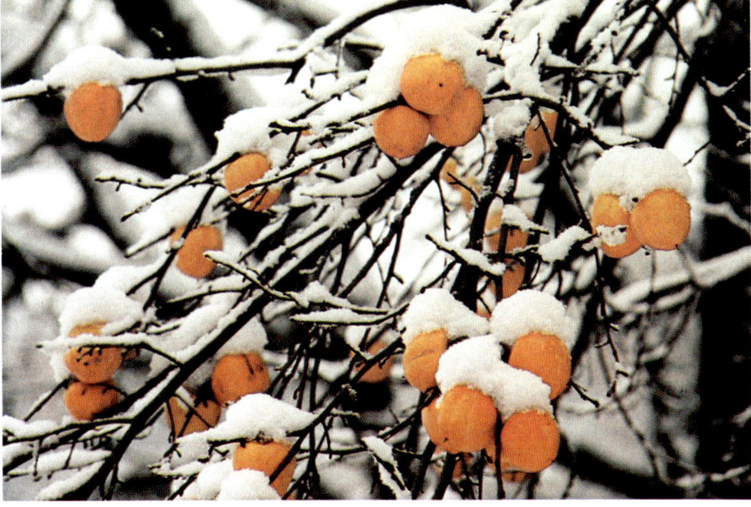

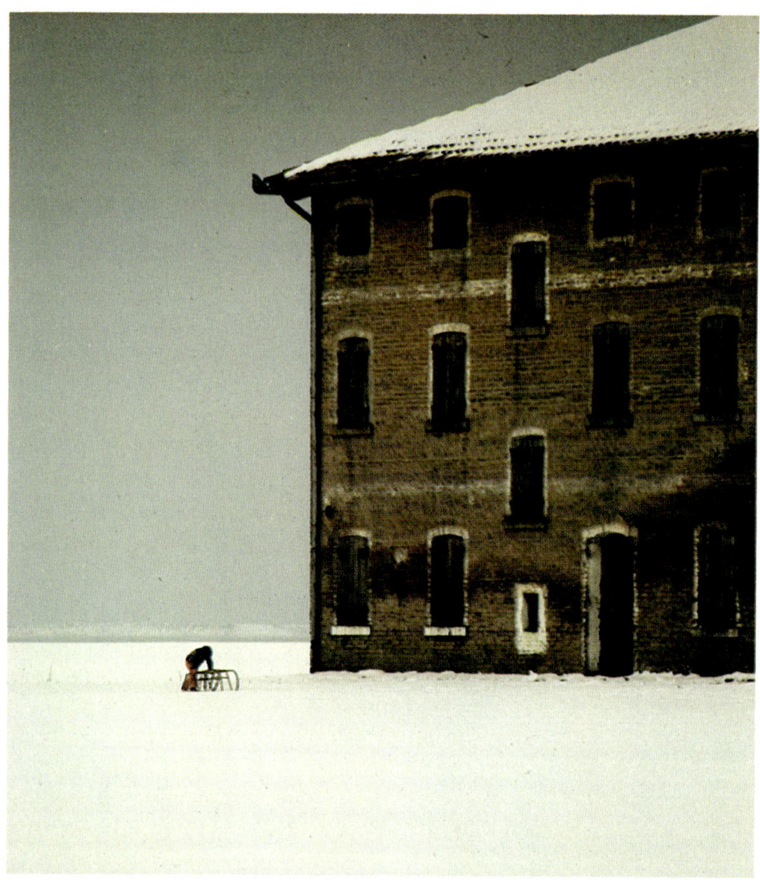

The image on the left is unusually effective and shows how important the interpretational skills of the photographer can be, faced here with a building devoid of any architectural merit and large areas of snow, also without any interesting details. The child with the sledge, framed at a suitable distance, has introduced a human reference to the scene, a proportion, further emphasizing the opposed masses of the house and snow and making them express the sense of wintry desolation.
In the photograph below, showing a lake in Carinthia with skaters, the frozen surface and patches of woodland give an idea of the cold in which the skaters are enveloped.

On the opposite page, the photograph above shows a typical effect of light and shade, due to the very great difference in brightness within a wood, between the areas reached by the sun's rays and those in shadow.
The photograph shows how even a grey day can be redeemed under special circumstances, by harmonious colours.

other brightly coloured motif is included, always taking care not to be too much attracted by facile effects and to limit and balance the amount of colour you wish to introduce.
Remember that the expressive force of any note of colour in a snowy landscape is enormously multiplied and can be overpowering.
A winter landscape does not just consist of expanses of snow. The effects of frost and ice offer a wealth of opportunities for the photographer, often enabling him to emphasize details which can convey the atmosphere of a scene more effectively than an overall view. Nor, of course, are winter landscapes always full of sunlight. This, in fact, is a characteristic of mountain landscapes where the air is very clear and the sky often limpid, whilst landscapes of plains or cities, for example,

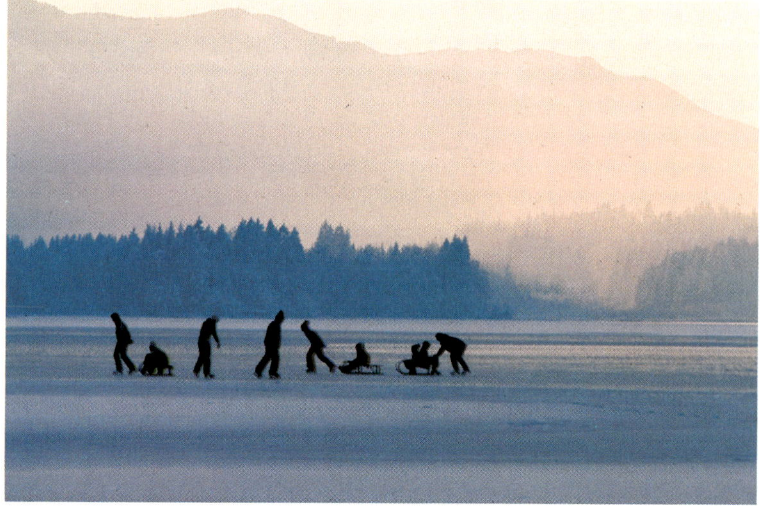

are primarily misty. Often, in fact, the greyness of winter seems the least inspiring to the photographer. But this is where he can exercise his powers of imagination and adaptability, trying to achieve a profound interpretation by entering into the spirit of the landscape.
When photographing falling snow, it is best to angle the frame in relation to the direction of the snow, remembering that while snow is falling, and immediately afterwards, a strong blue colour cast is produced in colour photographs which can be suitably exploited.
In winter landscapes, the photographer can be greatly assisted by the presence of people or animals – any details, in fact, which help to describe the type of life which people lead at that season. Other details, from frozen puddles to the weak, low light of the sun, or the immobility of plants locked in an icy grip, provide an endless source of inspiration.
Should the photographer have to operate in a particularly cold environment he must, of course, be suitably equipped and pay attention above all to gloves, which are certainly an obstacle when changing films. For this reason, many photographers wear a thin pair of gloves underneath their normal ones, to avoid touching the metal parts of the camera with the hands when outer gloves have to be removed. The camera, which would benefit from a suitable antifreeze treatment, must never be exposed to cold for longer than is strictly necessary and should be gradually transferred from a cold to a warm environment, to avoid condensation forming on the lens and films.

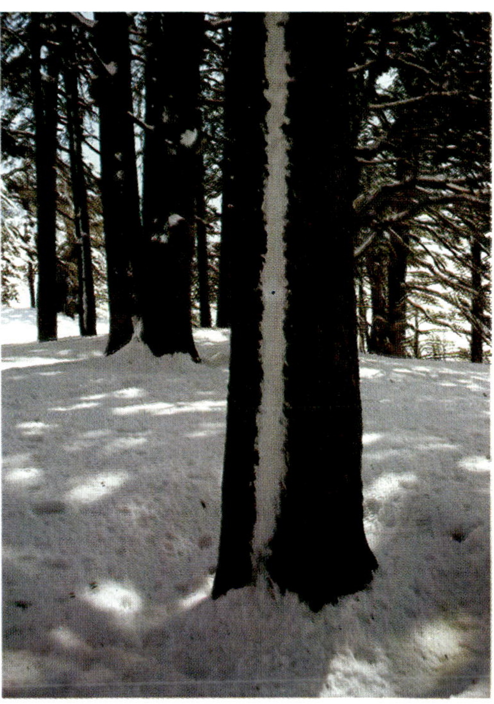

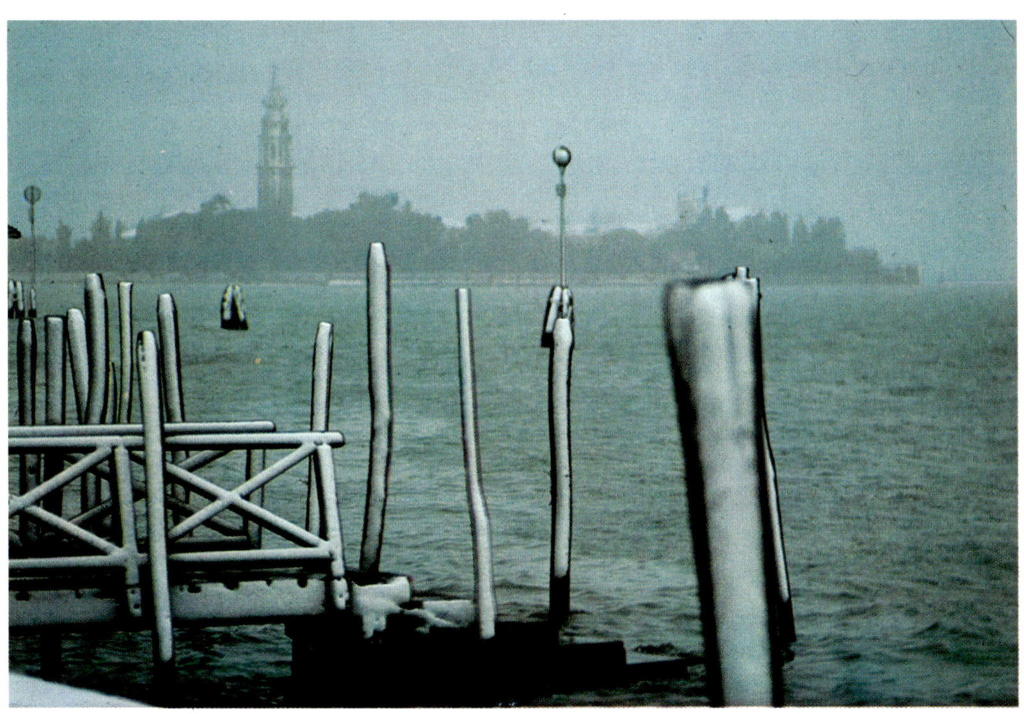

How to take photographs in fog and rain

Firstly, there is a very great contrast on wet days between the light of the sky and that of the ground and you therefore need to resort to the usual systems or reduce the area of sky to a minimum, or use filters, possibly graduated ones, given that in this case the reduction in brightness affects a clearly defined portion of the image. Another thing which can be useful if the photographer has to work in the rain is to fit an ordinary lens hood to the camera, to prevent drops of water falling on the lens.
Rainy days are the least favourable for photographs in natural surroundings, due both to the lack of depth the images show and their uniformity of colour, which seems to be unavoidable.
Naturally, a clever photographer will know how to make the most even of the greyness and monotony of such a landscape, accepting its characteristics or contrasting them with other elements which liven up the image.
Urban landscapes are easier to deal with, because in this case the human element can be given a major role. Furthermore, do not forget reflections in puddles or windows; those produced by rain in the presence of light; reflections from streetlamps and shop windows at nightfall. In short, even rain, like every other natural element, can inspire poetic values, as can be seen from the literature on

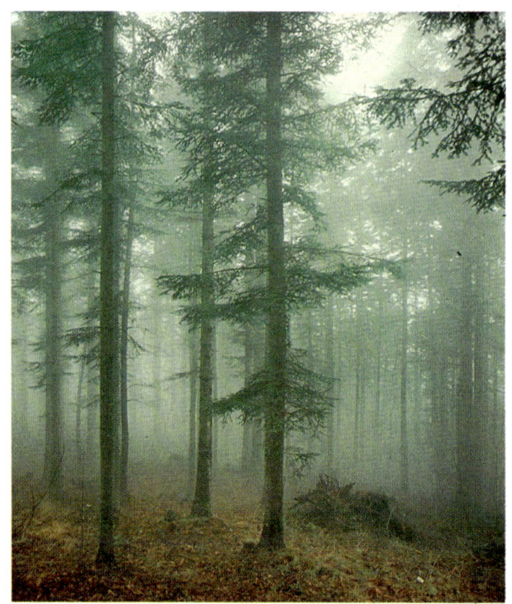

the subject, not to mention the moments immediately before rain, when a storm is imminent, or afterwards, when the sky clears up and the ground and everything else is still wet. Fog would appear to be a physical obstacle to the production of good photographs, but here too, the secret is to accept it and, if possible, use it to advantage.
Precisely because fog blurs outlines, it lends itself to fantastic and

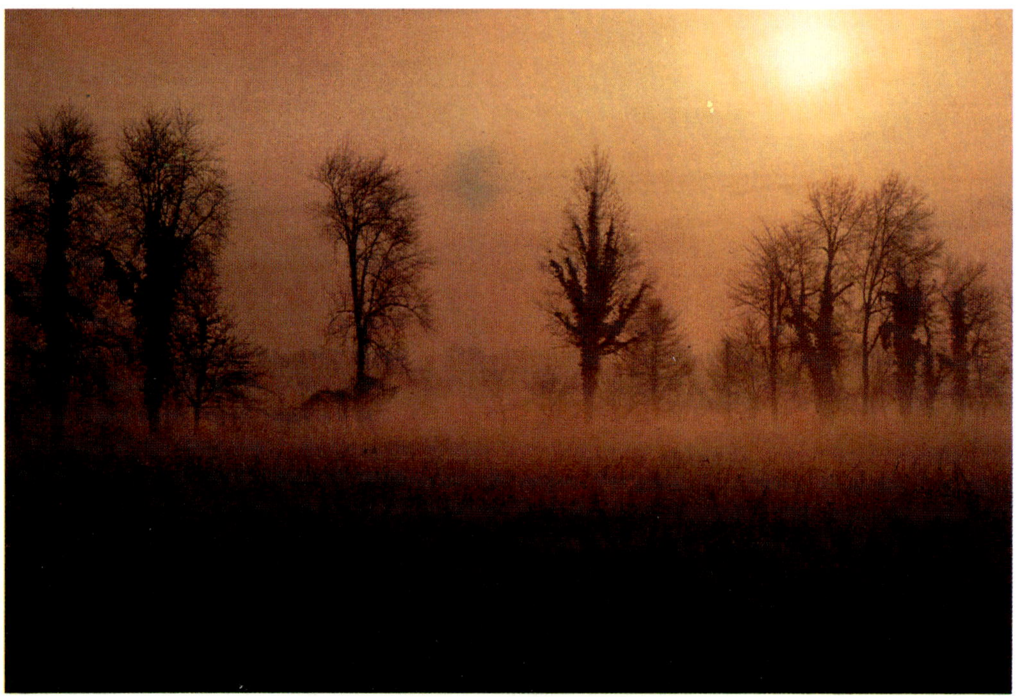

The photograph on the opposite page, above, illustrates the artistic potential of a light veil of mist in a wood. The presence of mist facilitates photography with backlighting. Note also how the skilful choice of frame and light helps create a sense of lyrical evanescence. While the photograph above explores the gradations in light, the one below underlines its soft, even distribution, recreating the unmistakeable atmosphere of the Lombard heathland.

Right, an amusing interpretation of a rainy day. In this case, the photographer is not interested in the size of the church of Santa Maria del Fiore (Florence cathedral), but in the intersection of spatial dimensions implicit in the movement of the two figures and the diagonal lines of the walls. The vividness of these contrasts is further emphasized by the greyness of the scene as a whole, and relieves its monotony.

Below, a picture taken from behind a car windscreen. The inevitable distortions of the image convey experiences and states of mind easily encountered on a wet day.

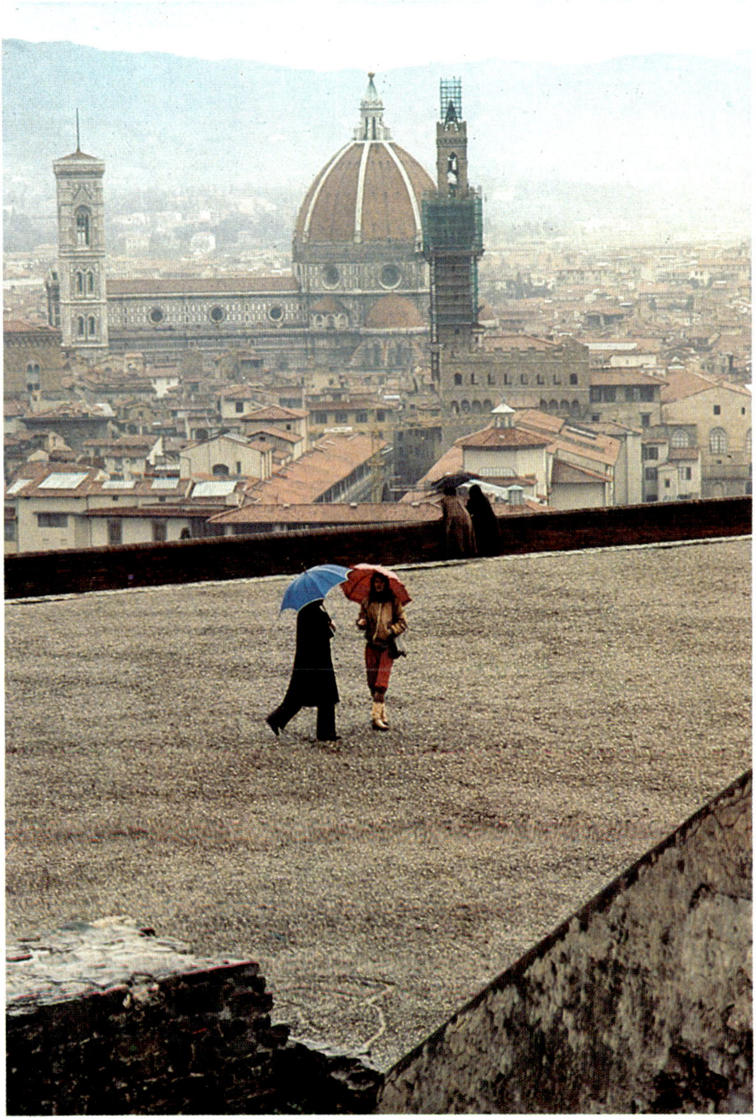

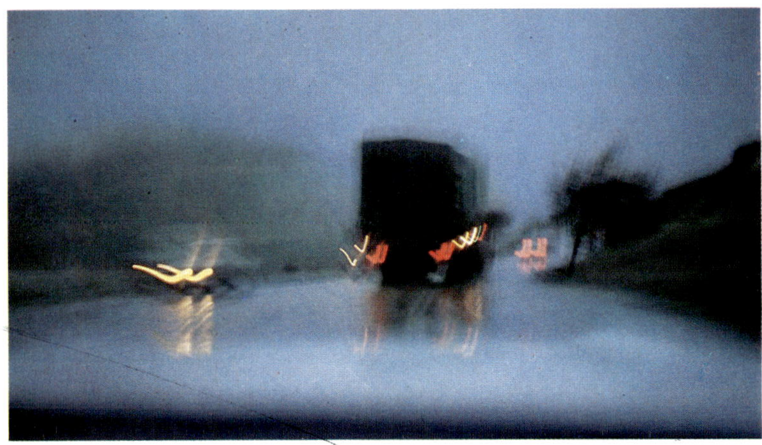

lyrical interpretations. Man has learned to live with fog and even capture the fantastic side of it. The photographer can do the same, as in the case of rain, which, whilst dull and depressing in itself, can offer interesting possibilities.

How to photograph the sky with clouds

Clouds are an important feature of landscape photography, whether they constitute the main theme or serve to enrich another subject. If the clouds are included in areas of blue sky, it will be a good idea to reduce their brightness with a yellow, or at any rate a coloured filter, if the photograph is in black-and-white, or a graduated neutral grey or polarizing filter in the case of colour. All this will have the effect of making the clouds more plastic and intensifying the colour of the sky, remembering that the most saturated blue will be in the part opposite the sun.

In countries with temperate climates, cumulo-cirrus clouds are the ones which create the most majestic, "architectural" effects, but all types of cloud can be interesting. The low, dense cloud, for example, of some storms, before and after rain, gives good backlighting effects with the sun's rays shining through breaks in the cloud or areas of clear sky above the horizon, and similar effects can be produced by clouds at sunset. Sometimes, the spectacle of clouds can be so interesting in itself that the rest of the landscape is reduced to a mere support. Finally, remember that clouds can increase the breadth of a landscape, by acting as virtual wings of perspective.

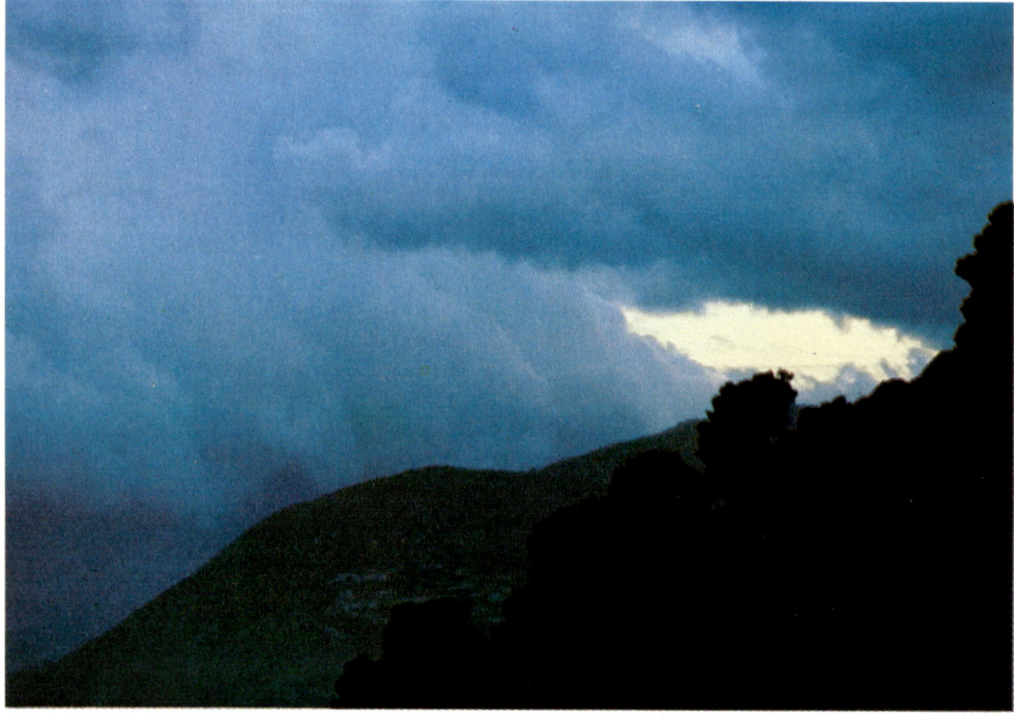

On the opposite page, above, an outstanding example of how effective a photograph wholly dedicated to clouds can be. It is a backlit nocturnal shot, which captures the radiance of the moon in a predominantly blue sky. The fantastic sense of night is heightened by this mobile, indistinct, profound symphony in blue, shot through by the intense light of the moon. Note the clever choice of frame, which by placing the moonlight at the top has succeeded in informing us of the depth of the night which is dominated, but not fully penetrated, by the circle of light.
The photograph below captures the moment of revelation as a rent appears in the cloud during a storm. The strong contrast of light and colour helps increase the sense of drama.

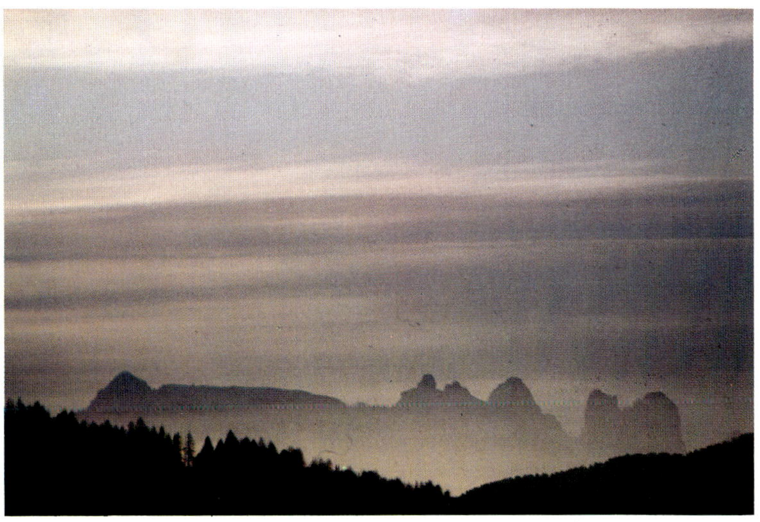

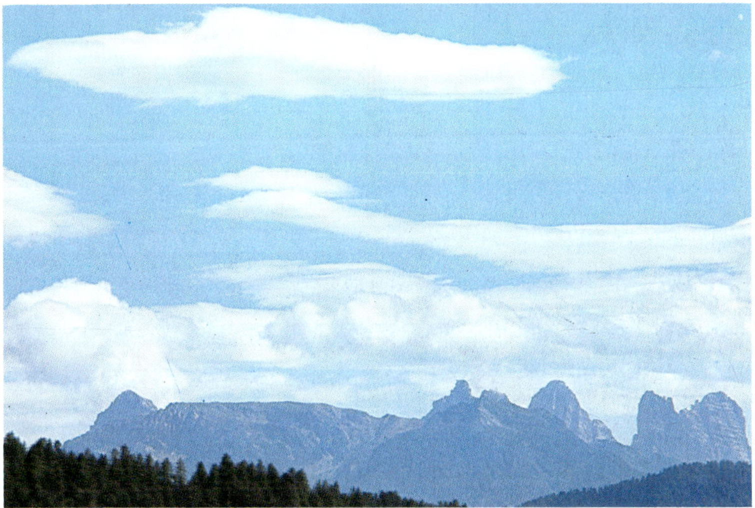

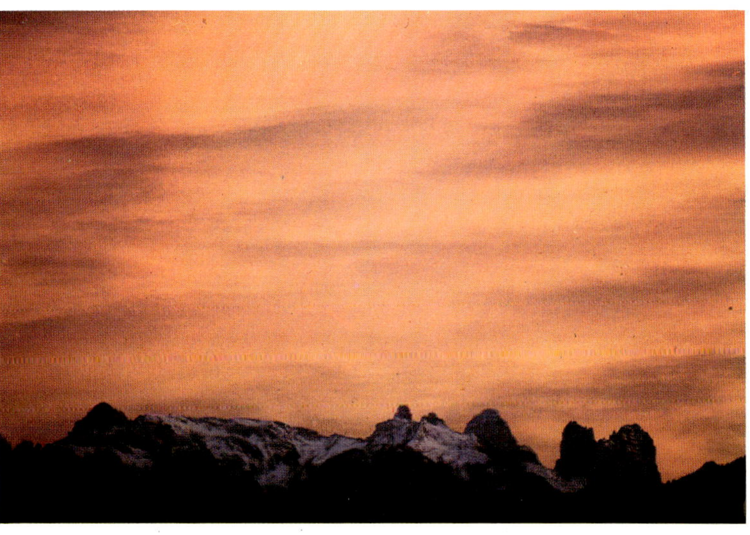

Right, the same alpine scene has been taken from the same point in three different sets of atmospheric conditions, each characterized by a different light and different cloud composition. Above, we have a description of a moment at dawn, with stratified cloud and a soft, delicately-toned light which is not yet able fully to reveal the face of the mountains.
The photograph, center, shows the scene in broad daylight, when the volume of the mountains is matched by more clearly modelled clouds.
The third photograph captures the hour of sunset, when the long shadows create more intense, dramatic contrasts and the entire sky is pervaded by reddish reflections.

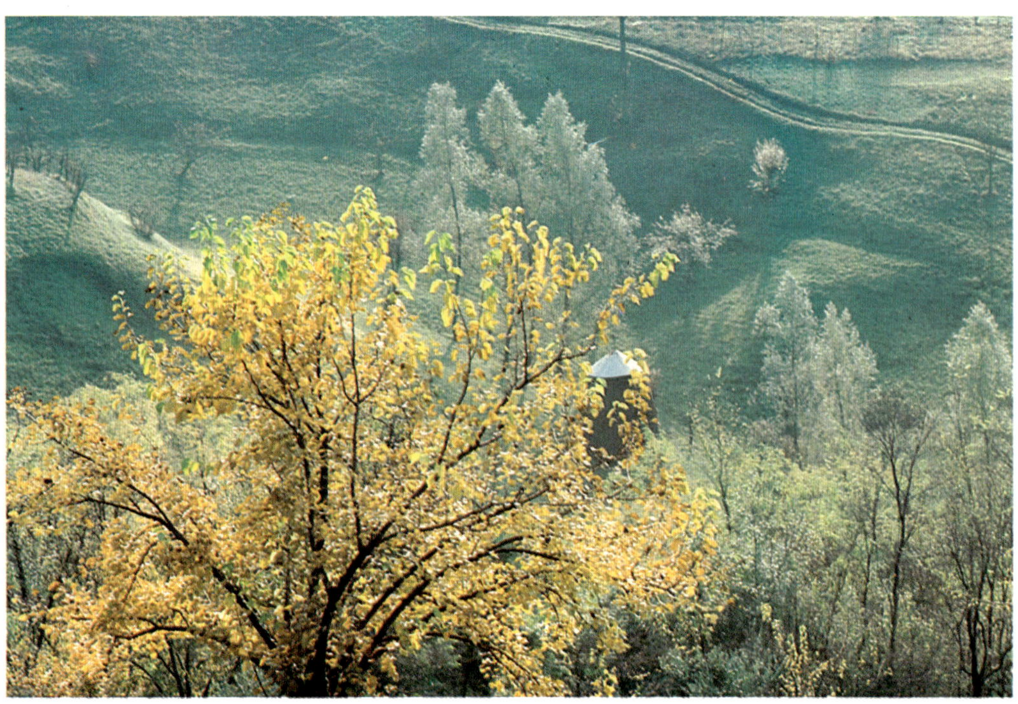

How to photograph with backlighting

A landscape can be differently illuminated by varying the position of the light source – that is, the sun. When the sun is behind us, we will have frontal lighting with very thin shadows. More substantial shadows will be obtained by having the sun behind us, but higher up. In these cases it is harder to achieve good results with black-and-white, because in the absence of relief from shadows the pictures will look flat, whilst better results will be obtained with colour photographs because frontal lighting intensifies colours and the details will be clear as well.

Three-quarter lighting is the type most used for both black-and-white and colour. In these cases, the sun is not exactly behind the photographer, but more to his right or left, whilst still being on his side. In these photographs, a balance is achieved between light and shade and this type of lighting is particularly suitable for showing the depth and richness of the view. Sidelighting is when the sun is completely to one side; particularly if it is low on the horizon this type of light will produce greatly elongated shadows. As we have seen, this type of lighting is effective when the landscape is in itself somewhat uniform, as in the case of expanses of snow, beaches or desert, or even countryside with very homogeneous crops, because the lateral angle will emphasize every detail.
If the sun is very high in the sky, the light will be similar to that of midday, and this type of lighting, which produces short but very dense shadows, helps create an impression of summer and heat.
Next we have various positions with backlighting, that is, when

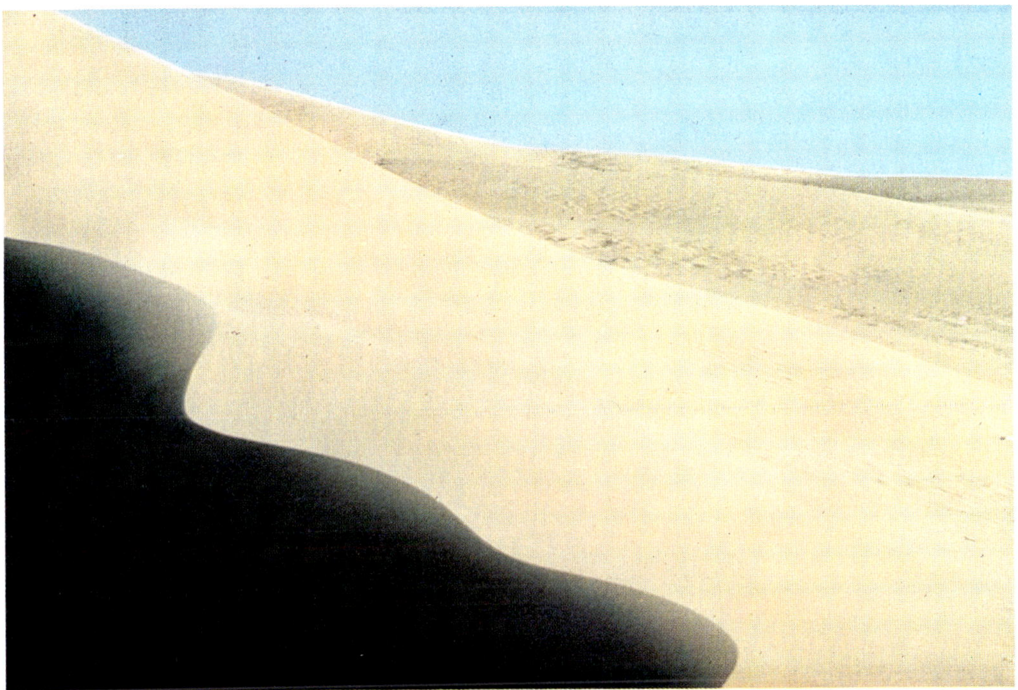

These photographs illustrate various ways of using backlighting.
On the opposite page, above, the sky has been totally excluded in order to enrich the tonal values of the part framed. Backlighting has helped in this case to give greater airiness and brilliance to the tree in the foreground.
The picture below includes a wide area of sky, necessary in this case to extend the play of reflections and balance the immobile outlines of the dark parts, increasing the sense of a deep, but perfectly motionless space.

the sun is facing, or to one side of, the photography but still in the area in front of the camera lens.
For the sake of convenience we have been referring all the time to sunlight, but obviously the same applies to any type of light source – which, in very many cases, may simply be the sky. Backlighting therefore applies not only when the camera is facing the area where the sun is, but also whenever the object one wishes to photograph is set against a very bright sky. As the light of the sky can be very intense, if the object in question is not suitably lit in turn, it can be eclipsed, thereby losing any possibility of being shown in detail.
The difficulties the photographer encounters in these cases are related to the sensitivity of the film, which while capable of tolerating quite a wide range of stimuli, is always necessarily limited. In other words it can only reproduce

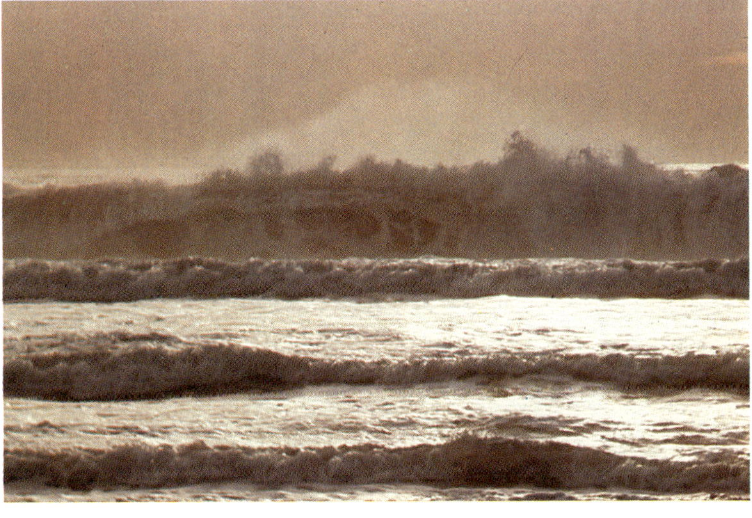

On this page, above, backlighting accentuates the extreme clarity of forms and sense of the absolute which accompanies their tone.
Right, backlighting has made it possible to capture the breakers of the Pacific, emphasizing their force, which is increased by the darker rendering of the mass of water.

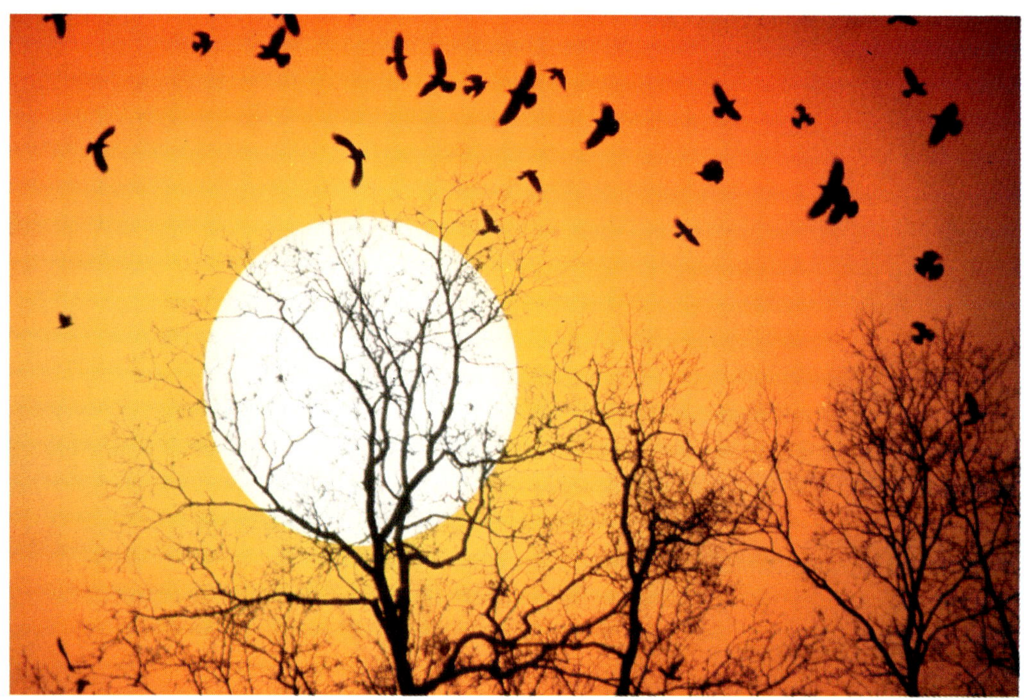

the image precisely within a certain brightness ratio. The parts in shade in a photograph against the light obviously fall outside these limits and can only leave a partial impression on the film in the necessarily short exposure time. By way of compensation, the objects present their shadow to the lens in these cases and this makes them more striking, even if only their outline is visible. Very often, the ground on to which the light is reflected is intensely bright, so that the difference between the areas of light and shade will be such as to cancel out colours and their intermediate shades.

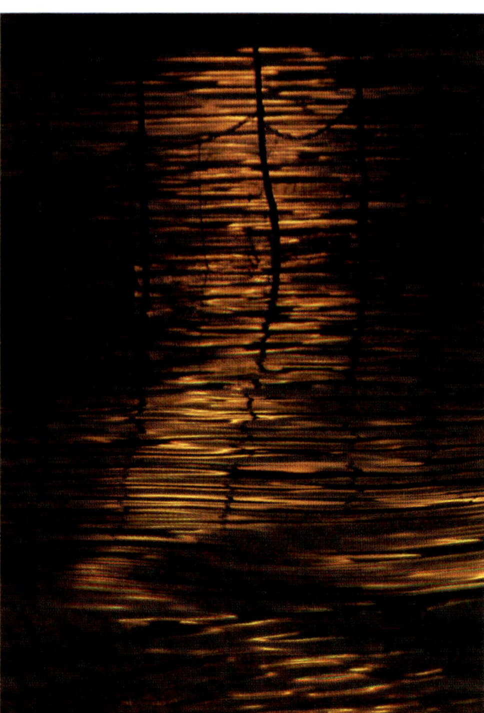

Naturally, if the light source is immediately behind the scene framed, attempts must be made to soften it or cover it up. The sun, for example, particularly if it is not too far above the horizon, can be covered by a detail in the foreground: the leafy branches of a tree, a building, or some other object. The difficulties are less when the sun is low on the horizon and veiled in cloud, as at

The pictures shown here are further evidence of the vast range of possible interpretations of backlighting.
The photograph above sets off the linear profiles of the bare branches of a tree. The strong contrasts in light permit this very clear graphic effect, to which the subject is, or course, particularly well suited. Equally evident is the photographer's intelligent choice of frame, with a sun magnified by telephoto lens, encircled by a flight of birds, which increase the depth and movement of the image.
The one on the left shows a play of reflections in a lagoon environment where molluscs are farmed. Here, the photographer has contrasted the horizontal movement of the stripes on the water with that of the vertical profiles of the stakes.

On the opposite page, Fulvio Roiter shows off the rich tones of sunset: the photograph has all the qualities of a painting, rendered with extremely subtle variations in colour.

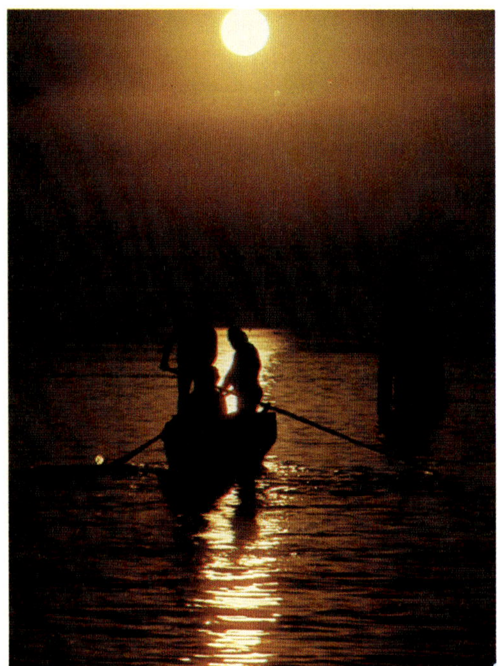

dawn or sunset. In these cases, the sun can be directly included in the frame, taking care to adjust the exposure times according to the details you wish to emphasize. Slight underexposure can in some cases facilitate a harmonious tonal rendering of the colours of the sky. In other cases, use of a wide-angle, by reducing the diameter of the sun, can make it easier to include.
Particularly favourable situations are when the sun is partially or totally shielded by cloud, adding scenographic effects to the advantages of photographing with backlighting. The photographer must be sure to calculate the brightness of the sky, which is often greater than it looks, even when the sun is hidden. Other favourable situations are with reflected light, from the sea, a lake, a pond, even a wet road or frozen surface. In this case, the camera lens can be aimed entirely at the reflections, excluding the direct light source from the picture. Naturally, in this and very many other cases,

Other examples of the use of backlighting. The photograph on the left is highly effective, the silhouettes of the fishermen having been set against the reflections in the water. In this way, the overall brightness is attenuated, remaining within sufficient limits to harmonize with the surrounding calm, and tranquil rhythm of the oars.
The picture below is devoted to the sky, but a sky which is exceptional in its relative uniformity, revealing the enormous fiery potential of a sunset in San Francisco Bay, California, rendered in shades of deepest violet to red.

On the opposite page, above, the already impressionistic effects of a sunset are further muted by a screen in the form of a glass covered in tiny drops of moisture, which introduce interesting motifs and very subtle reflections.
Below, a backlit scene showing the effects produced by diagonal light.

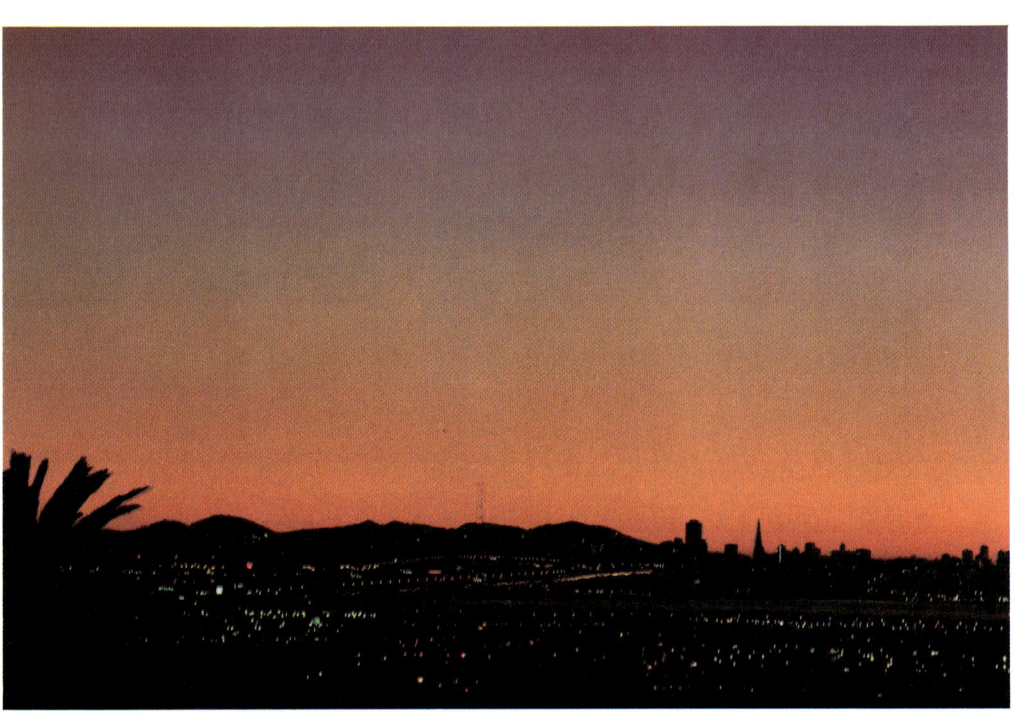

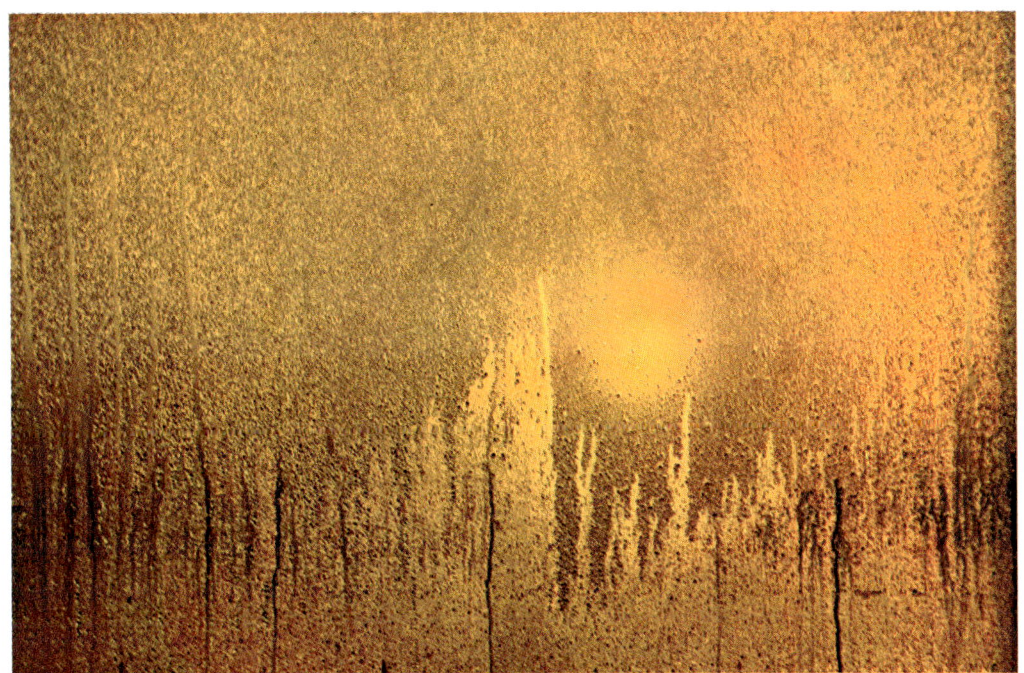

a lens hood can be very useful to avoid unwanted reflections. When greater detail is required of a photograph with backlighting, and no other procedure is possible, the best conditions will be on overcast days.
Remember that on such days the light is equally diffuse throughout and there are no shadows, therefore, pictures will tend to look monotonous, particularly in black-and-white, while colour photographs will lose much of their intensity.

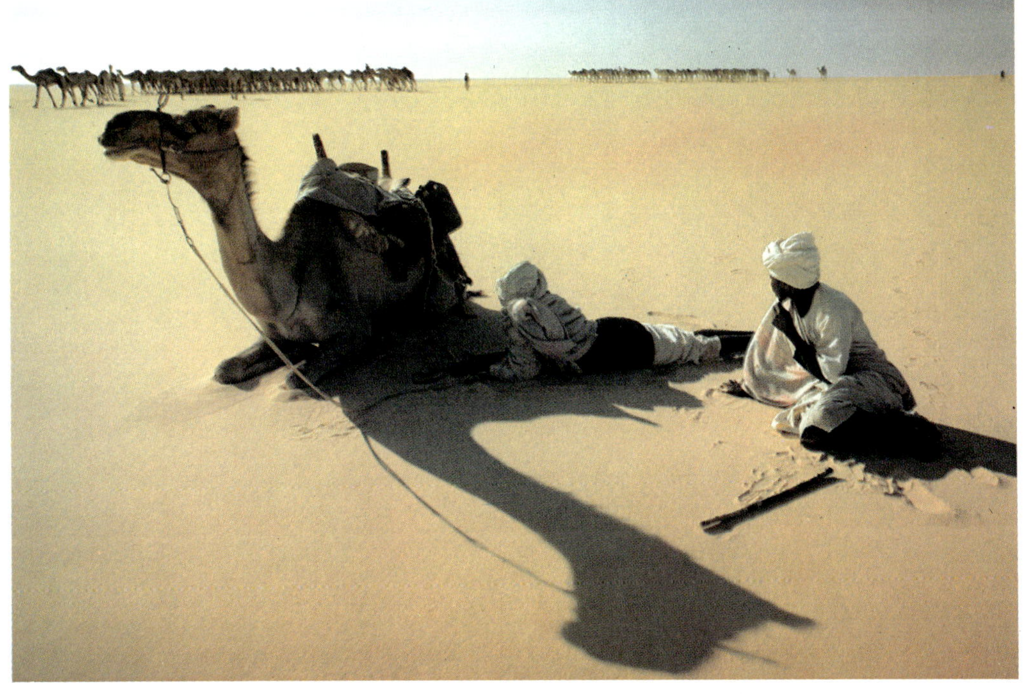

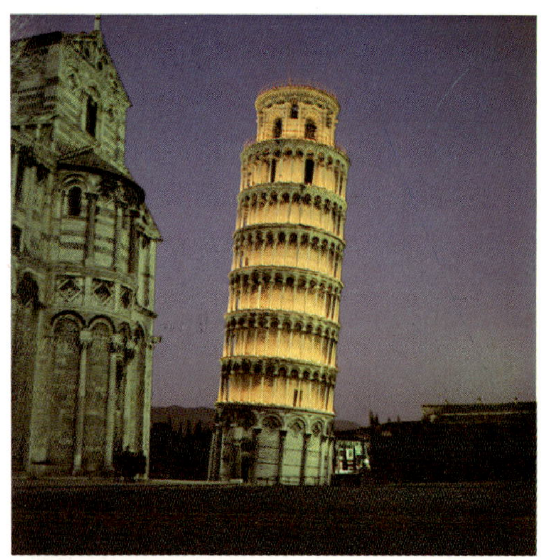

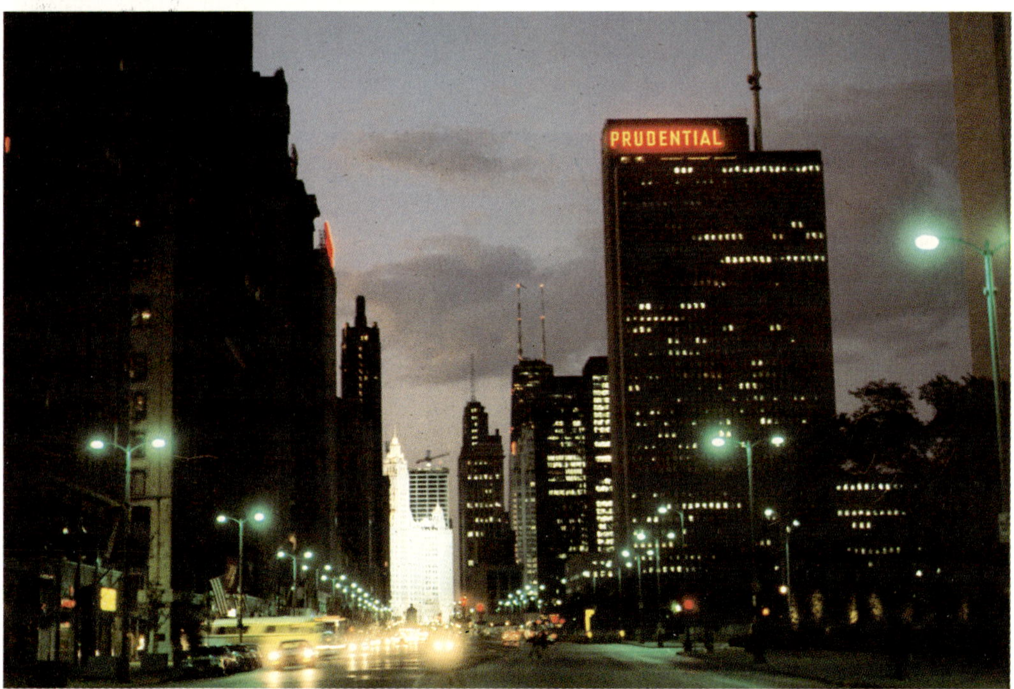

How to take nocturnal photographs

The first point about nocturnal photographs is the shortage of light available and hence the need for comparatively long exposure times and the absolute necessity of a support for the camera. Such a support, i.e. the conventional tripod, is in fact recommended if not strictly necessary, for all landscape photographs. Clearly, in fact, the image must be technically perfect, particularly when a small format film is required to undergo considerable enlargement. Good definition is essential here and it depends on the strength and clarity of the image, clear focusing and a perfectly immobile camera. The sole means of achieving this is by using a support. This is an indispensable piece of equipment. In fact, the photographer should not even regard it as an accessory, but as an integral part of the camera.

A tripod enables you to use medium and long exposure times, to stop down the lens, thereby increasing the depth of field, and to control the frame precisely. To perform these tasks it must be a genuine, good quality support, even if small, not just one of the multitude of cut-price contraptions available on the market which transmit all the vibrations due to the unavoidable work which has to be done on the camera prior to shutter release. A support also enables the camera to be placed in unusual positions, for example, higher up or lower down than physiclly possible if the camera is hand-held.

Naturally it slows down preparations, but while this could be a serious disadvantage with other types of photography, such as reporting, it hardly ever is with landscapes.

Special films for artificial light are available for night photography – that is, they are adapted to a particular colour rendering. There are, in fact, some types of lamps such as sodium vapour and mercury (the typical neon lights) which have an incomplete range of wavelengths, and will therefore give blueish or orange pictures

The best nocturnal photographs are often taken at dusk, when the last light of day, however feeble, can reconcile contrasts which would otherwise be insuperable.

On the opposite page, above, the leaning tower of Pisa is emphasized by floodlighting.
The photograph below shows the animation of a Chicago street lit up at night, while the one on the right of this page relies on a disquieting sense of mystery.
Below, the panorama of New York owes its effectiveness to the sparkle of a myriad lights.

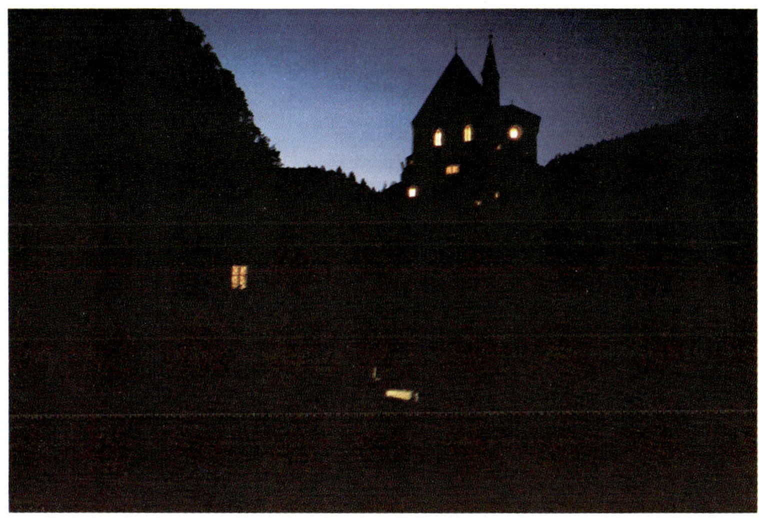

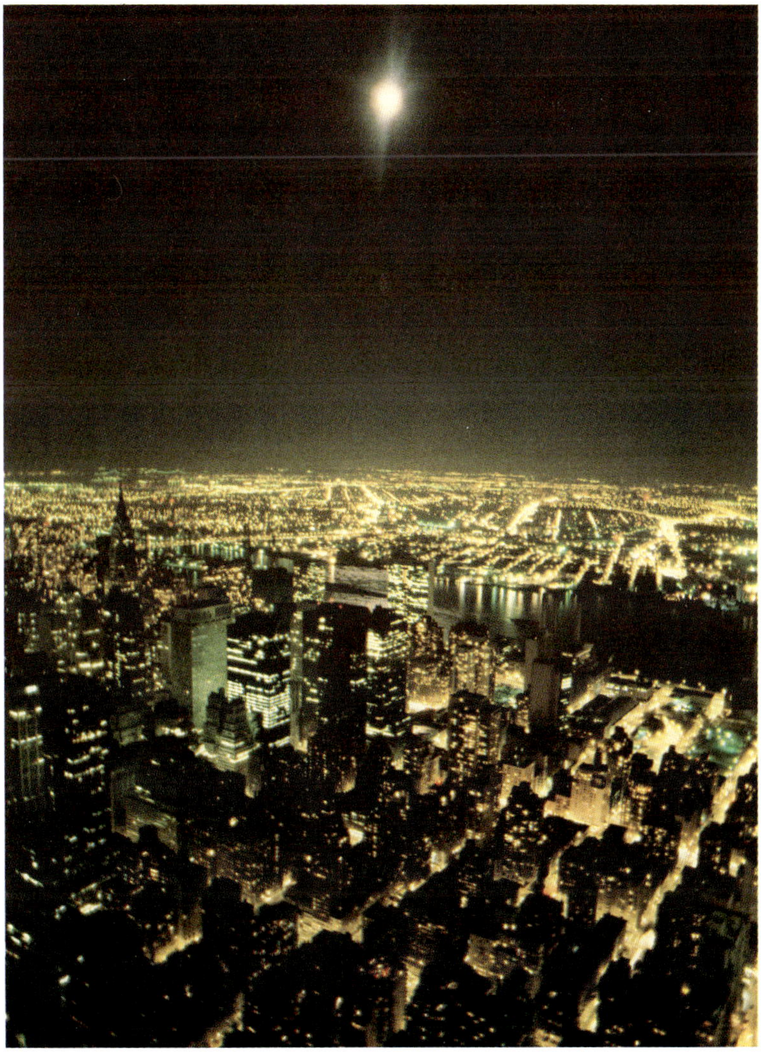

which will have to be corrected either by filters or by varying the types of film, if you do not wish them to have such an accentuated colour. Urban landscapes – or streets with lighted shop windows, for example – can include several different types of light source and in this case you will need to choose which type of light is to be given precedence.
By using films for artificial light and strong underexposure, nocturnal effects can be achieved even with pictures taken in broad daylight, particularly if a graduated polarizing filter is used for the sky. Another standard method is to take photographs in brilliant sunshine, with a blue sky, but using a very deep red filter, which gives effects typical of moonlight. Other techniques can of course be applied during developing and printing.
In mentioning the need to use the

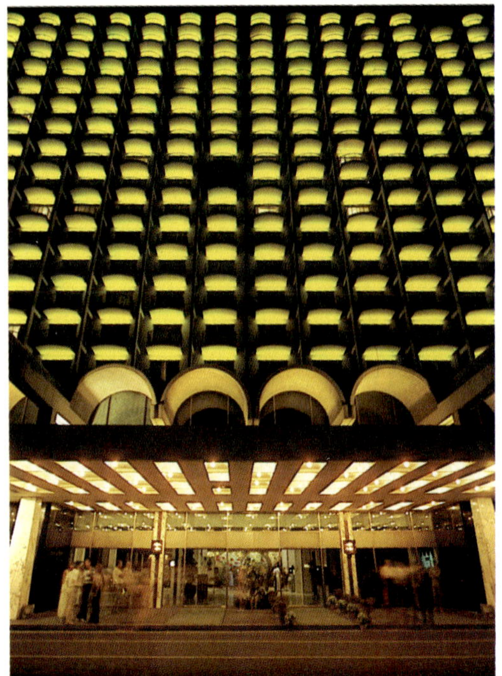

right films to achieve certain results, we are referring to films for artificial light, rather than very high-speed films, because where relatively short exposure times are not necessary to capture moving details, long exposures will always be preferable to the use of films with a grain that gives poorer definition and less good enlargements.

In a number of respects, the best time to achieve nocturnal effects is at dusk when the artificial lights are on and the moon and stars may already have appeared, but there is still some diffuse light. In this way, by varying the exposure times, it will be possible not only to convey the particular atmosphere of these moments – which have a character of their own – but also those of a deeper, nocturnal sky, avoiding those extremes of contrast between the light source and the rest of the landscape which are normally unavoidable.

During the night, for instance, it is absolutely impossible to photograph the disc of the moon and the landscape it illuminates together, because while an exposure of even less than a second can be sufficient for the moon, the rest of the landscape, under the same conditions, would require several minutes. Even in the case of buildings which are artificially illuminated, such as the very frequent examples of floodlit monuments, twilight is the most favourable time. Another difficulty when photographing the moon is its movement which, however slow, begins to show from an exposure of 30 seconds onwards, with the result that an elongated disc is produced. The problem is even more obvious when you wish to photograph a starry sky, as in this case the exposure times will have to be much longer, and therefore

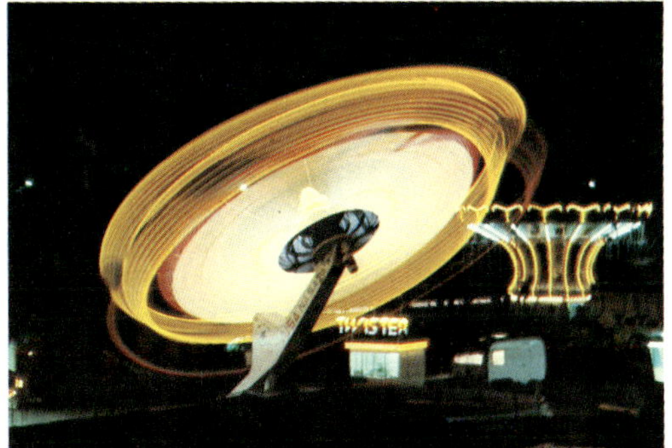

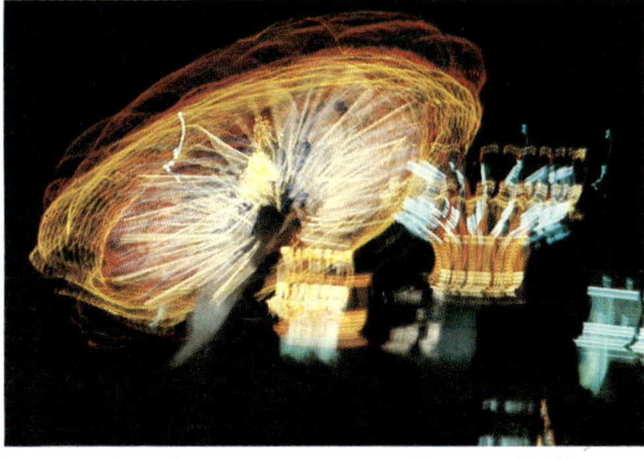

If lights can be set in frames, as in the photograph on the opposite page, above, the lively rhythms this produces can be an effective compositional element.
The photograph below, on the other hand, is so constructed that the contrast creates an almost magical halo of light.
On this page, above, two ways of photographing a fairground wheel, by varying the exposure time.
Below, the effects of passing car lights near a motorway, taken with a prolonged exposure.

the stars will show up not as pin-points, but lines. To remedy this, instruments are available which rotate the camera to follow the movement of the heavens. Although not hard to obtain, these instruments belong to the quite different field of astronomical photography.
To reproduce both moon and moonlit landscape together, two different negatives can be used, which can be superimposed at the moment of printing, or the same frame can be exposed twice, first slowly to reproduce the landscape, then rapidly, for the moon.
In the case of photographs of monuments, or other details submerged in darkness, when they are accessible you can also use several flash emissions, fired from different angles. It depends on the results you wish to obtain.
Night-time has a magic of its own and certain unreal effects such as the trails of light from passing cars can make interesting subjects.

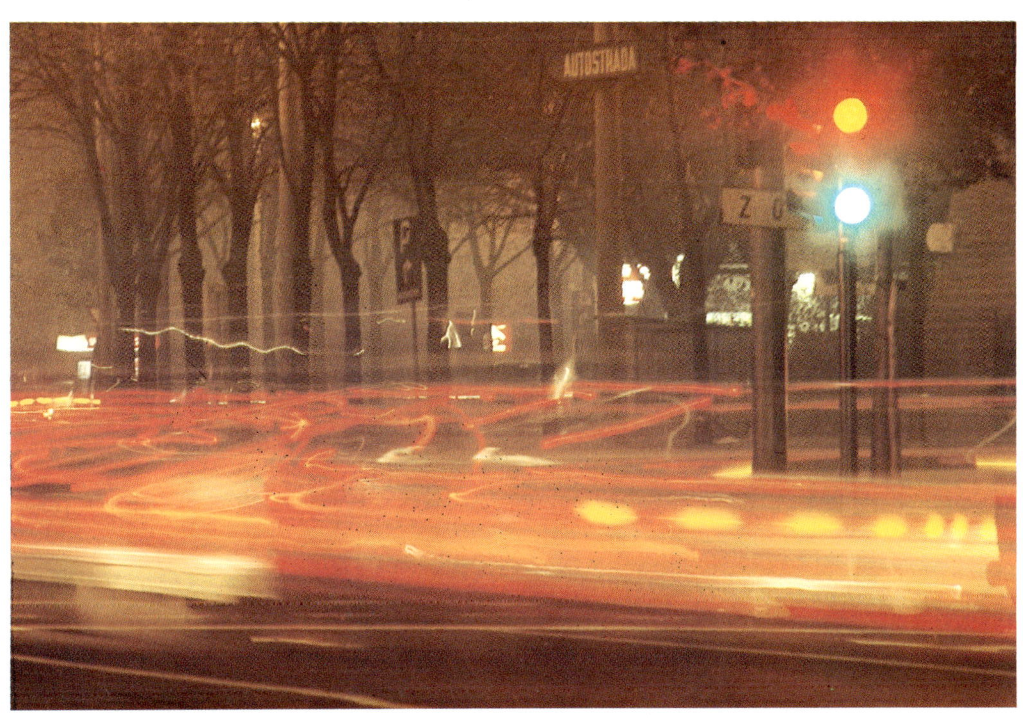

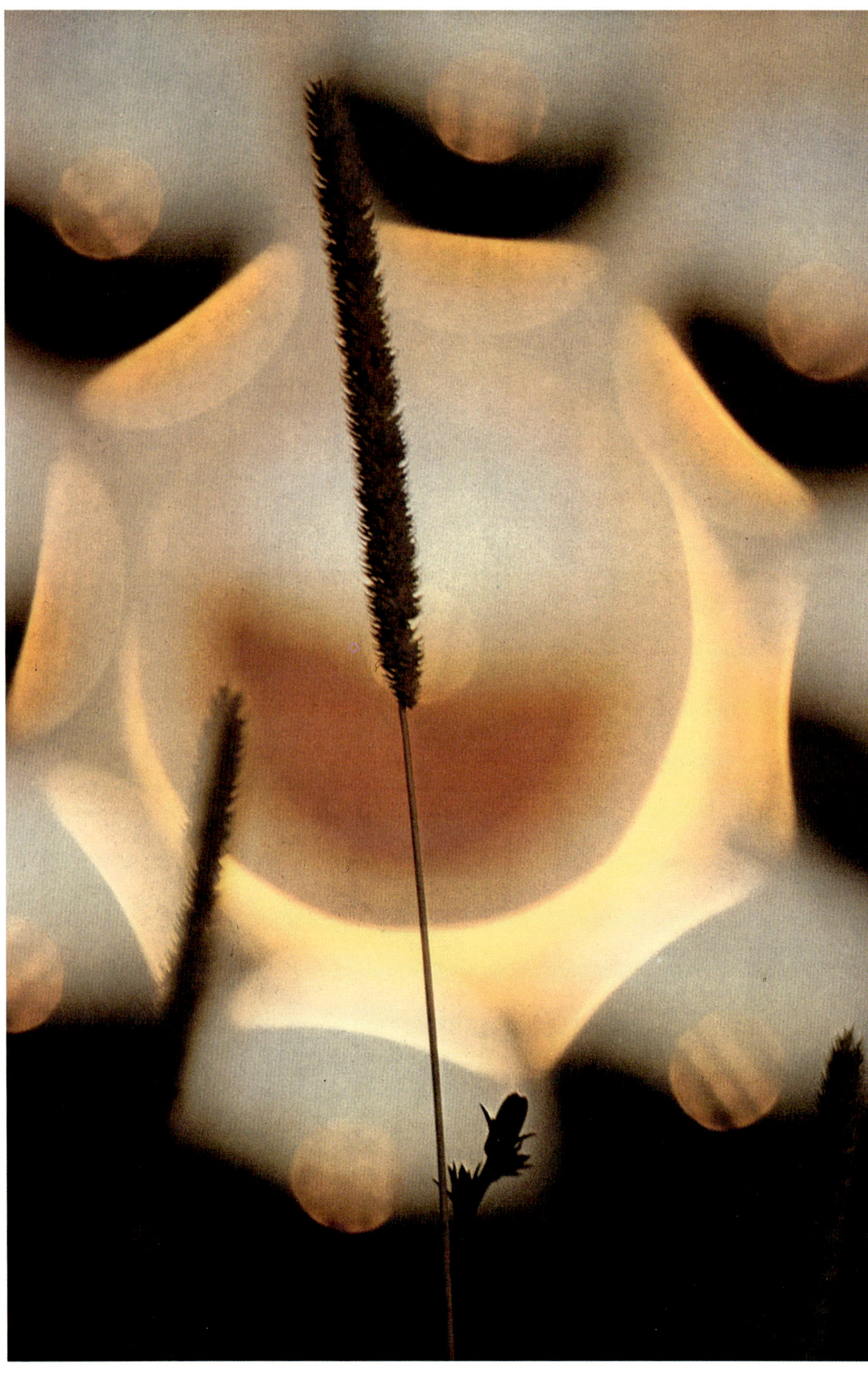

The microlandscape

It is but a short step from the landscape photograph in which a detail can assume particular significance and convey the atmosphere of an entire scene to the so-called microlandscape. The microlandscape uses a minimal, sometimes microscopic detail, to express the element contained in an environment. The picture often magnifies that detail a great deal, or simply isolates it, but emphasizing it in such a way that it assumes significance.
There are very many other cases in which the microlandscape, instead of being used to illustrate the environment in which it is contained, is autonomous, and becomes an end in itself. Its values assume an analogical significance, evoking lines, colours and shapes which we normally find in other experiences and which stimulate our imagination, introducing us to wholly unexpected dimensions and environments.
Note that the microlandscape must not be confused with photography under the microscope, which can also assume aesthetic values and can also be highly evocative. Microphotography has its own particular scientific technique, from which microlandscapes are excluded. The purpose of the microlandscape is not to show us the invisible, or help us perform an experimental survey, but merely to show us the fantastic side of details which escape our notice on account of their small size.
The microlandscape can therefore introduce us to fascinating aspects of the reality about us. Thus flowers in a vase, a trickle of water on a window pane or the reflections in a drinking glass will be sufficient to reveal vast panoramas and huge dimensions. But very often, the objects, spaces and forms will be largely fantastic and the spirit with which the photographer sets about discovering and choosing them can be as paradoxical, eccentric and fanciful as they are documentary and he will need all his discrimination not to get carried away.
The microlandscape nearly always involves a basic technical problem. As these photographs are taken at very close range, the focus of the image, the depth of field, can only cover a very small area, of no more than a few millimeters; hence the photographer must ensure that the parts which will be out of focus are not counterproductive.
On the other hand, precisely because his work covers a very small area, he will be able to avail himself of some advantages which normally only apply to photographs taken in other than natural light.

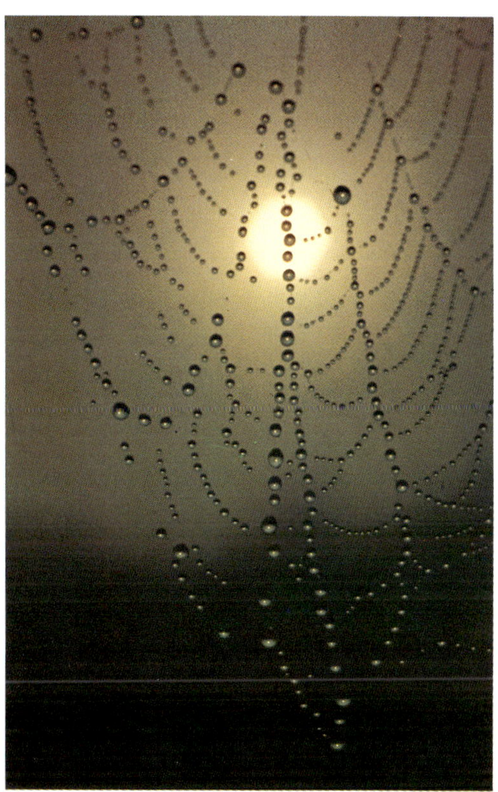

On the opposite page, a microlandscape built around a strand of flowering grass. The sharp and blurred parts are superbly balanced and the light lends particular magic to the composition.

Above, a cobweb viewed against the light, covered in drops of water which invest it with a jewel-like quality. Below, two strands of grass bathed in dew, a composition of extreme geometrical purity. Both pictures are highly evocative.

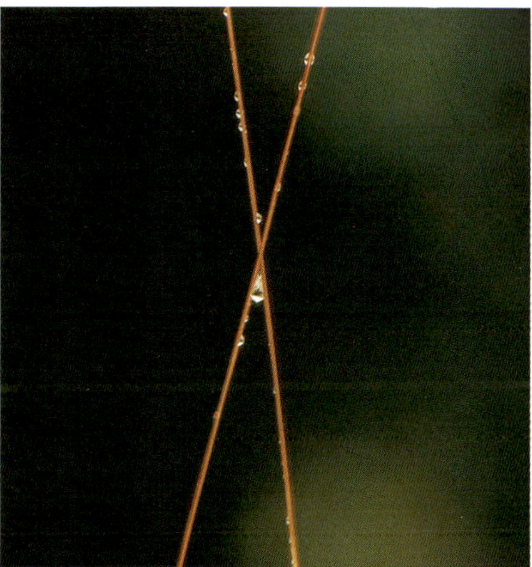

The choice of expressive elements

To prepare ourselves for landscape photography, we can proceed in two directions: one regarding technical procedures; the other, aspects of the configuration of the landscape. The first will give us interchangeable experience. The technical problems involved when dealing with a snowy landscape, for instance, can be the same for the whole variety of landscapes of this kind. It is the same when one wishes to show a rough sea, or a thicket, etc. But in the second direction, regarding the structure of the landscape, the problems will be different each time. When faced with a landscape it is very important to establish the correct angle for the lens and the best light. In short, even before choosing the frame, it will be important to understand which are the most expressive elements of that landscape. Understanding a landscape is the first, important operation to be performed. And to understand it, it may not be sufficient to admire it or be moved by it. You need to know how to capture the atmosphere and the infinite details which make it distinctive. Sometimes, experience of other art forms can offer unexpected help in this analysis. The verses of a poet, the lines of an author, can help us understand a landscape;

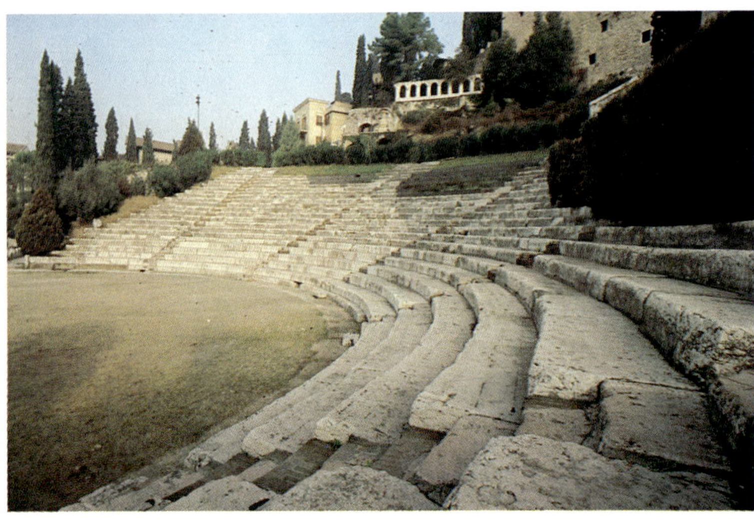

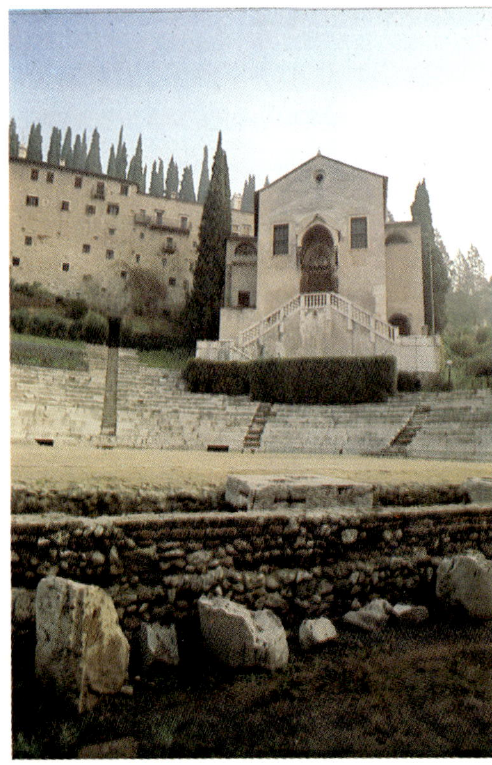

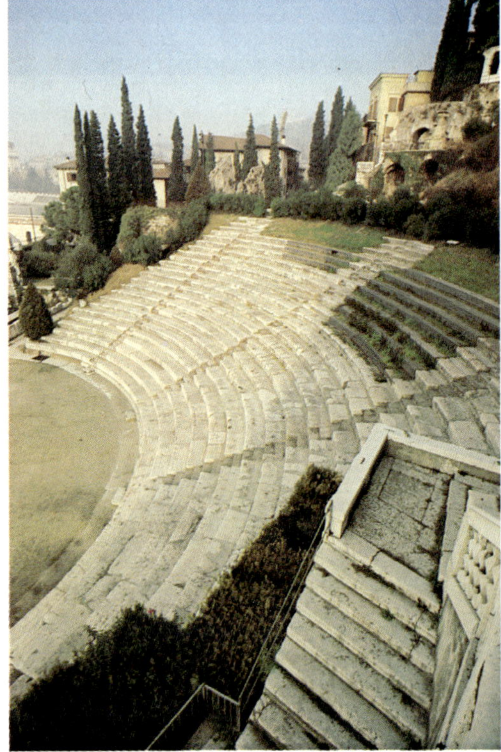

These photographs are not intended to be artistic. They serve to illustrate the wide variety of frames which can be taken of a single monument such as the Roman theater in Verona. The pictures were taken at the same time of day, as is apparent from the light. Naturally, the same photographs could have been further multiplied by taking them at different times or on different days and maybe animating the theater with a few figures. This could safely have been done without undermining its architectural quality, given that this is an important monument of greater historical than artistic interest.
Every monument, every environment, every landscape, can suggest innumerable photographs, and the beginner should practise finding them, by studying the subject attentively.

they may reveal a hidden meaning which had escaped us. Above all if a landscape carries the mark of past events, or the customs or mentality of the people still living there today, a knowledge of the history and traditions of the area can help us discover motifs, signs, colours and harmonies which we were at first quite unaware of.
From a formal point of view, it should be borne in mind that every work of art, every fine photograph has its own general harmony, which is also a sign of the completeness of a work. This is particularly important in landscape photography, which, by its very nature embraces a multiplicity of themes. This poses

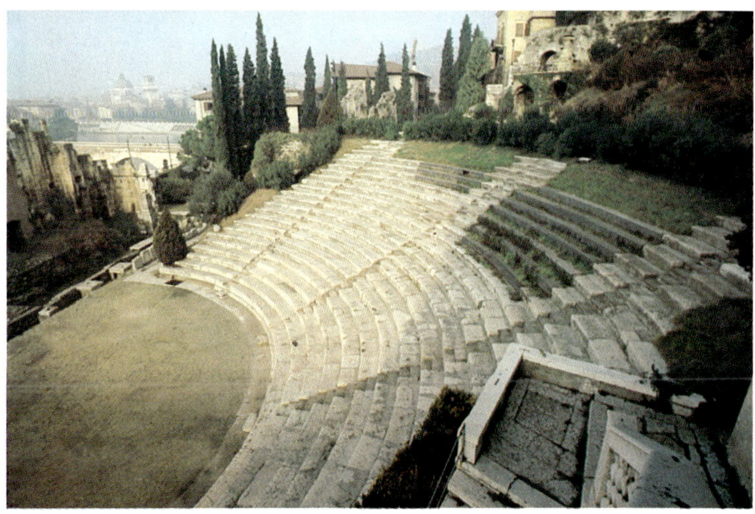

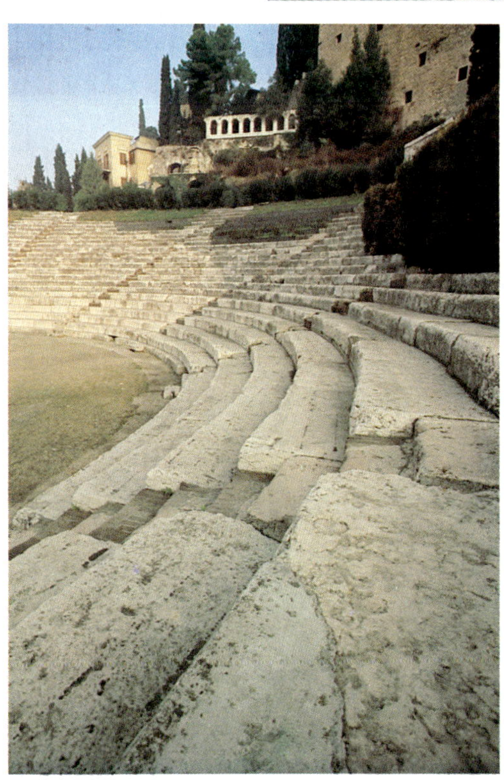

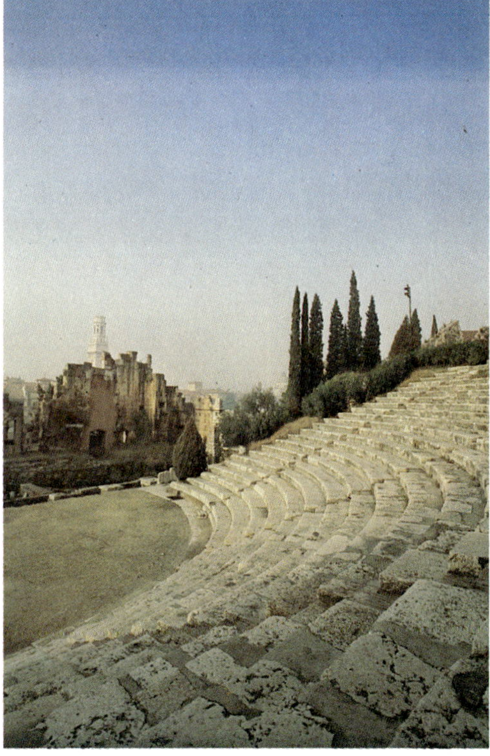

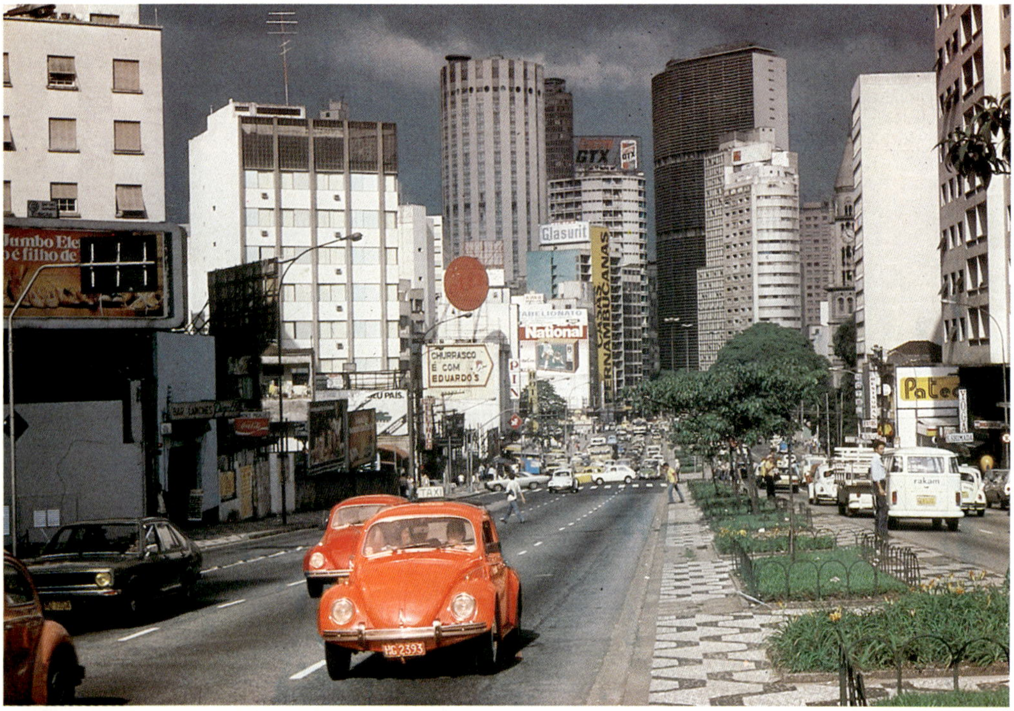

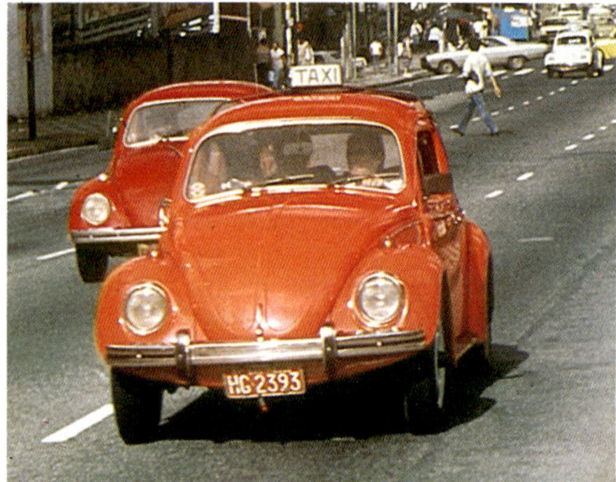

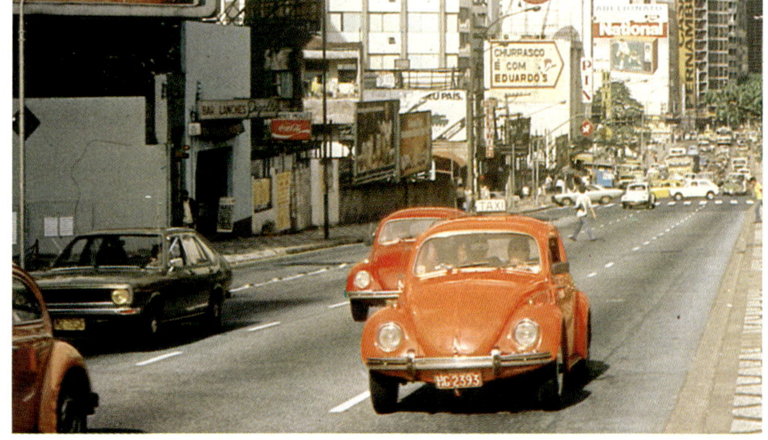

problems which seem to be inversely proportional to the enthusiasm with which very many approach them, attracted by their apparent simplicity, by the fascination the landscape exercises, almost invariably to be disillusioned by the results, if they are not adequately prepared. What could be more inspiring than the luxuriant vegetation of summer months? Yet an experienced photographer knows that those greens which are so pleasing to the eye are in fact a considerable obstacle to the production of a good photograph. What disappointment, to turn to another even more common example, a brilliantly clear, sunny day can produce. Many photographers prefer a slightly veiled sun or even an overcast sky to these radiant days, unless, of course, such effects defeat the very purpose of the photograph.

The experienced photographer knows in any case that he must adapt to very different situations and that he cannot always expect to accomplish what he

A good photograph, if technically correct and taken on large format or very fine grain film, can be enlarged during printing and even trimmed to produce independent pictures, as required.
Here we see the various possible versions of a good photograph taken in São Paolo, Brazil, which is particularly rich in interesting detail.

set out to achieve. Maybe, in fact, his very flexibility is a measure of his worth, his ability to adapt to the solutions which are presented to him, in such a way as to obtain the most effective results from them at all times. But remember that a photographer, any photographer, never reproduces reality as we see it, or are accustomed to seeing it, but in terms of relationships which are due to a multiplicity of factors — the type of frame, first and foremost, not to mention colours, proportions, etc. A subject, in the context of a landscape, can appear to have a given value,

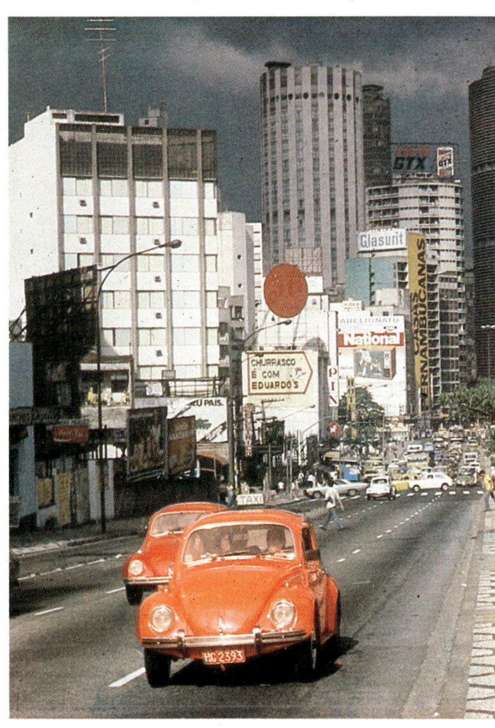

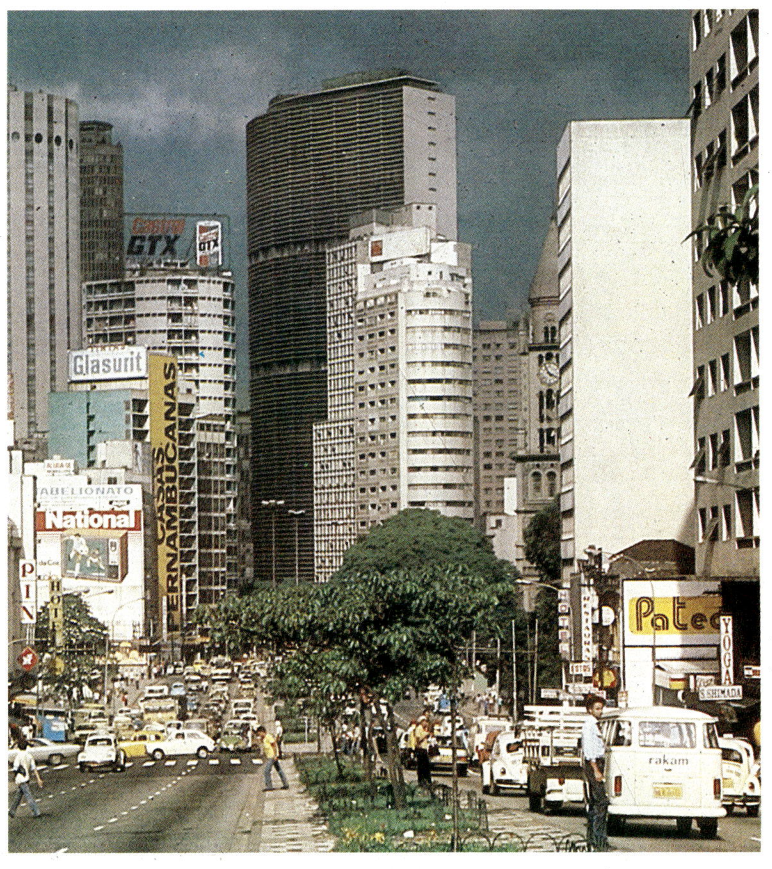

but when we come to isolate it, it assumes another. Conversely, a detail on which our eye comes to rest, which may seem vitally important, when placed together with other details, can almost disappear. The fact is that our eye does not just see, but reasons, selects, establishes hierarchies in turn. The beginner tends to be unaware of this problem and trusts ingenuously to what his eyes think they see, whilst the skilled photographer already knows what the results will be and has learned to adapt himself in such a way that he is able, instinctively, to translate the "real" image into the one which will be reproduced.

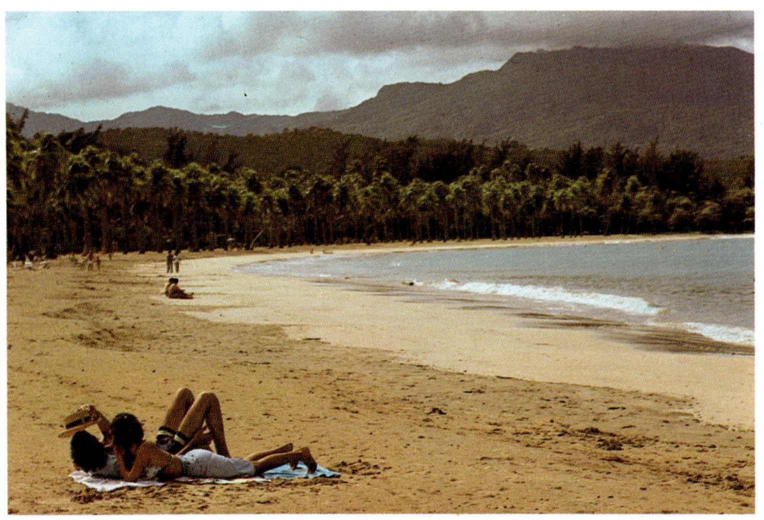

Left, a good photograph of a bay: the photographer has succeeded in interpreting the breadth of the beach, by placing the couple to one side and resisting the temptation to make them a central motif. It is a typical example of a photograph by a skilled photographer which raises no particular interpretational problems.
Below, a view of a rocky inlet, where the massed flowers have been shown to advantage, partly by contrast.

On the opposite page, above, in a somewhat dreary environment, the photographer has succeeded in setting off the otherwise insignificant motif of the palm, and in fact creating a striking ecological contrast.
The photograph below, showing the main square in Assisi, is effective as a living interpretation of the environment, even though its historical features are left unexplored.

Preparing oneself for the subject

To understand the landscape better, it would not be a bad idea for the photographer to turn up ready equipped with a fair amount of knowledge of the subject he is to be dealing with, irrespective of a physical acquaintance with it.

It may not be necessary, because intuition, inspiration and creative capacity can make up for many deficiencies, but it can also be extremely useful and never harmful to prepare onself. Knowing what one is going to see, so that there will not be the surprise of the unexpected (there will always be some degree of surprise because the imagination alone will never give us the fullness of reality) but so that the encounter can be almost familiar and facilitate our getting to grips with the environment.
Often, even the skilled photographer in

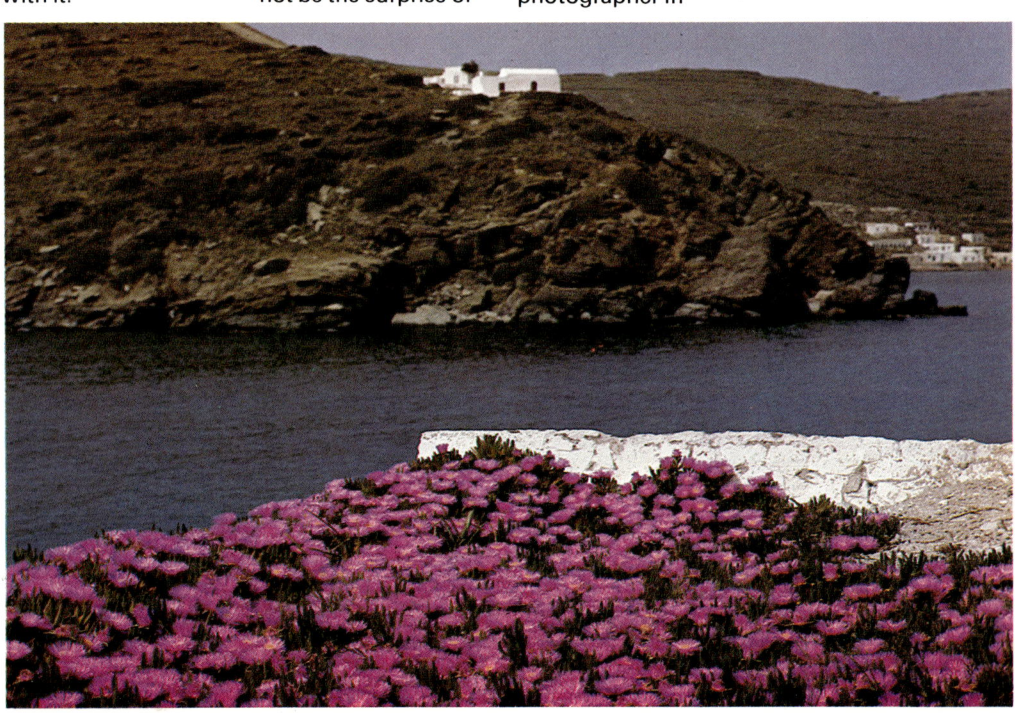

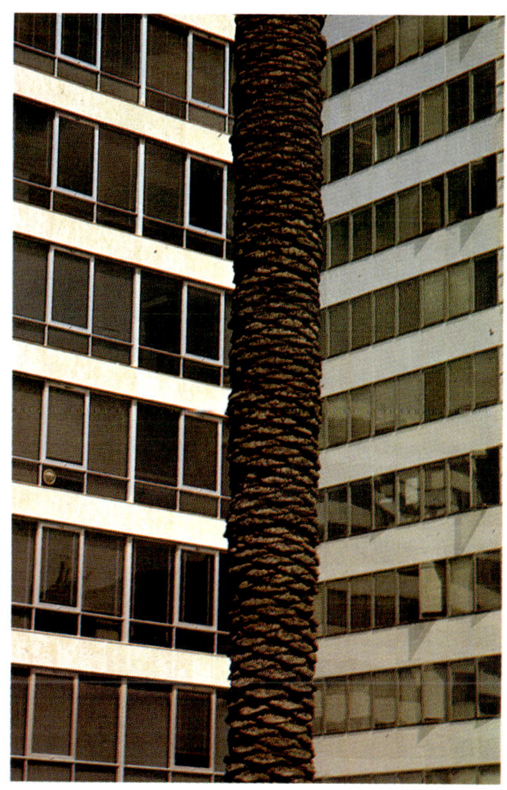

search of impressions risks being struck by interesting but superficial details. He sets out to photograph the slope of a hill and his eye is caught by a bird perched on a branch, or flowers peeping out of a bush. Those flowers and that bird are very lovely, but they could have been in any other place, on any other hillside. Had he known the place better, he would have been able to proceed without too many distractions, to much more distinctive views. It is as though a photographer, having been asked to show the appearance of a city, were to wander through it at random and lose himself in the broad avenues, before the great monuments, unaware that there were alleys, houses and details of monuments capable of revealing its innermost secrets. One can see very skilled photographers wandering unprepared through areas they do not know. They always end up by getting away with it, because their experience and technical capacity enable them to bring out the best in even the most mundane scenes. But they often remain sadly foreign to the spirit of those places or only touch on some of their characteristics by chance.

A photographer is not a mere seeker of curiosities, as in fact many amateurs are content to be, but an

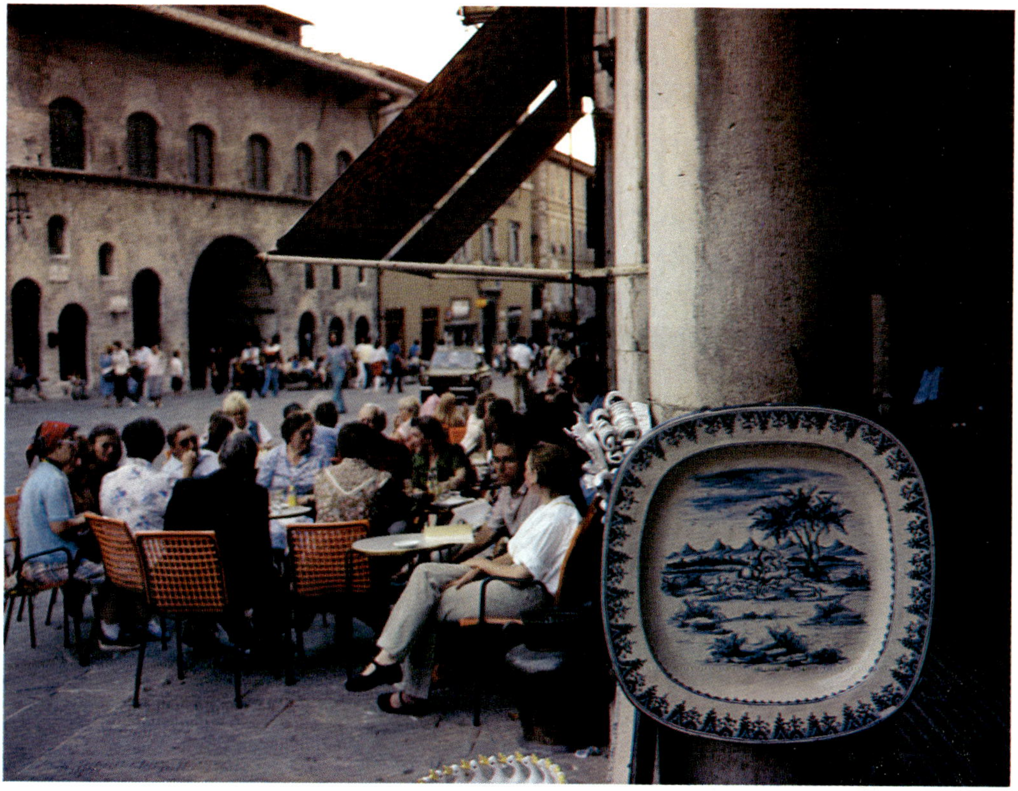

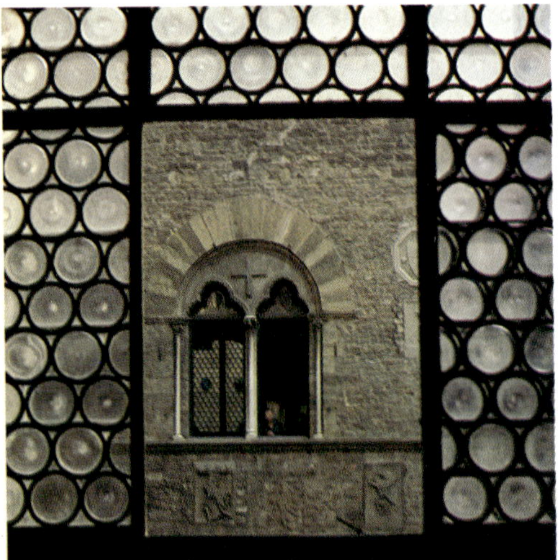

interpreter of situations and states of mind, a revealer of presences hidden from our all too often distracted view, and he can help us understand the harmonies of reality like a painter, and the symbolic meaning of things like a poet. To take good photographs, you need a trained eye and mind.
It is not enough, in fact, to discover objectively interesting themes; you need to know how to translate them into shapes, or rather, know the exact shapes into which they will be translated by the camera. One cannot shoot at random. It is a widespread belief that to take a few good photographs, all you need do is shoot tens, hundreds, thousands. This opinion does little credit to the photographer, because not only is it a waste, but by attributing the good photograph purely to chance, you degrade it to an effortless pastime devoid of any aesthetic value. In which case, one will have to admit that photography is far from being an art, as many people, quite superficially, maintain. Random shooting serves no purpose and is not even a useful exercise from a technical point of view. If you do not study the subject you are dealing with in some way, you will never learn anything.
You never see a good photographer shooting at random. He may behave quite differently before the scenes to be photographed. Some photographers dwell upon the subject at length, study it, weigh it up. In an entire day, they take very few pictures, most of them of a necessarily high standard. If a picture turns out less well, it does not do so by chance but because, in spite of all the care taken, some error was made, some light was over- or underestimated, some feature, or any one of the infinite number of surprises which lenses, filters and films can reserve for us and

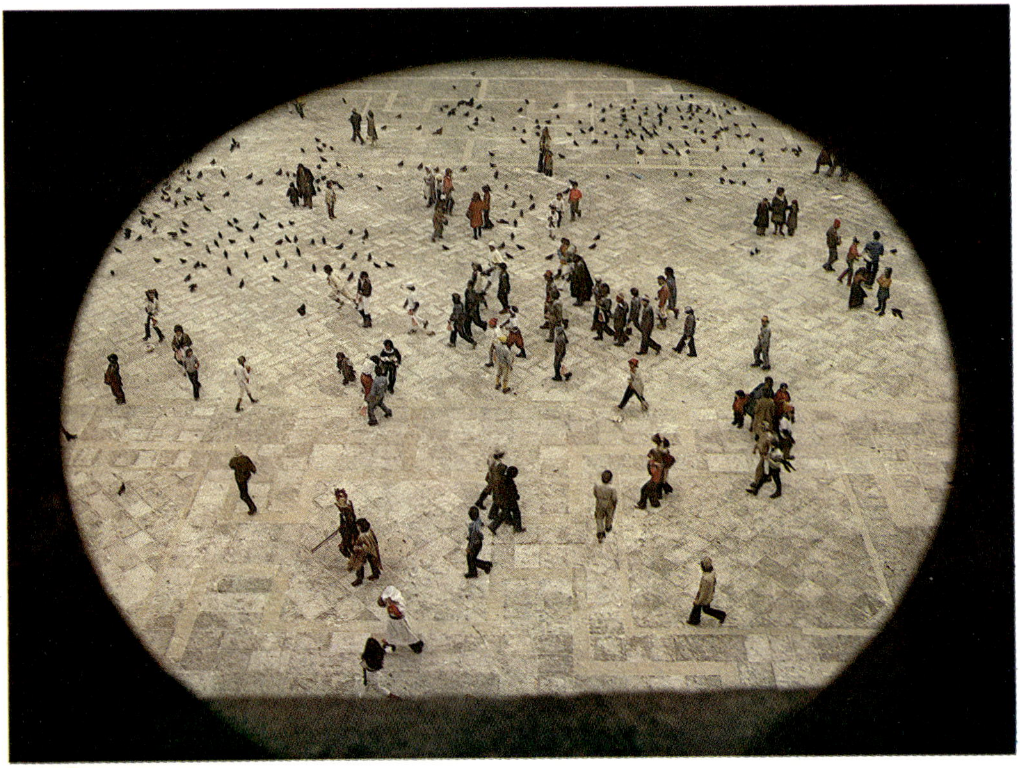

These pages show a series of clever environmental shots even if none of them presupposes any particular preparation. Only the photograph at the bottom of the opposite page, with the detail of St. Mark's Square, presupposes a familiarity with the square itself. The movement of people far and wide over the ancient pavement, mingling with the pigeons, is fairly typical.
The other pictures depend above all on the eye of the photographer, ready to capture a motif capable of setting off the picture.

For the photograph below right, with the Bedouin kneeling in the courtyard of a mosque, the photographer may well have intervened to place the figure in the correct pose, but the artifice is justified by the wisdom with which the scene has been framed, with a subtle balance of light and shade which increases the sense of space.
The photograph, above, right, has caught a gust of wind in a field of flax.

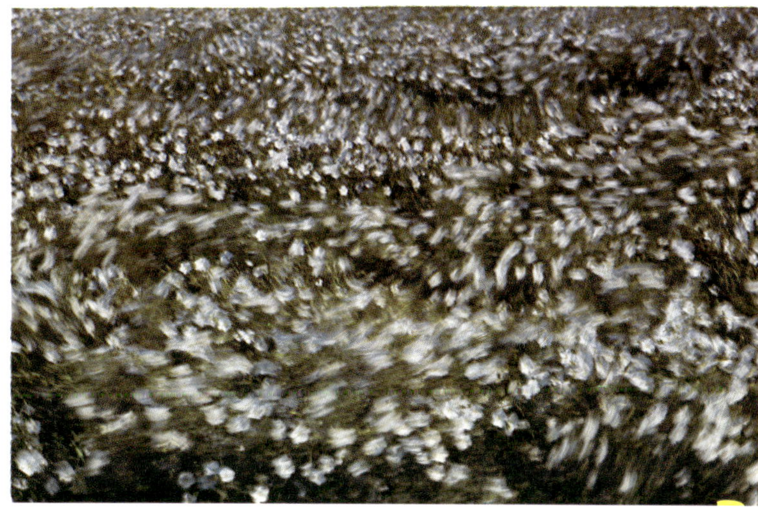

which photographers are familiar with and the casual amateur may not even be aware of.
Other photographers, however, are highly prolific and fast workers. For them, the biggest problem seems to be the need to change film constantly. But they do not take so many photographs to be sure of a few good ones among the many, but simply to pick out the best. To the mortification of the champions of the theory of chance, nearly all of the large number of pictures they take are indeed good.
Naturally, it can happen that even the most experienced photographer has doubts; he could be undecided, between the aperture and shutter speed for example;

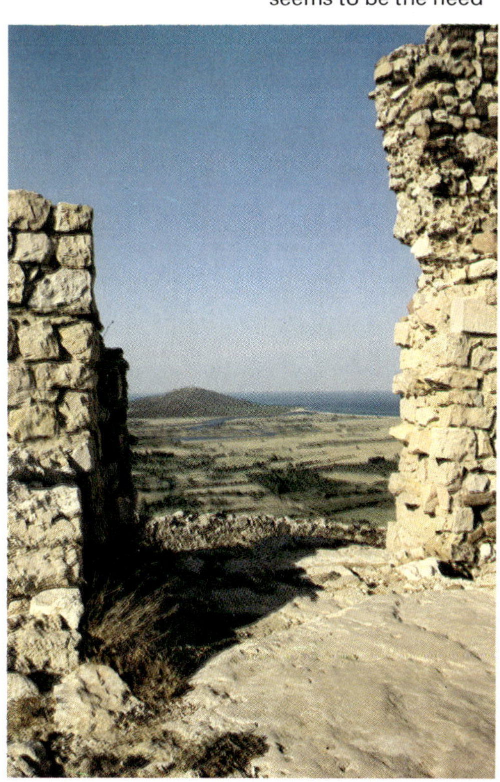

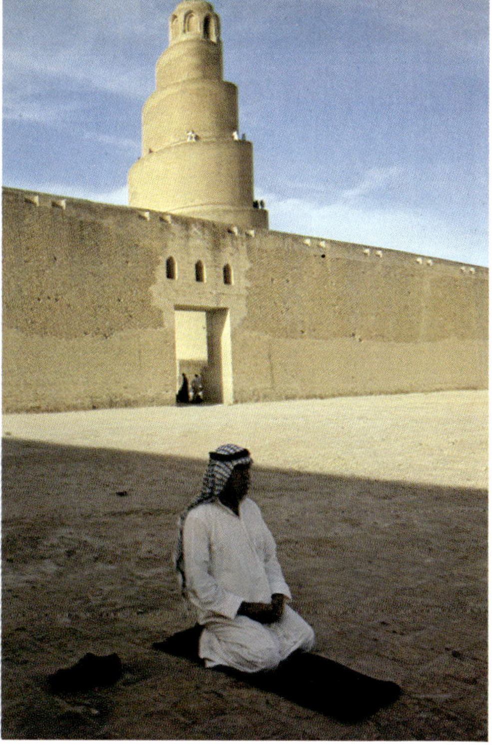

between one filter and another. Very often, he will solve the problem by shooting according to both systems between which he is undecided. Then, having obtained the results, he will choose the photograph which seems to him to be the best. Sometimes, the layman is not even in a position to notice these differences, which are scarcely perceptible. The frame is already so eloquent, the photograph so complete in every respect, that the differences may seem trivial, even if the photographers attach great importance to them.

The photographer can feel an artist's intolerance of certain tasks which seem to him to be superfluous and then, particularly if he is skilful, it will be harder to induce him to carry out a detailed preparation of the subjects he is to be dealing with. It will seem to him that his intuition will suffice and that a minimum of information can exhaust everything that is required of him. This can often be true of the environment in which he normally operates, where his cultural initiation can be accomplished in an infinite number of even indirect ways. One must also recognize that his skill, if he is a professional photographer, or a reporter, or a person with particular experience of the cultural world, will tend to make him learn faster, more spontaneously, more deeply what characterizes an environment. But very often, all this is not enough for a true knowledge and an authentic understanding. As the general level of photographic expression in the world improves, as it undoubtedly is doing, we feel an increasing need for photographers to provide us with something more than an aesthetic emotion, even if highly original, and we are increasingly inclined to notice the gaps they leave in many sectors, which their creativity is not sufficient to fill. It is regrettable that the interpretational skills of the photographer are not more often accompanied by a deeper knowledge of for example, historical or ecological matters. Not for the purpose of making a science of photography, but to bring to it even richer and more interesting creative stimuli. We are equally sorry that scientists themselves, the very people who are expert in so many areas of culture, are not or do not become good photographers in turn, capable of informing us, of educating us, through this very important modern medium.

We must not forget

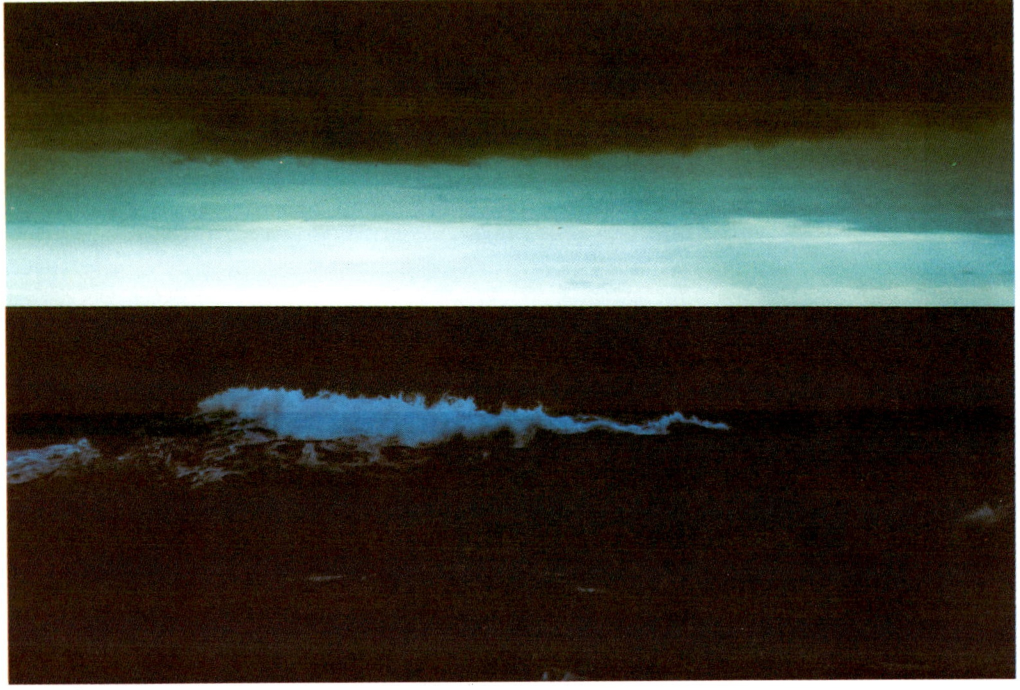

These pages show two photographs of completely different origin.
Above, the frame is designed to capture a natural phenomenon: the breaking of a wave, no matter where, and relies on the extraordinary lighting effect.

The picture on the opposite page shows a sunset from the island of Pellestrina, in the Venetian lagoon and explores the human dimension of an environment steeped in history.

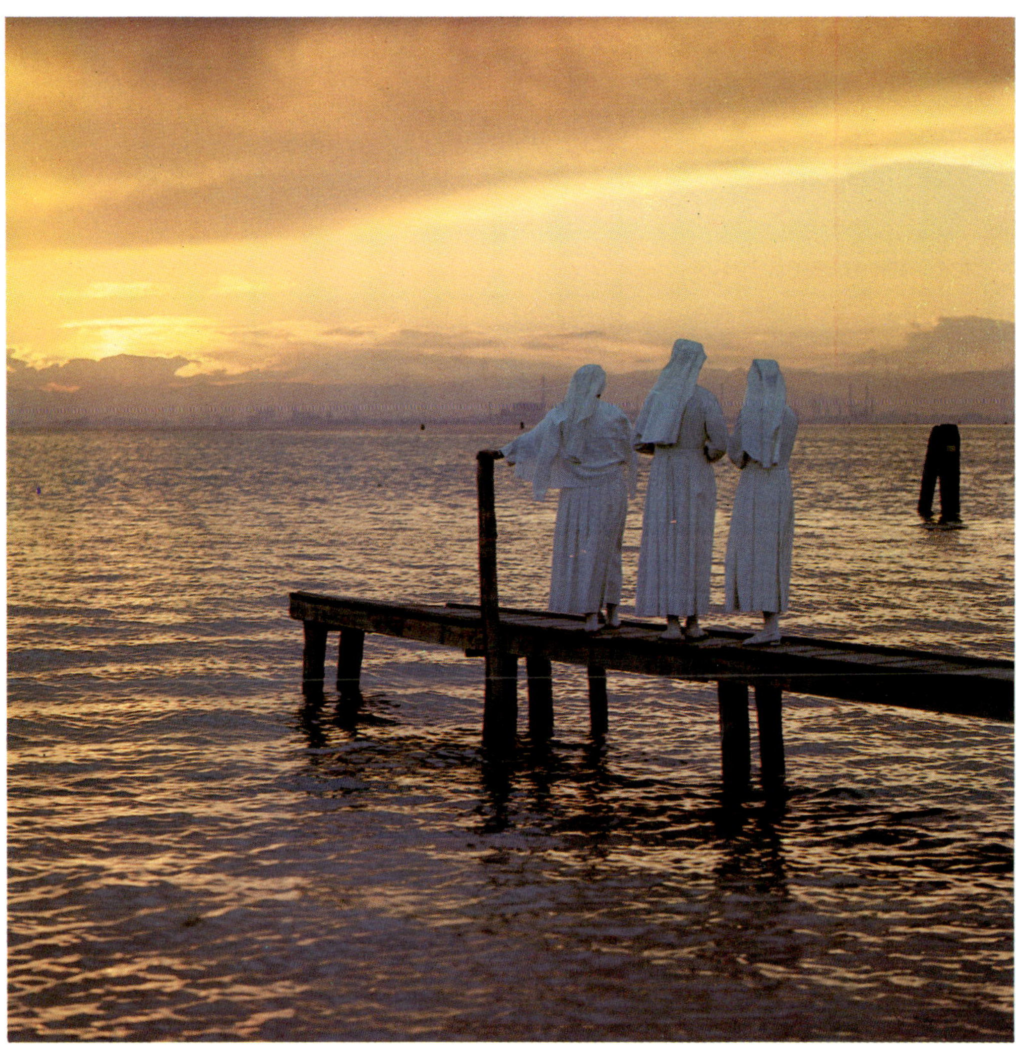

that photography can be a work of fantasy, in which case reality will often only be able to offer a support for a creation which can completely transfigure it. But photography can also be a work of documentation. In fact, in very many cases, it is the most effective and functional means of documentation we have. Just as one must not shoot at random, because nothing serious can be achieved without effort, similarly, no true documentation can be based on superficial knowledge. Even if self-preparation can cost the photographer some sacrifices and a certain amount of patience, he should still operate with his customary spontaneity – which is, of course, essential to success.
This kind of preparation and research, which is absolutely indispensable when the photographer is operating in new countries and environments, can also be valuable to him when dealing with the place where he lives, because it will always enable him to improve his knowledge.
Precisely because it contains the greatest number of geographical, geological, botanical, historical, social, etc. features, landscape photography is the type in which the photographer's knowledge is best able and most needs to assert itself. It will permit him not only to grasp data, aspects and details which could otherwise easily have escaped him, but also to avoid making banal and possibly misguided choices.
Naturally, any preparation must be purposeful: if one is interested in flora, it will need to be strictly botanical in character; if one is interested in history, it will be historical, and if only a general knowledge of the environment is required, many areas of research will prove useful.

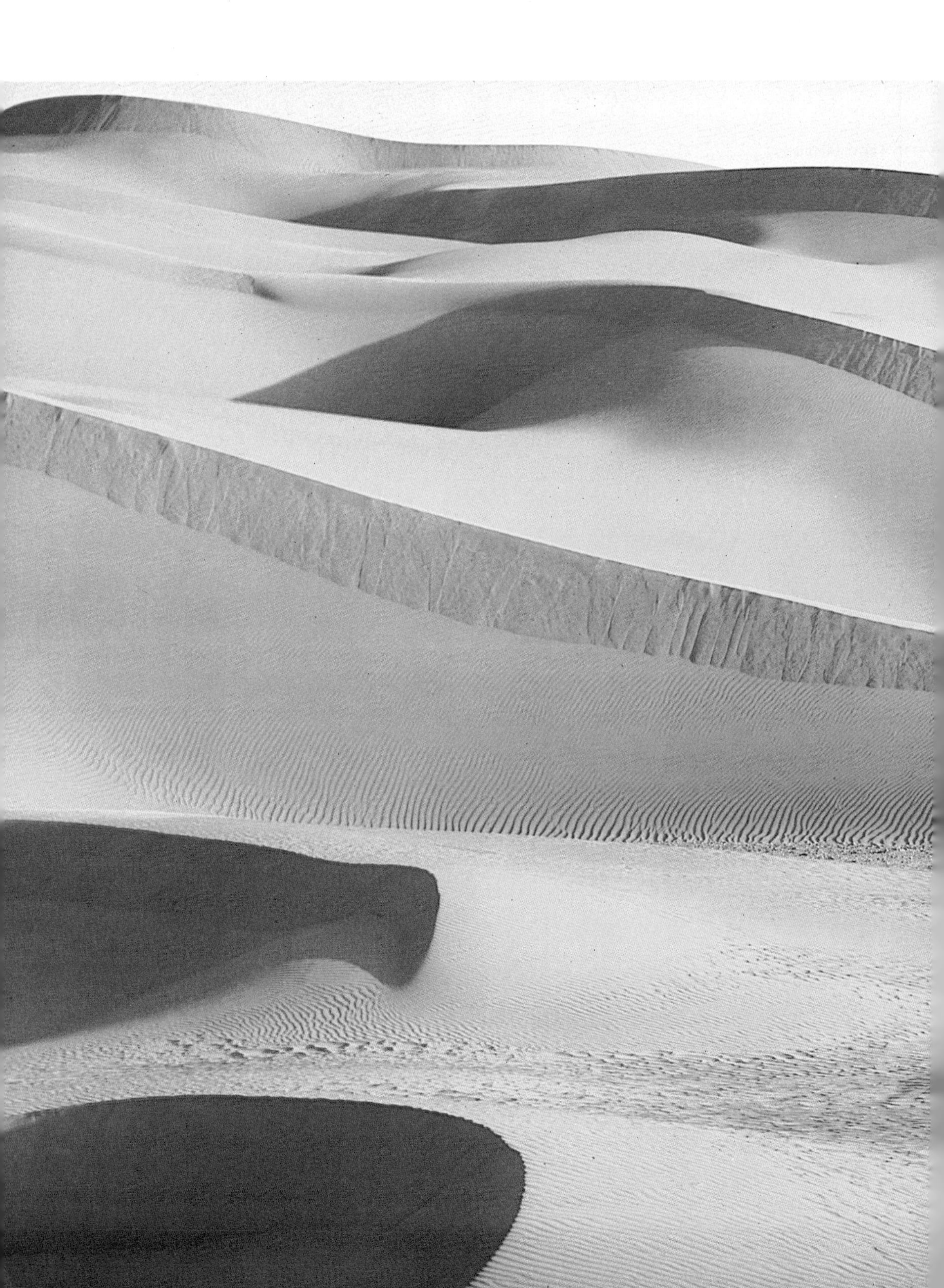

THE LANGUAGE OF SHAPES

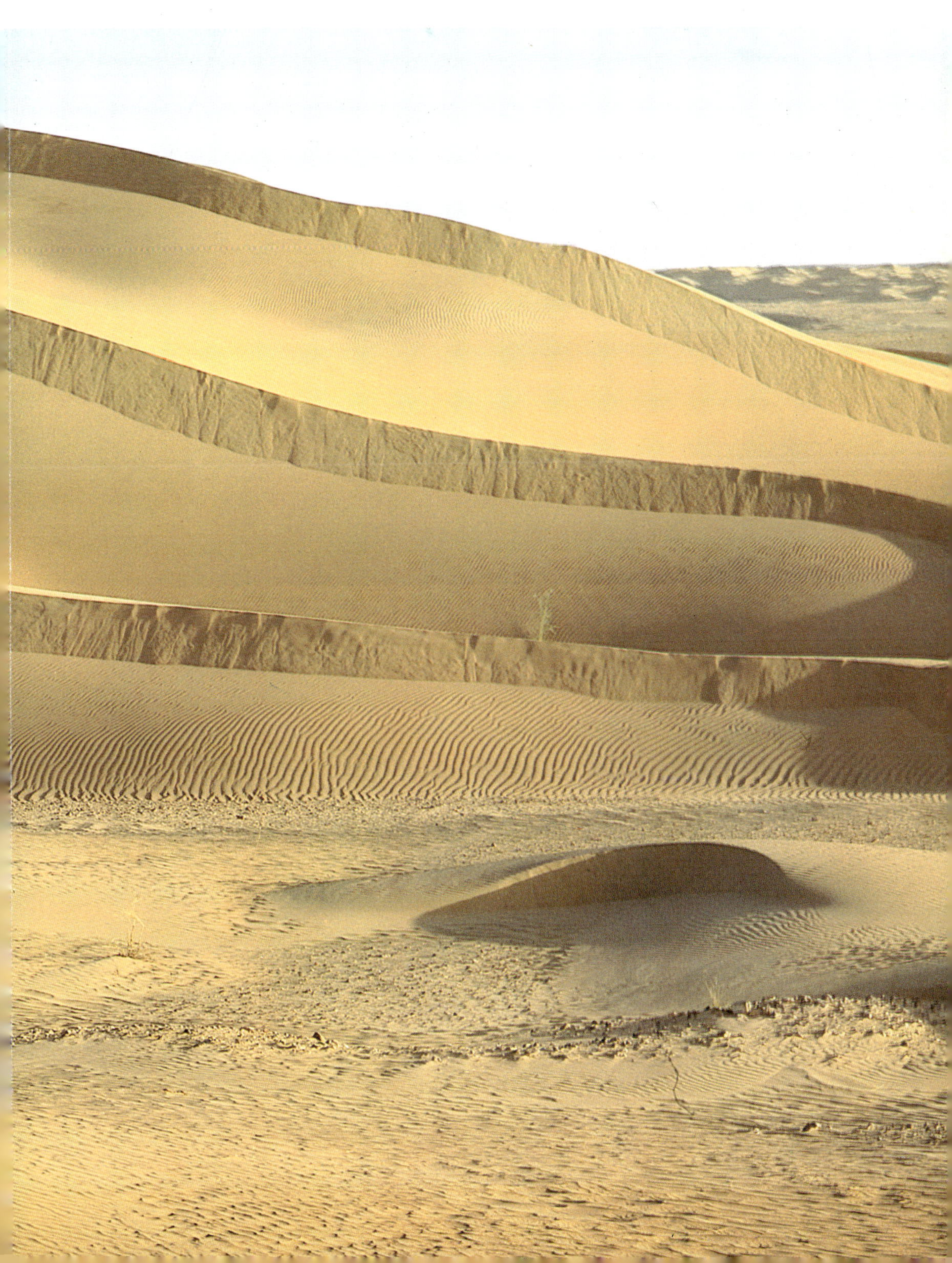

Reading shapes

Our eyes and camera lens see things: mountains, water, trees, flowers, houses, figures. The success of a photograph depends a great deal on the interest these things can arouse, the evocative value of the subject.
In reality, apart from the intrinsic interest the subject arouses, its manner of presentation and interpretation is of fundamental importance. It is from this that one sees the style of a photographer and it is in this way that he manages to convey the subjective side of the photograph which makes it truly original and represents the expression of the photographer's personality and his message. This language, which transcends straightforward reproduction of the objects, and is peculiar to all the figurative arts, is the language of shapes.
Shapes are the graphic and chromatic signs reality assumes when it is defined in the photographic image. In that image, there will no longer be just the object, but the shapes composing it. There will no longer be just the house, or tree, or figure, but the line, colours, rhythms of that house, that tree, that figure.
To understand the meaning of a work of art, we must read shapes. In painting, too, the choice of theme and evocative and symbolic force of the object is very important. In other words, its significance. But the thing which determines the quality of a painting is not the subject matter in itself, but its mode of execution. Now, these signs which constitute the dynamics of a painting and reveal its rhythms, richness and harmony, are also found in photographs. Here we are referring to the normal constituents of the image, and not just its formal emphases or the aestheticism in which the photographer may quite legitimately indulge, which are due to the conscious construction of certain artifices, as when one wishes to give the photograph a particularly surreal or expressionistic appear-

On the two preceding pages, dunes near Ghardaia, in the Sahara. The size and clarity of the desert emphasizes the expressive and decorative value of the great, harmonious masses and the long, flowing lines of the dunes.

Below, Study for autumn, *an oil painting by Kandinsky, 1910. On the threshold of Abstractionism, the painting synthesizes the landscape in a composition made up of lines and masses of colour. The language of shapes is particularly evident.*

On the opposite page, above, this landscape by Fontana is interpreted by extremely simple shapes, unbroken lines and homogeneous surfaces.
Below left, this aerial view depends on the colour contrast of irregular surfaces. Right, a nocturnal interpretation of Brasilia, the image is characterized by linear filaments.

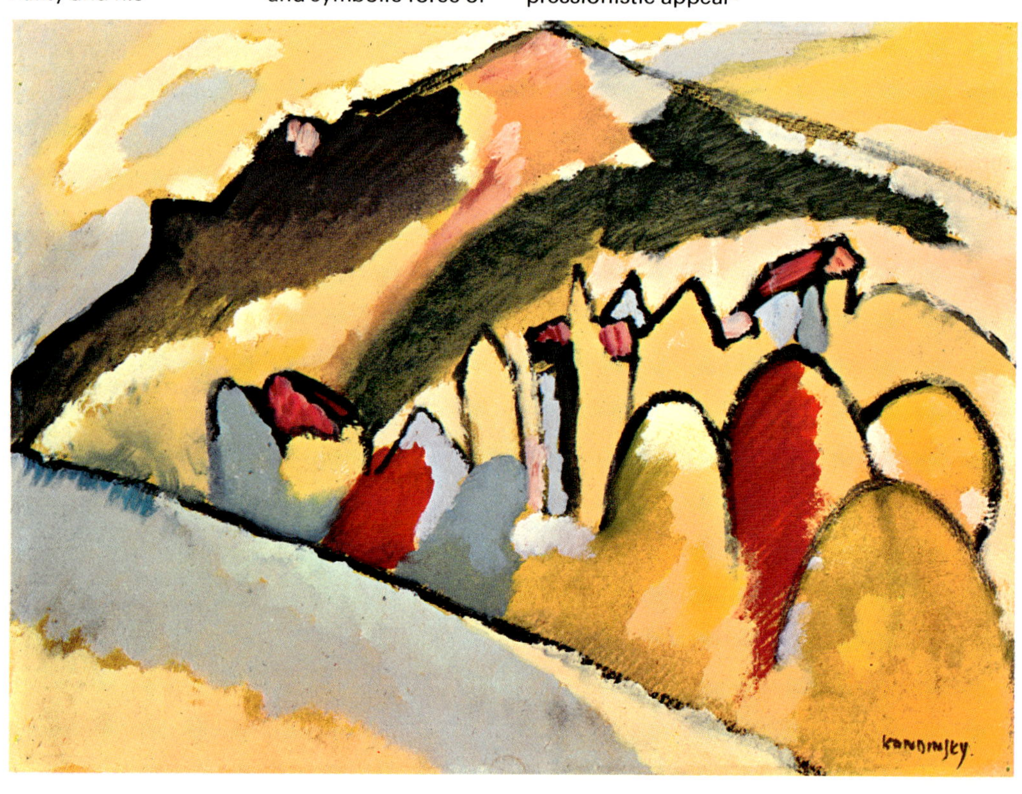

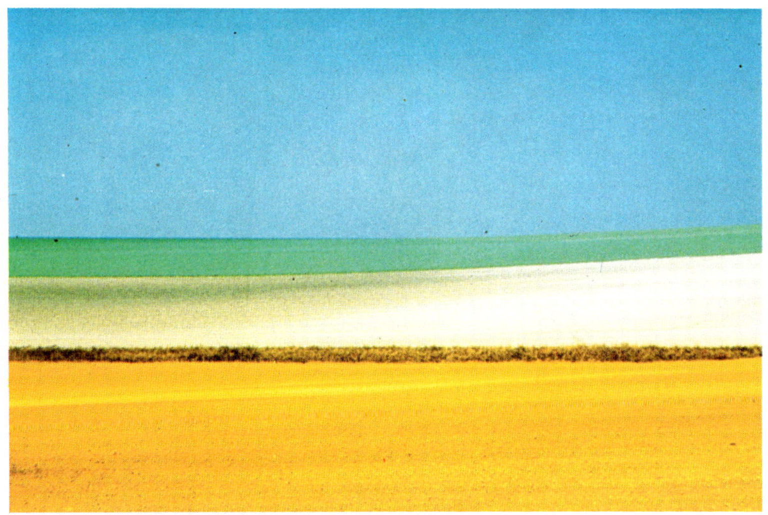

ance. These concepts are perfectly permissible and can sometimes lead to works which are excellent, but in which the value of the shapes has been deliberately underlined to the point where the objective references to the subject matter are greatly reduced or even eliminated. In a snowy landscape, for example, the contrast of shadows has been so much emphasized that anyone observing the photograph has the impression of looking at a type of checker-board in which the original sense of the wintry landscape almost disappears. Or the reflections of a ripple on the sea are so much emphasized that it ends up looking more like a mysterious fabric, making us forget its original nature.

One could continue these examples *ad infinitum* and they are constantly being suggested to us by photographic exhibitions. The language of shapes is abundantly clear in these cases, but there are many other cases of straightforward interpretation rather than stylization of an objective reality, in which the language of shapes translates the objective data without altering it too much, therefore without undue emphasis or the use of anything artificial. Even in these, more normal and undoubtedly more common cases, the language of shapes is clearly evident and by observing the photograph attentively, we

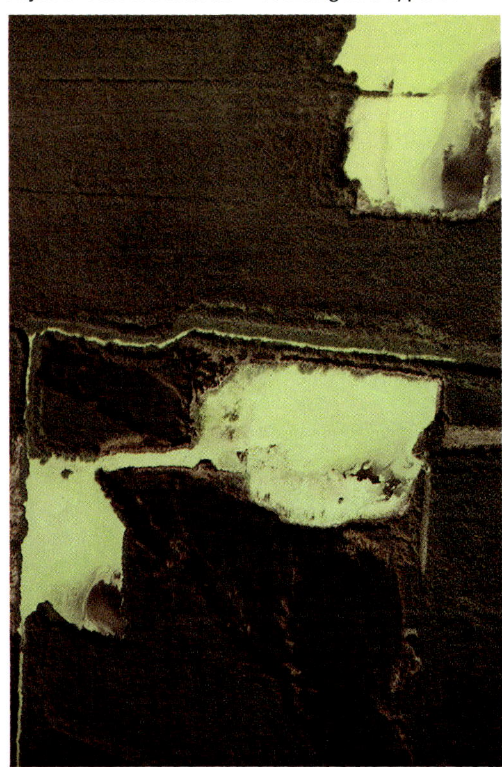

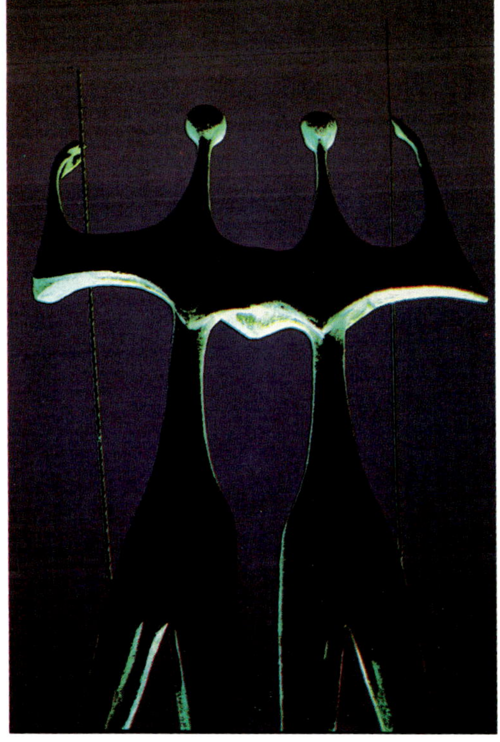

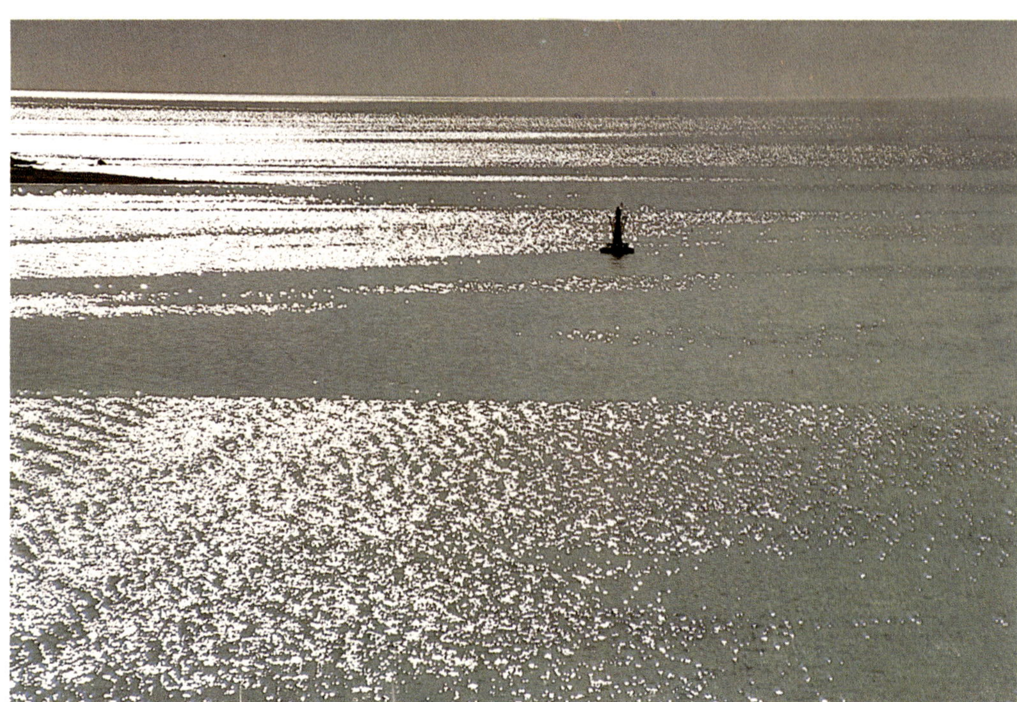

would discover its structure, tensions and harmonies and be able to see whether delicate or abrupt transitions prevailed, continuous or broken lines, calm or excited rhythms, etc.

These remarks should have clarified not only the importance of shapes, but the advantage of analyzing and understanding them. The language of signs must be recognized even before it is interpreted and it will be very useful to train the eye to do this on the works of the top photographers. In this way, we will discover the coherence of their language and also its richness. A photograph can be formally rich even when it contains few compositional elements. In this case, the quality of relationships can make up for quantity. The spatial and chromatic proportions and conciseness of a few signs can be richer and more expressive than a multiplicity of details.

Naturally, conciseness or breadth of description do not create a work of art. There are works of art based on synthesis, just as there are others based on an abundance of details. One can achieve equilibrium with few elements, as with many. What is important is for the work to achieve an equilibrium, a state of completeness, and this can vary in nature, being either static or dynamic, based on contrasts, or harmonies. There are clearly discernible harmonies, which invite the definition "classic," just as there are other, less obvious ones which arise out of discords, disproportions and juxtapositions of shapes which are apparently very different, but which find agreement and cohesion in the reality of the work. The number

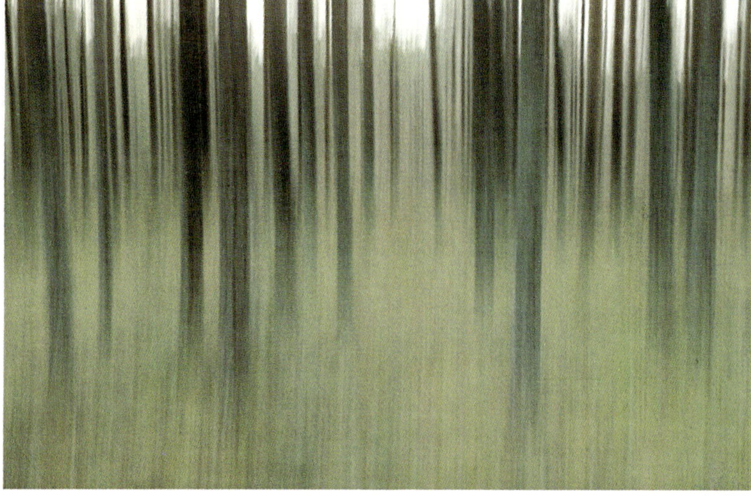

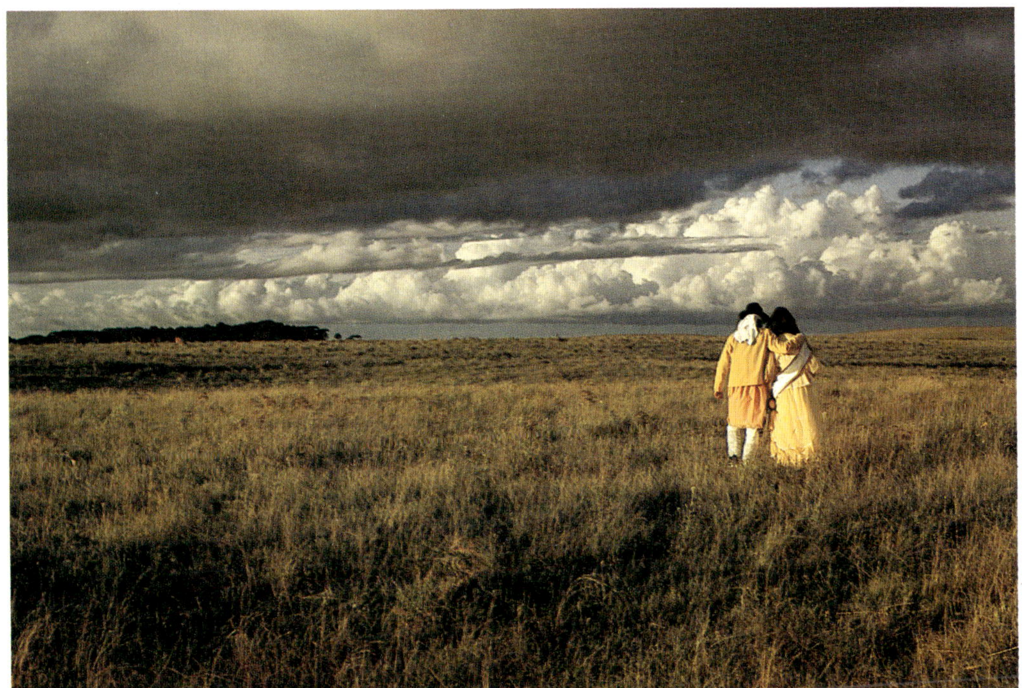

The expressive force of the photograph at the top of the facing page is due to the juxtaposition of broad areas of light with a varied shimmer of reflections. The breadth is so absolute that it gives an idea of the immensity of the sea even before the relationship with the solitary boat.
Below, a clear example of the prevalence of linear motifs, deliberately emphasized by the photographer moving the lens upwards during exposure.

of possible examples is infinite and can convince us that no starting point is inappropriate, neither one which attempts the most daring, unpredictable and paradoxical solutions, nor one which seems to lead us along well-trodden paths and is content with extremely simple, almost scholastic solutions. There are photographs and works of art which owe their beauty to their constituent order; others to their disorder. But we should avoid adopting one of these positions in the absence of either the necessary circumstances or vocation. The results would inevitably look forced. One cannot go against one's nature, not even with the noble intention of improvement. Once again, the comparison with painting and other areas of artistic activity can show us the results which can be achieved by expressive language.

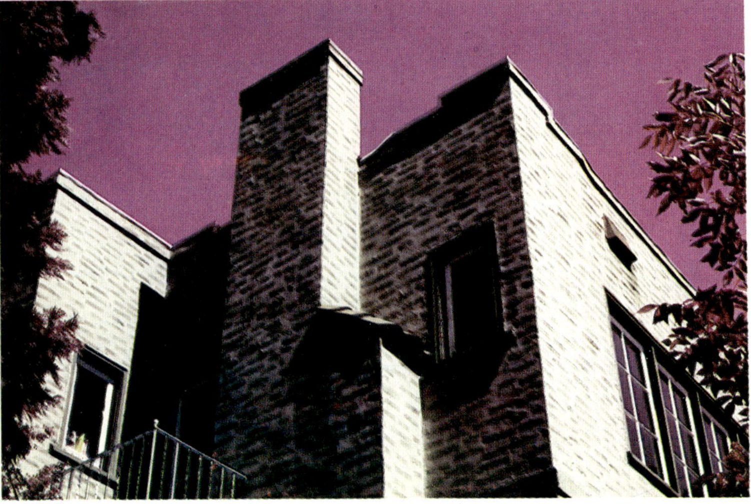

Above, a photograph based on lighting effects and intense colours rather than graphic motifs. The couple focus the light and their prominence emphasizes the contrasts already inherent in the composition.
The photograph on the right of the Heithaus building in Oakland, exemplifies the expressive use of colour, cleverly adapted here to the plastic force of architectural relief. The effects are accentuated by the use of infra-red film which introduces a note of anguish to the picture.

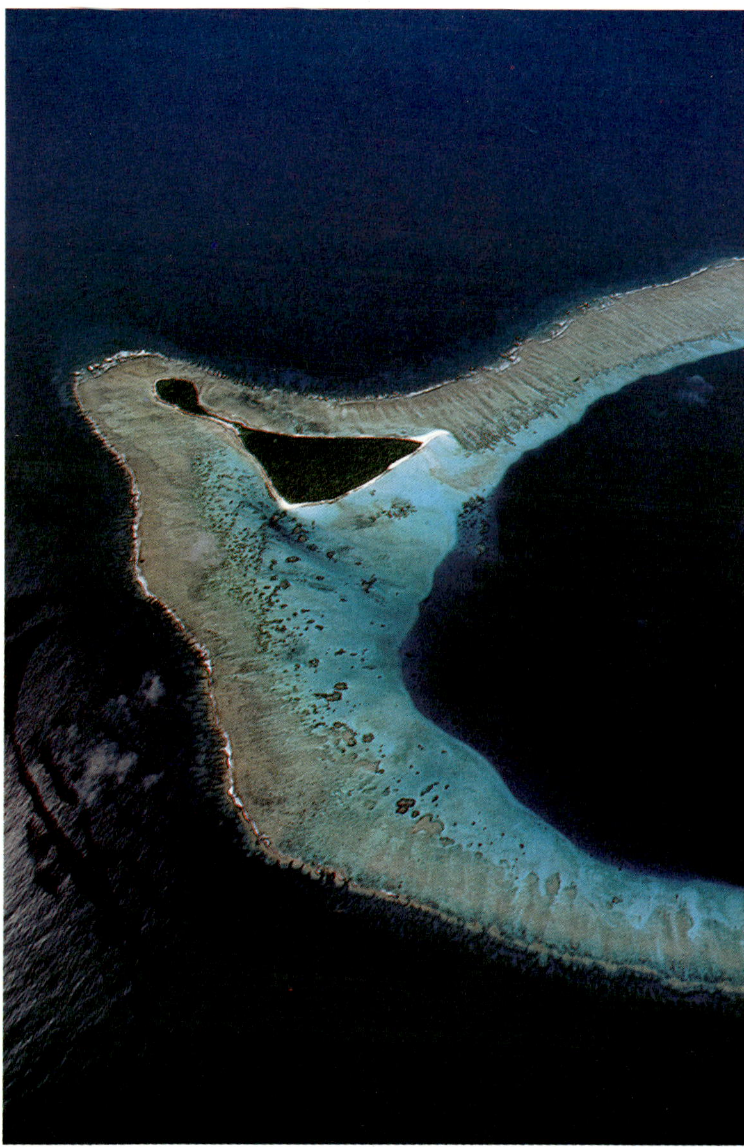

Aerial photography

If landscape photography has often followed in the footsteps of landscape painting, there are instances today where the opposite has occurred and painting has made use of the results of photography, above all on discovering the abstract values of pictures taken from aircraft.

This unusual view of reality – to which, however, we are becoming increasingly accustomed – can be extremely important for our scientific knowledge, enabling us to grasp a geography which no longer requires the normal aid of a map, but is reproduced in all its infinite nuances and with an incomparable degree of authenticity.

The photograph by Georg Gerster showing an atoll in the Fiji Islands, not only provides an exceptional view of the configuration of the island, but the intense shades of sky blue and indigo evoke the atmosphere of the sea.

On the opposite page, the same photographer shows us an African village on an island of the River Niger. Few abstract paintings could give us such a vivid and imaginative sense of "matter."

Apart from this valuable documentary role, aerial photography offers us a vast range of juxtapositions and arrangements with which only the most extreme examples of abstract painting would seem able to compete.
Special cameras are available for aerial photography, but the photographer can also use normal equipment, taking care to choose low-speed films with a very fine grain. He will have no difficulty with the aperture, given that there is no need to adjust the depth of field, as the distance will always correspond to infinity.
These photographs can be taken from special planes and helicopters, but if the lighting conditions, windows and seating arrangements for passengers permit, they can also be taken from normal, commercial aircraft.
The most interesting photographs are those taken at low altitude and with a low sun. The exposure times must always be minimal (from 1/250 to 1/1000).
The following pages are devoted to an anthology of landscape photographs by some famous photographers. We have sought to give an idea of how important it can be to be aware of what some artists have been capable of doing, in order to stimulate our own critical sense and creative capacities.

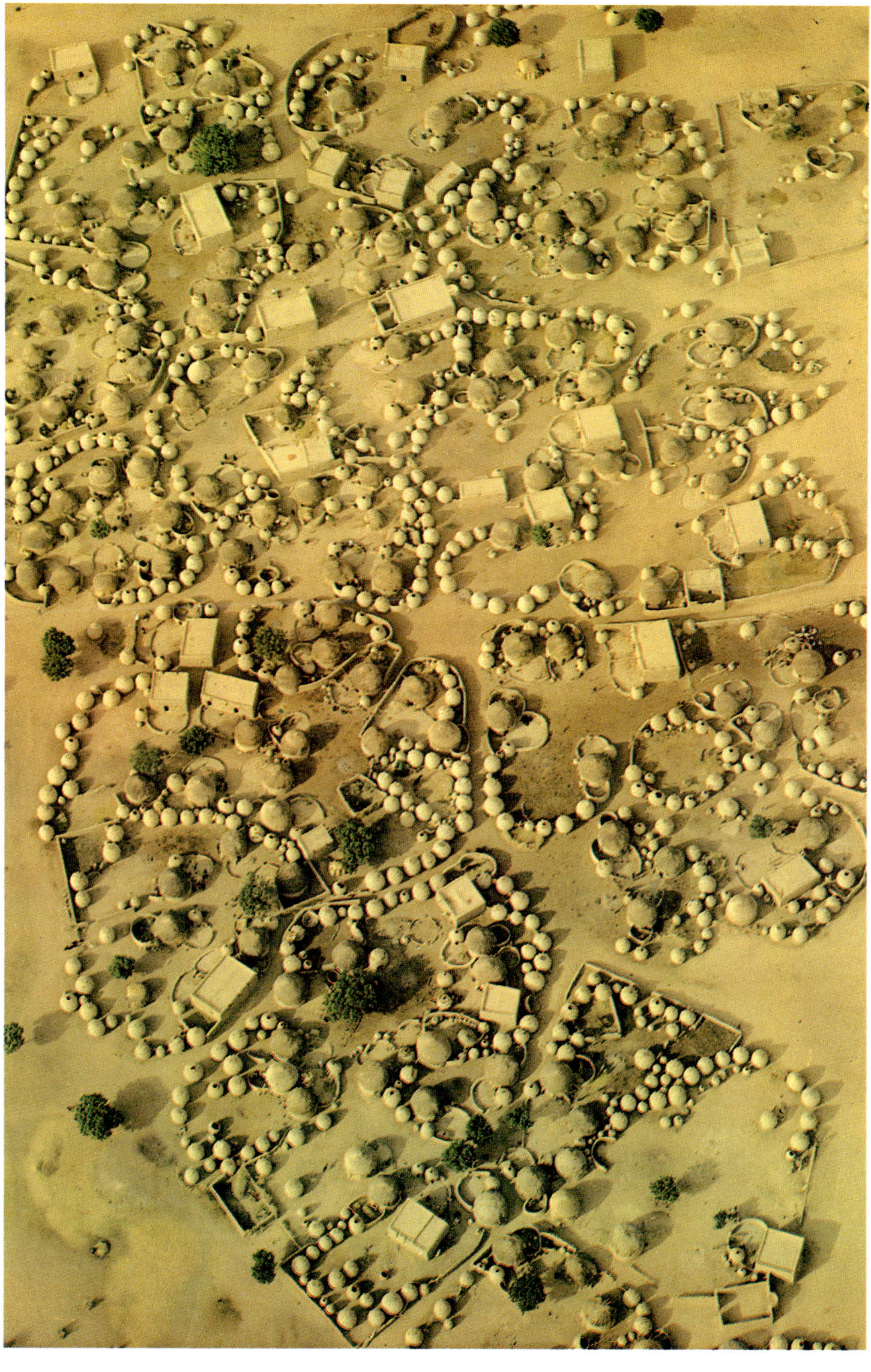

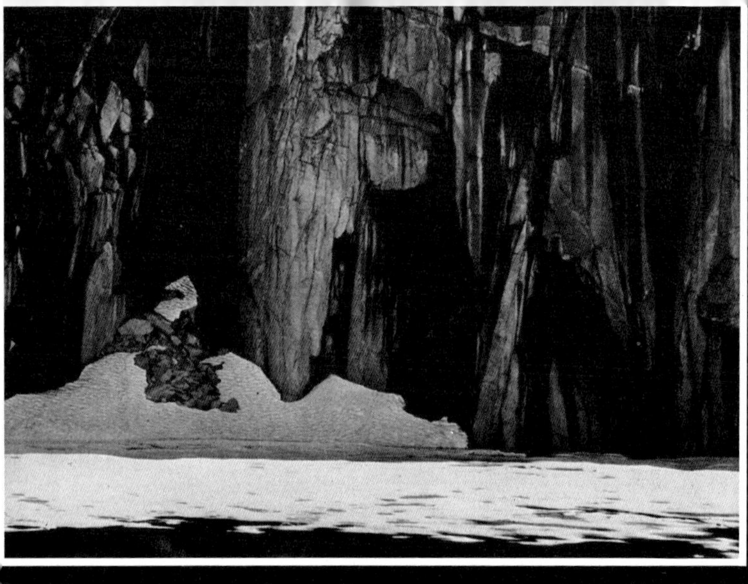

Ansel Adams

Generally regarded as one of the greatest American photographers, who has devoted himself almost exclusively to landscapes, to the point of being considered the most authentic interpreter of American scenery.
He studied music as a young man, and began taking photographs when still a boy, devoting himself to the Yosemite Valley, and has continued to concern himself above all with the scenery of the Far West.
In 1932, Ansel Adams founded the f/64 Group, together with six other photographers, whose aim was to emphasize the definition and depth of field to be obtained with small apertures.
Good definition is in fact one of Adams' basic precepts and he shuns artificial techniques.
The four photographs that are reproduced here are a demonstration of the results which can be obtained with black-and-white.
The wealth of greys, with sensitive harmonies and highly effective compositions, make up for the lack of colour. An eloquent, profound, and almost religious love of nature inspires this photographer, who is constantly looking for more interesting, more revealing pictures. His work is characterized by a sense of grandeur which conveys all the magnitude of the spaces he is portraying and elevating force of the atmosphere.

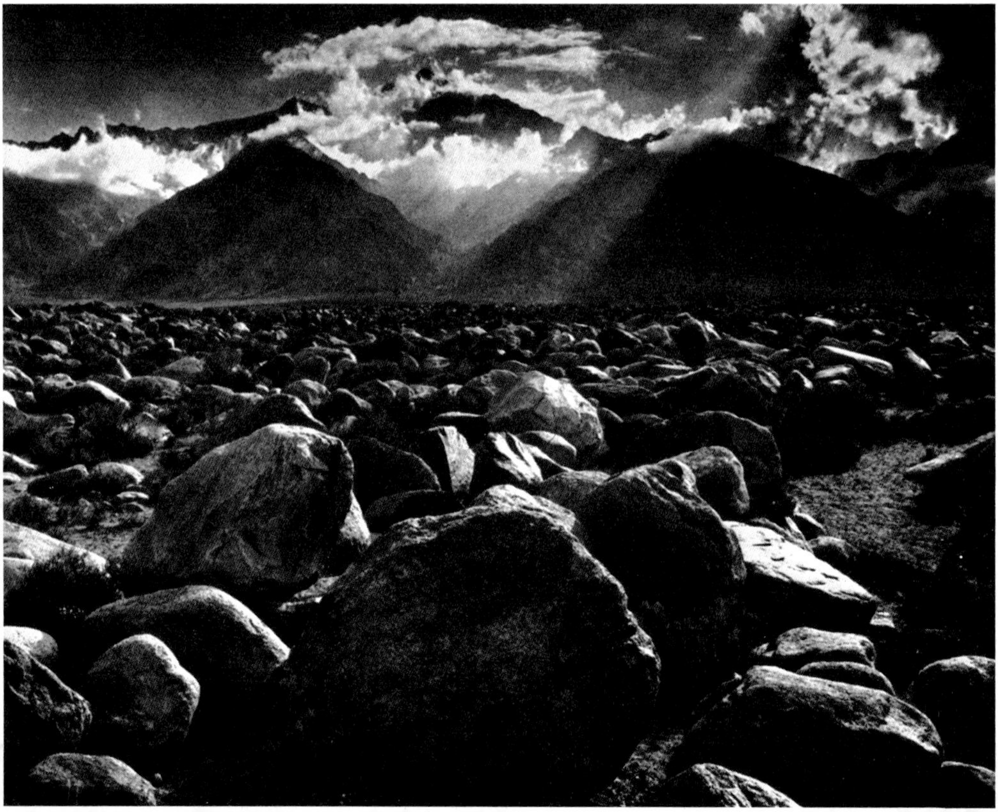

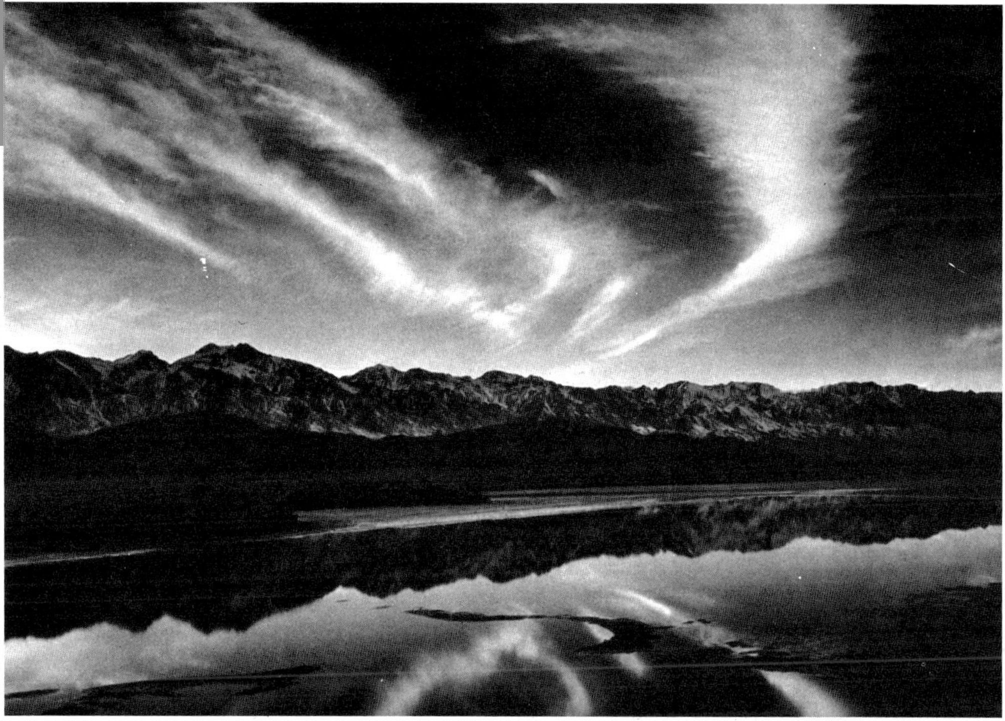

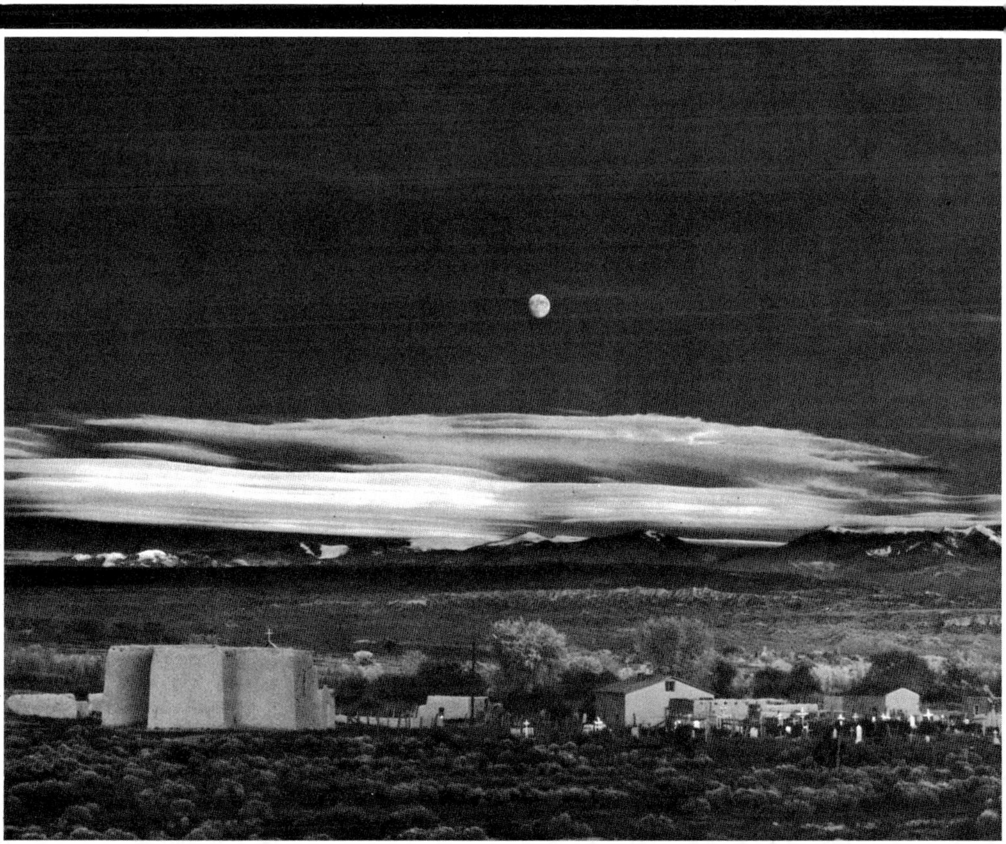

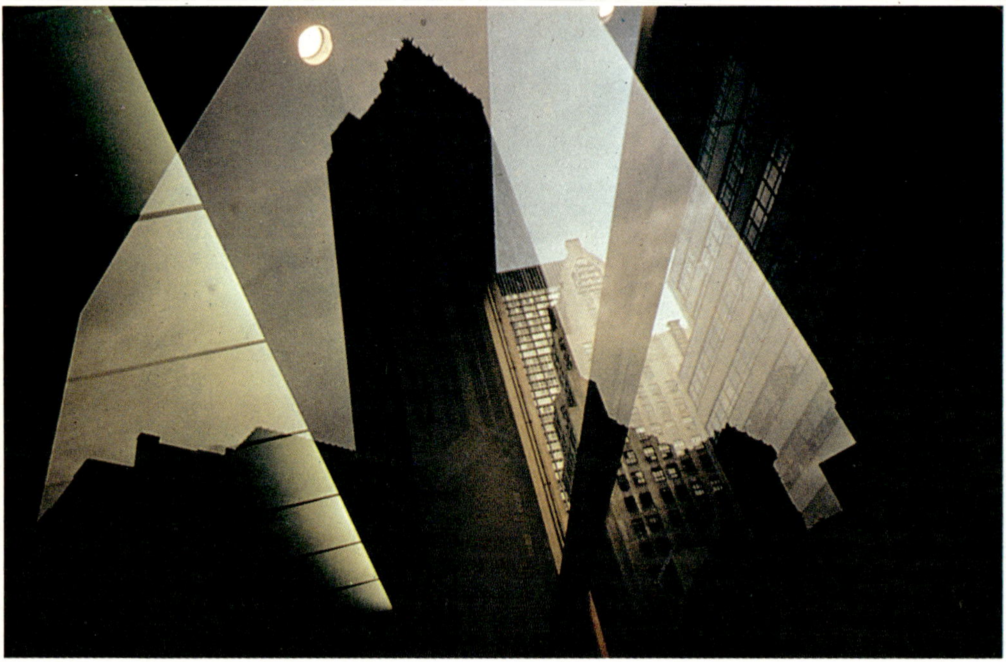

Ernst Haas

Of Austrian origin, he originally studied medicine.
He joined the Magnum group in 1949 – a studio which has had a fundamental influence on the history of photography in the post-war period.
He has devoted much time to photography in black-and-white, and subsequently colour, and regards them both as interesting and effective.
*It is worth recalling his advice to reduce equipment to a minimum, in order to concentrate fully on the subject in hand: "The camera should become an extension of the eye and nothing else."**
These photographs give an idea of Haas' creativity and interpretational skills. The first, above, shows skyscrapers reflected in a window, which breaks them up like a cubist or futurist painting, in an interesting play of superimposed lines, surfaces and colours.
The second photograph, below it, shows a wall with torn posters, a truly artificial landscape which this time is reminiscent of informal,

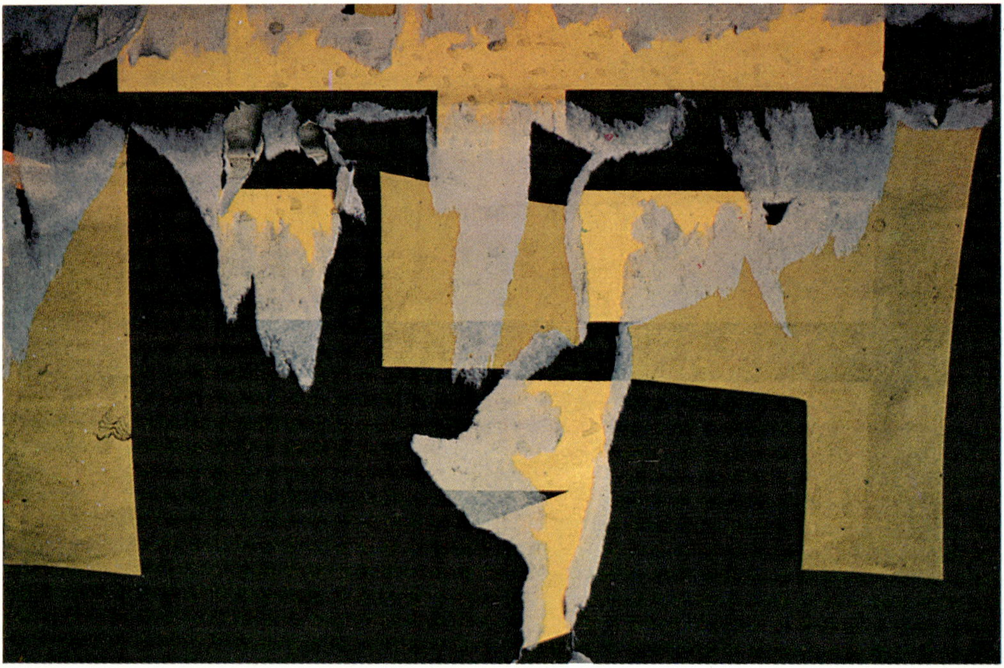

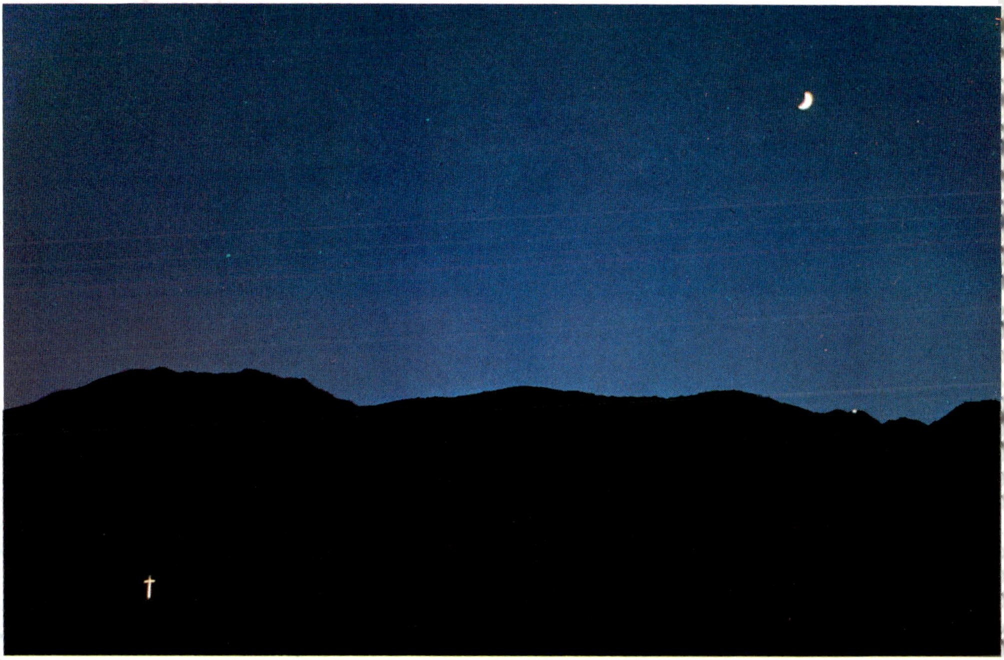

material paintings and gives a sense of the imperma- nence, but not necessarily sadness, of a modern city. Once again, the composition is clear and lively, with a very precise pattern.
The photograph at the top of this page, evokes the rapt, magical atmosphere of a nocturnal landscape, enlivened by the jewel-like presence of the moon and a cross.
The photograph below, in the typical monochrome blue of winter landscapes, emphasizes the "anatomi- cal" shapes of the snow.
Ernst Haas specializes in the use of 35 mm cameras, in particular the Leica and Leicaflex. He rarely uses filters apart from polarizers to cut down reflections. He is the author of well-known publications, such as Returning Prisoners of War *(1949)*, The Creation *(1971)*, In America *(1975)*.

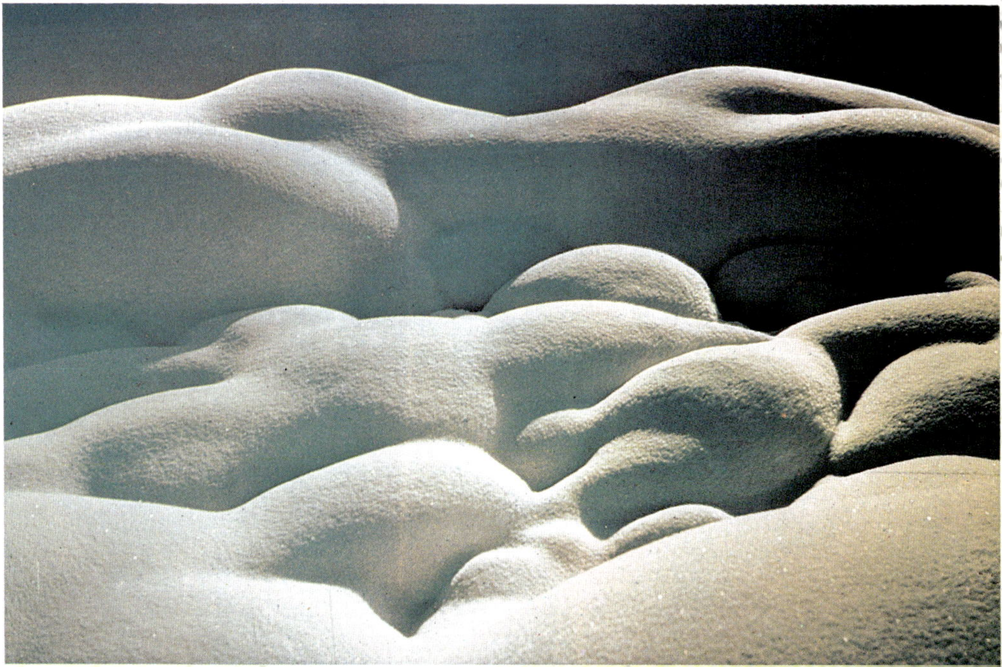

Burt Glinn

Another great American photographer, who was born in Pittsburg, Pennsylvania and studied at Harvard. Burt Glinn joined Magnum Photos at the start of his career and has been its president three times. Glinn has worked as a reporter throughout the world and mainly uses colour, of which he is particularly fond and which he handles with unmistakeable delicacy. The photographs shown here, whilst referring to different situations, have one characteristic in common: very subtle colours. Burt Glinn understands as few others do the value of tonal gradations, which are highly important when part of a unified pattern of colour, containing clearly dominant lights and tints, as for example in the watery atmosphere of the picture at the top of this page, or the greenish mist which dominates the photograph at the top of the opposite page. Together with this sense of vivid and at the same time delicate colour, relying on broad atmospheric spaces, Burt Glinn also knows the value of lines and profiles, which whilst equally sensitively developed, introduce a more precise sense of rhythm to the picture.

We find these lines everywhere, in the photograph of the rice pickers where they circumscribe the colours of the hats, or draw in the patterns of the basket and dress in the foreground, or indicate the depth of perspective through the lines of the crops or enclose the background with their regular repetition. In the photograph below left, the pattern of these lines symbolically circumscribes the two umbrellas, draws round the profiles of the figures, seems to repeat itself in the objects, and closes the image with the window frame. The entire scene is emphasized by the white of the snow, with the result that the composition both stands out clearly and is balanced and gentle. In the photograph at the top of the next page, the very thin outlines of the reeds are delicately drawn in the soft misty expanse, steeped in colour.

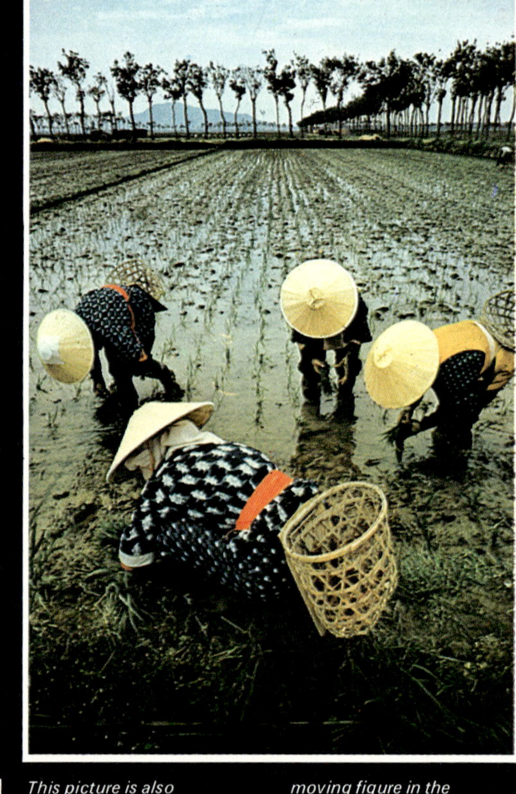

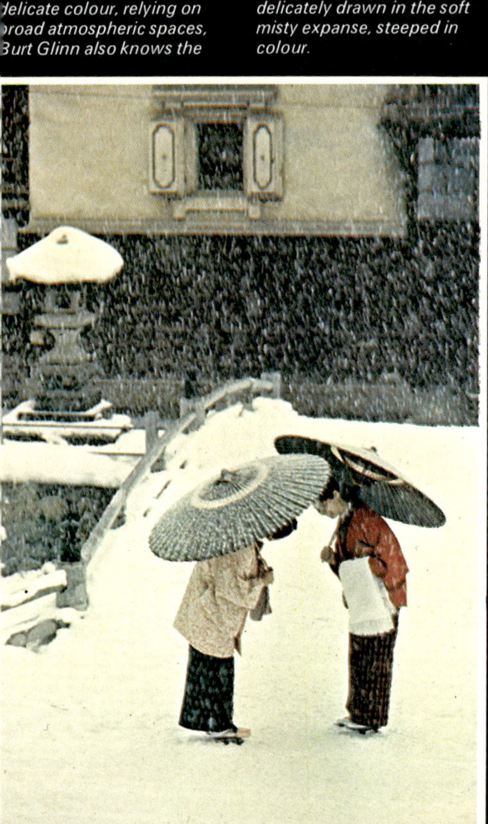

This picture is also dominated by broad rhythms, definite motifs which clearly occupy the frame, simplifying its expressiveness. It is interesting to note that the style, manner and shapes according to which these photographs have been produced are very reminiscent of Chinese painting in their delicacy of colour and refinement of contour. They reveal an exceptional understanding of certain profound characteristics of oriental painting which the photographer has revived, not to obtain facile folklore effects, as so often happens, but to show us the essence and structure of that world. The same sensitivity and compositional taste, based on light and lively rhythms, are found in the photograph opposite, below, reproducing a snowy landscape in Siberia. The way in which the depth of perspective is suggested by horizontal bands (another entirely oriental way of rendering space) rather than lines and vanishing points is highly original. The presence of moving figure in the foreground is effective too. Whilst no more three-dimensional than the rows of fences, its foreignness of size and movement seems to provide a focal point on which the wandering and imprecise rhythms of the rest of the picture can converge. Glinn became famous through his pictures of the south seas, Japan, Russia, Mexico and California which were published in Holiday Magazine. One of the best known American photographers, Burt Glinn is president of the American Society of Magazine Photographers.

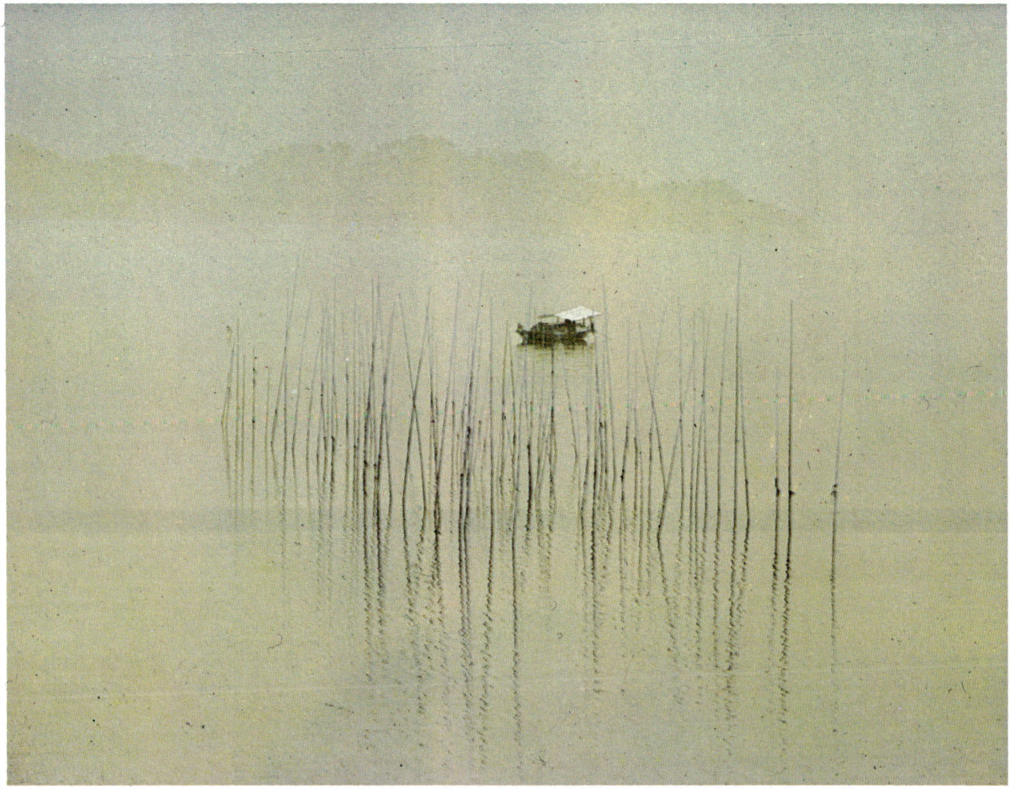

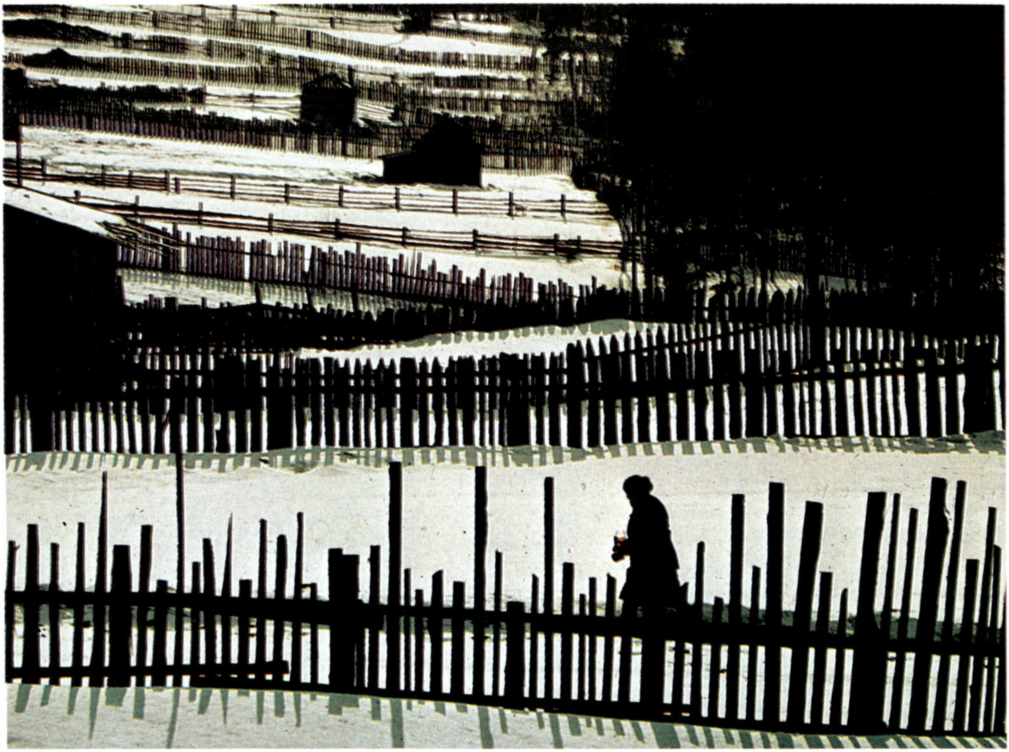

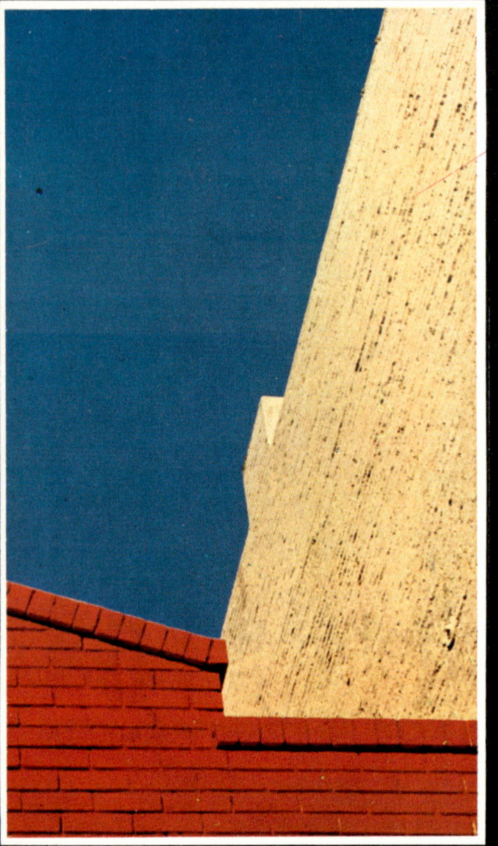

Franco Fontana

Born in Modena, his entire career has been devoted to landscape photography. Nowadays, he may be regarded as one of those who bring the landscape closest to being an abstract composition, imposing their own interpretation to the point of elaborating it with considerable technical aids.

In short, Fontana is a photographer who does not despise artificial techniques and they are in fact made to play a major role in his work.

At the same time, however, it must be recognized that this artificiality, this subjective interpretational approach and taste for abstraction, tend to an extreme simplification of forms. The artifice, the adulteration, are made to serve simplicity.

Few abstract painters have achieved such compositional purity, whilst managing to convey such richness of expression.

Fontana aims to reduce the passage of lines to a minimum. They therefore tend to be geometrical and uncluttered, making the areas of colour as homogeneous as possible, flattening their relief and juxtaposing them in broad areas like a piece of marquetry.

The power of his images is due to this essential purity, this stylistic rigour and at the same time, to the suggestion of broad, absolute, incontrovertible measurements.

Fontana always starts from a real landscape and his photographs are often an interpretation of an aspect of that landscape.

But in the process of simplification it undergoes, losing all accidental details which do not absolutely fit in with the principal motifs, the landscape assumes decorative values, becomes a support for harmonies of planes and colours which transcend their ties with the environment, suggesting a play of ideal beauties and theoretical formulae.

The photographs reproduced here, whilst clearly similar in style, show radically different combinations.

Note the effect of clashing colours of the photograph at the top of the left-hand page accompanied by an angular interlocking of planes, while the photograph beneath it is based on harmonious colours.

Likewise soft blends of

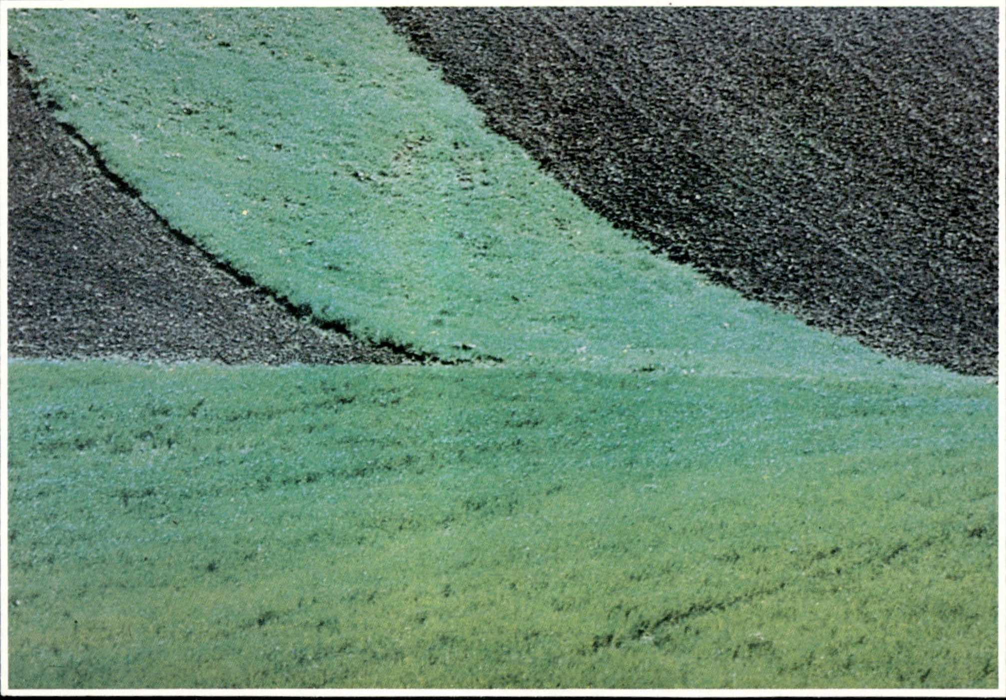

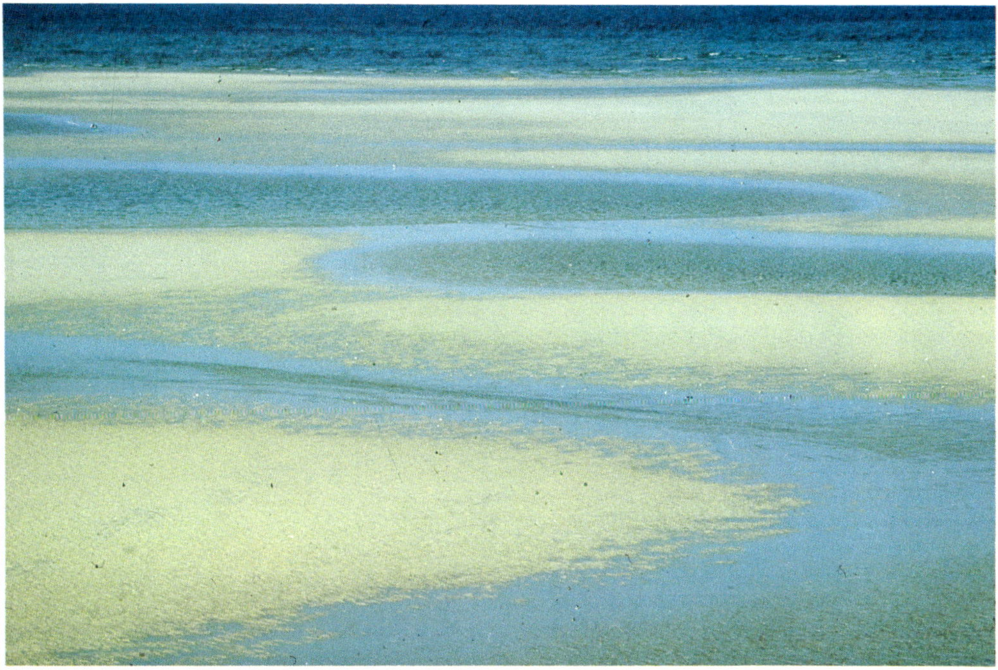

colour prevail in the photograph above, on the right hand page, but are organized into interpenetrating, meandering loops.
In the picture below, the contrast in colour is extremely clear-cut, as is the line which separates them.
The resulting landscapes are completely transformed and as it were rebuilt, by a process which has revealed a secret and powerful nature.
Works by Franco Fontana are now found in all the major photographic collections throughout the world.

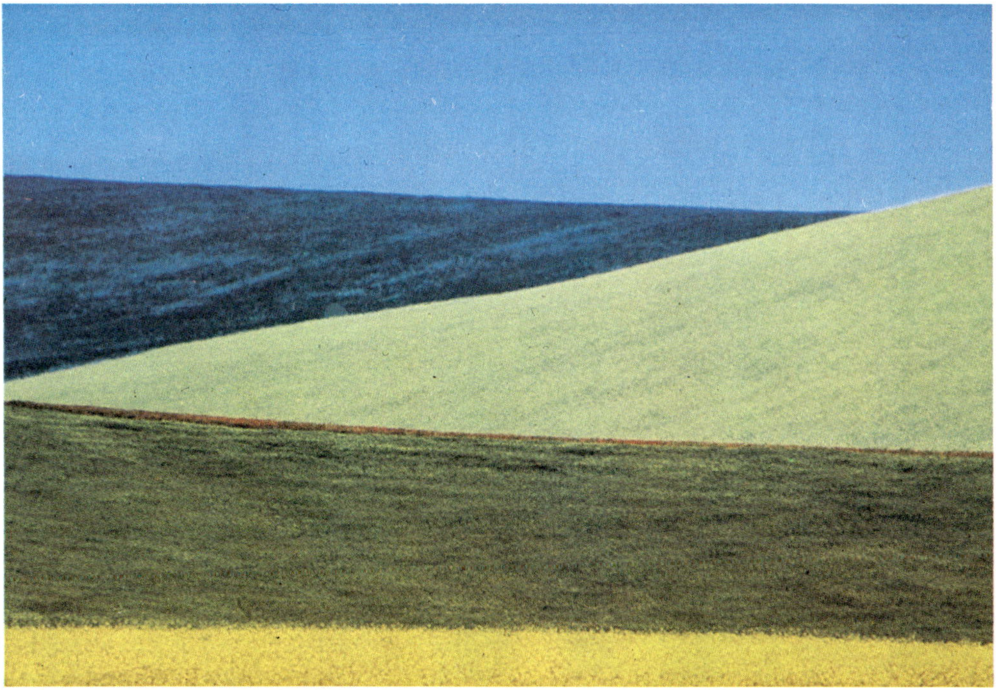

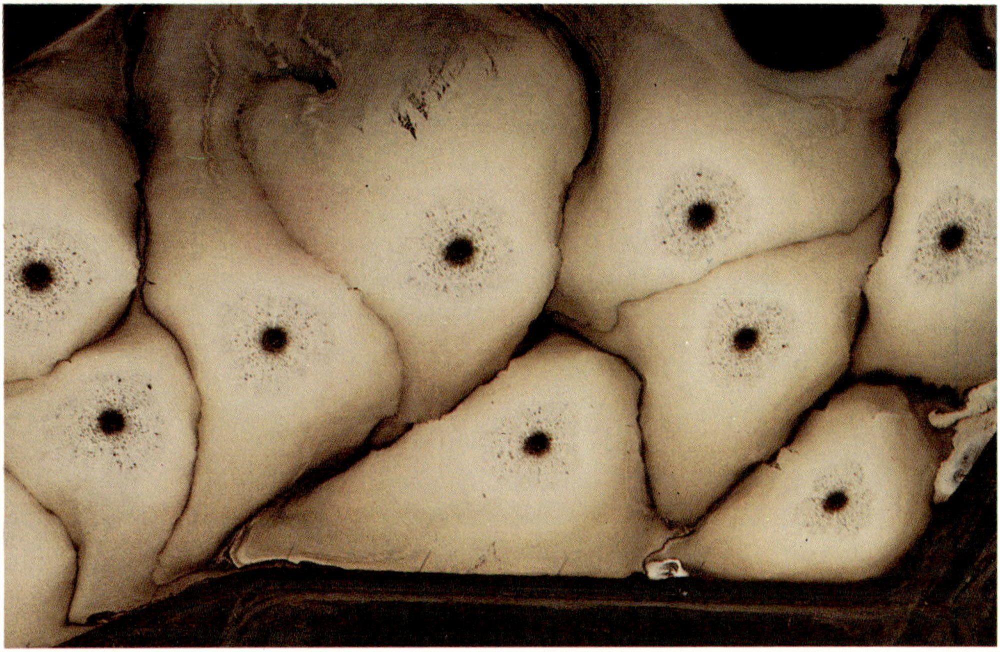

Georg Gerster

The power of photography to transform reality reaches some of its highest peaks in the work of Georg Gerster, for whom the landscape often abandons its natural connotations, to become something different, giving rise to shapes which are indefinable, but vivid in their organic unity, now entertaining, now disconcerting. We are referring to aerial photographs, of which Gerster is a very famous interpreter, and which are the type which lend themselves best to the most varied interpretations. The photograph above shows a lagoon in Lewiston, Idaho, USA, and the photographer has mischievously entitled it Honi soit qui mal y pense. *The photograph below shows a farm near Palouse, while the one opposite shows rice terracing in Java. Georg Gerster was born in Winterthur, Switzerland, graduated from the University of Zurich and took up photography when working as an editor for a scientific journal. All these photographs were taken with 35 mm Kodachrome film and an exposure of 1/500 second.*

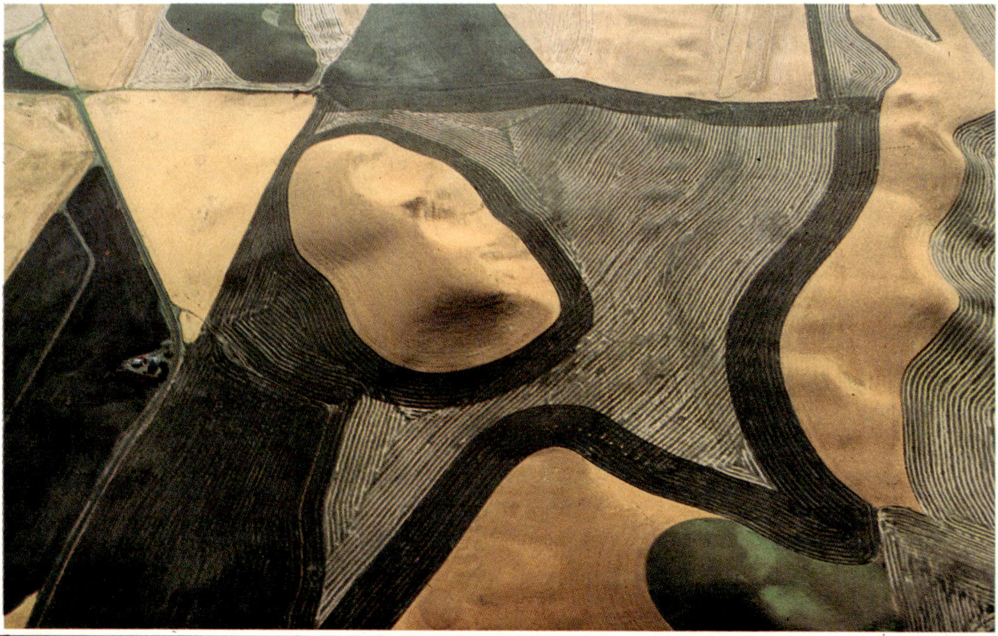

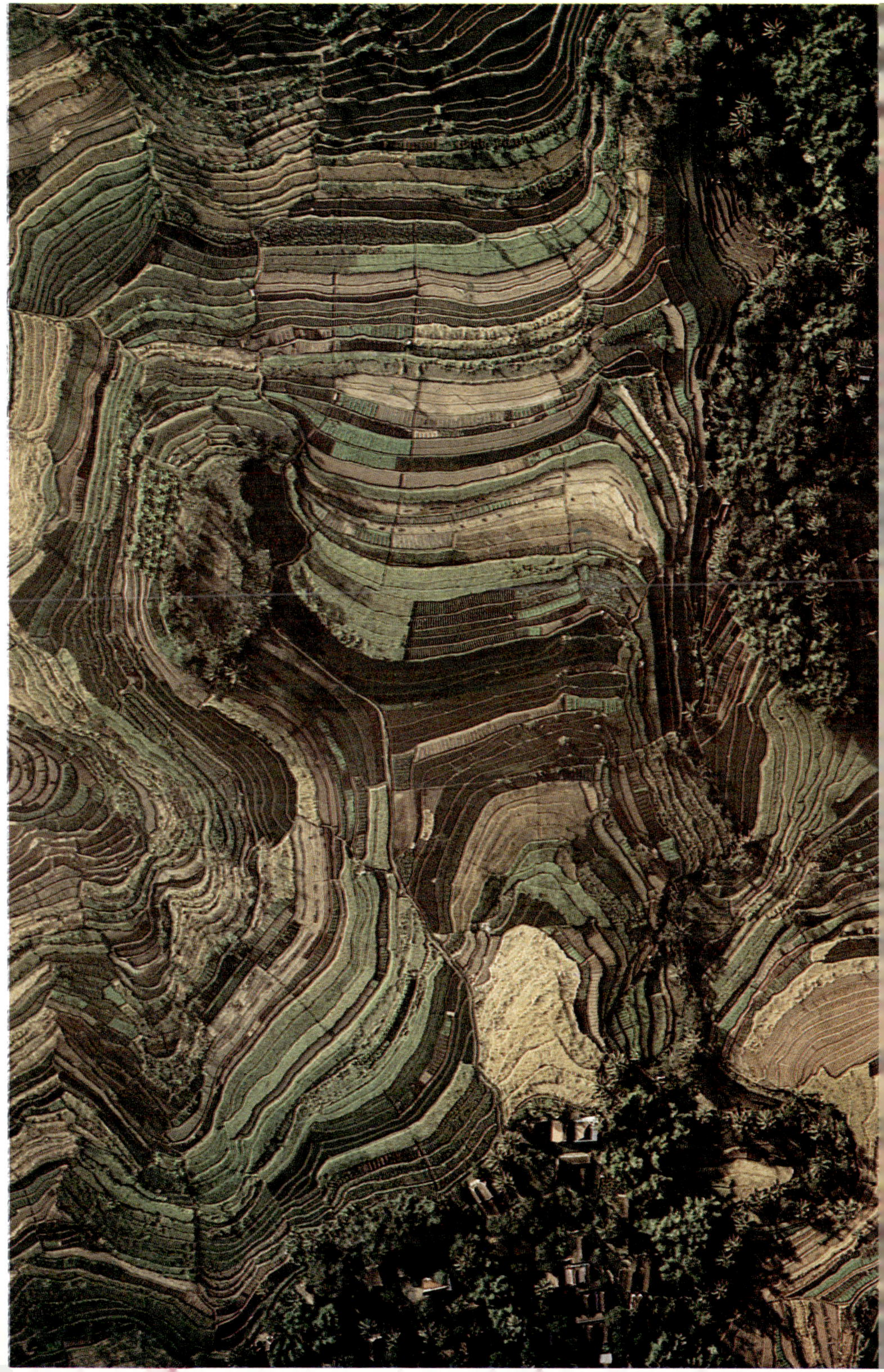

Fulvio Roiter

Born in Meolo in the Veneto, he was first better-known and appreciated abroad than in Italy, where, however, he has now achieved popularity, following his excellent publications on Venice and her lagoon. Roiter is an eclectic photographer by temperament, sensitive to all aspects of photography, one moment the interpreter of social and human situations, the next the imaginative creator of polished, formal compositions. He has devoted much time to landscapes. Despite the multiplicity of themes which inspires him, Roiter shows a constant characteristic: his frankness, the simplicity of his language, his adherence to reality, in order to explore it, heighten it, select it, but never superimpose himself on it, with the result that technically, he is one of those photographers who most avoid artificiality. Roiter has expressed himself with equal ability in black-and-white and colour. The photograph on the right, of an Umbrian landscape in winter, is a classic example from his repertoire and combines a rare interpretation of the environment with a very well-balanced, formally fluent composition. The photograph below, showing intersecting lines of wake on the sea, is typical of Roiter's ability to capture in passing highly original motifs without the slightest distortion. The domes of St. Mark's, seen against the light, on the opposite page, are one of the most unusual interpretations of the historic heart of Venice. Below, Roiter shows us on the left the grandiose definition of an architectural detail (note the clever inclusion of human figures to establish a scale of reference), while the photograph on the right depends on an exceptional and amusing situation, one of those "finds" which are a source of tremendous satisfaction to the reporter-photographer.

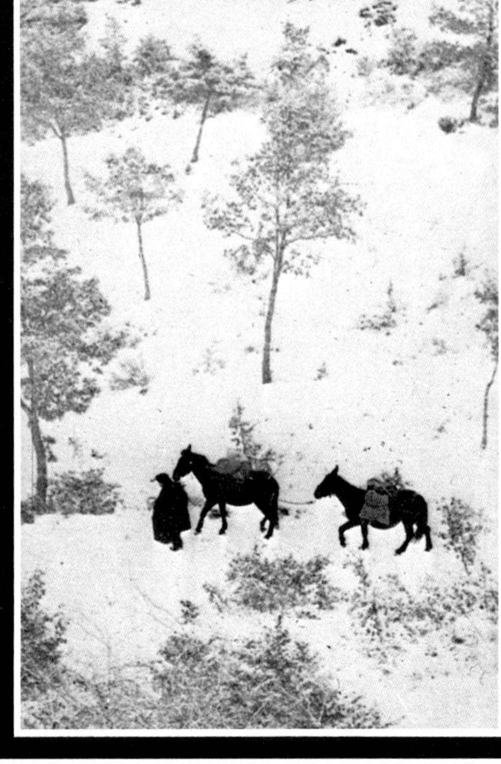

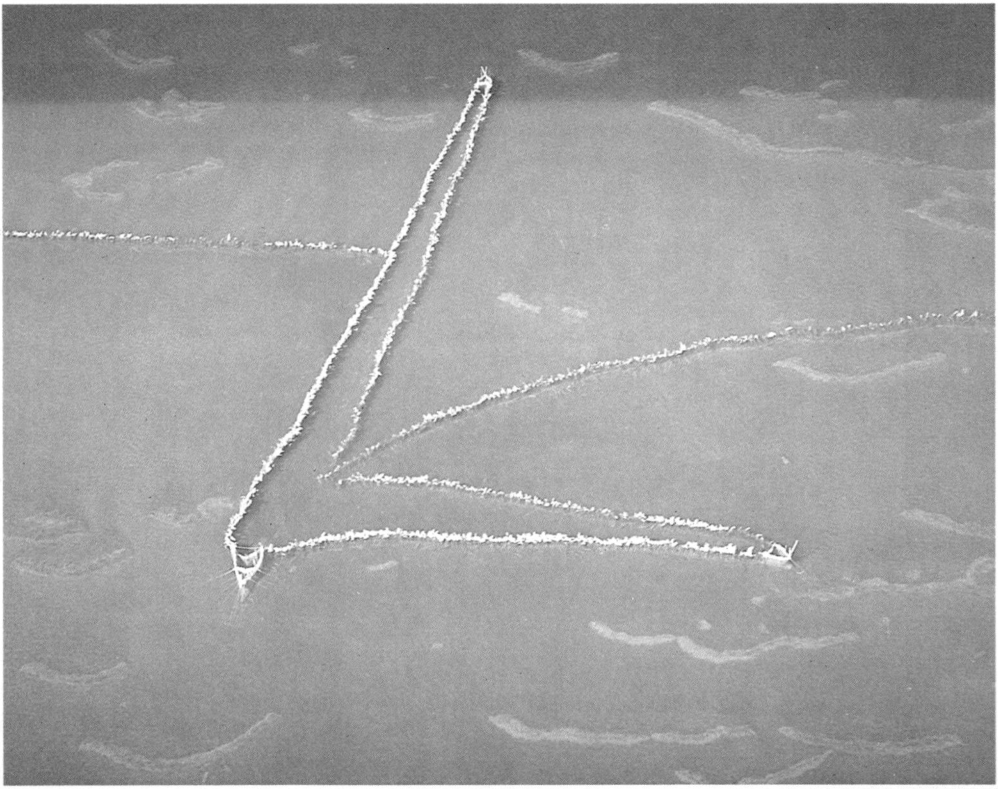

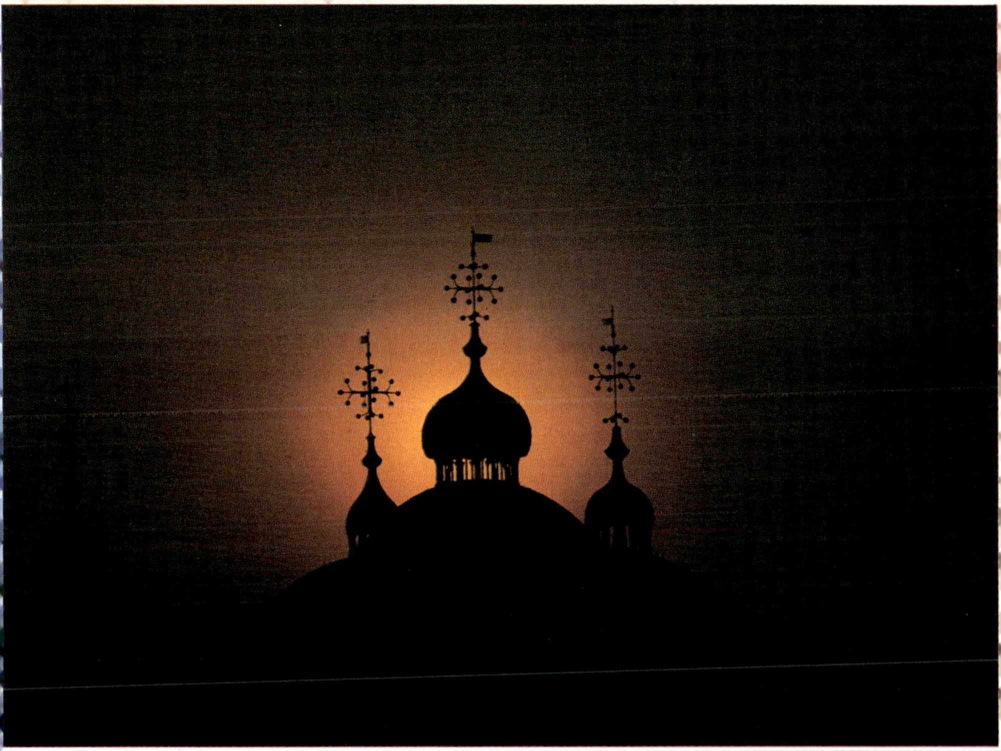

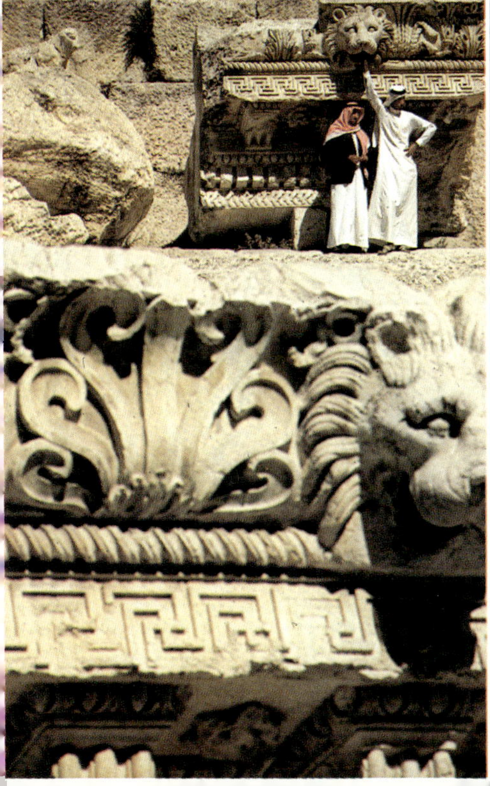

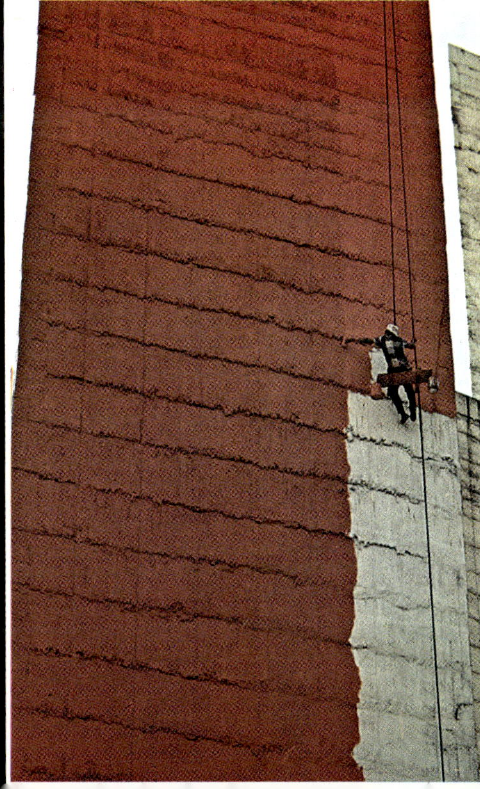

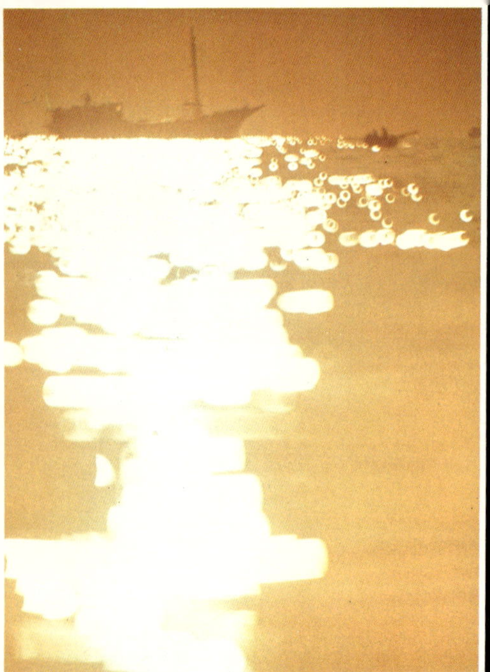

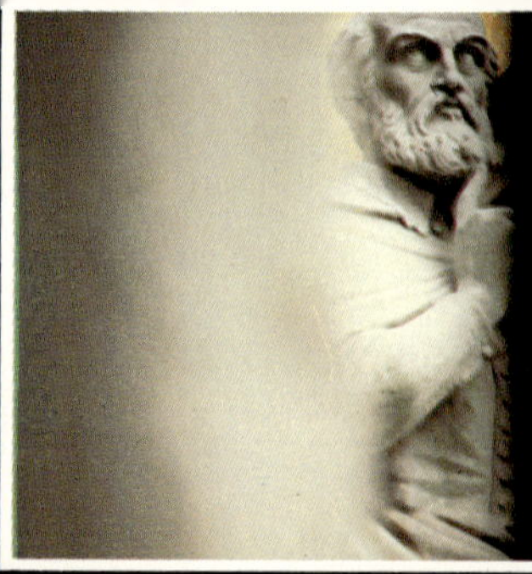

Giorgio Lotti

A native of Emilia, with long experience of publishing, he is one of the photographers most sensitive to the language of shapes and most capable of extracting from a landscape those details, those rhythms, those elements with which to build a new image, linked to reality by a significance which is no longer purely descriptive, but strongly symbolic.
In this quest for formal syntheses, in which Lotti is certainly not alone today, he is distinguished by the variety of his solutions and his ability to explore a different structure in each image.
In short, Lotti is not a photographer who relies on a formula which, however well tested, polished and effective, can be repetitive, but one who finds a fresh characterization each time.
Take, for example, the photographs shown here. The sea view, top left, is based on optical effects which are not found in any of the other photographs reproduced here; the reflections have the form and thickness of the brush strokes of an impressionist painter.
The photograph below, showing the movement of a wave, draws on three-dimensional elasticity and chromatic tension.
The photograph on the opposite page, above is based on the atmospheric separation of planes, while the one below it makes use of the elegant play of the undulating curvature of shadows.
It goes without saying that a photographer so intent on highly-polished compositions will be less committed to other types of subject – historical, for example – as can be seen from the photograph of Palladio which could (but should not) be an interpretation of history. This composition is based on a statue of him and

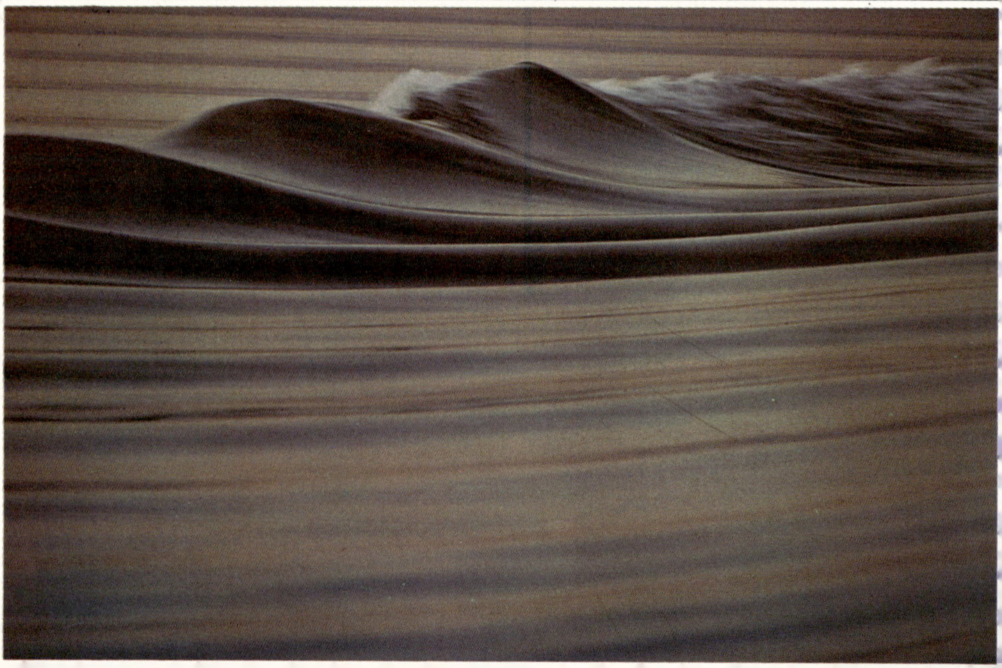

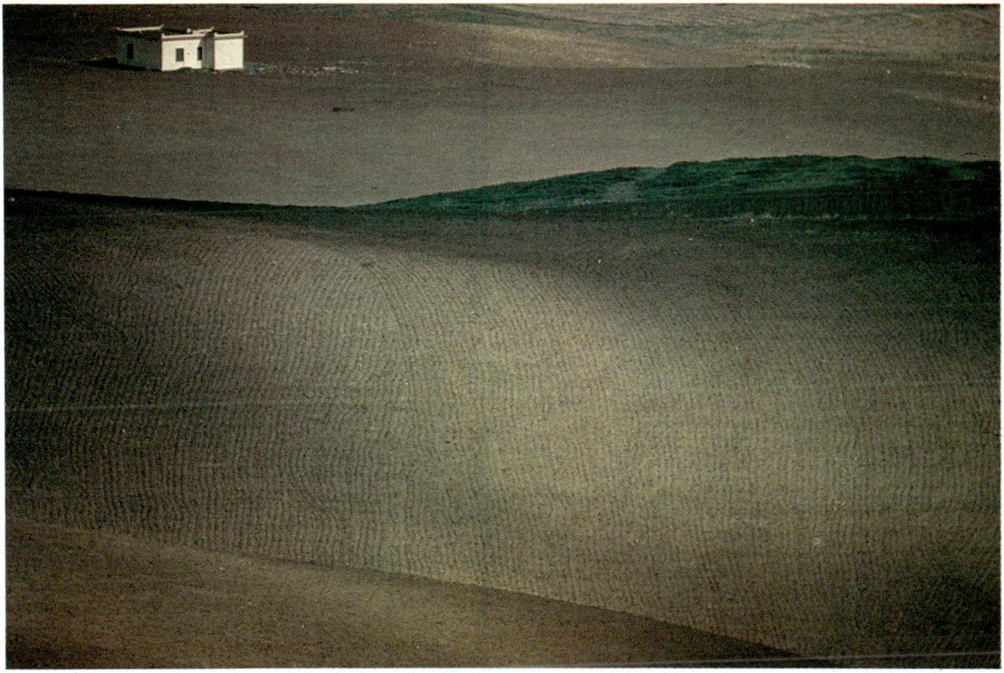

a few, indistinct lights, in which, however, all that there is of Palladio – and the result is very clever and successful – is purely rhetorical.
Light and shade conflict beside the immobility of a portrait.
Lotti's style consists of reducing basic motifs, not to make them artificial, but to intensify their content and expressive force. He achieves a concentration in which the most vital elements of the landscape are sublimated with a rigour proportional to his inventive power.
The elegant outer surface of his compositions is in fact always intensely alive.

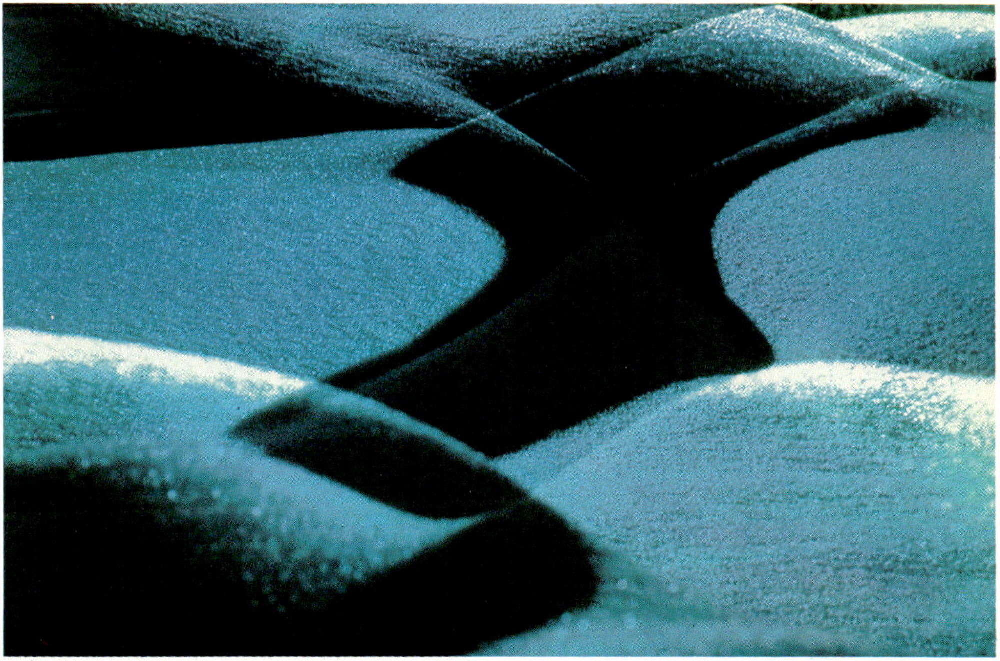

Mario de Biasi

A true inventor, or discoverer as the case may be, of the most sophisticated compositions is Mario de Biasi.
Born in Belluno and Milanese by adoption, he has been head of the photographic department of the Italian magazine Epoca for many years.
And yet this photographer of very wide experience and familiar with all the techniques, likes to produce his own images with the simplest equipment, of the type accessible to all, and avoids trick photography, despite being conversant with it.
Above right, the photograph shows trees in the garden in front of the Municipal Hall in Vienna. It was taken with an exposure of 180 seconds and the colour of the background is due to the many lights reflected over the city of Vienna. The duration of the exposure permitted the slight blurring of the foliage, producing the infinite gradations of green.
The photograph below shows a nocturnal landscape with the profile of Sella seen from Selva.
The exposure lasted for several minutes and the photographer only uncovered the lens when clouds were passing over the moon, which is why they look so extensive, emphasizing their fantastic appearance.
The photograph on the opposite page, above, shows a detail of the windscreen of a parked car in Amsterdam.
As on other occasions, de Biasi's photographs regard details which are so limited that the location of the photograph becomes superfluous, even if the sense of winter of this image and the presence of the car windscreen are environmental elements not to be underestimated. But the evocative force of the image is primarily due to the abstract composition of the lines and colours on a single plane where they form a sort of accidental calligraphy.
Anyone familiar with painting will know the extent to which abstract artists have made us of these motifs, rarely achieving, however, such richness and vivacity of notation.
The results of the photograph below are similar, even if there is a more definite link with the environment. The formal quality of the image relies to the same extent on the linear geometry of the stalks imprisoned in a

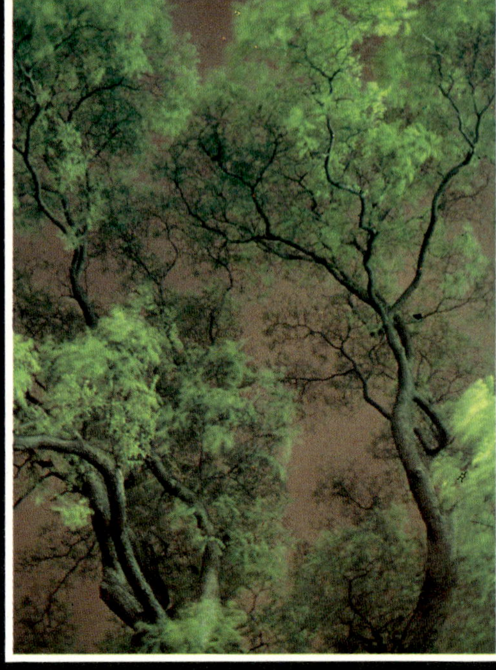

small, frozen lake near Milan.
One only need glance at the titles of some of de Biasi's photographs to have an idea of his favourite themes: lichens on the bark of a tree; stone with lichens; lace effect created on sand by a wandering insect; spray from a fountain; rhododendron pistils; details of charred wood, etc.
These often border on the microlandscape, but are always handled with

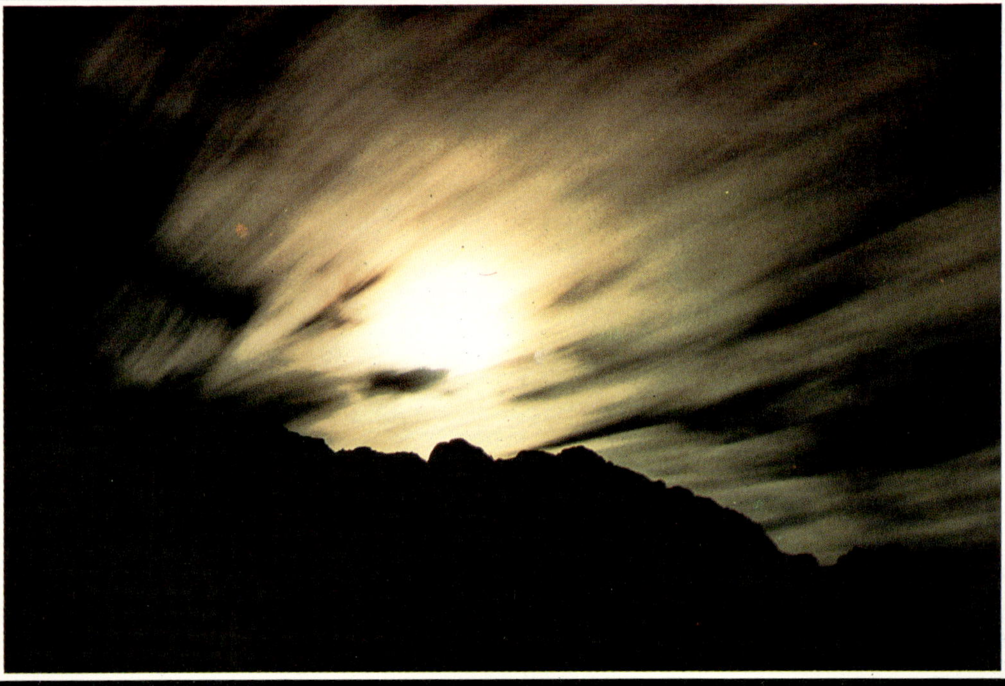

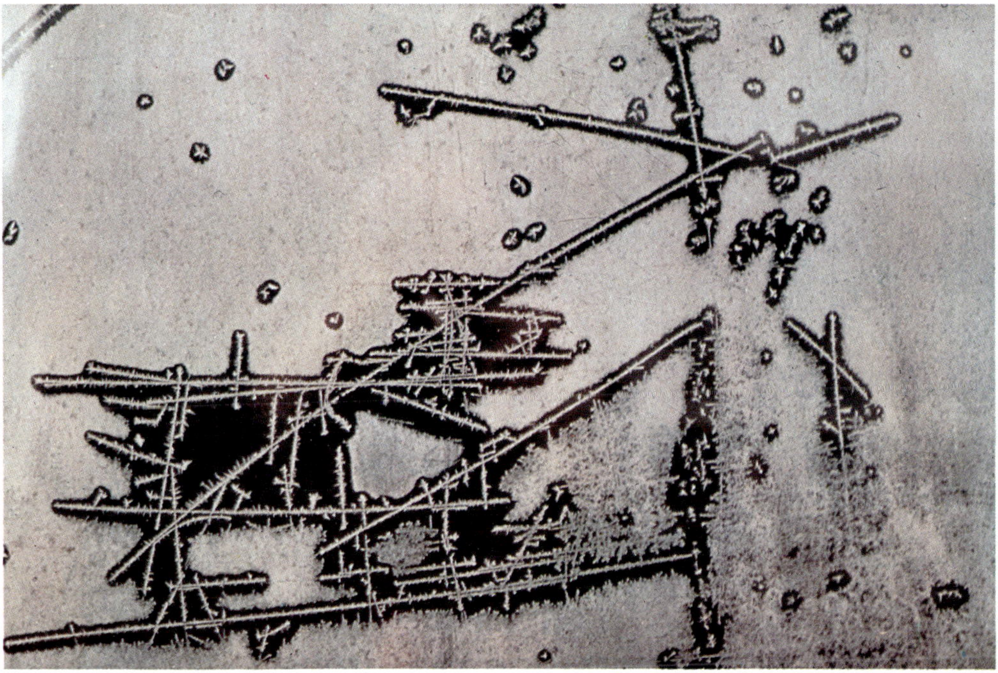

emotions which go well beyond a taste for analysis and always yield the stimulus of a discovery. But de Biasi is not just attracted by small, often hidden items. He also willingly undertakes shots of wide open spaces, provided an intimate vibration can be mirrored there; a secret confession can be echoed. Creativity is his password.

De Biasi has photographed in all countries. He prefers the 24 × 36 format, and makes extensive use of a tripod and long exposures by which he avoids resorting to reflectors or electronic flash.

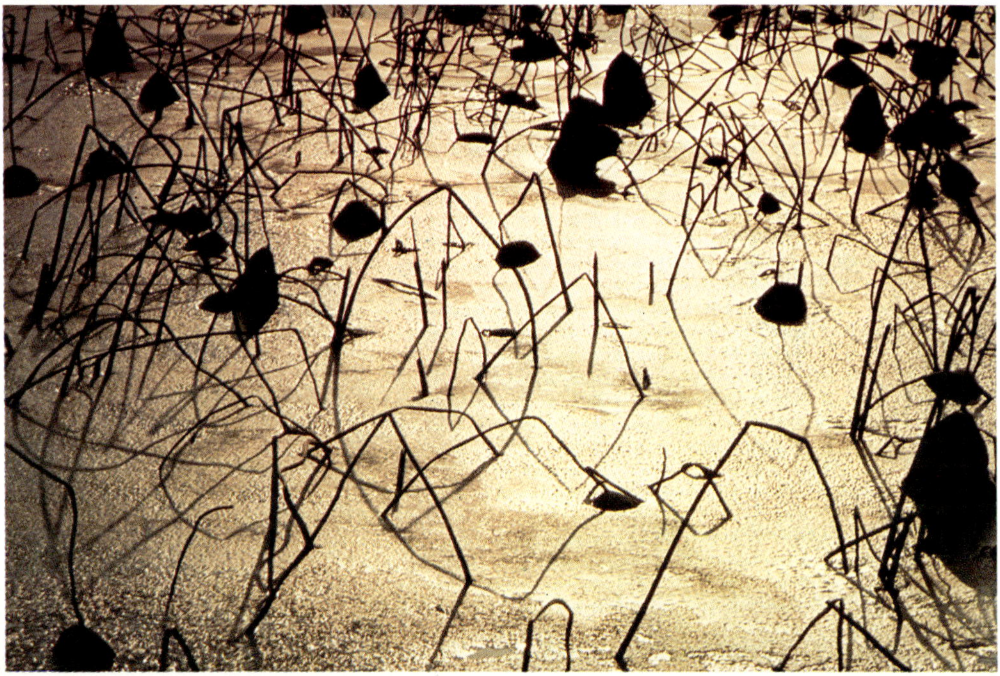

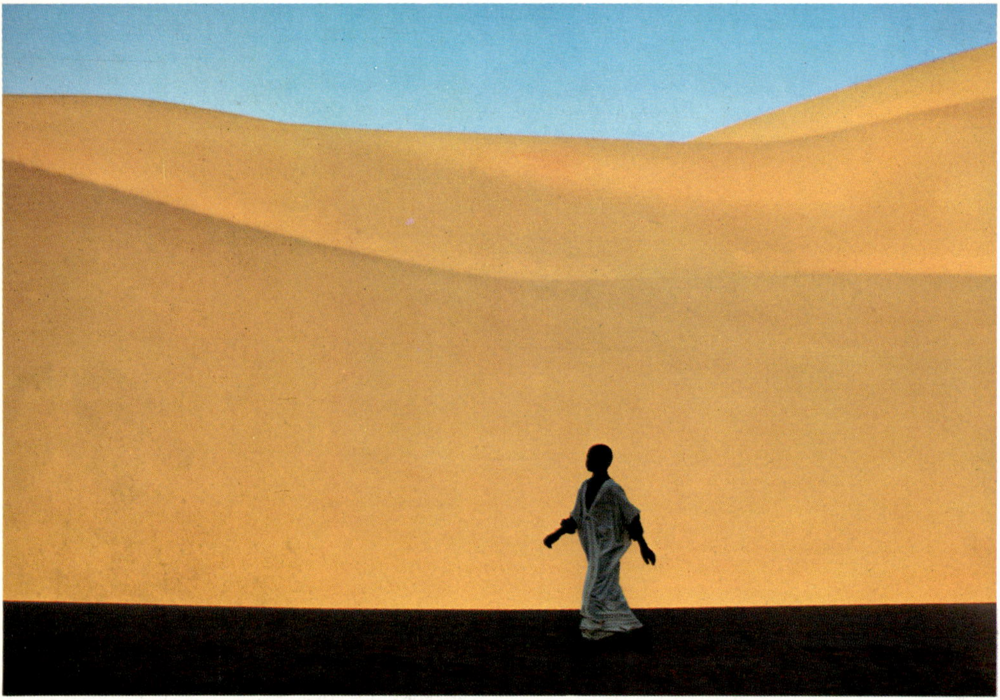

Kazuyoshi Nomachi

To understand a Japanese photographer, it is perhaps important to know something of the tradition of that country's painting, the typical way the Japanese make images stand out, giving them great chromatic force; the value that profiles and lines assume in their compositions and the taste for the idyllic and the monstrous which often characterizes their works. The photographs reproduced here are taken from a book on the Sahara. The photograph above was taken in Algeria, the one below in Gezzan, in Libya.

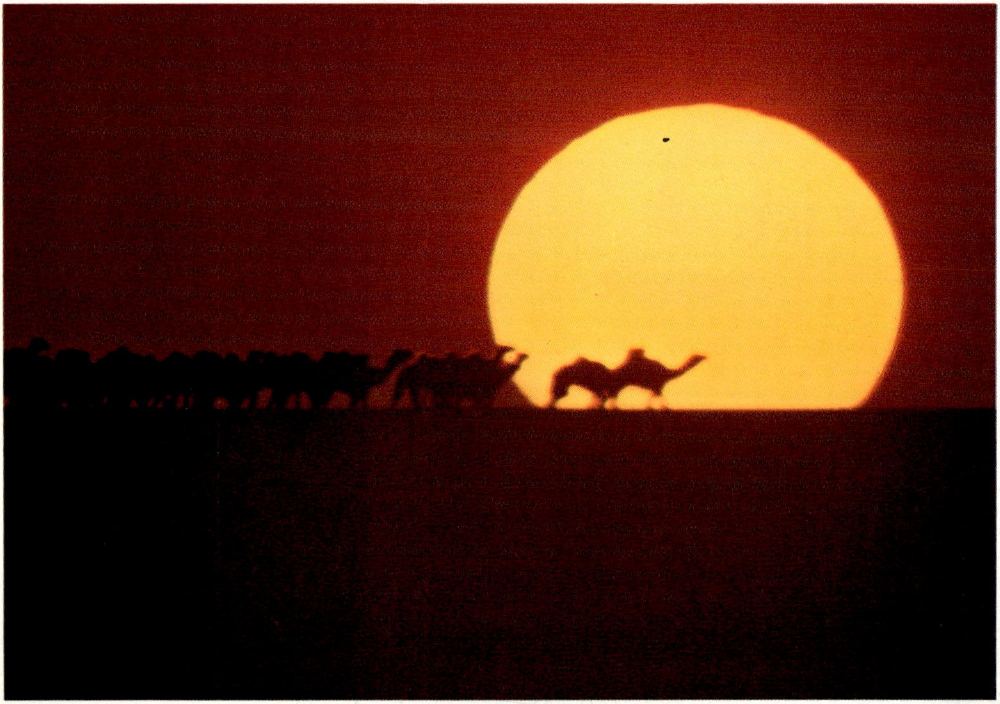

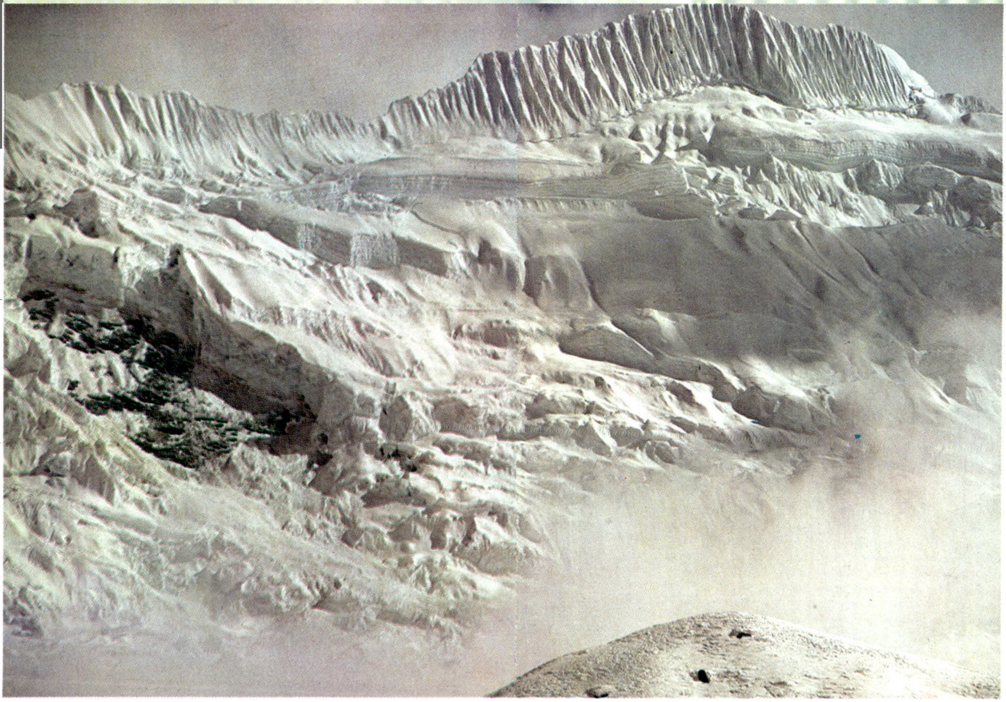

Yoshikazu Shirakawa

A photographer and journalist, a graduate of the University of Nihon and also an expert mountaineer, his favourite subjects are mountains.
The photographs on this page are the fruit of various expeditions to the Himalayas. The one above was taken from the Chukhung glacier and the one below shows the east face of Machapuchare. In both, the powerful relief which characterizes the photographs is much in evidence and seems to express the superhuman character of these magnificent and awe-inspiring mountains.

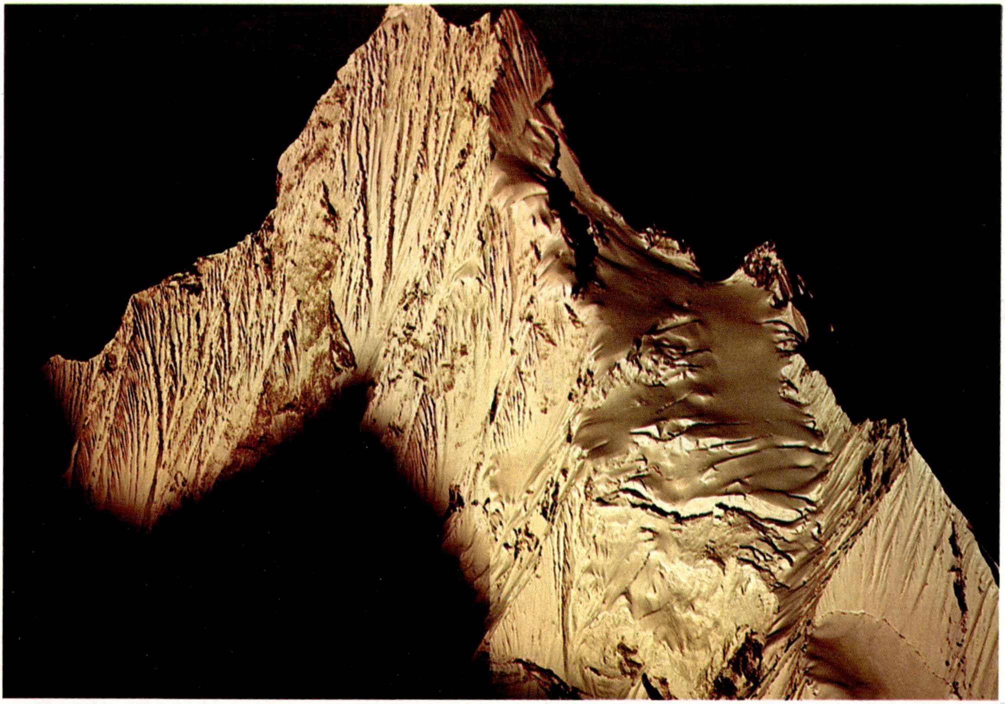

THE URBAN LANDSCAPE

Peculiarities of the historical landscape

So far we have been dealing with an eminently natural landscape, dominated by the spontaneity of nature. But there are landscapes in which nature is "historicized" that is, they carry traces of history, of human activity. These traces may be completely immersed in the natural elements. The scattered houses of a highland valley, seen as a whole, certainly tell a human story, but they can also be completely subjected to the natural elements, to the vastness and grandeur of the valley, for example. Likewise, the crops on a stretch of Appenine hillside are undoubtedly an historical and human sign, but they can be completely subordinated to the undulating profile of those hills, to the sense of distances, etc.
There are very many other cases in which these pieces of historical and human evidence assume much greater value, either because they are more extensive or more decisive, or because they are observed from closer range (the houses of that valley seen from closer up, so that the breadth of the valley becomes a secondary or collateral fact).
Views of cities are a typical case in point. What happens when a photographer has to give a typical rendering of an historical environment? Obviously, he will then be faced with different problems from those we have been dealing with so far.

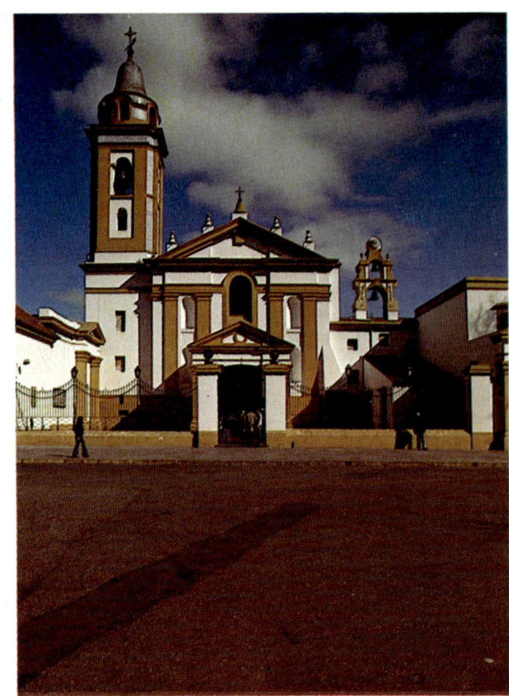

In the case of a natural landscape, the photographer has a great deal of interpretational freedom. He is, of course, restricted by certain types of objective conditioning here as well. If a mountain landscape is rugged, he will have to convey its ruggedness; if a hilly landscape

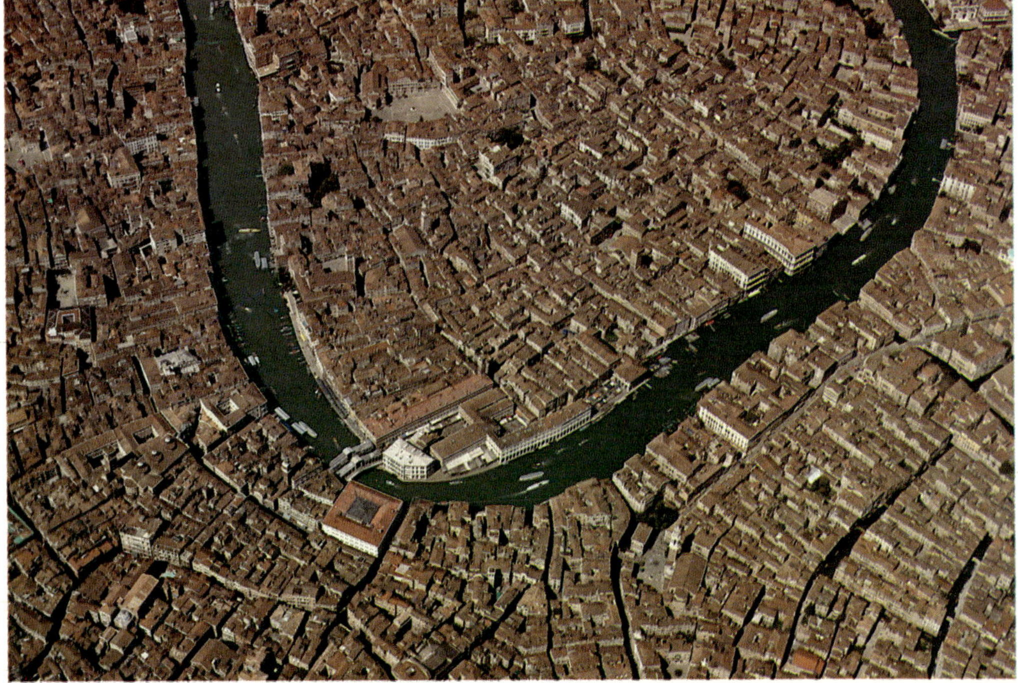

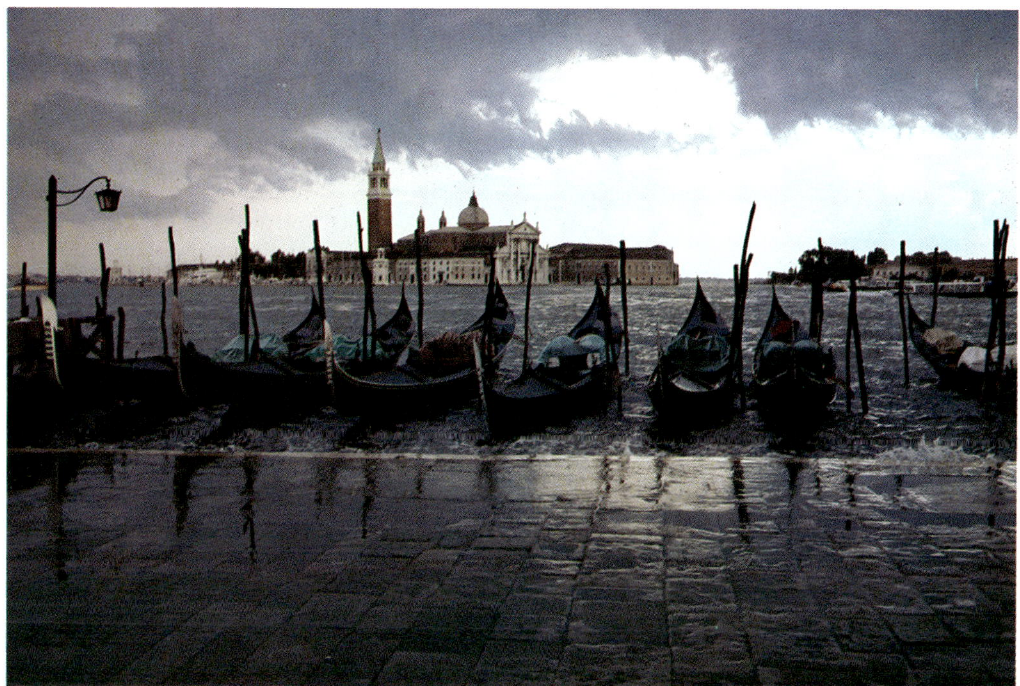

is gentle, it is unlikely that he will be able to avoid characterizing it as such. In fact, if he wishes to keep to reality, or rather to the feelings that landscape normally arouses, he will have to play it up. But within these limitations, he can enjoy considerable freedom all the same, in the sense that he can choose the motifs available to him, draw attention to some and forget others. But with an historical landscape, he may be obliged to show the elements which characterize its history and sometimes even leave out of account its natural attractions, however interesting.

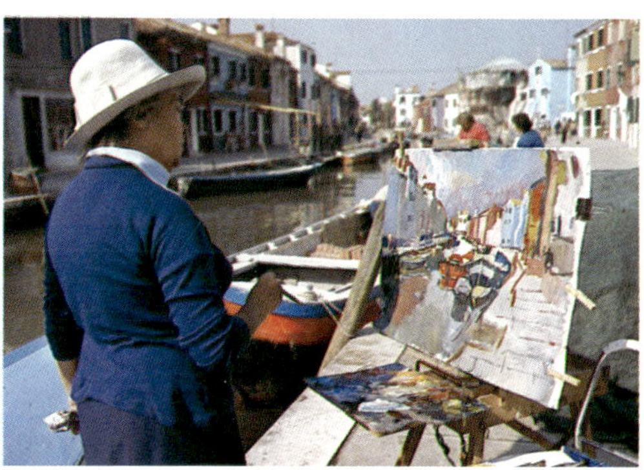

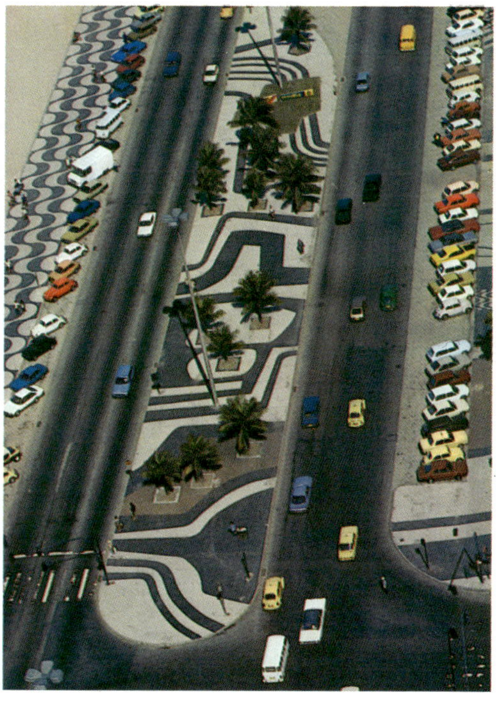

On the two preceding pages, an urban landscape in Brazil. On the opposite page, above, an urban landscape (Baires) composed of very clearly defined historico-architectural elements. Below, an aerial view of Venice. The historical structure of the city is crystal clear, but at the same time the photograph achieves a decorative, almost abstract effect.

On this page, top, a typical view of Venice at high water. Above, a clever interpretation of Venice, "city of art," in which an artist at work has been added to the picturesque environment. Right, the dynamic features near the beach at Copacabana.

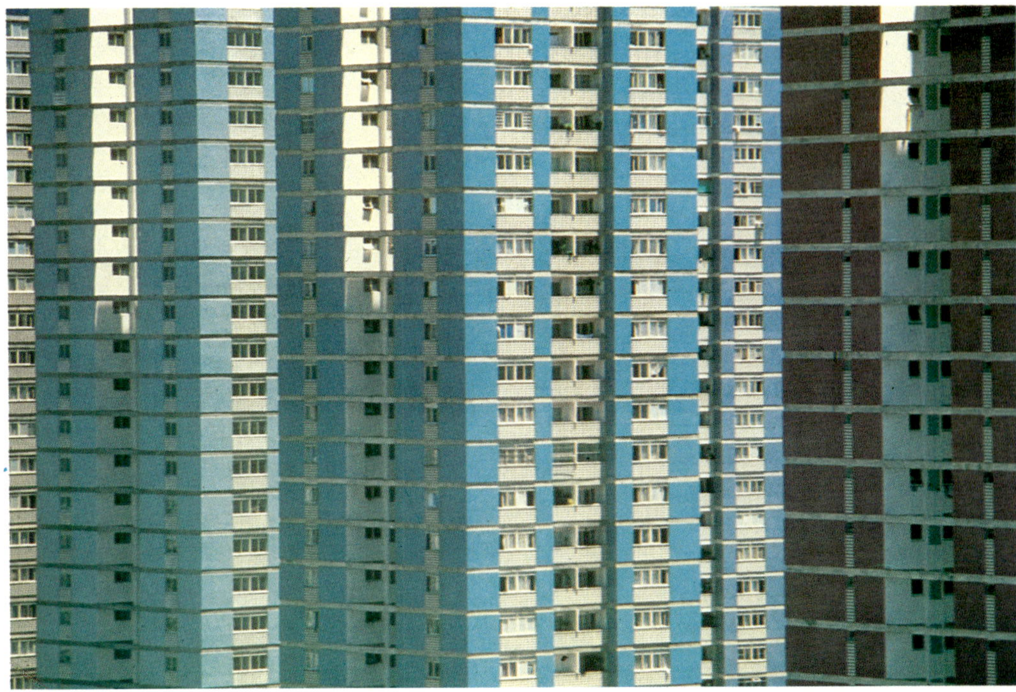

Traces of history

An historical landscape does not just consist of shapes and objects but also of what history has left behind in it, which has determined its atmosphere and its character. At this point, the photographer cannot only have an eye for shapes; he must also sense which of the elements before him are the most suitable for defining the historical individuality of that place.
He may be endowed with exceptional intuition and immediately understand, in a place he may never have been to before, which are the salient features from an historical point of view. But very often, however gifted he may be, intuition alone will not suffice and unless that town or city is familiar to him in other ways, he will need to supplement it with suitable preparation. Historical knowledge, in fact, cannot be improvised. Anyone arriving in Milan will go to see the cathedral, and quite rightly so, because this building is a fundamental, irreplaceable element of the physical appearance and history of Milan. But is the cathedral enough to define Milan and its history? And which, and how many, monuments are needed then to give an adequate idea of it? (This reminds me of a picture postcard I came across one afternoon at a stationer's in Liverpool. I was looking for a few souvenir photographs to send, when a somewhat

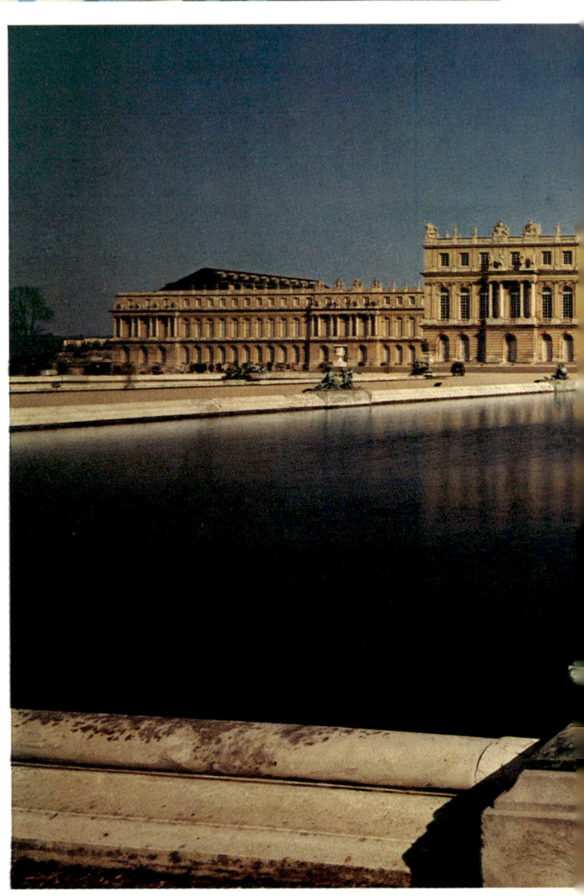

On the opposite page, an architectural detail at Salvador de Bahia in Brazil. However anonymous contemporary architecture may tend to look, this clever shot succeeds in giving an idea of the imposing, functional, obsessive nature of a modern quarter. The photograph on the right, of Times Square in New York, seen through a powerful telephoto lens, conveys all the frenzy of the big city.
Below is a view of Versailles. The breadth of the image, the presence of a precise and interesting foreground and the clever choice of light, all contribute to the success of this photograph which interprets the sense of sumptuous, theatrical decor of this very famous palace.

unusual photograph caught my eye. It did not show either a street or a monument of Liverpool, but one of those big iron mooring posts by which ship's hawsers are tied to wharves. It seemed to me that the whole atmosphere of Liverpool was expressed in that grey post: its industry, its seriousness, its nineteenth-century traditions, its activities as a great seaport, even the degree of humidity of the air. And even today when I think of Liverpool, I associate it with that photograph, which seemed to reveal the entire character of the city to me).

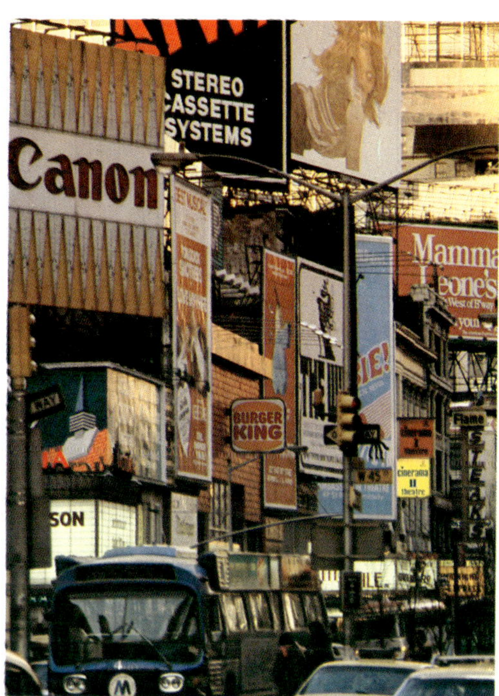

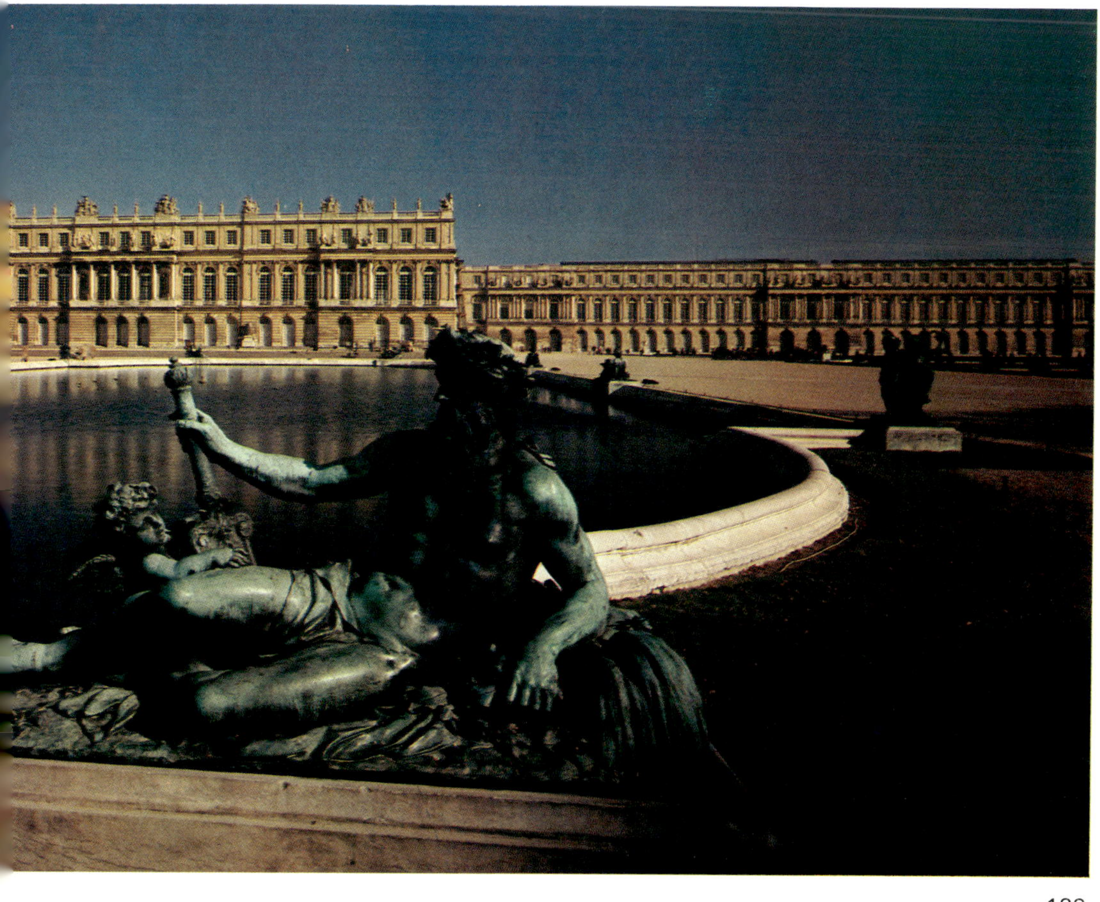

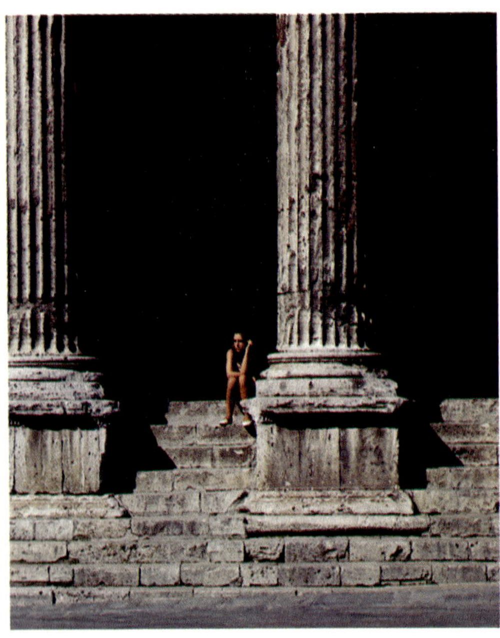

One might ask why at least the more important cities do not take the trouble to publish photographs like the one of Liverpool. It is incredible, in fact, the amount of second-rate material there is on sale, sufficient to justify the very low opinion one generally has of picture post-cards as such. Post-cards are often as trite as they could be. But, regretfully, it must be said that even the magnificent photographs of a great photographer may not be at all characteristic. I will always remember the desperation of the director of a big agency which had sent a very famous photographer to the Dolomites, with high hopes, and virtually giving him carte blanche. He came back with a few hundred photographs, but only about ten or so could satisfy the requirements of that agency, which naturally wanted to publicize the uniqueness of the environment. The others were very beautiful in themselves, but they could have been taken in the Dolomites or any other alpine valley. To stay away from the banal and the expected, our photographer had conscientiously avoided all the most obvious landscapes. The results were magnificent details of winter scenes, sports and tourism, but there was not a single locality which distinguished itself from the others. What can happen with natural environments happens all the more easily with historical ones. Publishers often do not know who to turn to when they need photographs of cities or famous monuments. Before surrendering to an indisputable fact, i.e. that it is difficult, if not impossible, to get a famous photographer to photograph things he does not wish to or is not accustomed to photographing, one has to survive a number of harsh encounters with reality. The historical and artistic interpretation of a city or monument

Above, the figure of the girl between the columns is very useful to proportion the monument, without depriving it of its heroic character. Right, an amusing environmental interpretation. Below, Piazza delle Erbe in Padua, a cheerful union of different periods. The clutter of bicycles is matched by the throng of people.

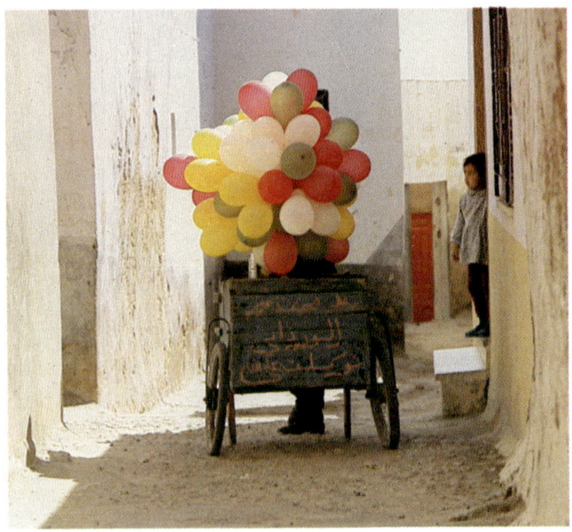

Right, an effective interpretation of Piazza della Frutta, in Padua. The bunches of asparagus arranged on the stall are much more than a still life detail. They reflect a commercial custom, a social relationship, an economic activity which is an integral part of the history of the city, for many centuries heavily dependent on agriculture.
Below, an exceptional interpretation of a Neapolitan scene. The disorder of the shop signs is matched by the lively, appearance of the middle-aged couple and the obstruction of the cars. Naples: a city where everything speaks and everything is intermingled.

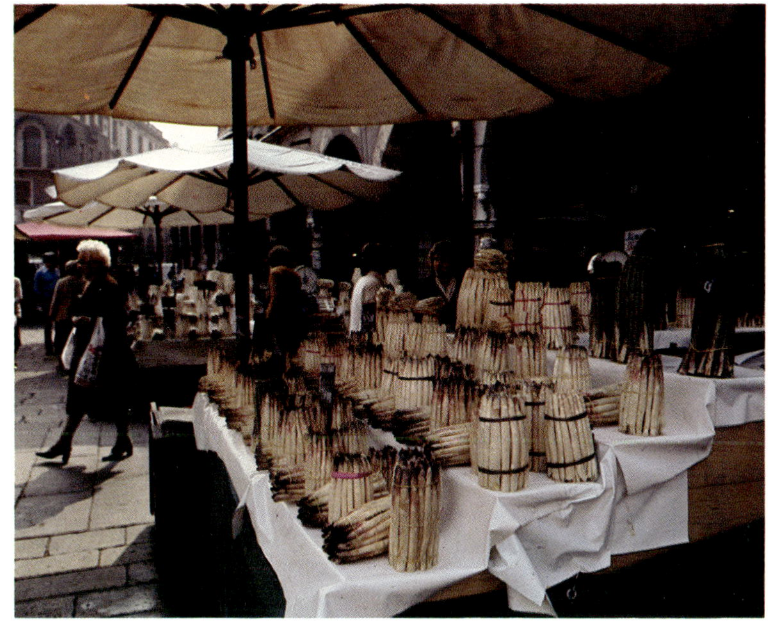

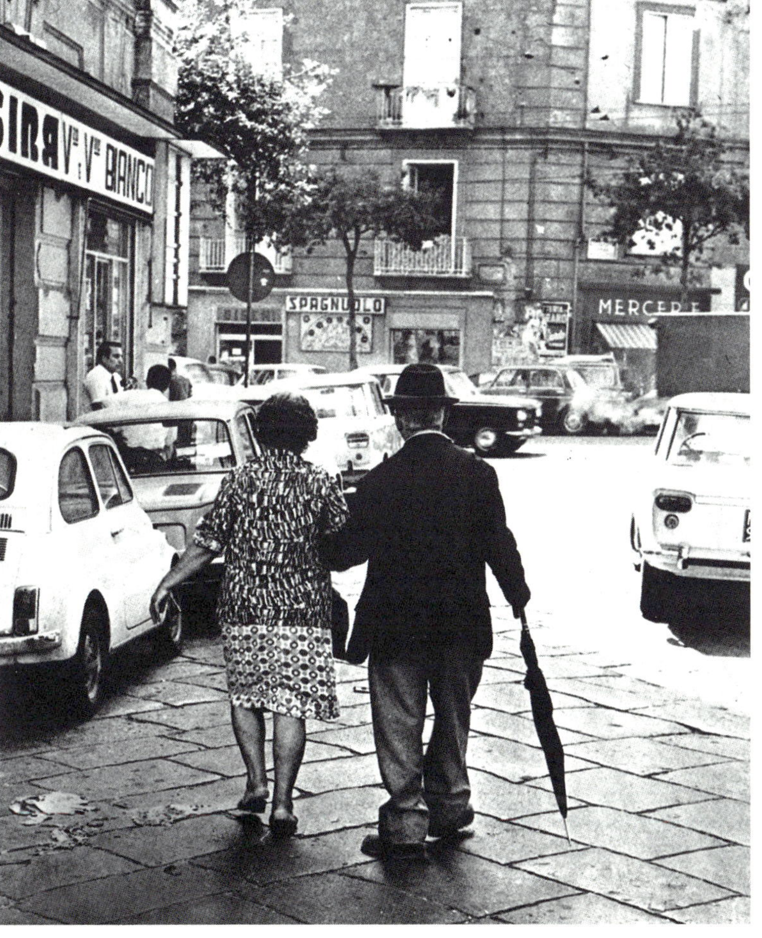

calls for a type of preparation which is often beyond the powers of the photographer. In these cases, he could fill the gaps in his knowledge by preparing himself deliberately then and there, given that outstanding solutions are not normally required for him, but just that minimum of familiarity which with his undoubted professional skills will enable him to tackle a particular environmental situation, which may initially be foreign to him. The trouble is that the need for such preparation often does not even enter the photographer's head. So that even true artists, capable of creating masterpieces out of less substantial material with ease, can come to grief over works which, if better identified and understood, could provide them with greater inspiration.

Architectural monuments

The ultimate example and, in a sense, the acid test on this subject are photographs of architectural monuments. We are including them here even if they are not landscape photographs in the strict sense of the word.
It is not inappropriate to discuss them here, because, they bring to light certain problems which involve historical landscapes to a greater or lesser degree. We are referring to architectural monuments as such and not as part of a landscape, because they too, can form part of an environment, help create an atmosphere and therefore be regarded like any other natural element. An architectural monument is the specific work of an artist who has left the mark of his style on it. A photograph of an architectural monument cannot as such ignore a reading of this style, the at least partial transmission of the message the architect has left in those stones, in those modules, in that composition of his. It cannot be just any interpretation, but an interpretation of his particular language. In these cases, the photograph becomes "critical," it must make one understand the essence of that work, of that style. Clearly at this point

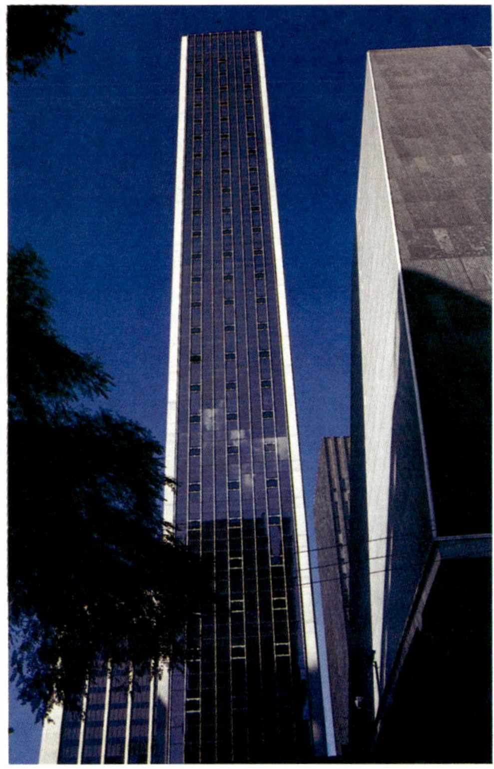

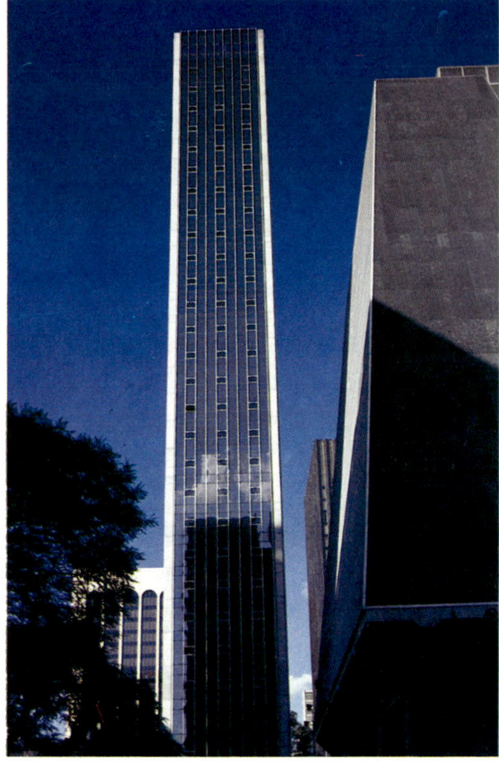

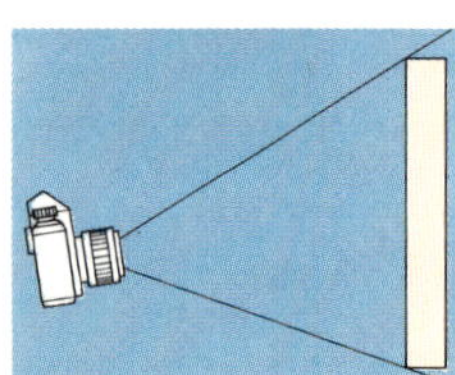

Linear distortion is one of the major problems a photographer has to face in urban views, particularly if architectural works are strongly emphasized. In the two photographs of the skyscraper shown on this page the distortion of perspective is clearly seen in the one on the left. This can be corrected either during printing or by using a corrective device (shift or rising front) not found on small cameras but fitted to medium and large format ones. The distortion is the greater the shorter the focal length of the lens and is therefore at a maximum with wide-angles. There are cases, such as the one examined, where the distortion effect is not serious (it serves to accentuate the vertical mass and the height of the skyscraper) · but in many others, it can be intolerable

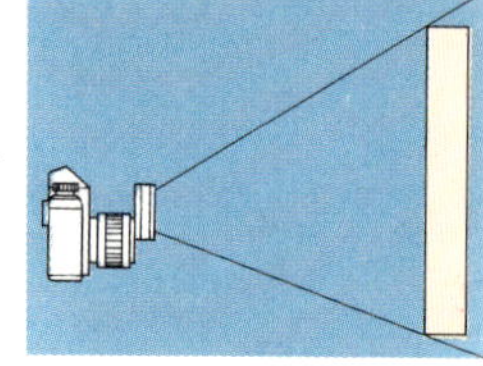

and the photographer must at all costs take account of it. The photograph on the right shows the skyscraper taken with a shift lens.
On the opposite page, a detail of Rio de Janeiro, which is effective in giving an idea of the historical transformation of the city, apart from balancing in formal terms a contrast which could be irreconcilable in reality. Even if the church has no great architectural merit, it still represents a more imaginative world which the overbearing mass of the skyscraper seems to stifle.

the photographer must not only be suitably prepared, but also capable of performing that precise critical reading.
One must admit that such critical photographs, taken with adequate preparation or intuition, are rare, and are not often found even in manuals on the history of architecture or monographs by architects.
The casualness of photographers, and often their incompetence, is such that they sometimes do not even bother to correct the angular distortion which without suitable precautions almost invariably disfigures photographs of buildings taken at close range.
There are, it is true, also specialist photographers accustomed to working on these subjects. Very often they are the architects themselves, who can be experienced photographers, but in many cases even this material is somewhat mediocre, because the historical and critical background may be there, but it is not matched by a high degree of interpretational ability.
Admittedly, these photographs are somewhat difficult, even ignoring the cultural ability they demand.
First of all, there is the problem of angular distortion, because, especially if the monument is in a city, there is simply not enough room to take it from a suitable distance. Often, even when the monument is in a more open space, other buildings have risen up near it, which can look out of place in the frame, or ruin it. The space surrounding the monument is rarely empty: the least that can happen is for there to be copious festoons of telephone wires, electricity wires, or other similar ingredients such as streetlamps or television aerials. Then, the point where it touches the ground will nearly always be obstructed by cars – a fault which cannot be rectified even by using a telephoto, as the photographer will often be tempted to do to avoid other problems.
The problem of producing "clean" pictures absolutely must not be neglected. It becomes glaringly obvious in the case of a monument, but is ever present. The beginner, in particular, must always pay great attention to it. Often, those counterproductive details, which we have just defined as "unclean," are little noticed by our eye

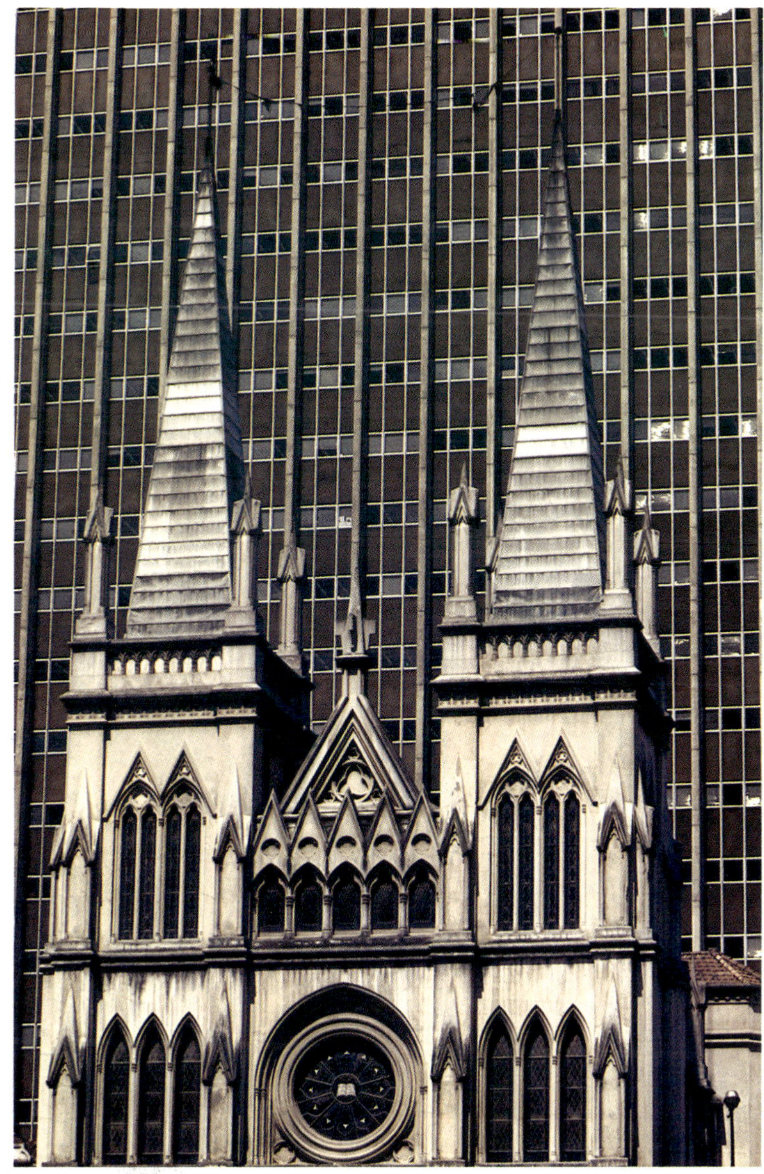

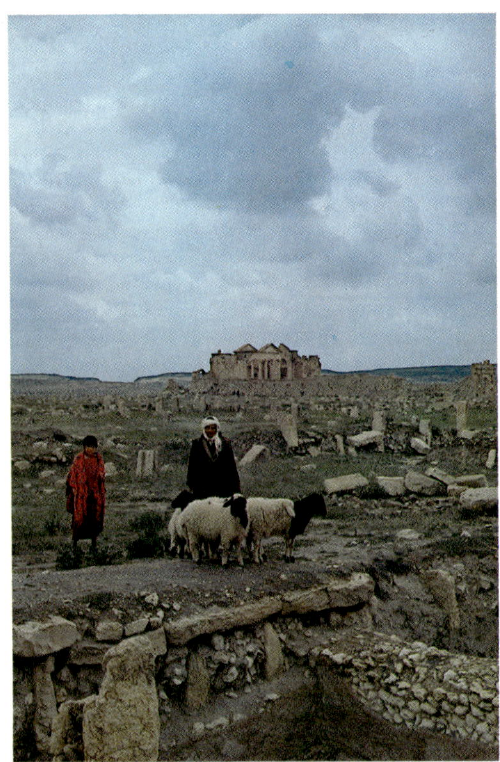

which is accustomed to their pollution to the point of being almost indifferent to them. But to our dismay, even when we had not even noticed them with the naked eye, they will look painfully obtrusive in the photograph. They are found not only in photographs of monuments, where a telephone wire or a parked car becomes intolerable, but in any other type of landscape.

Any detail which conflicts with the meaning of the photograph must be carefully avoided. It is impossible to make a list here, which would cover billboards (unless there are intended to be the subject of the photograph) to building sites, the rubbish which sometimes litters even the most beautiful natural environments, and other signs of human industry when they are incongruous. They include deplorable examples of modern architecture in the middle of an historic city center, or even an area characterized by the restraint of an ancient or natural order: or a stone quarry shattering the harmony of a hillside... But interpretational difficulties pose the worst problems. Artistic monuments come in an enormous variety and the keys to understanding them are very different.

Often, even a good photographer is inclined to appreciate certain precise solutions and to be totally unaware of others. There are architectural forms related to movement, to the opposition of large masses which are easily noticeable at least in part, but there are others which depend on lights, on the movement of subtle planes, which escape the untrained or unpractised eye.

A very famous architect, for example, who has had little fortune photographically, is Palladio. The first impression his works give to the layman is one of great order and a continuous reference to classicism (columns, tympana, friezes, trabeations), bordering on academicism. Only the most experienced critic knows that this is only one aspect of Palladio's architecture and that his most original contribution consists of the planes of light, the volumetric expanses which the light manages to create as it runs over the surface of his buildings, which being of different depths, produce a whole scenography of wings and spatial allusions.

The best interpretations of Palladio I have seen were taken at the Villa in Masèr. I should perhaps add that the photographer had been drawn to the place not by the desire to interpret Palladio, but by a fashion show and he had in fact photographed a fantastic sequence of models. But, being a sensitive, intelligent

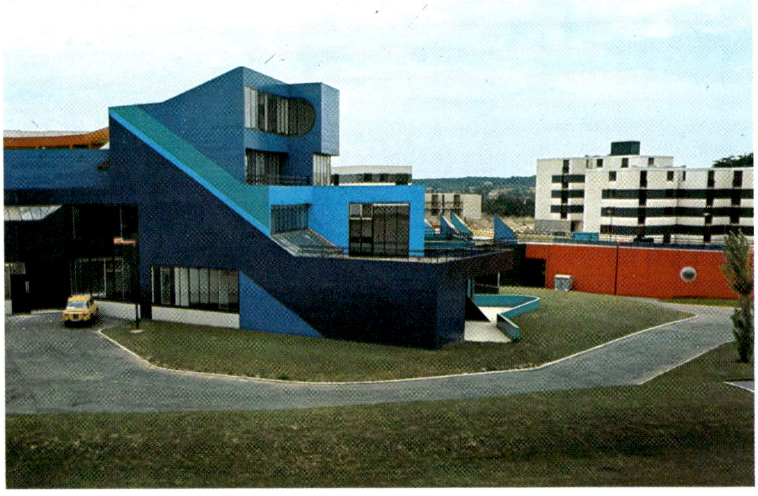

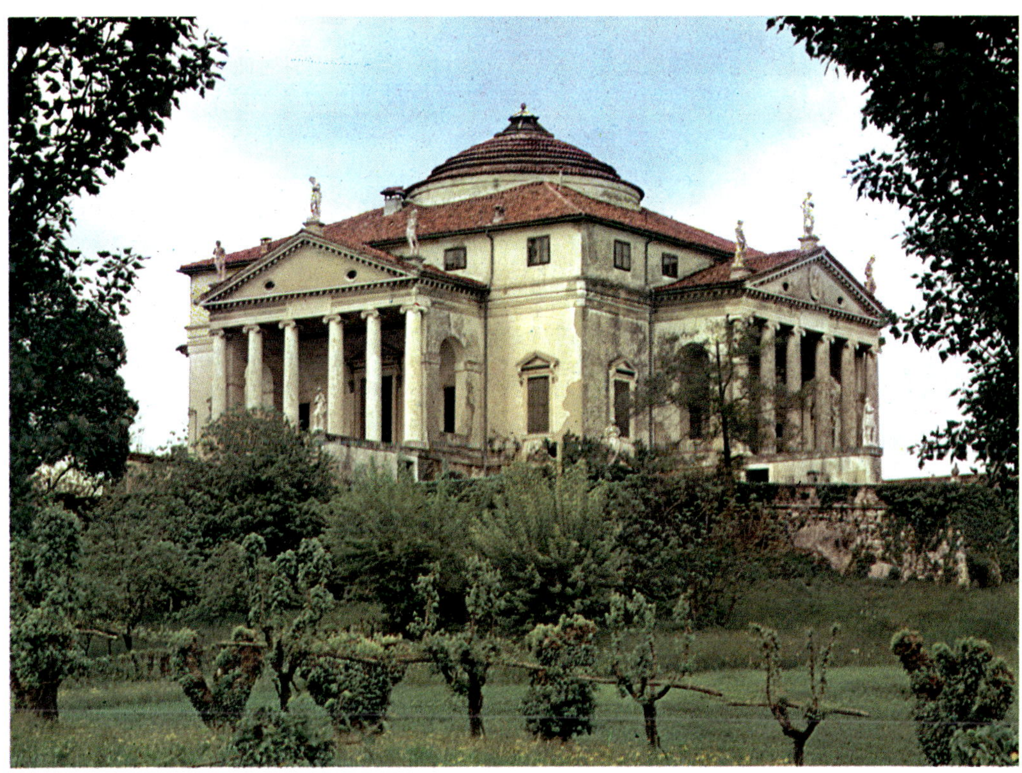

On the opposite page, above, an archeological site at Sbeitla in Tunisia. However important they may be historically, ruins often look anonymous and the photographer therefore has greater scope for exploring the environment.

Below, a good photograph of a building in which the architect has tackled the problem of the use of colour. The photograph has considerable documentary value. Above, the Rotunda, by Palladio, one of the most famous architectural works of the sixteenth century. The photograph shows in detail both the structure of the building and its setting, but fails to reveal the innermost meaning of Palladio's language, which depends on a sense of atmosphere, barely detectable here. To capture this, the photographer would have needed adequate historical and critical preparation.

photographer, he had not been indifferent to the setting in which the show was taking place and whilst successfully devoting most of his attention to the young ladies, he had also sublimated the environment in which they appeared.

On another occasion, I had the task of directing a skilful photographer for a documentary on a sixteenth-century mansion. It was an extremely difficult subject, a type of architecture which at first sight had very little to interest the layman. But he succeeded in producing a series of pictures of very high interpretational quality. Only he could not take a single frame of the floor at street level without it including some bicycle: one minute propped casually against the wall; the next, ridden by a cyclist. For a present day photograph, those bicycles were certainly a very useful ingredient. Apart from anything else, they were a peculiar expression of the provincial nature of that environment, of the drowsy atmosphere which lingered in its streets. The photographer had been clever in perceiving this and had he needed to give a picture of that city, he could not have done without one of those photographs with the bicycle. The trouble was that we had set out to do something else. I believe that he drew upon all his resources to cope with those bicycles, because many photographs had been taken at special times, when there must have been very little traffic around and goodness knows how long he might have waited to find the right cyclist, short of bringing one with him (he came from another town). I recall this episode not to give vent to my possible exasperation at the time, (even with the bicycle, those photographs were good) but to show how far even first-rate photographers are from realizing the need for critical and interpretational photographs – a type which is still almost non-existent in photographic manuals.

Having kept the reader occupied for so long with such elevated discourse and so many examples, now that the moment of leave-taking has come, we wish him every success and offer him all our sympathy.
Perhaps still encumbered by the small but important set of instruments with which we have advised him to equip his camera and perhaps undecided as to which lens and filter to use, deeply perplexed about the best frame to choose and perhaps dismayed at the task of discovering certain formal motifs, which initially will seem thoroughly daunting to him, he already belongs, although he may not know it, to a select group.
He belongs to that rare category of people who put beauty before profit and contemplation before interest – people for whom beauty is profitable and contemplation is a fundamental attitude for the enrichment of life.
In this group he will find himself in the company of the most elevated and generous minds, of those who, be they artists or not, have offered us the means of feeling at peace with the universe, of feeling the trace of the infinite and the presence of the eternal. Certainly they are a composite group and those who lead it will seem way above us, but the important thing is to feel that one is marching under the same banner, to the sound of the same fanfare.
Nature awaits him with her infinite variety; the discovery of distant lands, or opportunities no less important or desired for, which may be just round the corner. Enjoyable walks await him; stimulating journeys; the priceless satisfaction whatever may be the outcome of his photography, of a day well spent.

PICTURE SOURCES

Photographic agencies:
Kodansha Ltd, Tokyo
Magnum Photos, New York
Luisa Ricciarini, Milan
Sygma, Paris
Vautier-De Nanxe-Decool, Paris.

The following abbreviations have been used to indicate the position of the photographs: *a*, above; *b*, below; *c*, center; *l*, left; *r*, right.

p. 2 Fulvio Roiter, Venice
3 P2 (Luisa Ricciarini)
6 Holmes-Lebel/Edwards
8-9 Franco Fontana, Cognento (Modena)
10 Paolo Belloni/Marzia Malli, Milan
11 *a*, Fabio Simion (L. Ricciarini)
b, Stelvio Andreis, Verona
12 *a*, Mondadori Archives, Milan
b, F. Simion (L. Ricciarini)
13 Mondadori Archives
14 U.S. Coast and Geodetic Survey
15 Mondadori Archives
16 Mario De Biasi, Milan
17 Giuliano Cappelli, Florence
18 Mondadori Archives
19 *a*, F. Simion (L. Ricciarini)
b, Mondadori Archives
20-21 Mondadori Archives
22 *a*, Mondadori Archives
b, Mondadori Archives
23 *a*, Giorgio Lotti, Milan
b, F. Roiter
24 Mondadori Archives
26-27 Vautier-De Nanxe, Paris
28 Vautier-De Nanxe
29 *a*, Vautier-De Nanxe
b, Pino Dal Gal, Verona
30-31 Mondadori Archives
32 *a*, F. Roiter
l, Enzo Arnone, Milan
33 E. Arnone
34 *a*, Gian Paolo Cavallero, Savona
b, P2 (L. Ricciarini)
35 Vautier-De Nanxe
36 *a*, Mondadori Archives
b, F. Roiter
37 *a*, F. Roiter
bl, G. P. Cavallero
br, F. Fontana
38 *a*, Giancarlo Molinari, Verona
b, S. Andreis
39 *a*, Vautier-De Nanxe
b, P2 (L. Ricciarini)
40 F. Roiter
41 Mondadori Archives
42 F. Roiter
43 S. Andreis
44-45 Vautier-De Nanxe
46 F. Fontana
47 *a*, Vautier-De Nanxe
b, F. Roiter
48 F. Roiter
49 G. Cappelli
50 E. Arnone
51 Guglielmo Izzi, St. Paul, USA
52 *a*, courtesy of Canon Italy S.p.A., Bussolengo (Verona)
b, Mondadori Archives
53 *b*, courtesy of Canon Italy S.p.A.
55 *al*, G. Cappelli
56 G. Izzi
57 *a*, G. P. Cavallero
c, Vautier-De Nanxe
b, F. Roiter
58 S. Andreis
60 F. Roiter
61 *a*, F. Roiter
b, Vautier-De Nanxe
62-63 P. Dal Gal
64-65 S. Andreis
67 Vautier-De Nanxe
68 *b*, G. Lotti
69 F. Roiter
70 Vincenzo Naddeo, Rome
71 G. Lotti
72-73 S. Andreis
74 *a*, Vautier-De Nanxe
cl, Vautier-De Nanxe
cr, Roberto Mennella, Venice
b, R. Mennella
75 F. Roiter
76 Livio Nogarin, Verona
77 *a*, L. Nogarin
b, G. Lotti
78-79 Carlo delle Cese, Verona
81 Vautier-De Nanxe
82-83 S. Andreis
84 *a*, G. Cappelli
c, G. Cappelli
b, Vautier-De Nanxe
85 Vautier-De Nanxe
86 *a*, Ce. delle Cese
cl, M. De Biasi
cr, C. delle Cese
87 *a*, P2 (L. Ricciarini)
b, M. De Biasi
88 *a*, M. De Biasi
b, G. Lotti
89 M. De Biasi
90 *a*, Minor White
b, R. Benny
91 *a*, Bob Clemens and Frederick C. Enrich
b, Keith Boas
92 M. Malli
93 *a*, Barbara Jean/Eastman Kodak Company, 1975
b, E. Arnone
94 M. Malli
95 *a*, Vautier-De Nanxe
b, Dennis Stock (Magnum Photos)
96-97 *a*, Emil Schultess
b, Mondadori Archives
b, Fairchild Space and Defense Systems
98 E. Arnone
99 *a*, F. Roiter
b, G. Lotti
100 F. Roiter
101 *a*, Vautier-De Nanxe
b, Roberto Vatalaro, Bologna
102 F. Roiter
103 *a*, F. Roiter
b, M. De Biasi
104 *a*, F. Roiter
104-105 *b*, G. Lotti
105 *a*, F. Roiter
106 G.P. Cavallero
107 *a*, F. Roiter
b, Vautier-De Nanxe
108 *a*, F. Fontana
b, M. De Biasi
109 *al*, G. Lotti
ar, M. De Biasi
cr, E. Arnone
b, F. Roiter
110 G. Cappelli
111 *a*, G.P. Cavallero
b, F. Roiter
112 *a*, G.P. Cavallero
b, F. Simion (L. Ricciarini)
113 *a*, Bruno Barbey (Magnum Photos)
114 *a*, F. Roiter
b, Folco Quilici, Rome
115 *a*, F. Roiter
b, Kazuyoshi Nomachi
116 Georg Gerster, Zurich
117 *a*, Vautier-Decool
b, F. Roiter
118 *a*, E. Arnone
b, G. Chauvel (Sygma)
119 *a*, S. Andreis
b, F. Roiter
120-121 Yoshikazu Shirakawa
122 *a*, Gigi Craighero, Tolmezzo (Udine)
b, R. Mennella
123 *a*, F. Roiter
b, E. Arnone
124 *a*, R. Mennella
b, G. Cappelli
125 F. Roiter
126 *a*, G. Cappelli
b, E. Arnone
127 F. Roiter
128 *a*, F. Roiter
b, G. Lotti
129 E. Arnone
130 F. Roiter
131 *a*, F. Fontana
b, Paolo Semenzato, Padua
132 *a*, G. Lotti
b, F. Roiter
133 F. Roiter
134 *a*, R. Mennella
b, P. Semenzato
135 *a*, Dennis Stock (Magnum Photos)
b, Kazuyoshi Nomachi
136 *a*, G. Cappelli
b, Vautier
137 *a*, G. Lotti
b, G. Izzi
138 *a*, Vautier-De Nanxe
b, S. Andreis
139 S. Andreis
140 Dennis Stock (Magnum Photos)
141 M. De Biasi
142-143 S. Andreis
144-145 Vautier-De Nanxe
146-147 F. Roiter
148 F. Roiter
149 *a*, F. Roiter
bl, Giuseppe Agostini, Verona
br, F. Roiter
150 P. Dal Gal
151 F. Roiter
152-153 P2 (L. Ricciarini)
154 Mondadori Archives
155 *a*, F. Fontana
bl, F. Roiter
br, Vautier-De Nanxe
156 *a*, P. dal Gal
b, G. Cappelli
157 *a*, F. Roiter
b, P. Semenzato
158-159 G. Gerster
160-161 Ansel Adams
162-163 Ernst Haas (Magnum Photos)
164-165 Burt Glinn (Magnum Photos)
166-167 F. Fontana
168-169 G. Gerster
170-171 F. Roiter
172-173 G. Lotti
174-175 M. De Biasi
176 Kazuyoshi Nomachi
177 Yoshikazu Shirakawa
178-179 Vautier-De Nanxe
180 F. Roiter
181 *a*, F. Roiter
bl, F. Roiter
br, Vautier-De Nanxe
182 *a*, Vautier-De Nanxe
182-183 F. Simion (L. Ricciarini)
183 *a*, Vautier-De Nanxe
184 F. Roiter
185 *a*, F. Roiter
b, Mondadori Archives
186-187 Vautier-De Nanxe
188 *a*, F. Roiter
b, J.F. Gaudinean (© Kodansha Ltd.)
189 Mondadori Archives

The drawings are by Andrea Corbella (Milan).